RICHARD BRINSLEY SHERIDAN

"What things have we seen
Done at the Mermaid! heard words that have been
So nimble, and so full of subtle flame,
As if that every one from whence they came
Had meant to put his whole wit in a jest,
And had resolved to live a fool the rest
Of his dull life."

Master Francis Beaumont to Ben Jonson

"Souls of Poets dead and gone,
    What Elysium have ye known,
    Happy field or mossy cavern,
    Choicer than the Mermaid Tavern?"

Keats

Richard Brinsley Sheridan

(SIX PLAYS)

Edited, with an Introduction

by

LOUIS KRONENBERGER

A MERMAID DRAMABOOK

Advisory Editor, Eric Bentley

"I lie and dream of your full Mermaid wine."—*Beaumont*

HILL AND WANG, INC. · NEW YORK · 1957

The text and notes for "The School for Scandal" is reprinted from *British Dramatists from Dryden to Sheridan*, edited by George H. Nettleton and Arthur E. Case. It is reprinted in this edition by special arrangement with Houghton Mifflin Company and through the courtesy of Georgetown University, owner of the original Crewe manuscript.

Louis Kronenberger is Professor of Theatre Arts at Brandeis University; he has also been Visiting Lecturer on drama at Columbia University and Visiting Professor of English at The City College, New York. Since 1938 Mr. Kronenberger has been drama critic of *Time;* since 1953 he has edited the *Best Plays.* He is the author of a book on English stage comedy, *The Thread of Laughter,* and also *Kings and Desperate Men.* In addition he has edited the work of Pope, Johnson, Boswell, and other eighteenth-century figures. At the present time he is writing a life of an eighteenth-century woman, the first Duchess of Marlborough.

Library of Congress Catalog Card Number: 57–5842
Copyright © 1957 by Hill and Wang, Inc.
Manufactured in the United States of America

CONTENTS

INTRODUCTION

THOUGH all Sheridan's real writing for the theatre was crowded into a mere five years, there are few people over whom the sense of the stage hovers more insistently. It was not just that the stage was in his blood, that his mother was a playwright and his father an actor, or that long after he stopped writing plays he continued to produce them; it is also that he had the kind of romantic nature that frequently saw life in terms of theatre, and the kind of rhetorical instinct that saw language as dialogue and communication as public speaking. And when, indeed, he gave up writing for the theater it was to turn actor upon a more lustrous stage and in a more momentous drama: it was to enter the House of Commons and become part—with Burke and the younger Pitt—of the most resplendent of all ages of oratory. In political thinking Sheridan was not much more than the devoted follower of Charles Fox; in political acting, however—whether in the great India Bill speech in the Commons, or in the superb histrionics of the Warren Hastings trial—he was of a kind and class with Garrick.

To this born feeling for situation and gift for the spoken word Sheridan added an ample Irish inheritance of wit. And he had, or early acquired, one thing more—a sense of the great world, a natural polish and grace; and these four qualities sufficed to make him a playwright of lasting appeal. He had more than his share of bad luck in life, but he also had the good luck to be born into an age of limp playwriting that craved something stylish and starched. The assault against sentimentalism that Goldsmith opened in *The Good-Natured Man* and *She Stoops to Conquer,* Sheridan now extended; but he did more than help discredit sentimental comedy; he at one blow restored the comedy of manners.

In terms of appraisal, Sheridan is a very simple playwright because, beyond the four impressive talents mentioned above, he had no others at all; and because—though he gained enormously in the handling of gifts that were at the outset used impurely—his career provides no striking intellectual development, no sudden deepening of perception or widening of scope. There is simply a discarding of the sentimental hand-me-downs and theatrical commonplaces that served him badly, and a sharpening of the satiric eye and polished style that still serve him well. To the very end, however—and his reward is to have been the only playwright in England between Elizabethan and modern times with two plays that have consistently held the boards—he put the theater ahead of life, the vivid effect ahead of the revealing essence. His, accordingly, is a view of human nature that is curiously undistinctive and even shallow; his brilliance itself is only phrase deep. Thus his plays are easily, almost necessarily, judged as individual stage pieces; they are not evolutionary or linked or interlocking; they are the children of one parent but not the parents of one another.

Sheridan opened his career, and quickly won considerable fame, with a play written at twenty-three, *The Rivals.* And in the popular—as, indeed, the academic—view it has accounted ever since for half his celebrity. This is not too hard to explain, even though merit is no part of the explanation. Actually, one of the great faults of *The Rivals*—its lacking all unity of tone—has in the popular view been no fault at all: its being such a grab bag of attractions has made it a great catch-all of admirers. Half the play's creative impetus derived, of course, from Sheridan's purposing to make fun of sentimental comedy; and the fun he made of romantical Lydia Languish, who would rather elope than be married in church, or marry an obscure ensign than a splendid *parti*, is much of it still good broad spoofing. And as *The Rivals* nowhere soars up to real satire, neither does it make its way as true comedy of manners. Considering that the scene is Bath at a time when Bath still followed, if it no longer quite set, the fashions, we could scarcely be offered less that seems modish or even polite: the only comedy-of-manners talk comes at the very outset, in the conversation of servants.

There is an obvious reason for all this: for too many of his characters Sheridan had fallen back on the merest stage types, the pure staples of the comedy of humors—whether in his silly heroine, his heavy father, his bragging coward, his blustering Irishman, or his man-hunting (whom he also made a word-massacring) hag. At the other extreme, Falkland and Julia—whether adjudged straight holdovers from sentimental comedy or contrivances for ridiculing it—serve the comedy of manners, properly regarded, little better. Yet the play is just sufficiently well-bred, it smacks just enough of the drawing room, to avoid (what actually it might better attempt) the full flavor of farce.

It is indeed a hodgepodge, a theatrical coat-of-many-colors that has most of all, today, a kind of musical-comedy air; its level of jesting, its style of plot, its cast of characters all would consort agreeably with tunes. The people involved constitute, one after another, solid, serviceable character parts, as much what most actors love to play as audiences to watch. Though they are none of them quite original with Sheridan himself, few roles have won more lasting favor than Bob Acres or Sir Lucius or Mrs. Malaprop.

That in his first play Sheridan was almost nowhere original counts less against him than that he was only fitfully his happier self. Of the bright wit that Sheridan could command in private life as well as on the stage, there are only mild foretastes in *The Rivals:* The best of the writing—

> Zounds! don't enter the same hemisphere with me! don't dare to breathe the same air, or use the same light with me; but get an atmosphere and a sun of your own! I'll strip you of your commission; I'll lodge a five-and-threepence in the hands of trustees, and you shall live on the interest. I'll disown you, I'll disinherit you, I'll unget you! and d--n me! if ever I call you Jack again

—has verve, certainly, but no more sheen than bite; and much oftener the dialogue whimsies into

> I own I should rather choose a wife of mine to have the usual number of limbs, and a limited quantity of back; and tho' *one* eye may be very agreeable, yet as the prejudice has always run in favor of *two*, I would not wish to affect a singularity in that article.

It is indeed whimsicality, and not wit, that Sheridan achieved throughout; something vanilla-flavored to please the Victorian-minded. If *The Rivals* has a certain playfulness and sprightliness quite foreign to the sentimental comedy it was inveighing against, it is yet—compared with true unsentimental comedy in earlier days, or later ones—thoroughly larkish, frisky, and given to playing safe. It is perhaps, less the play itself, than its great reputation, that needs to be disparaged: but surely, besides lacking the originality to create, Sheridan brought no real boldness to what he borrowed, and the real offense of *The Rivals* is its dogged inoffensiveness.

St. Patrick's Day, produced shortly after *The Rivals*, was a "benefit play," aimed at helping the actor (one Larry Clinch) who had just been playing Sir Lucius O'Trigger. We can as easily believe that *St. Patrick's Day* sought to capitalize on Clinch's talents as that Sheridan contrived the whole thing in forty-eight hours. And so far as Clinch went, the play did handsomely: it enabled him, by virtue of some lightning quick-changes, to impersonate not only a lively Irish officer but an English booby and a German quack. And as a short farce of simple-minded deceptions and disguises, *St. Patrick's Day* is decent enough in its craftsmanship, rich in actable character parts, and endowed in spots with spirited and even gifted dialogue. The knack for phrase, for stylish drollery, that is one of Sheridan's hallmarks—"We'll argue in platoons"; "Put on your mutiny looks"; "Such a circumvallation of hoop, with a breastwork of whalebone"—is frequently evident. There are amusing effects, as when Justice Credulous cannot get his wife and daughter—busy talking among themselves—to listen to what he is saying. And in Dr. Rosy, whose every speech —and figure of speech—must touch upon medicine, Sheridan has produced an entertaining comedy-of-humors figure (most reminiscent of Wycherley's Widow Blackacre who must as insistently revert to the law). "Brave as a lion, gentle as a saline draught," Rosy characterizes the disguised Lieutenant, and eulogizes his own deceased wife Dolly: "Such an arm for a bandage—veins that seemed to invite the lancet!" If *St. Patrick's Day* can be acclaimed as no more than passably entertaining, that is not such faint praise as may appear: not very much hackwork so venerable can be called entertaining at all.

The Duenna—which in terms of production belongs, like its two predecessors, to 1775—was so huge a success that it initially ran longer than the century's other comic-

opera sensation, *The Beggars' Opera*. "Nowadays," ran the
song

> as 'twas in Gay's
> The world's run mad agen-a;
> From morn to night, its whole delight
> To cry up *The Duenna*.

Nor was such success ephemeral. So late as 1819, Hazlitt
pronounced *The Duenna* "a perfect work of art" and its
songs "the best that were ever written, except those in
The Beggars' Opera." And when revived in England in
the 1920's, first at Norwich, later at Birmingham, and most
memorably by Nigel Playfair at the Lyric, Hammersmith,
it again managed to give pleasure.

It is necessary, of course, to appraise it not as comedy
but as comic opera, and (in the absence of music) to ask
for suspended judgment on some of its "weaknesses." The
plot, though no worse and decidedly no worse contrived,
than the plot of a good many straight comedies of intrigue,
cannot really hold its head up on a purely dramatic
basis. The monastery episodes aside, everything takes place
in an atmosphere where much must be sung rather than
spoken, where music needs charms to rouse the sluggish
text. Sheridan has loaded his narrative with every possible
ambiguity and misapprehension in a milieu where human
beings display a positive compulsion to be misled. There
is no timid compromising with the improbable, no diffidence with regard to the absurd; and on its own unblushing, old-fashioned terms *The Duenna* is very happily managed.

Still, Time has plainly been at work on *The Duenna*,
and even for those of us who are amused by eighteenth-
century machinery, rust and all, the play is quite often
stubbornly unamusing. However much or little it may be
indebted to Dryden's *Spanish Friar* or any other prede-
cessor, it is obvious that, even when written, *The Duenna*
was already part of a passing tradition. But at any rate
it is all of an age throughout. Sheridan brought little more
than sound workmanship to it; not, surely, much wit; and
nowhere, the least originality. We can properly plead the
great importance of music for *The Duenna*, but in doing
so cannot but stress that it is rather a libretto than a play.
Understandably the world ran mad in Gay's time when

> All day long, its sole sing-song
> Was pretty, pretty Polly

—for *The Beggars' Opera* brought something wonderfully new, and vital, and pungent to the stage, and the tunes that Gay went borrowing, attractive though they are, merely enhance the book that Gay himself brought forth. But between Sheridan's work and Gay's there is more, even, than the difference between an eloping miss disguised as her duenna in cardboard Seville, and a life-breathing gang of underworld characters in sharp-etched London. There are for one thing the songs that Hazlitt put only second to *The Beggars'* songs, but which are scarcely to be mentioned in the same breath with them.

In Sheridan's day, to be sure—and to a degree in Sheridan's own talent—there still lingered, among all the stock eighteenth-century poetizing, a faint accent of poetry. Sheridan's comic-opera lyrics were still—as almost none are today—remotely, vestigially lyrical. But though the offspring of a superior tradition to ours, they were the anemic, washed-out last of their line; and Sheridan's lyrics, it must be confessed, are more rewarding when they anticipate Gilbert & Sullivan than when they echo Herrick or Carew:

> Tho' cause for suspicion appears,
> Yet proofs of her love too are strong;
> I'm a wretch if I'm right in my fears,
> And unworthy of bliss if I'm wrong.

Even a famous Ogden Nash couplet finds a sort of distant ancestor in:

> A bumper of good liquor
> Will end a contest quicker
> Than justice, judge or vicar.

The best character in *The Duenna* is surely the complacent Isaac, another of those own-petard-hoisted sharpers, and by so much the less distinctive. This converted Jew inspires some amusing lines, as in the well-known description of him as "the blank leaves between the Old and New Testament." But the wit of *The Duenna* is a matter of here a phrase and there a repartee, and oftener of such merely pretty hand-me-downs as "If we grumbled a little now and then, it was soon over, for we were never fond enough to quarrel." Faint praise is as much as can be accorded *The Duenna* also; but it is yet real praise of a kind. For the wonder, certainly, is not that *The Duenna* is no better than it is, but that it is on the whole so adequate.

Sheridan's *A Trip to Scarborough* isn't properly Sheridan's at all, being a cleaned-up—which is to say a watered-down—version of Vanbrugh's *The Relapse*. Wherever possible, which was for most of the time, Sheridan retained Vanbrugh's actual dialogue; it is only where the telling turned glaringly prolix and Sheridan abridged it, or the plot turned sexually dangerous and Sheridan rerouted it, or the talk turned indecent and Sheridan disinfected it, that Vanbrugh's text was recast. This was sufficiently often, however, to give the plot a different impulsion and the play a much seemlier tone. All this acquires added interest when it is recalled that Vanbrugh wrote *The Relapse* as a hardheaded sequel to, and retort upon, Cibber's *Love's Last Shift,* the play in which the sentimental comedy that was in time to pack the stage first really tenanted it. *The Relapse* thus tried to strangle at birth the sentimentalism that *The Rivals*, some eighty years later, would seek to dislodge. And it had better be confessed that in *A Trip to Scarborough* Sheridan did more to encourage gentility than in *The Rivals* he had done to expel it. Shifting Vanbrugh's scene from London to Scarborough is the most negligible of his changes. He has in addition made everyone in the new play not only well-behaved but well-spoken; and has not simply modified conduct but has altered motives. Nor was this fortuitous; Garrick thrust into the prologue he wrote for *A Trip to Scarborough:*

> As change thus circulates throughout the nation
> Some plays may justly call for alteration . . .
> Those writers well and wisely use their pens
> Who turn our wantons into Magdalens

and Sheridan wrote into the very body of the play: " 'Twould surely be a pity to exclude the productions of some of our best writers for want of a little pruning." But pruning is not the most accurate word for what Sheridan did: it is not just that "son of a whore" is changed to

"knave," or "lie with" to "make love to." Ignoble sentiments are as much frowned upon as unseemly language;
where in Vanbrugh, Lord Foppington admits he is gratified by his father's death, for now he will inherit his estate,
in Sheridan father is made into uncle. Still other impro-
prieties, rather than amended, are wholly expunged.

More important, however, are the plot alterations. To
mention but one: where in Vanbrugh, Berinthia actually
goes to bed with Loveless; was formerly the mistress of
Amanda's present suitor; and now turns procuress for him
with Amanda: in Sheridan she will not succumb to Loveless, and indeed she only leads him on so that Amanda's
suitor—whose mistress she has not been—may want her
the more for a wife. A change of this sort does more, of
course, than affect plot; it greatly alters character.

In some respects Sheridan's changes, whatever the motive behind them, are for the better. Vanbrugh's Berinthia,
by her treachery and utter baseness, is too wicked for
an otherwise good-natured enough comedy. In Vanbrugh
again, the vicious Berinthia and the virtuous Amanda seem
far more out of Victorian melodrama than they do in
Sheridan. And Sheridan has Lord Foppington so behave
at the end that Tom's amusingly unscrupulous ruse for
marrying Miss Hoyden goes down better. Sheridan is also
wise in eliminating all the blank-verse passages (most of
them soliloquies) that already in Vanbrugh's time seem
archaic and inconsonant; and Sheridan's cuts make for
greater compactness. But though he has genuinely im-
proved Vanbrugh's play at this point or that, he has clearly
harmed it as a whole. He has not only (rather to one's
surprise) weakened the dialogue or diluted the wit even
where the matter of decorum does not enter; he has not
only, again, cut it in such a way as to largely banish the
sort of talk that is the very soul of the comedy of manners:
ultimately he has done more than emasculate *The Relapse*,
he has falsified it. Artifice passes over into staginess, and
in banishing pornography, Sheridan has evicted psychol-
ogy as well. But on one count at least we can be very
grateful to him. From this single adaptation of his we
can learn more of what changes had come over society—
and hence over its mirror, the stage—than from half-a-
dozen critical tomes.

There can be little question that of all comedies of manners written in English *The School for Scandal,* no less in public fame than theatrical popularity, stands easily first. And here indeed the man of the world in Sheridan came into his own and brought back into the theater a degree of wit it had not known since Vanbrugh, and of style and polish since Congreve. Here besides—in terms of sheer stagecraft—the theater must acknowledge a surer hand than either's. Sheridan's carpentry is always expert, his theatre sense acute; he also knew how to write rewarding roles and where to find actors to play them. Of the original production of *The School for Scandal* Horace Walpole wrote that "there were more parts performed admirably . . . than I almost ever saw in any play."

The play richly deserved to succeed: in fact, it could hardly not. Very great indeed was the demand for a first-rate comedy of manners in a society whose own manners, if rococo, were elegant and whose inclinations were worldly; and for three-quarters of a century no playwright had supplied one. As for theme, though tattle and *Tatlers* had long engrossed the town, there was beyond that a more topical impetus for a comedy pivoting on scandal-mongers. As the notable Sheridan scholar, R. Crompton Rhodes, has made clear, there had recently arisen in London a new kind of slanderous journalism, initiated by the *Town and Country* magazine and perfected by the *Morning Post* newspaper. Such scandal sheets carried innuendo to the point of libel; made tattle not just an art but an industry; and had everyone in society in a panic over his own reputation while delighting in the shattered reputations of others.

Scandal being an art, its manipulation could challenge such a word artist as Sheridan. As a theme, moreover—something that Sheridan must at least subconsciously have grasped—it went far toward solving a difficulty born of a decorous age. The age—or at least the stage—had grown too prissy to deal happily, even to deal honestly, with sin. Not only could no maiden surrender her virtue and keep the title of heroine; no wife could deceive her husband and be permitted to prosper; indeed, no widow (consider Berinthia in *A Trip to Scarborough*) could sin her way to matrimony. But in proportion as it failed of license, sin had increased in lure; and though vice might not triumph, female virtue could seem, again and again, to totter. In other words, there was to be no sin whatever, but all possible imputation of sinning; and just this *The School for Scandal* provided in an eminent degree. And it does so altogether in the interest of morality: the screen scene, the most famous scene of its kind in the language, exists not to ruin Lady Teazle's good name but to unmask Joseph Surface's evil nature.

Sheridan's play, by reason of Sheridan's theme, thus capitalizes brilliantly on the name without the game; and can thus as legitimately have recourse to talk as to action. And the talk is superior to the action: the scandalmongers are the finer and fresher part of things; it is in being shown their operations, in seeing how—like any other important commodity—scandal is brewed, bottled, labeled, purveyed, that Sheridan best catches the tone, best achieves the enameling of the true comedy of manners. Here the prose, at once starched and informal, most enhances a tradition; here the wit is equally a matter of expression and idea. Sheridan stands closest here, in manner as in merit, to Congreve; and like Congreve epitomizes the worldling's point of view. For virtually the last time in England comedy catches a certain crisped and elegant tone: a Wilde or Maugham fails to catch it and Shaw never tries.

When we turn from the play's manner to its substance our reactions become considerably more mixed. If we are to judge a story only by its storytelling, high praise is still in order, for Sheridan's sense of plot carries us with real ease and genuine expectation from one scene to another. Perhaps no English comic playwright since Ben Jonson had shown nimbler craftsmanship: despite how many characters are involved in *The School for Scandal*, there are no distracting subplots or confusing complications: the play is of inventiveness all compact. And as with the plotting, so with the pace—despite the many purely conversational scenes, there is always a sense of movement and, almost, of activity.

But this could only be had at a price; and along with being so engagingly animated the story of *The School for Scandal* is also almost obstreperously fictional. It belongs wholly to the stage, with no overtones of real life. What I mean by this has nothing to do with surface realism, but with essential veracity. The comedy of manners has no use for surface realism: being, indeed, concerned with the shams and pretenses of human beings, it has as great need of artifice as have the lungs of oxygen. But since its very orbit is a world of masks, what it must always be moving toward is a general unmasking, so that we see at last the faces that lurk beneath. When a Congreve, or even an Etherege, has brought things to an end we have a proper sense of what true and often ugly instincts underlie such exquisite and obliging manners; we comprehend by how narrow a margin virtue survives, and with what sleepless pertinacity vanity conspires; we watch the eyes of Innocence first widen and then contract; we note the polished in process of becoming the tarnished, and how the heart, like the cheeks, has need of rouge. Above all, since the real dramatis personae of the comedy of manners are the practices of Society itself, we see in what ways they alter and contaminate and corrupt; and though wickedness need certainly not triumph, a sense of man's dark, tempted nature must somehow obtrude. Artifice, when expertly applied, is perhaps the shortest cut to truth.

But between artifice and the sheer staginess we find at times in *The School for Scandal* there is a notable difference. Sheridan heightens scenes and situations not to become more expressive, but only to be more effective. His is a real "fiction" plot in which, rather than the audience finding out the truth about human nature, the characters find out—in the nick of time—the truth about one another. In the picture scene, a rich uncle learns how good the bad brother is; as other characters, in the screen scene, learn how bad is the good one. Where Sheridan has earlier dug a little deeper, as with Lady Teazle's inclination toward sin, we are shown (and expected to believe) that she is now sick of scandal and social pretense: there is not even a hint that this may only be a temporary repentance born of fright, and that tomorrow week the blooming young wife of a man more than twice her age will be tempted anew. In another way, Maria—from an adherence to vapid stage conventions—becomes almost the dullest of ingénues; she, who might be the Millamant of the piece, is not allowed (as though the presence of wit implied the absence of virtue) to be pert or amusing at all.

For all its narrative vivacity, its verbal sheen, its drawing-room grace; and indeed for all its genuine air of worldliness and dazzling suggestion of scandal, the play, in the final sense, is simply a very brilliant stage piece, a superlative box-office comedy. This is to classify, not condemn. We are in a world, that is to say, of conventional rewards and punishments, of old-fashioned heroes and heroines, of rich uncles and falling screens. And all this, it is only fair to add, is what Sheridan himself half believed in. E. M. Forster speaks somewhere of a man who made him feel that his books contained him and not he his books. But Sheridan's plays do perhaps contain him; he is in many ways no larger than they are. There was much of the true romantic in the Sheridan who himself fought duels and eloped, who himself was overdazzled by the great world, who himself looked out upon life as a kind of spectacle. The gentility of the age clearly did him harm; but there is more involved than conformity or compromise, for even as he conformed, Sheridan somehow expressed an inherent part of himself. His wit always tends to face south and toward the sun; in his portrayal of venom there is nothing venomous; he had only worldly tastes, not—like Congreve or Molière or LaRochefoucauld—an incorruptibly worldly mind. Hence *The School for Scandal* has manner, but not really point of view.

Sheridan will always be best known—and even perhaps be most admired—for *The School for Scandal* and *The Rivals*. They are always named together, but are no more equal in merit than those other ill-bracketed twins, *Huckleberry Finn* and *Tom Sawyer*. The truer bracketing with Mark Twain is *Huck Finn* and *Life on the Mississippi*, as with Sheridan it is *The School for Scandal* and *The Critic*. Where *The Rivals* seems often tame and wishy-washy, *The Critic* is very probably the best, which means also the most playable, stage burlesque in the language. Shaw's *The Admirable Bashville* is frequently as funny, but is not strictly a burlesque—in his re-do of *Cashel Byron's Profession* Shaw appears *in impropria persona*, bits of his real beard mingling with the false Victorian whiskers; and the rhetorical blank verse is used a little for its own sake as well as for periphrasis, bathos and garbled quotations. In a purely literary sense Max Beerbohm may have managed subtler and wittier touches in 'Savonarola' Brown; but Beerbohm's very best effects, such as his wonderful stage directions, are not playable. But what Sheridan wrote in *The Critic*, as anyone who saw the Old Vic production (New York, 1946) will bear out, carries over perfectly to the stage.

Stage parody and burlesque must not only face the danger of all parody and burlesque—that, when no longer topical, its allusions fail very often of comprehension and almost always of laughter. Stage burlesque must also, from the very outset, be largely unsubtle and broad, its business and speeches and allusions easily acted and spouted and grasped. (Even the most cultivated audience, having to catch things on the run, differs greatly from a cultivated person reading a book.) Hence a stage burlesque, to survive, must seize on something theatrically durable—an actor's vanity or an author's bombast, avant-gardism at its silliest or pedantry at its worst. Stylistic parody, again, can only survive through being very specific or very general— through parodying Milton's blank verse or all blank verse, Dr. Johnson's ponderosity or ponderosity in general. The finest parody is almost always the most specific, for it thus displays real insight into an author's shortcomings, and is nothing less than first-rate criticism. But while bad *styles* of writing oftenest lend themselves to crude forms of parodying, they can with the least knowledge prove the most fun. Victorian melodrama or high-society twaddle—just because what is being parodied is itself so nearly absurd —frequently come off very well. But where what is being spoofed has real merit as well as patent faults, the parodist must get below the surface and beyond the obvious: it takes more than just alliteration to hit off Swinburne, or than archaism to hit off Spenser, or than long words to do in Dr. Johnson or than long sentences to do in Henry James.

And when not the style alone is involved, but the whole paraphernalia of stagecraft; when it is necessary to think of the actor as well as the playwright, the stagehands no less than the audience, there can result something quite maddeningly complex. At this level the successes have been notably few. In Buckingham's famous Restoration spoof— which travestied, on the one hand, the highfalutin' of heroic drama and, on the other, the servile following or whimsical flouting of "rules"—not too much survives that is fun. But *The Rehearsal* comes off better on the whole than, say, Fielding's *Tom Thumb* just because it *does* pivot on a rehearsal, does introduce a very vocal playwright as well as a play, does provide discussion of the text as well as the text itself. *Tom Thumb*, by hurling its burlesque straight at the audience, is denied the commentary that can both point up the goings-on and enhance the fun. In

The Critic Sheridan has contrived a very effective framework, which among other things reduces the need for too protracted a "play." His framework is superior to Buckingham's, for *The Critic*—by making fun of a number of things, such as the art of puffing—doesn't throw all its eggs at one target. And Sheridan, unlike Buckingham, miswrote not for an age, but for all time. Where *The Rehearsal* chiefly spoofs a now archaic heroic drama, *The Critic* spoofs a very recognizable Elizabethan manner, and the all too recurrent costume play. As for the Elizabethan manner, its use of blank verse—as opposed to *The Rehearsal's* use of the heroic couplet—certifies more catastrophic anticlimaxes and wilder dives into bathos. As for the costume play, nothing is easier to burlesque because nothing, really, is harder not to. Often, at a seriously intended period drama, one has only to read one's program with its list of famous names to start smiling; while a whole assemblage of such persons on the stage—bearded and brogued and bewigged, full of quotations from their own works or of allusions to their own deeds—can become stark unintentional travesty. Sheridan made a good choice, in style and subject alike, for a burlesque drama, and his general success follows from it. All the same, the constant shifting (within *The Critic*) from stage to sidelines, the frequent counterpointing of side-remarks and text, is of the greatest value. The play-within-the-play has its right quota of good things—whether the superbly irrelevant subplot, or Sir Walter Raleigh and Sir Christopher Hatton informing each other of the obvious, or Tilburnia's Lycidean flower passage (particularly, the repeat), or Whiskerando's dying in mid-syllable (with the Beefeater's addendum), or the stage business of the nieces and the uncles, or the final nonsense of the Thames with its procession of tributaries. But the fun of the thing is enormously enhanced by the sidelines commentary and the sidelines characters—by Sneer's "A very cautious conjecture that"; by the matter of a heroine having to go mad in white satin, or the business of how to get kneeling performers offstage, or the question of cuts that make utter mincemeat of the text. If *The Critic* takes potshots at something eternal in some kinds of playwriting, it also takes them at what is eternal in *every* kind of production.

But Sheridan has more to offer still—has, at the very least, the character of Mr. Puff. The first scene of Act I, given over to the Dangles and Sir Fretful, is conceivably something of a mistake. Or perhaps it was not so much a mistake to spoof a busybody amateur and a madly vain author (who are incidental to the action) as it was simply that Sheridan was less than inspired in dealing with them —though they do *play*. But Mr. Puff is a truly inspired added attraction; not just another mere butt, however good, but someone who fizzes and aerates the entire action. Even if the first scene falls a little short, and Time has left this passage or that a little sallow, *The Critic* is still, after a century and three-quarters, very amusing in book form, as it can prove hilarious in the theatre. In spoofing outmoded language and ludicrous attitudes, capricious workmanship and desperate stage business, Sheridan contrived something that theatrically stands on its own legs, and even walks and runs. *The School for Scandal* graces a distinguished tradition, but *The Critic* stands alone.

LOUIS KRONENBERGER

THE RIVALS

A Comedy

PREFACE

A PREFACE to a play seems generally to be considered as a kind of closet-prologue, in which—if his piece has been successful—the author solicits that indulgence from the reader which he had before experienced from the audience: but as the scope and immediate object of a play is to please a mixed assembly in *representation* (whose judgment in the theatre at least is decisive), its degree of reputation is usually as determined by the public, before it can be prepared for the cooler tribunal of the study. Thus any further solicitude on the part of the writer becomes unnecessary at least, if not an intrusion: and if the piece has been condemned in the performance, I fear an address to the closet, like an appeal to posterity, is constantly regarded as the procrastination of a suit, from a consciousness of the weakness of the cause. From these considerations, the following comedy would certainly have been submitted to the reader, without any further introduction than what it had in the representation, but that its success has probably been founded on a circumstance which the author is informed has not before attended a theatrical trial, and which consequently ought not to pass unnoticed.

I need scarcely add, that the circumstance alluded to was the withdrawing of the piece, to remove those imperfections in the first representation which were too obvious to escape reprehension, and too numerous to admit of a hasty correction. There are few writers, I believe, who, even in the fullest consciousness of error, do not wish to palliate the faults which they acknowledge; and, however trifling the performance, to second their confession of its deficiencies, by whatever plea seems least disgraceful to their ability. In the present instance, it cannot be said to amount either to candour or modesty in me, to acknowledge an extreme inexperience and want of judgment on matters, in which, without guidance from practice, or spur from success, a young man should scarcely boast of being an adept. If it be said that under such disadvantages no one should attempt to write a play, I must beg leave to dissent from the position, while the first point of experience that I have gained on the subject is, a knowledge of the candour and judgment with which an impartial public distinguishes between the errors of inexperience and incapacity, and the indulgence which it shows even to a disposition to remedy the defects of either.

It were unnecessary to enter into any further extenuation of what was thought exceptionable in this play, but that it has been said, that the managers should have prevented some of the defects before its appearance to the public—and in particular the uncommon length of the piece as represented the first night. It were an ill return for the most liberal and gentlemanly conduct on their side, to suffer any censure to rest where none was deserved. Hurry in writing has long been exploded as an excuse for an author;—however, in the dramatic line, it may happen, that both an author and a manager may wish to fill a chasm in the entertainment of the public with a hastiness not altogether culpable. The season was advanced when I first put the play into Mr. Harris's hands: it was at that time at least double the length of any acting comedy. I profited by his judgment and experience in the curtailing of it—till, I believe, his feeling for the vanity of a young author got the better of his desire for correctness, and he left many excrescences remaining, because he had assisted in pruning so many more. Hence, though I was not uninformed that the acts were still too long, I flattered myself that, after the first trial, I might with safer judgment proceed to remove what should appear to have been most dissatisfactory. Many other errors there were, which might in part have arisen from my being by no means conversant with plays in general, either in reading or at the theatre. Yet I own that, in one respect, I did not regret my ignorance: for as my first wish in attempting a play was to avoid every appearance of plagiary, I thought I should stand a better chance of effecting this from being in a walk which I had not frequented, and where, consequently, the progress of invention was less likely to be interrupted by starts of recollection: for on subjects on which the mind has been much informed, invention is slow of exerting itself. Faded ideas float in the fancy like half-forgotten dreams; and the imagination in its fullest enjoyments becomes suspicious of its offspring, and doubts whether it has created or adopted.

With regard to some particular passages which on the first night's representation seemed generally disliked, I confess that if I felt any emotion of surprise at the disapprobation, it was not that they were disapproved of, but that I had not before perceived that they deserved it. As some part of the attack on the piece was begun too early to pass for the sentence of *judgment,* which is ever tardy in condemning, it has been suggested to me that much of the disapprobation must have arisen from virulence of malice, rather than severity of criticism: but as I was more apprehensive of there being just grounds to excite the latter than conscious of having deserved the former, I continue not to believe that probable which I am sure must have been unprovoked. However, if it was so, and I could even mark the quarter from whence it came, it would be ungenerous to retort; for no passion suffers more than malice from disappointment. For my own part, I see no reason why the author of a play should not regard a first night's audience as a candid and judicious friend attending, in behalf of the public, at his last rehearsal. If he can dispense with flattery, he is sure at least of sincerity, and even though the annotation be rude, he may rely upon the justness of the comment. Considered in this light, that audience, whose *fiat* is essential to the poet's claim, whether his object be fame or profit, has surely a right to expect some deference to its opinion, from principles of politeness at least, if not from gratitude.

As for the little puny critics, who scatter their peevish strictures in private circles, and scribble at every author who has the eminence of being unconnected with them, as they are usually spleen-swoln from a vain idea of increasing their consequence, there will always be found a petulance and illiberality in their remarks, which should place them as far beneath the notice of a gentleman as their original dulness had sunk them from the level of the most unsuccessful author.

It is not without pleasure that I catch at an opportunity of justifying myself from the charge of intending any national reflection in the character of Sir Lucius O'Trigger. If any gentlemen opposed the piece from that idea, I thank them sincerely for their opposition; and if the condemnation of this comedy (however misconceived the provocation) could have added one spark to the decaying flame of national attachment to the country supposed to be reflected on, I should have been happy in its fate, and might with truth have boasted that it had done more real service in its failure than the successful morality of a thousand stage-novels will ever effect.

It is usual, I believe, to thank the performers in a new play for the exertion of their several abilities. But where (as in this instance) their merit has been so striking and uncontroverted as to call for the warmest and truest applause from a number of judicious audiences, the poet's after-praise comes like the feeble acclamation of a child to close the shouts of a multitude. The conduct, however, of the principals in a theatre cannot be so apparent to the public. I think it therefore but justice to declare, that from this theatre (the only one I can speak of from experience) those writers who wish to try the dramatic line will meet with that candour and liberal attention which are generally allowed to be better calculated to lead genius into excellence than either the precepts of judgment or the guidance of experience.

THE AUTHOR

DRAMATIS PERSONÆ

AS ACTED AT COVENT GARDEN THEATRE
ON JANUARY 17, 1775

SIR ANTHONY ABSOLUTE	*Mr. Shuter*
CAPTAIN ABSOLUTE	*Mr. Woodward*
FAULKLAND	*Mr. Lewis*
ACRES	*Mr. Quick*
SIR LUCIUS O'TRIGGER	*Mr. Lee*
FAG	*Mr. Lee Lewes*
DAVID	*Mr. Dunstal*
THOMAS	*Mr. Fearon*
MRS. MALAPROP	*Mrs. Green*
LYDIA LANGUISH	*Miss Barsanti*
JULIA	*Mrs. Bulkley*
LUCY	*Mrs. Lessingham*

Maid, Boy, Servants, &c.

SCENE—BATH

Time of Action—Within one day

PROLOGUE

By the Author

SPOKEN BY MR. WOODWARD AND MR. QUICK

Enter SERJEANT-AT-LAW, *and* ATTORNEY *following, and giving a paper.*

SERJEANT. What's here!—a vile cramp hand! I cannot see
Without my spectacles.
    Attorney.   He means his fee.
Nay, Mr. Serjeant, good sir, try again.   [*Gives money.*
    Serjeant. The scrawl improves! [*more*] O come, 'tis
        pretty plain.
Hey! how's this? Dibble!—sure it cannot be!
A poet's brief! a poet and a fee!
    Attorney. Yes, sir! though you without reward, I know,
Would gladly plead the Muse's cause.
    Serjeant.   So!—So!
    Attorney. And if the fee offends, your wrath should fall
On me.
    Serjeant. Dear Dibble, no offence at all.
    Attorney. Some sons of Phœbus in the courts we meet,
    Serjeant. And fifty sons of Phœbus in the Fleet!
    Attorney. Nor pleads he worse, who with a decent sprig
Of bays adorns his legal waste of wig.
    Serjeant. Full-bottomed heroes thus, on signs, unfurl
A leaf of laurel in a grove of curl!
Yet tell your client, that, in adverse days,
This wig is warmer than a bush of bays.
    Attorney. Do you, then, sir, my client's place supply,
Profuse of robe, and prodigal of tie——
Do you, with all those blushing powers of face,
And wonted bashful hesitating grace,
Rise in the court and flourish on the case.   [*Exit.*
    Serjeant. For practice then suppose—this brief will show
        it,—
Me, Serjeant Woodward,—counsel for the poet.
Used to the ground, I know 'tis hard to deal

With this dread court, from whence there's no appeal;
No tricking here, to blunt the edge of law,
Or, damn'd in equity, escape by flaw:
But judgment given, your sentence must remain;
No writ of error lies—to Drury-lane!
    Yet when so kind you seem, 'tis past dispute
We gain some favour, if not costs of suit.
No spleen is here! I see no hoarded fury;—
I think I never faced a milder jury!
Sad else our plight! where frowns are transportation,
A hiss the gallows, and a groan damnation!
But such the public candour, without fear
My client waives all right of challenge here.
No newsman from our session is dismiss'd,
Nor wit nor critic we scratch off the list;
His faults can never hurt another's ease,
His crime, at worst, a bad attempt to please:
Thus, all respecting, he appeals to all,
And by the general voice will stand or fall.

PROLOGUE

By the Author

SPOKEN ON THE TENTH NIGHT, BY MRS. BULKLEY

GRANTED our cause, our suit and trial o'er,
The worthy serjeant need appear no more:
In pleasing I a different client choose,
He served the Poet—I would serve the Muse.
Like him, I'll try to merit your applause,
A female counsel in a female's cause.
    Look on this form,[1]—where humour, quaint and sly,
Dimples the cheek, and points the beaming eye;
Where gay invention seems to boast its wiles
In amorous hint, and half-triumphant smiles;
While her light mask or covers satire's strokes,
Or hides the conscious blush her wit provokes.
Look on her well—does she seem form'd to teach?
Should you expect to hear this lady preach?
Is grey experience suited to her youth?

[1] Pointing to the figure of Comedy.

Do solemn sentiments become that mouth?
Bid her be grave, those lips should rebel prove
To every theme that slanders mirth or love.
    Yet, thus adorn'd with every graceful art
To charm the fancy and yet reach the heart——
Must we displace her, and instead advance
The goddess of the woful countenance—
The sentimental Muse?—Her emblems view,
The Pilgrim's Progress, and a sprig of rue!
View her—too chaste to look like flesh and blood—
Primly portray'd on emblematic wood!
There, fix'd in usurpation, should she stand,
She'll snatch the dagger from her sister's hand:
And having made her votaries weep a flood,
Good heaven! she'll end her comedies in blood—
Bid Harry Woodward break poor Dunstal's crown
Imprison Quick, and knock Ned Shuter down;
While sad Barsanti, weeping o'er the scene,
Shall stab herself—or poison Mrs. Green.
    Such dire encroachments to prevent in time,
Demands the critic's voice—the poet's rhyme.
Can our light scenes add strength to holy laws!
Such puny patronage but hurts the cause:
Fair virtue scorns our feeble aid to ask;
And moral truth disdains the trickster's mask.
For here their favourite stands,[1] whose brow, severe
And sad, claims youth's respect, and pity's tear;
Who, when oppress'd by foes her worth creates,
Can point a poniard at the guilt she hates.

[1] Pointing to Tragedy.

THE RIVALS

ACT ONE

SCENE I—*A Street*

Enter THOMAS; *he crosses the Stage;* FAG *follows, looking after him.*

FAG. What! Thomas! Sure 'tis he?—What! Thomas! Thomas!

Thomas. Hey!—Odd's life! Mr. Fag!—give us your hand, my old fellow-servant.

Fag. Excuse my glove, Thomas:—I'm devilish glad to see you, my lad. Why, my prince of charioteers, you look as hearty!—but who the deuce thought of seeing you in Bath?

Thomas. Sure, master, Madam Julia, Harry, Mrs. Kate, and the postilion, be all come.

Fag. Indeed!

Thomas. Ay, master thought another fit of the gout was coming to make him a visit; so he'd a mind to gi't the slip, and whip! we were all off at an hour's warning.

Fag. Ay, ay, hasty in everything, or it would not be Sir Anthony Absolute!

Thomas. But tell us, Mr. Fag, how does young master? Odd! Sir Anthony will stare to see the captain here!

Fag. I do not serve Captain Absolute now.

Thomas. Why sure!

Fag. At present I am employed by Ensign Beverley.

Thomas. I doubt, Mr. Fag, you ha'n't changed for the better.

Fag. I have not changed, Thomas.

Thomas. No! Why didn't you say you had left young master?

Fag. No.—Well, honest Thomas, I must puzzle you no farther:—briefly then—Captain Absolute and Ensign Beverley are one and the same person.

Thomas. The devil they are!

Fag. So it is indeed, Thomas; and the ensign half of my master being on guard at present—the captain has nothing to do with me.

Thomas. So, so!—What, this is some freak, I warrant!—Do tell us, Mr. Fag, the meaning o't—you know I ha' trusted you.

Fag. You'll be secret, Thomas?

Thomas. As a coach-horse.

Fag. Why then the cause of all this is—Love[1]—Love, Thomas, who (as you may get read to you) has been a masquerader ever since the days of Jupiter.

Thomas. Ay, ay;—I guessed there was a lady in the case:—but pray, why does your master pass only for an ensign?—Now if he had shammed general indeed——

Fag. Ah! Thomas, there lies the mystery o' the matter. Hark'ee, Thomas, my master is in love with a lady of a very singular taste: a lady who likes him better as a half-pay ensign than if she knew he was son and heir to Sir Anthony Absolute, a baronet of three thousand a year.

Thomas. That is an odd taste indeed!—But has she got the stuff, Mr. Fag? Is she rich, hey?

Fag. Rich!—Why, I believe she owns half the stocks! Zounds! Thomas, she could pay the national debt as easily as I could my washerwoman! She has a lap-dog that eats out of gold,—she feeds her parrot with small pearls,—and all her thread-papers are made of banknotes!

Thomas. Bravo, faith!—Odd! I warrant she has a set of thousands at least:—but does she draw kindly with the captain?

Fag. As fond as pigeons.

Thomas. May one hear her name?

Fag. Miss Lydia Languish.—But there is an old tough aunt in the way; though, by-the-by, she has never seen my master—for we got acquainted with miss while on a visit in Gloucestershire.

Thomas. Well—I wish they were once harnessed together in matrimony.—But pray, Mr. Fag, what kind of a place is this Bath?—I ha' heard a deal of it—here's a mort o' merry-making, hey?

Fag. Pretty well, Thomas, pretty well—'tis a good lounge; in the morning we go to the pump-room (though neither my master nor I drink the waters); after breakfast

[1] i.e.—he spells the word.

we saunter on the parades, or play a game at billiards; at night we dance; but damn the place, I'm tired of it: their regular hours stupefy me—not a fiddle nor a card after eleven!—However Mr. Faulkland's gentleman and I keep it up a little in private parties;—I'll introduce you there, Thomas—you'll like him much.

Thomas. Sure I know Mr. Du-Peigne—you know his master is to marry Madam Julia.

Fag. I had forgot.—But, Thomas, you must polish a little—indeed you must.—Here now—this wig! What the devil do you do with a wig, Thomas?—None of the London whips of any degree of *ton* wear wigs now.

Thomas. More's the pity! more's the pity! I say.—Odd's life! when I heard how the lawyers and doctors had took to their own hair, I thought how 'twould go next:—odd rabbit it! when the fashion had got foot on the bar, I guessed 'twould mount to the box!—but 'tis all out of character, believe me, Mr. Fag: and look'ee, I'll never gi' up mine—the lawyers and doctors may do as they will.

Fag. Well, Thomas, we'll not quarrel about that.

Thomas. Why, bless you, the gentlemen of the professions ben't all of a mind—for in our village now, thoff Jack Gauge, the exciseman, has ta'en to his carrots, there's little Dick the farrier swears he'll never forsake his bob, though all the college should appear with their own heads!

Fag. Indeed! well said, Dick!—but hold—mark! mark! Thomas.

Thomas. Zooks! 'tis the captain.—Is that the Lady with him?

Fag. No, no, that is Madam Lucy, my master's mistress's maid. They lodge at that house—but I must after him to tell him the news.

Thomas. Odd! he's given her money!—Well, Mr. Fag——

Fag. Good-bye, Thomas. I have an appointment in Gyde's porch this evening at eight; meet me there, and we'll make a little party.   [*Exeunt severally.*

SCENE II—*A Dressing-room in* Mrs. Malaprop's
Lodgings

Lydia *sitting on a sofa, with a book in her hand.* Lucy,
as just returned from a message.

Lucy. Indeed, ma'am, I traversed half the town in search
of it! I don't believe there's a circulating library in Bath I
han't been at.

Lydia. And could not you get *The Reward of Constancy?*

Lucy. No, indeed, ma'am.

Lydia. Nor *The Fatal Connexion?*

Lucy. No, indeed, ma'am.

Lydia. Nor *The Mistakes of the Heart?*

Lucy. Ma'am, as ill luck would have it, Mr. Bull said
Miss Sukey Saunter had just fetched it away.

Lydia. Heigh-ho! Did you inquire for *The Delicate
Distress?*

Lucy. Or, *The Memoirs of Lady Woodford?* Yes, indeed,
ma'am. I asked everywhere for it; and I might have
brought it from Mr. Frederick's, but Lady Slattern
Lounger, who had just sent it home, had so soiled and
dog's-eared it, it wa'n't fit for a Christian to read.

Lydia. Heigh-ho! Yes, I always know when Lady Slattern has been before me. She has a most observing thumb;
and, I believe, cherishes her nails for the convenience of
making marginal notes.—Well, child, what have you
brought me?

Lucy. Oh! here, ma'am.—[*Taking books from under her
cloak and from her pockets.*] This is *The Gordian Knot,*—
and this *Peregrine Pickle.* Here are *The Tears of Sensibility,* and *Humphrey Clinker.* This is *The Memoirs of a
Lady of Quality, written by Herself,* and here the second
volume of *The Sentimental Journey.*

Lydia. Heigh-ho!—What are those books by the glass?

Lucy. The great one is only *The Whole Duty of Man,*
where I press a few blonds, ma'am.

Lydia. Very well—give me the *sal volatile.*

Lucy. Is it in a blue cover, ma'am?

Lydia. My smelling-bottle, you simpleton!

Lucy. Oh, the drops—here, ma'am.

Lydia. Hold!—here's some one coming—quick! see who
it is.—

[*Exit* Lucy.] Surely I heard my cousin Julia's voice.

Re-enter LUCY.

Lucy. Lud! ma'am, here is Miss Melville.
Lydia. Is it possible?—   [*Exit* LUCY.

Enter JULIA.

Lydia. My dearest Julia, how delighted am I!—[*Embrace.*] How unexpected was this happiness!

Julia. True, Lydia—and our pleasure is the greater.—But what has been the matter?—you were denied to me at first!

Lydia. Ah, Julia, I have a thousand things to tell you!—But first inform me what has conjured you to Bath?—Is Sir Anthony here?

Julia. He is—we are arrived within this hour—and I suppose he will be here to wait on Mrs. Malaprop as soon as he is dressed.

Lydia. Then before we are interrupted, let me impart to you some of my distress!—I know your gentle nature will sympathize with me, though your prudence may condemn me! My letters have informed you of my whole connection with Beverley; but I have lost him, Julia! My aunt has discovered our intercourse by a note she intercepted, and has confined me ever since! Yet, would you believe it? she has absolutely fallen in love with a tall Irish baronet she met one night since she has been here, at Lady Macshuffle's rout.

Julia. You jest, Lydia!

Lydia. No, upon my word.—She really carries on a kind of correspondence with him, under a feigned name though, till she chooses to be known to him: but it is a Delia or a Celia, I assure you.

Julia. Then, surely, she is now more indulgent to her niece.

Lydia. Quite the contrary. Since she has discovered her own frailty, she is become more suspicious of mine. Then I must inform you of another plague! That odious Acres is to be in Bath to-day: so that I protest I shall be teased out of all spirits!

Julia. Come, come, Lydia, hope for the best—Sir Anthony shall use his interest with Mrs. Malaprop.

Lydia. But you have not heard the worst. Unfortunately I had quarrelled with my poor Beverley, just before my

aunt made the discovery, and I have not seen him since
to make it up.

Julia. What was his offence?

Lydia. Nothing at all! But, I don't know how it was, as
often as we had been together, we had never had a
quarrel, and, somehow, I was afraid he would never give
me an opportunity. So, last Thursday, I wrote a letter to
myself, to inform myself that Beverley was at that time
paying his addresses to another woman. I signed it *your
friend unknown,* showed it to Beverley, charged him with
his falsehood, put myself in a violent passion, and vowed
I'd never see him more.

Julia. And you let him depart so, and have not seen him
since?

Lydia. 'Twas the next day my aunt found the matter
out. I intended only to have teased him three days and a
half, and now I've lost him for ever.

Julia. If he is as deserving and sincere as you have
represented him to me, he will never give you up so. Yet,
consider, Lydia, you tell me he is but an ensign, and you
have thirty thousand pounds.

Lydia. But you know I lose most of my fortune if I
marry without my aunt's consent, till of age; and that is
what I have determined to do, ever since I knew the
penalty. Nor could I love the man who would wish to
wait a day for the alternative.

Julia. Nay, this is caprice!

Lydia. What, does Julia tax me with caprice? I thought
her lover Faulkland had inured her to it.

Julia. I do not love even his faults.

Lydia. But àpropos—you have sent to him, I suppose?

Julia. Not yet, upon my word—nor has he the least idea
of my being in Bath. Sir Anthony's resolution was so sudden, I could not inform him of it.

Lydia. Well, Julia, you are your own mistress (though
under the protection of Sir Anthony), yet have you, for
this long year, been a slave to the caprice, the whim, the
jealousy of this ungrateful Faulkland, who will ever delay
assuming the right of a husband, while you suffer him to
be equally imperious as a lover.

Julia. Nay, you are wrong entirely. We were contracted
before my father's death. That, and some consequent em-
barrassments, have delayed what I know to be my Faulk-

land's most ardent wish. He is too generous to trifle on
such a point—and for his character, you wrong him there,
too. No, Lydia, he is too proud, too noble, to be jealous;
if he is captious, 'tis without dissembling; if fretful, without rudeness. Unused to the fopperies of love, he is
negligent of the little duties expected from a lover—but
being unhackneyed in the passion, his affection is ardent
and sincere; and as it engrosses his whole soul, he expects
every thought and emotion of his mistress to move in
unison with his. Yet, though his pride calls for this full
return, his humility makes him undervalue those qualities
in him which would entitle him to it; and not feeling why
he should be loved to the degree he wishes, he still suspects that he is not loved enough. This temper, I must
own, has cost me many unhappy hours; but I have learned
to think myself his debtor, for those imperfections which
arise from the ardour of his attachment.

Lydia. Well, I cannot blame you for defending him. But
tell me candidly, Julia, had he never saved your life, do
you think you should have been attached to him as you
are?—Believe me, the rude blast that overset your boat
was a prosperous gale of love to him.

Julia. Gratitude may have strengthened my attachment
to Mr. Faulkland, but I loved him before he had preserved
me; yet surely that alone were an obligation sufficient.

Lydia. Obligation! why a water spaniel would have
done as much!—Well, I should never think of giving my
heart to a man because he could swim.

Julia. Come, Lydia, you are too inconsiderate.

Lydia. Nay, I do but jest—What's here?

Re-enter Lucy *in a hurry.*

Lucy. O ma'am, here is Sir Anthony Absolute just come
home with your aunt.

Lydia. They'll not come here.—Lucy, do you watch.

[*Exit* Lucy.

Julia. Yet I must go. Sir Anthony does not know I am
here, and if we meet, he'll detain me, to show me the town.
I'll take another opportunity of paying my respects to Mrs.
Malaprop, when she shall treat me, as long as she chooses,
with her select words so ingeniously misapplied, without
being mispronounced.

Re-enter LUCY.

Lucy. O Lud! ma'am, they are both coming upstairs.

Lydia. Well, I'll not detain you, coz.—Adieu, my dear Julia. I'm sure you are in haste to send to Faulkland.—There, through my room you'll find another staircase.

Julia. Adieu! [*Embraces* LYDIA, *and exit.*

Lydia. Here, my dear Lucy, hide these books. Quick, quick!—Fling *Peregrine Pickle* under the toilet—throw *Roderick Random* into the closet—put *The Innocent Adultery* into *The Whole Duty of Man*—thrust *Lord Aimworth* under the sofa—cram *Ovid* behind the bolster—there—put *The Man of Feeling* into your pocket—so, so—now lay *Mrs. Chapone* in sight, and leave *Fordyce's Sermons* open on the table.

Lucy. O burn it, ma'am! the hair-dresser has torn away as far as *Proper Pride*.

Lydia. Never mind—open at *Sobriety*.—Fling me *Lord Chesterfield's Letters*. Now for 'em. [*Exit* LUCY.

Enter MRS. MALAPROP *and* SIR ANTHONY ABSOLUTE.

Mrs. Malaprop. There, Sir Anthony, there sits the deliberate simpleton who wants to disgrace her family, and lavish herself on a fellow not worth a shilling.

Lydia. Madam, I thought you once—

Mrs. Malaprop. You thought, miss! I don't know any business you have to think at all—thought does not become a young woman. But the point we would request of you is, that you will promise to forget this fellow—to illiterate him, I say, quite from your memory.

Lydia. Ah, madam! our memories are independent of our wills. It is not so easy to forget.

Mrs. Malaprop. But I say it is, miss; there is nothing on earth so easy as to forget, if a person chooses to set about it. I'm sure I have as much forgot your poor dear uncle as if he had never existed—and I thought it my duty so to do; and let me tell you, Lydia, these violent memories don't become a young woman.

Sir Anthony. Why sure she won't pretend to remember what she's ordered not!—ay, this comes of her reading!

Lydia. What crime, madam, have I committed, to be treated thus?

Mrs. Malaprop. Now don't attempt to extirpate yourself from the matter; you know I have proof controvertible of it.—But tell me, will you promise to do as you're bid? Will you take a husband of your friends' choosing?

Lydia. Madam, I must tell you plainly, that had I no preference for any one else, the choice you have made would be my aversion.

Mrs. Malaprop. What business have you, miss, with preference and aversion? They don't become a young woman; and you ought to know, that as both always wear off, 'tis safest in matrimony to begin with a little aversion. I am sure I hated your poor dear uncle before marriage as if he'd been a blackamoor—and yet, miss, you are sensible what a wife I made!—and when it pleased Heaven to release me from him, 'tis unknown what tears I shed! But suppose we were going to give you another choice, will you promise us to give up this Beverley?

Lydia. Could I belie my thoughts so far as to give that promise, my actions would certainly as far belie my words.

Mrs. Malaprop. Take yourself to your room. You are fit company for nothing but your own ill-humours.

Lydia. Willingly, ma'am—I cannot change for the worse.   [*Exit.*

Mrs. Malaprop. There's a little intricate hussy for you!

Sir Anthony. It is not to be wondered at, ma'am,—all this is the natural consequence of teaching girls to read. Had I a thousand daughters, by Heaven! I'd as soon have them taught the black art as their alphabet!

Mrs. Malaprop. Nay, nay, Sir Anthony, you are an absolute misanthropy.

Sir Anthony. In my way hither, Mrs. Malaprop, I observed your niece's maid coming forth from a circulating library!—She had a book in each hand—they were half-bound volumes, with marble covers!—From that moment I guessed how full of duty I should see her mistress!

Mrs. Malaprop. Those are vile places, indeed!

Sir Anthony. Madam, a circulating library in a town is as an evergreen tree of diabolical knowledge! It blossoms through the year!—and depend on it, Mrs. Malaprop, that they who are so fond of handling the leaves, will long for the fruit at last.

Mrs. Malaprop. Fy, fy, Sir Anthony, you surely speak laconically.

Sir Anthony. Why, Mrs. Malaprop, in moderation now, what would you have a woman know?

Mrs. Malaprop. Observe me, Sir Anthony. I would by no

means wish a daughter of mine to be a progeny of learning; I don't think so much learning becomes a young woman; for instance, I would never let her meddle with Greek, or Hebrew, or algebra, or simony, or fluxions, or paradoxes, or such inflammatory branches of learning—neither would it be necessary for her to handle any of your mathematical, astronomical, diabolical instruments. —But, Sir Anthony, I would send her, at nine years old, to a boarding-school, in order to learn a little ingenuity and artifice. Then, sir, she should have a supercilious knowledge in accounts;—and as she grew up, I would have her instructed in geometry, that she might know something of the contagious countries;—but above all, Sir Anthony, she should be mistress of orthodoxy, that she might not mis-spell, and mis-pronounce words so shamefully as girls usually do; and likewise that she might reprehend the true meaning of what she is saying. This, Sir Anthony, is what I would have a woman know;—and I don't think there is a superstitious article in it.

Sir Anthony. Well, well, Mrs. Malaprop, I will dispute the point no further with you; though I must confess that you are a truly moderate and polite arguer, for almost every third word you say is on my side of the question. But, Mrs. Malaprop, to the more important point in debate —you say you have no objection to my proposal?

Mrs. Malaprop. None, I assure you. I am under no positive engagement with Mr. Acres, and as Lydia is so obstinate against him, perhaps your son may have better success.

Sir Anthony. Well, madam, I will write for the boy directly. He knows not a syllable of this yet, though I have for some time had the proposal in my head. He is at present with his regiment.

Mrs. Malaprop. We have never seen your son, Sir Anthony; but I hope no objection on his side.

Sir Anthony. Objection!—let him object if he dare!—No, no, Mrs. Malaprop, Jack knows that the least demur puts me in a frenzy directly. My process was always very simple—in their younger days, 'twas "Jack do this";—if he demurred, I knocked him down—and if he grumbled at that, I always sent him out of the room.

Mrs. Malaprop. Ah, and the properest way, o' my conscience!—nothing is so conciliating to young people as severity.—Well, Sir Anthony, I shall give Mr. Acres his discharge, and prepare Lydia to receive your son's invocations;—and I hope you will represent her to the captain as an object not altogether illegible.

Sir Anthony. Madam, I will handle the subject prudently.—Well, I must leave you; and let me beg you, Mrs. Malaprop, to enforce this matter roundly to the girl.— Take my advice—keep a tight hand; if she rejects this proposal, clap her under lock and key; and if you were just to let the servants forget to bring her dinner for three or four days, you can't conceive how she'd come about.   [*Exit.*

Mrs. Malaprop. Well, at any rate, I shall be glad to get her from under my intuition. She has somehow discovered my partiality for Sir Lucius O'Trigger—sure, Lucy can't have betrayed me!—No, the girl is such a simpleton, I should have made her confess it.—Lucy!—Lucy!—[*Calls.*] Had she been one of your artificial ones, I should never have trusted her.

Re-enter LUCY.

Lucy. Did you call, ma'am?

Mrs. Malaprop. Yes, girl.—Did you see Sir Lucius while you was out?

Lucy. No, indeed, ma'am, not a glimpse of him.

Mrs. Malaprop. You are sure, Lucy, that you never mentioned——

Lucy. Oh, gemini! I'd sooner cut my tongue out.

Mrs. Malaprop. Well, don't let your simplicity be imposed on.

Lucy. No, ma'am.

Mrs. Malaprop. So, come to me presently, and I'll give you another letter to Sir Lucius; but mind, Lucy—if ever you betray what you are entrusted with (unless it be other people's secrets to me), you forfeit my malevolence for ever, and your being a simpleton shall be no excuse for your locality.   [*Exit.*

Lucy. Ha! ha! ha!—So, my dear Simplicity, let me give you a little respite.—[*Altering her manner.*] Let girls in my station be as fond as they please of appearing expert, and knowing in their trusts; commend me to a mask of silliness, and a pair of sharp eyes for my own interest under it!—Let me see to what account have I turned my simplicity lately.—[*Looks at a paper.*] For *abetting Miss Lydia Languish in a design of running away with an*

*ensign!—in money, sundry times, twelve pound twelve;
gowns, five; hats, ruffles, caps, etc., etc., numberless!—
From the said ensign, within this last month, six guineas
and a half.*—About a quarter's pay!—Item, *from Mrs.
Malaprop, for betraying the young people to her*—when I
found matters were likely to be discovered—*two guineas
and a black paduasoy.*—Item, *from Mr. Acres, for carrying divers letters*—which I never delivered—*two guineas
and a pair of buckles*—Item, *from Sir Lucius O'Trigger,
three crowns, two gold pocket-pieces, and a silver snuff-
box!*—Well done, Simplicity!—Yet I was forced to make
my Hibernian believe that he was corresponding, not with
the aunt, but with the niece; for though not over rich, I
found he had too much pride and delicacy to sacrifice the
feelings of a gentleman to the necessities of his fortune.

[*Exit.*

ACT TWO

SCENE I—Captain Absolute's *Lodgings*

Captain Absolute *and* Fag.

Fag. Sir, while I was there, Sir Anthony came in: I told
him you had sent me to inquire after his health, and to
know if he was at leisure to see you.

Absolute. And what did he say, on hearing I was at
Bath?

Fag. Sir, in my life I never saw an elderly gentleman
more astonished! He started back two or three paces,
rapped out a dozen interjectural oaths, and asked what
the devil had brought you here.

Absolute. Well, sir, and what did you say?

Fag. Oh, I lied, sir—I forget the precise lie; but you
may depend on't, he got no truth from me. Yet, with submission, for fear of blunders in future, I should be glad to
fix what has brought us to Bath, in order that we may
lie a little consistently. Sir Anthony's servants were curious,
sir, very curious indeed.

Absolute. You have said nothing to them?

Fag. Oh, not a word, sir,—not a word! Mr. Thomas,
indeed, the coachman (whom I take to be the discreetest
of whips)——

Absolute. 'Sdeath!—you rascal! you have not trusted him!

Fag. Oh, no, sir—no—no—not a syllable, upon my veracity!—He was, indeed, a little inquisitive; but I was sly, sir—devilish sly! My master (said I), honest Thomas (you know, sir, one says honest to one's inferiors), is come to Bath to recruit.—Yes, sir, I said to recruit—and whether for men, money, or constitution, you know, sir, is nothing to him nor any one else.

Absolute. Well, recruit will do—let it be so.

Fag. Oh, sir, recruit will do surprisingly—indeed, to give the thing an air, I told Thomas that your honour had already enlisted five disbanded chairmen, seven minority waiters, and thirteen billiard-markers.

Absolute. You blockhead, never say more than is necessary.

Fag. I beg pardon, sir—I beg pardon—but, with submission, a lie is nothing unless one supports it. Sir, whenever I draw on my invention for a good current lie, I always forge indorsements as well as the bill.

Absolute. Well, take care you don't hurt your credit by offering too much security.—Is Mr. Faulkland returned?

Fag. He is above, sir, changing his dress.

Absolute. Can you tell whether he has been informed of Sir Anthony and Miss Melville's arrival?

Fag. I fancy not, sir; he has seen no one since he came in but his gentleman, who was with him at Bristol.—I think, sir, I hear Mr. Faulkland coming down—

Absolute. Go tell him I am here.

Fag. Yes, sir.—[*Going.*] I beg pardon, sir, but should Sir Anthony call, you will do me the favour to remember that we are recruiting, if you please.

Absolute. Well, well.

Fag. And, in tenderness to my character, if your honour could bring in the chairmen and waiters, I should esteem it as an obligation; for though I never scruple a lie to serve my master, yet it hurts one's conscience to be found out. [*Exit.*

Absolute. Now for my whimsical friend—if he does not know that his mistress is here, I'll tease him a little before I tell him——

Enter FAULKLAND.

Faulkland, you're welcome to Bath again; you are punctual in your return.

Faulkland. Yes; I had nothing to detain me when I had finished the business I went on. Well, what news since I left you? how stand matters between you and Lydia?

Absolute. Faith, much as they were; I have not seen her since our quarrel; however, I expect to be recalled every hour.

Faulkland. Why don't you persuade her to go off with you at once?

Absolute. What, and lose two-thirds of her fortune? You forget that, my friend.—No, no, I could have brought her to that long ago.

Faulkland. Nay, then, you trifle too long—if you are sure of her, propose to the aunt in your own character, and write to Sir Anthony for his consent.

Absolute. Softly, softly; for though I am convinced my little Lydia would elope with me as Ensign Beverley, yet am I by no means certain that she would take me with the impediment of our friends' consent, a regular humdrum wedding, and the reversion of a good fortune on my side: no, no; I must prepare her gradually for the discovery, and make myself necessary to her, before I risk it.—Well, but Faulkland; you'll dine with us to-day at the hotel?

Faulkland. Indeed, I cannot; I am not in spirits to be of such a party.

Absolute. By heavens! I shall forswear your company. You are the most teasing, captious, incorrigible lover!— Do love like a man.

Faulkland. I own I am unfit for company.

Absolute. Am I not a lover; ay, and a romantic one too? Yet do I carry everywhere with me such a confounded farrago of doubts, fears, hopes, wishes, and all the flimsy furniture of a country miss's brain!

Faulkland. Ah! Jack, your heart and soul are not, like mine, fixed immutably on one only object. You throw for a large stake, but losing, you could stake and throw again:—but I have set my sum of happiness on this cast, and not to succeed were to be stripped of all.

Absolute. But, for heaven's sake! what grounds for apprehension can your whimsical brain conjure up at present?

Faulkland. What grounds for apprehension, did you say? Heavens! are there not a thousand! I fear for her spirits—her health—her life!—My absence may fret her; her anxiety for my return, her fears for me, may oppress her gentle temper: and for her health, does not every hour bring me cause to be alarmed? If it rains, some shower may even then have chilled her delicate frame. If the wind be keen, some rude blast may have affected her! The heat of noon, the dews of the evening, may endanger the life of her for whom only I value mine. O Jack! when delicate and feeling souls are separated, there is not a feature in the sky, not a movement of the elements, not an aspiration of the breeze, but hints some cause for a lover's apprehension!

Absolute. Ay, but we may choose whether we will take the hint or not.—So, then, Faulkland, if you were convinced that Julia were well and in spirits, you would be entirely content?

Faulkland. I should be happy beyond measure—I am anxious only for that.

Absolute. Then to cure your anxiety at once—Miss Melville is in perfect health, and is at this moment in Bath.

Faulkland. Nay, Jack—don't trifle with me.

Absolute. She is arrived here with my father within this hour.

Faulkland. Can you be serious?

Absolute. I thought you knew Sir Anthony better than to be surprised at a sudden whim of this kind.—Seriously, then, it is as I tell you—upon my honour.

Faulkland. My dear friend!—Hollo, Du-Peigne! my hat. —My dear Jack—now nothing on earth can give me a moment's uneasiness.

Re-enter FAG.

Fag. Sir, Mr. Acres, just arrived, is below.

Absolute. Stay, Faulkland, this Acres lives within a mile of Sir Anthony, and he shall tell you how your mistress has been ever since you left her. Fag, show this gentleman up.   [*Exit* FAG.

Faulkland. What, is he much acquainted in the family?

Absolute. Oh, very intimate: I insist on your not going: besides, his character will divert you.

Faulkland. Well, I should like to ask him a few questions.

Absolute. He is likewise a rival of mine—that is, of my other self's, for he does not think his friend Captain Absolute ever saw the lady in question; and it is ridiculous

enough to hear him complain to me of one Beverley, a
concealed skulking rival, who——

Faulkland. Hush!—he's here.

Enter ACRES.

Acres. Ha! my dear friend, noble captain, and honest
Jack, how do'st thou? just arrived, faith, as you see.—
Sir, your humble servant. Warm work on the roads,
Jack!—Odds whips and wheels! I've travelled like a
comet, with a tail of dust all the way as long as the Mall.

Absolute. Ah! Bob, you are indeed an eccentric planet,
but we know your attraction hither.—Give me leave to
introduce Mr. Faulkland to you; Mr. Faulkland, Mr. Acres.

Acres. Sir, I am most heartily glad to see you: sir, I
solicit your connections.—Hey, Jack—what, this is Mr.
Faulkland, who——

Absolute. Ay, Bob, Miss Melville's Mr. Faulkland.

Acres. Odso! she and your father can be but just arrived before me?—I suppose you have seen them. Ah! Mr.
Faulkland, you are indeed a happy man.

Faulkland. I have not seen Miss Melville yet, sir;—I
hope she enjoyed full health and spirits in Devonshire?

Acres. Never knew her better in my life, sir,—never
better. Odds blushes and blooms! she has been as healthy
as the German Spa.

Faulkland. Indeed! I did hear that she had been a little
indisposed.

Acres. False, false, sir—only said to vex you: quite the
reverse, I assure you.

Faulkland. There, Jack, you see she has the advantage
of me; I had almost fretted myself ill.

Absolute. Now are you angry with your mistress for not
having been sick?

Faulkland. No, no, you misunderstand me: yet surely a
little trifling indisposition is not an unnatural consequence
of absence from those we love.—Now confess—isn't there
something unkind in this violent, robust, unfeeling health?

Absolute. Oh, it was very unkind of her to be well in
your absence, to be sure!

Acres. Good apartments, Jack.

Faulkland. Well, sir, but you were saying that Miss
Melville has been so exceedingly well—what then she has
been merry and gay, I suppose?—Always in spirits—
hey?

Acres. Merry, odds crickets! she has been the belle and spirit of the company wherever she has been—so lively and entertaining! so full of wit and humour!

Faulkland. There, Jack, there.—Oh, by my soul! there is an innate levity in woman that nothing can overcome.— What! happy, and I away!

Absolute. Have done!—How foolish this is! just now you were only apprehensive for your mistress' spirits.

Faulkland. Why, Jack, have I been the joy and spirit of the company?

Absolute. No, indeed, you have not.

Faulkland. Have I been lively and entertaining?

Absolute. Oh, upon my word, I acquit you.

Faulkland. Have I been full of wit and humour?

Absolute. No, faith, to do you justice, you have been confoundedly stupid indeed.

Acres. What's the matter with the gentleman?

Absolute. He is only expressing his great satisfaction at hearing that Julia has been so well and happy—that's all —hey, Faulkland?

Faulkland. Oh! I am rejoiced to hear it—yes, yes, she has a happy disposition!

Acres. That she has indeed—then she is so accomplished—so sweet a voice—so expert at her harpsichord— such a mistress of flat and sharp, squallante, rumblante, and quiverante!—There was this time month—odds minums and crotchets! how she did chirrup at Mrs. Piano's concert!

Faulkland. There again, what say you to this? you see she has been all mirth and song—not a thought of me!

Absolute. Pho! man, is not music the food of love?

Faulkland. Well, well, it may be so.—Pray, Mr.——, what's his damned name?—Do you remember what songs Miss Melville sung?

Acres. Not I indeed.

Absolute. Stay, now, they were some pretty melancholy purling-stream airs, I warrant; perhaps you may recollect; —did she sing, *When absent from my soul's delight?*

Acres. No, that wa'n't it.

Absolute. Or, *Go, gentle dales!*   [*Sings.*

Acres. Oh, no! nothing like it. Odds! now I recollect one of them—*My heart's my own, my will is free.* [*Sings.*

Faulkland. Fool! fool that I am! to fix all my happiness on such a trifler! 'Sdeath! to make herself the pipe and ballad-monger of a circle to soothe her light heart with catches and glees!—What can you say to this, sir?

Absolute. Why, that I should be glad to hear my mistress had been so merry, sir.

Faulkland. Nay, nay, nay—I'm not sorry that she has been happy—no, no, I am glad of that—I would not have had her sad or sick—yet surely a sympathetic heart would have shown itself even in the choice of a song—she might have been temperately healthy, and somehow, plaintively gay;—but she has been dancing too, I doubt not!

Acres. What does the gentleman say about dancing?

Absolute. He says the lady we speak of dances as well as she sings.

Acres. Ay, truly, does she—there was at our last race ball——

Faulkland. Hell and the devil!—There!—there—I told you so! I told you so! Oh! she thrives in my absence!—Dancing! But her whole feelings have been in opposition with mine;—I have been anxious, silent, pensive, sedentary—my days have been hours of care, my nights of watchfulness.—She has been all health! spirit! laugh! song! dance!—Oh! damned, damned levity!

Absolute. For heaven's sake, Faulkland, don't expose yourself so!—Suppose she has danced, what then?—does not the ceremony of society often oblige——

Faulkland. Well, well, I'll contain myself—perhaps as you say—for form sake.—What, Mr. Acres, you were praising Miss Melville's manner of dancing a minuet—hey?

Acres. Oh, I dare insure her for that—but what I was going to speak of was her country dancing. Odds swimmings! she has such an air with her!

Faulkland. Now disappointment on her!—Defend this, Absolute; why don't you defend this?—Country-dances! jigs and reels! am I to blame now? A minuet I could have forgiven—I should not have minded that—I say I should not have regarded a minuet—but country-dances!—Zounds! had she made one in a cotillon—I believe I could have forgiven even that—but to be monkey-led for a night!—to run the gauntlet through a string of amorous palming puppies!—to show paces like a managed filly!—Oh, Jack, there never can be but one man in the world whom a truly modest and delicate woman ought to pair with in a country-dance; and, even then, the rest of the couples should be her great-uncles and aunts!

Absolute. Ay, to be sure!—grandfathers and grandmothers!

Faulkland. If there be but one vicious mind in the set, 'twill spread like a contagion—the action of their pulse beats to the lascivious movement of the jig—their quivering, warm-breathed sighs impregnate the very air—the atmosphere becomes electrical to love, and each amorous spark darts through every link of the chain!—I must leave you—I own I am somewhat flurried—and that confounded looby has perceived it.   [*Going.*

Absolute. Nay, but stay, Faulkland, and thank Mr. Acres for his good news.

Faulkland. Damn his news!   [*Exit.*

Absolute. Ha! ha! ha! poor Faulkland five minutes since —"nothing on earth could give him a moment's uneasiness!"

Acres. The gentleman wa'n't angry at my praising his mistress, was he?

Absolute. A little jealous, I believe, Bob.

Acres. You don't say so? Ha! ha! jealous of me—that's a good joke.

Absolute. There's nothing strange in that, Bob! let me tell you, that sprightly grace and insinuating manner of yours will do some mischief among the girls here.

Acres. Ah! you joke—ha! ha! mischief—ha! ha! but you know I am not my own property, my dear Lydia has forestalled me. She could never abide me in the country, because I used to dress so badly—but odds frogs and tambours! I shan't take matters so here, now ancient madam has no voice in it: I'll make my old clothes know who's master. I shall straightway cashier the hunting-frock, and render my leather breeches incapable. My hair has been in training some time.

Absolute. Indeed!

Acres. Ay—and tho'ff the side curls are a little restive, my hind-part takes it very kindly.

Absolute. Oh, you'll polish, I doubt not.

Acres. Absolutely I propose so—then if I can find out this Ensign Beverley, odds triggers and flints! I'll make him know the difference o't.

Absolute. Spoke like a man! But pray, Bob, I observe you have got an odd kind of a new method of swearing——

Acres. Ha! ha! you've taken notice of it—'tis genteel,

isn't it!—I didn't invent it myself though; but a commander in our militia, a great scholar, I assure you, says that there is no meaning in the common oaths, and that nothing but their antiquity makes them respectable; because, he says, the ancients would never stick to an oath or two, but would say, by Jove! or by Bacchus! or by Mars! or by Venus! or by Pallas, according to the sentiment: so that to swear with propriety, says my little major, the oath should be an echo to the sense; and this we call the *oath referential,* or *sentimental swearing*—ha! ha! 'tis genteel, isn't it.

Absolute. Very genteel, and very new, indeed!—and I dare say will supplant all other figures of imprecation.

Acres. Ay, ay, the best terms will grow obsolete.—Damns have had their day.

Re-enter FAG.

Fag. Sir, there is a gentleman below desires to see you.—Shall I show him into the parlour?

Absolute. Ay—you may.

Acres. Well, I must be gone——

Absolute. Stay; who is it, Fag?

Fag. Your father, sir.

Absolute. You puppy, why didn't you show him up directly?   [*Exit* FAG.

Acres. You have business with Sir Anthony.—I expect a message from Mrs. Malaprop at my lodgings. I have sent also to my dear friend, Sir Lucius O'Trigger. Adieu, Jack! we must meet at night, when you shall give me a dozen bumpers to little Lydia.

Absolute. That I will with all my heart.—[*Exit* ACRES.] Now for a parental lecture—I hope he has heard nothing of the business that brought me here—I wish the gout had held him fast in Devonshire, with all my soul!

Enter SIR ANTHONY ABSOLUTE.

Sir, I am delighted to see you here; looking so well! your sudden arrival at Bath made me apprehensive for your health.

Sir Anthony. Very apprehensive, I dare say, Jack.—What, you are recruiting here, hey?

Absolute. Yes, sir, I am on duty.

Sir Anthony. Well, Jack, I am glad to see you, though I

did not expect it, for I was going to write to you on a little matter of business.—Jack, I have been considering that I grow old and infirm, and shall probably not trouble you long.

Absolute. Pardon me, sir, I never saw you look more strong and hearty; and I pray frequently that you may continue so.

Sir Anthony. I hope your prayers may be heard, with all my heart. Well, then, Jack, I have been considering that I am so strong and hearty I may continue to plague you a long time. Now, Jack, I am sensible that the income of your commission, and what I have hitherto allowed you, is but a small pittance for a lad of your spirit.

Absolute. Sir, you are very good.

Sir Anthony. And it is my wish, while yet I live, to have my boy make some figure in the world. I have resolved, therefore, to fix you at once in a noble independence.

Absolute. Sir, your kindness overpowers me—such generosity makes the gratitude of reason more lively than the sensations even of filial affection.

Sir Anthony. I am glad you are so sensible of my attention—and you shall be master of a large estate in a few weeks.

Absolute. Let my future life, sir, speak my gratitude; I cannot express the sense I have of your munificence.—Yet, sir, I presume you would not wish me to quit the army?

Sir Anthony. Oh, that shall be as your wife chooses.

Absolute. My wife, sir!

Sir Anthony. Ay, ay, settle that between you—settle that between you.

Absolute. A wife, sir, did you say?

Sir Anthony. Ay, a wife—why, did not I mention her before?

Absolute. Not a word of her, sir.

Sir Anthony. Odd so!—I mus'n't forget her though.—Yes, Jack, the independence I was talking of is by marriage—the fortune is saddled with a wife—but I suppose that makes no difference.

Absolute. Sir! sir!—you amaze me!

Sir Anthony. Why, what the devil's the matter with the fool? Just now you were all gratitude and duty.

Absolute. I was, sir—you talked to me of independence and a fortune, but not a word of a wife.

Sir Anthony. Why—what difference does that make?

Odds life, sir! if you have the estate, you must take it with the live stock on it, as it stands.

Absolute. If my happiness is to be the price, I must beg leave to decline the purchase.—Pray, sir, who is the lady?

Sir Anthony. What's that to you, sir?—Come, give me your promise to love, and to marry her directly.

Absolute. Sure, sir, this is not very reasonable, to summon my affections for a lady I know nothing of!

Sir Anthony. I am sure, sir, 'tis more unreasonable in you to object to a lady you know nothing of.

Absolute. Then, sir, I must tell you plainly that my inclinations are fixed on another—my heart is engaged to an angel.

Sir Anthony. Then pray let it send an excuse. It is very sorry—but business prevents its waiting on her.

Absolute. But my vows are pledged to her.

Sir Anthony. Let her foreclose, Jack; let her foreclose; they are not worth redeeming; besides, you have the angel's vows in exchange, I suppose; so there can be no loss there.

Absolute. You must excuse me, sir, if I tell you, once for all, that in this point I cannot obey you.

Sir Anthony. Hark'ee, Jack;—I have heard you for some time with patience—I have been cool—quite cool; but take care—you know I am compliance itself—when I am not thwarted;—no one more easily led—when I have my own way;—but don't put me in a frenzy.

Absolute. Sir, I must repeat—in this I cannot obey you.

Sir Anthony. Now damn me! if ever I call you Jack again while I live!

Absolute. Nay, sir, but hear me.

Sir Anthony. Sir, I won't hear a word—not a word! not one word! so give me your promise by a nod—and I'll tell you what, Jack—I mean, you dog—if you don't, by——

Absolute. What, sir, promise to link myself to some mass of ugliness! to——

Sir Anthony. Zounds! sirrah! the lady shall be as ugly as I choose: she shall have a hump on each shoulder; she shall be as crooked as the crescent; her one eye shall roll like the bull's in Cox's Museum; she shall have a skin like a mummy, and the beard of a Jew—she shall be all this, sirrah!—yet I will make you ogle her all day, and sit up all night to write sonnets on her beauty.

Absolute. This is reason and moderation indeed!

Sir Anthony. None of your sneering, puppy! no grinning, jackanapes!

Absolute. Indeed, sir, I never was in a worse humour for mirth in my life.

Sir Anthony. 'Tis false, sir. I know you are laughing in your sleeve; I know you'll grin when I am gone, sirrah!

Absolute. Sir, I hope I know my duty better.

Sir Anthony. None of your passion, sir! none of your violence, if you please!—It won't do with me, I promise you.

Absolute. Indeed, sir, I never was cooler in my life.

Sir Anthony. 'Tis a confounded lie!—I know you are in a passion in your heart; I know you are, you hypocritical young dog! but it won't do.

Absolute. Nay, sir, upon my word——

Sir Anthony. So you will fly out! can't you be cool like me? What the devil good can passion do?—Passion is of no service, you impudent, insolent, overbearing reprobate! —There, you sneer again! don't provoke me!—but you rely upon the mildness of my temper—you do, you dog! you play upon the meekness of my disposition!—Yet take care—the patience of a saint may be overcome at last! —but mark! I give you six hours and a half to consider of this: if you then agree, without any condition, to do everything on earth that I choose, why—confound you! I may in time forgive you.—If not, zounds! don't enter the same hemisphere with me! don't dare to breathe the same air, or use the same light with me; but get an atmosphere and a sun of your own! I'll strip you of your commission; I'll lodge a five-and-threepence in the hands of trustees, and you shall live on the interest.—I'll disown you, I'll disinherit you, I'll unget you! and damn me! if ever I call you Jack again! [*Exit* SIR ANTHONY.

Absolute. Mild, gentle, considerate father—I kiss your hands!—What a tender method of giving his opinion in these matters Sir Anthony has! I dare not trust him with the truth.—I wonder what old wealthy hag it is that he wants to bestow on me!—Yet he married himself for love! and was in his youth a bold intriguer, and a gay companion!

Re-enter FAG.

Fag. Assuredly, sir, your father is wrath to a degree; he comes down stairs eight or ten steps at a time—muttering, growling, and thumping the banisters all the way: I and the cook's dog stand bowing at the door—rap! he gives me a stroke on the head with his cane; bids me carry that to my master; then kicking the poor turnspit into the area, damns us all, for a puppy triumvirate!— Upon my credit, sir, were I in your place, and found my father such very bad company, I should certainly drop his acquaintance.

Absolute. Cease your impertinence, sir, at present.— Did you come in for nothing more?—Stand out of the way!　　　　　　　　　　　　*[Pushes him aside, and exit.*

Fag. So! Sir Anthony trims my master; he is afraid to reply to his father—then vents his spleen on poor Fag! —When one is vexed by one person, to revenge one's self on another, who happens to come in the way, is the vilest injustice! Ah! it shows the worst temper—the basest——

Enter BOY.

Boy. Mr. Fag! Mr. Fag! your master calls you.

Fag. Well, you little dirty puppy, you need not bawl so!—The meanest disposition! the——

Boy. Quick, quick, Mr. Fag!

Fag. Quick! quick! you impudent jackanapes! am I to be commanded by you too? you little, impertinent, insolent, kitchen-bred——　　　　　　*[Exit kicking and beating him.*

SCENE II—*The North Parade*

Enter LUCY.

Lucy. So—I shall have another rival to add to my mistress's list—Captain Absolute. However, I shall not enter his name till my purse has received notice in form. Poor Acres is dismissed!—Well, I have done him a last friendly office, in letting him know that Beverley was here before him.—Sir Lucius is generally more punctual, when he expects to hear from his *dear Dalia,* as he calls her: I wonder he's not here!—I have a little scruple of conscience from this deceit; though I should not be paid so well, if my hero knew that Delia was near fifty, and her own mistress.

Enter SIR LUCIUS O'TRIGGER.

Sir Lucius. Ha! my little ambassadress—upon my conscience, I have been looking for you; I have been on the South Parade this half hour.

Lucy. [*Speaking simply.*] O gemini! and I have been waiting for your lordship here on the North.

Sir Lucius. Faith!—may be that was the reason we did not meet; and it is very comical too, how you could go out and I not see you—for I was only taking a nap at the Parade Coffee-house, and I chose the window on purpose that I might not miss you.

Lucy. My stars! Now I'd wager a sixpence I went by while you were asleep.

Sir Lucius. Sure enough it must have been so—and I never dreamt it was so late, till I waked. Well, but my little girl, have you got nothing for me?

Lucy. Yes, but I have—I've got a letter for you in my pocket.

Sir Lucius. O faith! I guessed you weren't come empty-handed—Well—let me see what the dear creature says.

Lucy. There, Sir Lucius.   [*Gives him a letter.*

Sir Lucius. [Reads.] *Sir—there is often a sudden incentive impulse in love, that has a greater induction than years of domestic combination: such was the commotion I felt at the first superfluous view of Sir Lucius O'Trigger.* —Very pretty, upon my word.—*Female punctuation forbids me to say more; yet let me add, that it will give me joy infallible to find Sir Lucius worthy the last criterion of my affections.*

DELIA.

Upon my conscience! Lucy, your lady is a great mistress of language. Faith, she's quite the queen of the dictionary! —for the devil a word dare refuse coming at her call— though one would think it was quite out of hearing.

Lucy. Ay, sir, a lady of her experience——

Sir Lucius. Experience! what, at seventeen?

Lucy. O true, sir—but then she reads so—my stars! how she will read off hand!

Sir Lucius. Faith, she must be very deep read to write this way—though she is rather an arbitrary writer too— for here are a great many poor words pressed into the service of this note, that would get their *habeas corpus* from any court in Christendom.

Lucy. Ah! Sir Lucius, if you were to hear how she talks of you!

Sir Lucius. Oh, tell her I'll make her the best husband in the world, and Lady O'Trigger into the bargain!—But we must get the old gentlewoman's consent—and do everything fairly.

Lucy. Nay, Sir Lucius, I thought you wa'n't rich enough to be so nice.

Sir Lucius. Upon my word, young woman, you have hit it:—I am so poor, that I can't afford to do a dirty action. —If I did not want money, I'd steal your mistress and her fortune with a great deal of pleasure.—However, my pretty girl [*Gives her money*], here's a little something to buy you a ribbon; and meet me in the evening, and I'll give you an answer to this. So, hussy, take a kiss beforehand to put you in mind.   [*Kisses her.*

Lucy. O Lud! Sir Lucius—I never seed such a gemman! My lady won't like you if you're so impudent.

Sir Lucius. Faith she will, Lucy!—That same—pho! what's the name of it?—modesty—is a quality in a lover more praised by the women than liked; so, if your mistress asks you whether Sir Lucius ever gave you a kiss, tell her fifty—my dear.

Lucy. What, would you have me tell her a lie?

Sir Lucius. Ah, then, you baggage! I'll make it a truth presently.

Lucy. For shame now! here is some one coming.

Sir Lucius. Oh, faith, I'll quiet your conscience!

                    [*Exit humming a tune.*

Enter FAG.

Fag. So, so, ma'am! I humbly beg pardon.

Lucy. O Lud! now, Mr. Fag, you flurry one so.

Fag. Come, come, Lucy, here's no one by—so a little less simplicity, with a grain or two more sincerity, if you please.—You play false with us, madam.—I saw you give the baronet a letter.—My master shall know this—and if he don't call him out, I will.

Lucy. Ha! ha! ha! you gentlemen's gentlemen are so hasty. That letter was from Mrs. Malaprop, simpleton.— She is taken with Sir Lucius's address.

Fag. How! what tastes some people have!—Why, I suppose I have walked by her window a hundred times.

—But what says our young lady? any message to my master?

Lucy. Sad news, Mr. Fag.—A worse rival than Acres! Sir Anthony Absolute has proposed his son.

Fag. What, Captain Absolute?

Lucy. Even so—I overheard it all.

Fag. Ha! ha! ha! very good, faith. Good bye, Lucy, I must away with this news.

Lucy. Well, you may laugh—but it is true, I assure you.—[*Going.*] But, Mr. Fag, tell your master not to be cast down by this.

Fag. Oh, he'll be so disconsolate!

Lucy. And charge him not to think of quarrelling with young Absolute.

Fag. Never fear! never fear!

Lucy. Be sure—bid him keep up his spirits.

Fag. We will—we will.   [*Exeunt severally.*

ACT THREE

SCENE I—*The North Parade*

Enter CAPTAIN ABSOLUTE.

ABSOLUTE. 'Tis just as Fag told me, indeed. Whimsical enough, faith. My father wants to force me to marry the very girl I am plotting to run away with! He must not know of my connection with her yet awhile. He has too summary a method of proceeding in these matters. However, I'll read my recantation instantly. My conversion is something sudden, indeed—but I can assure him it is very sincere. So, so—here he comes. He looks plaguy gruff.   [*Steps aside.*

Enter SIR ANTHONY ABSOLUTE.

Sir Anthony. No—I'll die sooner than forgive him. Die, did I say? I'll live these fifty years to plague him. At our last meeting, his impudence had almost put me out of temper. An obstinate, passionate, self-willed boy! Who can he take after? This is my return for getting him before all his brothers and sisters!—for putting him, at twelve years old, into a marching regiment, and allowing him fifty pounds a year, besides his pay, ever since! But I have done with him; he's anybody's son for me. I never will see him more, never—never—never.

Absolute. [*Aside, coming forward.*] Now for a penitential face.

Sir Anthony. Fellow, get out of my way.

Absolute. Sir, you see a penitent before you.

Sir Anthony. I see an impudent scoundrel before me.

Absolute. A sincere penitent. I am come, sir, to acknowledge my error, and to submit entirely to your will.

Sir Anthony. What's that?

Absolute. I have been revolving, and reflecting, and considering on your past goodness, and kindness, and condescension to me.

Sir Anthony. Well, sir?

Absolute. I have been likewise weighing and balancing what you were pleased to mention concerning duty, and obedience, and authority.

Sir Anthony. Well, puppy?

Absolute. Why, then, sir, the result of my reflections is— a resolution to sacrifice every inclination of my own to your satisfaction.

Sir Anthony. Why now you talk sense—absolute sense. —I never heard anything more sensible in my life. Confound you! you shall be Jack again.

Absolute. I am happy in the appellation.

Sir Anthony. Why, then, Jack, my dear Jack, I will now inform you who the lady really is. Nothing but your passion and violence, you silly fellow, prevented my telling you at first. Prepare, Jack, for wonder and rapture—prepare. What think you of Miss Lydia Languish?

Absolute. Languish! What, the Languishes of Worcestershire?

Sir Anthony. Worcestershire! no. Did you ever meet Mrs. Malaprop and her niece, Miss Languish, who came into our country just before you were last ordered to your regiment?

Absolute. Malaprop! Languish! I don't remember ever to have heard the names before. Yet stay—I think I do recollect something. Languish! Languish! She squints, don't she? A little red-haired girl?

Sir Anthony. Squints! A red-haired girl! Zounds! no.

Absolute. Then I must have forgot; it can't be the same person.

Sir Anthony. Jack! Jack! what think you of blooming, love-breathing seventeen?

Absolute. As to that, sir, I am quite indifferent. If I can please you in the matter, 'tis all I desire.

Sir Anthony. Nay, but, Jack, such eyes! such eyes! so innocently wild! so bashfully irresolute! not a glance but speaks and kindles some thought of love! Then, Jack, her cheeks! her cheeks, Jack! so deeply blushing, at the insinuations of her tell-tale eyes! Then, Jack, her lips! O, Jack, lips smiling at their own discretion; and if not smiling, more sweetly pouting; more lovely in sullenness.

Absolute. That's she, indeed. Well done, old gentleman.
[*Aside.*

Sir Anthony. Then, Jack, her neck! O Jack! Jack!

Absolute. And which is to be mine, sir; the niece or the aunt?

Sir Anthony. Why, you unfeeling, insensible puppy, I despise you! When I was of your age, such a description would have made me fly like a rocket! The aunt, indeed! Odds life! when I ran away with your mother, I would not have touched anything old or ugly to gain an empire.

Absolute. Not to please your father, sir?

Sir Anthony. To please my father! zounds! not to please —Oh, my father—odd so!—yes—yes; if my father indeed had desired—that's quite another matter. Though he wa'n't the indulgent father that I am, Jack.

Absolute. I dare say not, sir.

Sir Anthony. But, Jack, you are not sorry to find your mistress is so beautiful?

Absolute. Sir, I repeat it—if I please you in this affair, 'tis all I desire. Not that I think a woman the worse for being handsome; but, sir, if you please to recollect, you before hinted something about a hump or two, one eye, and a few more graces of that kind—now, without being very nice, I own I should rather choose a wife of mine to have the usual number of limbs, and a limited quantity of back: and though one eye may be very agreeable, yet as the prejudice has always run in favour of two, I would not wish to affect a singularity in that article.

Sir Anthony. What a phlegmatic sot it is! Why, sirrah, you're an anchorite!—a vile, insensible stock. You a soldier!—you're a walking block, fit only to dust the company's regimentals on! Odds life! I have a great mind to marry the girl myself!

Absolute. I am entirely at your disposal, sir: if you should think of addressing Miss Languish yourself, I suppose you would have me marry the aunt; or if you should change your mind, and take the old lady—'tis the same to me— I'll marry the niece.

Sir Anthony. Upon my word, Jack, thou'rt either a very great hypocrite, or—but, come, I know your indifference on such a subject must be all a lie—I'm sure it must— come, now—damn your demure face!—come, confess, Jack—you have been lying, ha'n't you? You have been playing the hypocrite, hey!—I'll never forgive you, if you ha'n't been lying and playing the hypocrite.

Absolute. I'm sorry, sir, that the respect and duty which I bear to you should be so mistaken.

Sir Anthony. Hang your respect and duty! But come along with me, I'll write a note to Mrs. Malaprop, and you shall visit the lady directly. Her eyes shall be the Promethean torch to you—come along, I'll never forgive you, if you don't come back stark mad with rapture and impatience—if you don't, egad, I will marry the girl myself!
　　　　　　　　　　　　　　　　　　　　　　　[*Exeunt.*

SCENE II—*Julia's Dressing-Room*

FAULKLAND *discovered alone.*

Faulkland. They told me Julia would return directly; I wonder she is not yet come! How mean does this captious, unsatisfied temper of mine appear to my cooler judgment! Yet I know not that I indulge it in any other point: but on this one subject, and to this one subject, whom I think I love beyond my life, I am ever ungenerously fretful and madly capricious! I am conscious of it— yet I cannot correct myself! What tender honest joy sparkled in her eyes when we met! how delicate was the warmth of her expression! I was ashamed to appear less happy—though I had come resolved to wear a face of coolness and upbraiding. Sir Anthony's presence prevented my proposed expostulations: yet I must be satisfied that she has not been so very happy in my absence. She is coming! Yes!—I know the nimbleness of her tread, when she thinks her impatient Faulkland counts the moments of her stay.

Enter JULIA.

Julia. I had not hoped to see you again so soon.

Faulkland. Could I, Julia, be contented with my first welcome—restrained as we were by the presence of a third person?

Julia. O Faulkland, when your kindness can make me thus happy, let me not think that I discovered something of coldness in your first salutation.

Faulkland. 'Twas but your fancy, Julia. I was rejoiced to see you—to see you in such health. Sure I had no cause for coldness?

Julia. Nay, then, I see you have taken something ill. You must not conceal from me what it is.

Faulkland. Well, then—shall I own to you that my joy at hearing of your health and arrival here, by your neighbour Acres, was somewhat damped by his dwelling much on the high spirits you had enjoyed in Devonshire—on your mirth—your singing—dancing, and I know not what! For such is my temper, Julia, that I should regard every mirthful moment in your absence as a treason to constancy. The mutual tear that steals down the cheek of parting lovers is a compact, that no smile shall live there till they meet again.

Julia. Must I never cease to tax my Faulkland with this teasing minute caprice? Can the idle reports of a silly boor weigh in your breast against my tried affections?

Faulkland. They have no weight with me, Julia: No, no —I am happy if you have been so—yet only say, that you did not sing with mirth—say that you thought of Faulkland in the dance.

Julia. I never can be happy in your absence. If I wear a countenance of content, it is to show that my mind holds no doubt of my Faulkland's truth. If I seemed sad, it were to make malice triumph; and say, that I fixed my heart on one, who left me to lament his roving, and my own credulity. Believe me, Faulkland, I mean not to upbraid you, when I say, that I have often dressed sorrow in smiles, lest my friends should guess whose unkindness had caused my tears.

Faulkland. You were ever all goodness to me. Oh, I am a brute, when I but admit a doubt of your true constancy!

Julia. If ever without such cause from you, as I will not suppose possible, you find my affections veering but a point, may I become a proverbial scoff for levity and base ingratitude.

Faulkland. Ah! Julia, that last word is grating to me. I would I had no title to your gratitude! Search your heart, Julia; perhaps what you have mistaken for love, is but the warm effusion of a too thankful heart.

Julia. For what quality must I love you?

Faulkland. For no quality! To regard me for any quality of mind or understanding, were only to esteem me. And for person—I have often wished myself deformed, to be convinced that I owe no obligation there for any part of your affection.

Julia. Where nature has bestowed a show of nice attention in the features of a man, he should laugh at it as misplaced. I have seen men, who in this vain article, perhaps, might rank above you; but my heart has never asked my eyes if it were so or not.

Faulkland. Now this is not well from you, Julia—I despise person in a man—yet if you loved me as I wish, though I were an Æthiop, you'd think none so fair.

Julia. I see you are determined to be unkind! The contract which my poor father bound us in gives you more than a lover's privilege.

Faulkland. Again, Julia, you raise ideas that feed and justify my doubts. I would not have been more free—no —I am proud of my restraint. Yet—yet—perhaps your high respect alone for this solemn compact has fettered your inclinations, which else had made a worthier choice. How shall I be sure, had you remained unbound in thought and promise, that I should still have been the object of your persevering love?

Julia. Then try me now. Let us be free as strangers as to what is past: my heart will not feel more liberty!

Faulkland. There now! so hasty, Julia! so anxious to be free! If your love for me were fixed and ardent, you would not lose your hold, even though I wished it!

Julia. Oh! you torture me to the heart! I cannot bear it.

Faulkland. I do not mean to distress you. If I loved you less I should never give you an uneasy moment. But hear me. All my fretful doubts arise from this. Women are not used to weigh and separate the motives of their affections: the cold dictates of prudence, gratitude, or filial duty, may sometimes be mistaken for the pleadings of the heart. I would not boast—yet let me say, that I have neither age, person, nor character, to found dislike on; my fortune such as few ladies could be charged with indiscretion in the match. O Julia! when love receives such countenance from prudence, nice minds will be suspicious of its birth.

Julia. I know not whither your insinuations would tend: —but as they seem pressing to insult me, I will spare you the regret of having done so.—I have given you no cause for this!   [*Exit in tears.*

Faulkland. In tears! Stay, Julia: stay but for a moment. —The door is fastened!—Julia!—my soul!—but for one moment!—I hear her sobbing!—'Sdeath! what a brute am I to use her thus! Yet stay! Ay—she is coming now:—how little resolution there is in a woman!—how a few soft words can turn them!—No, faith!—she is not coming either.—Why, Julia—my love—say but that you forgive me—come but to tell me that—now this is being too resentful. Stay! she is coming too—I thought she would —no steadiness in anything: her going away must have been a mere trick then—she sha'n't see that I was hurt by it—I'll affect indifference—[*Hums a tune; then listens.*] No—zounds! she's not coming!—nor don't intend it, I suppose.—This is not steadiness, but obstinacy! Yet I deserve it.—What, after so long an absence to quarrel with her tenderness!—'twas barbarous and unmanly!—I should be ashamed to see her now.—I'll wait till her just resentment is abated—and when I distress her so again, may I lose her for ever! and be linked instead to some antique virago, whose gnawing passions, and long hoarded spleen, shall make me curse my folly half the day and all the night.   [*Exit.*

SCENE III—Mrs. Malaprop's *Lodgings*

Mrs. Malaprop, *with a letter in her hand, and* Captain Absolute.

Mrs. Malaprop. Your being Sir Anthony's son, captain, would itself be a sufficient accommodation; but from the ingenuity of your appearance, I am convinced you deserve the character here given of you.

Absolute. Permit me to say, madam, that as I never yet have had the pleasure of seeing Miss Languish, my principal inducement in this affair at present is the honour of being allied to Mrs. Malaprop; of whose intellectual accomplishments, elegant manners, and unaffected learning, no tongue is silent.

Mrs. Malaprop. Sir, you do me infinite honour! I beg, captain, you'll be seated.—[*They sit.*] Ah! few gentlemen, now-a-days, know how to value the ineffectual qualities in a woman!—few think how a little knowledge becomes a gentlewoman.—Men have no sense now but for the worth-less flower of beauty!

Absolute. It is but too true, indeed, ma'am;—yet I fear our ladies should share the blame—they think our admira-tion of beauty so great, that knowledge in them would be superfluous. Thus, like garden-trees, they seldom show fruit, till time has robbed them of more specious blossom. —Few, like Mrs. Malaprop and the orange-tree, are rich in both at once!

Mrs. Malaprop. Sir, you overpower me with good-breeding.—He is the very pine-apple of politeness!—You are not ignorant, captain, that this giddy girl has somehow contrived to fix her affections on a beggarly, strolling, eavesdropping ensign, whom none of us have seen, and nobody knows anything of.

Absolute. Oh, I have heard the silly affair before.—I'm not at all prejudiced against her on that account.

Mrs. Malaprop. You are very good and very considerate, captain. I am sure I have done everything in my power since I exploded the affair; long ago I laid my positive conjunctions on her, never to think on the fellow again; —I have since laid Sir Anthony's preposition before her; but, I am sorry to say, she seems resolved to decline every particle that I enjoin her.

Absolute. It must be very distressing, indeed, ma'am.

Mrs. Malaprop. Oh! it gives me the hydrostatics to such a degree.—I thought she had persisted from corresponding with him; but, behold, this very day, I have interceded another letter from the fellow; I believe I have it in my pocket.

Absolute. Oh, the devil! my last note.   [*Aside.*

Mrs. Malaprop. Ay, here it is.

Absolute. Ay, my note indeed! Oh, the little traitress Lucy.   [*Aside.*

Mrs. Malaprop. There, perhaps you may know the writ-ing.   [*Gives him the letter.*

Absolute. I think I have seen the hand before—yes, I certainly must have seen this hand before—

Mrs. Malaprop. Nay, but read it, captain.

Absolute. [Reads.] *My soul's idol, my adored Lydia!*—Very tender, indeed!

Mrs. Malaprop. Tender, ay, and profane too, o' my conscience.

Absolute. [Reads.] *I am excessively alarmed at the intelligence you send me, the more so as my new rival*——

Mrs. Malaprop. That's you, sir.

Absolute. [Reads.] *Has universally the character of being an accomplished gentleman and a man of honour.*—Well, that's handsome enough.

Mrs. Malaprop. Oh, the fellow has some design in writing so.

Absolute. That he had, I'll answer for him, ma'am.

Mrs. Malaprop. But go on, sir—you'll see presently.

Absolute. [Reads.] *As for the old weather-beaten she-dragon who guards you.*—Who can he mean by that?

Mrs. Malaprop. Me, sir!—me!—he means me!—There—what do you think now?—but go on a little further.

Absolute. Impudent scoundrel!—[Reads.] *it shall go hard but I will elude her vigilance, as I am told that the same ridiculous vanity, which makes her dress up her coarse features, and deck her dull chat with hard words which she don't understand*——

Mrs. Malaprop. There, sir, an attack upon my language! what do you think of that?—an aspersion upon my parts of speech! was ever such a brute! Sure, if I reprehend any thing in this world it is the use of my oracular tongue, and a nice derangement of epitaphs!

Absolute. He deserves to be hanged and quartered! let me see—[Reads.] *same ridiculous vanity*——

Mrs. Malaprop. You need not read it again, sir.

Absolute. I beg pardon, ma'am.—[Reads.] *does also lay her open to the grossest deceptions from flattery and pretended admiration*—an impudent coxcomb!—*so that I have a scheme to see you shortly with the old harridan's consent, and even to make her a go-between in our interview.*—Was ever such assurance!

Mrs. Malaprop. Did you ever hear anything like it?—he'll elude my vigilance, will he?—Yes, yes! ha! ha! he's very likely to enter these doors;—we'll try who can plot best!

Absolute. So we will, ma'am—so we will! Ha! ha! ha! a conceited puppy, ha! ha! ha!—Well, but, Mrs. Malaprop, as the girl seems so infatuated by this fellow, suppose you were to wink at her corresponding with him for a little time—let her even plot an elopement with him—then do you connive at her escape—while I, just in the nick, will have the fellow laid by the heels, and fairly contrive to carry her off in his stead.

Mrs. Malaprop. I am delighted with the scheme; never was anything better perpetrated!

Absolute. But, pray, could not I see the lady for a few minutes now?—I should like to try her temper a little.

Mrs. Malaprop. Why, I don't know—I doubt she is not prepared for a visit of this kind. There is a decorum in these matters.

Absolute. O Lord! she won't mind me—only tell her Beverley——

Mrs. Malaprop. Sir!

Absolute. Gently, good tongue.   [*Aside.*

Mrs. Malaprop. What did you say of Beverley?

Absolute. Oh, I was going to propose that you should tell her, by way of jest, that it was Beverley who was below; she'd come down fast enough then—ha! ha! ha!

Mrs. Malaprop. 'Twould be a trick she well deserves; besides, you know the fellow tells her he'll get my consent to see her—ha! ha! Let him if he can, I say again. Lydia, come down here!—[*Calling.*] He'll make me a go-between in their interviews!—ha! ha! ha! Come down, I say, Lydia! I don't wonder at your laughing, ha! ha! ha! his impudence is truly ridiculous.

Absolute. 'Tis very ridiculous, upon my soul, ma'am, ha! ha! ha!

Mrs. Malaprop. The little hussy won't hear. Well, I'll go and tell her at once who it is—she shall know that Captain Absolute is come to wait on her. And I'll make her behave as becomes a young woman.

Absolute. As you please, madam.

Mrs. Malaprop. For the present, captain, your servant. Ah! you've not done laughing yet, I see—elude my vigilance; yes, yes; ha! ha! ha!   [*Exit.*

Absolute. Ha! ha! ha! one would think now that I might throw off all disguise at once, and seize my prize with security; but such is Lydia's caprice, that to undeceive were probably to lose her. I'll see whether she knows me.

          [*Walks aside, and seems engaged in looking at the pictures.*

Enter LYDIA.

Lydia. What a scene am I now to go through! surely nothing can be more dreadful than to be obliged to listen to the loathsome addresses of a stranger to one's heart. I have heard of girls persecuted as I am, who have appealed in behalf of their favoured lover to the generosity of his rival; suppose I were to try it—there stands the hated rival—an officer too;—but oh, how unlike my Beverley! I wonder he don't begin—truly he seems a very negligent wooer!—quite at his ease, upon my word! I'll speak first—Mr. Absolute.

Absolute. Ma'am.   [*Turns round.*

Lydia. O heavens! Beverley!

Absolute. Hush;—hush, my life! softly! be not surprised!

Lydia. I am so astonished! and so terrified! and so overjoyed!—for Heaven's sake! how came you here?

Absolute. Briefly, I have deceived your aunt—I was informed that my new rival was to visit here this evening, and contriving to have him kept away, have passed myself on her for Captain Absolute.

Lydia. O charming! And she really takes you for young Absolute.

Absolute. Oh, she's convinced of it.

Lydia. Ha! ha! ha! I can't forbear laughing to think how her sagacity is overreached!

Absolute. But we trifle with our precious moments—such another opportunity may not occur; then let me conjure my kind, my condescending angel, to fix the time when I may rescue her from undeserving persecution, and with a licensed warmth plead for my reward.

Lydia. Will you then, Beverley, consent to forfeit that portion of my paltry wealth?—that burden on the wings of love?

Absolute. Oh, come to me—rich only thus—in loveliness! Bring no portion to me but thy love—'twill be generous in you, Lydia,—for well you know it is the only dower your poor Beverley can repay.

Lydia. How persuasive are his words!—how charming will poverty be with him!   [*Aside.*

Absolute. Ah! my soul, what a life will we then live! Love shall be our idol and support! we will worship him with a monastic strictness; adjuring all worldly toys, to centre every thought and action there. Proud of calamity, we will enjoy the wreck of wealth; while the surrounding gloom of adversity shall make the flame of our pure love show doubly bright. By Heavens! I would fling all goods of fortune from me with a prodigal hand, to enjoy the scene where I might clasp my Lydia to my bosom, and say, the world affords no smile to me but here—[*Embracing her.*] If she holds out now, the devil is in it!   [*Aside.*

Lydia. Now could I fly with him to the antipodes! but my persecution is not yet come to a crisis.   [*Aside.*

Re-enter MRS. MALAPROP, *listening.*

Mrs. Malaprop. I am impatient to know how the little hussy deports herself.   [*Aside.*

Absolute. So pensive, Lydia!—is then your warmth abated?

Mrs. Malaprop. Warmth abated!—so!—she has been in a passion, I suppose.   [*Aside.*

Lydia. No—nor ever can while I have life.

Mrs. Malaprop. An ill-tempered little devil! She'll be in a passion all her life—will she?   [*Aside.*

Lydia. Think not the idle threats of my ridiculous aunt can ever have any weight with me.

Mrs. Malaprop. Very dutiful, upon my word!   [*Aside.*

Lydia. Let her choice be Captain Absolute, but Beverley is mine.

Mrs. Malaprop. I am astonished at her assurance!—to his face—this is to his face.   [*Aside.*

Absolute. Thus then let me enforce my suit.   [*Kneeling.*

Mrs. Malaprop. [*Aside.*] Ay, poor young man!—down on his knees entreating for pity!—I can contain no longer. —[*Coming forward.*] Why, thou vixen!—I have overheard you.

Absolute. Oh, confound her vigilance!   [*Aside.*

Mrs. Malaprop. Captain Absolute, I know not how to apologize for her shocking rudeness.

Absolute. [*Aside.*] So all's safe, I find.—[*Aloud.*] I have hopes, madam, that time will bring the young lady——

Mrs. Malaprop. Oh, there's nothing to be hoped for from her! she's as headstrong as an allegory on the banks of Nile.

Lydia. Nay, madam, what do you charge me with now?

Mrs. Malaprop. Why, thou unblushing rebel—didn't you tell this gentleman to his face that you loved another better?—didn't you say you never would be his?

Lydia. No, madam—I did not.

Mrs. Malaprop. Good heavens! what assurance!—Lydia, Lydia, you ought to know that lying don't become a young woman!—Didn't you boast that Beverley, that stroller Beverley, possessed your heart?—Tell me that, I say.

Lydia. 'Tis true, ma'am, and none but Beverley——

Mrs. Malaprop. Hold!—hold, Assurance!—you shall not be so rude.

Absolute. Nay, pray, Mrs. Malaprop, don't stop the young lady's speech: she's very welcome to talk thus—it does not hurt me in the least, I assure you.

Mrs. Malaprop. You are too good, captain—too amiably patient—but come with me, miss.—Let us see you again soon, captain—remember what we have fixed.

Absolute. I shall, ma'am.

Mrs. Malaprop. Come, take a graceful leave of the gentleman.

Lydia. May every blessing wait on my Beverley, my loved Bev——

Mrs. Malaprop. Hussy! I'll choke the word in your throat!—come along—come along.

[*Exeunt severally;* CAPTAIN ABSOLUTE *kissing his hand to*
        LYDIA—MRS. MALAPROP *stopping her from speaking.*

SCENE IV—ACRES' *Lodgings*

ACRES, *as just dressed, and* DAVID.

Acres. Indeed, David—do you think I become it so?

David. You are quite another creature, believe me, master, by the mass! an' we've any luck we shall see the Devon monkeyrony in all the print-shops in Bath!

Acres. Dress does make a difference, David.

David. 'Tis all in all, I think.—Difference! why, an' you were to go now to Clod Hall, I am certain the old lady wouldn't know you: Master Butler wouldn't believe his own eyes, and Mrs. Pickle would cry, Lard presarve me! our dairy-maid would come giggling to the door, and I warrant Dolly Tester, your honour's favourite, would blush like my waistcoat.—Oons! I'll hold a gallon, there an't a dog in the house but would bark, and I question whether Phillis would wag a hair of her tail!

Acres. Ay, David, there's nothing like polishing.

David. So I says of your honour's boots; but the boy never heeds me!

Acres. But, David, has Mr. De-la-grace been here? I must rub up my balancing, and chasing, and boring.

David. I'll call again, sir.

Acres. Do—and see if there are any letters for me at the post-office.

David. I will.—By the mass, I can't help looking at your head!—if I hadn't been by at the cooking, I wish I may die if I should have known the dish again myself.   [*Exit.*

Acres. [*Practising a dancing-step.*] Sink, slide—coupee. —Confound the first inventors of cotillons! say I—they are as bad as algebra to us country gentlemen.—I can walk a minuet easy enough when I am forced!—and I have been accounted a good stick in a country-dance.— Odds jigs and tabors! I never valued your cross-over to couple—figure in—right and left—and I'd foot it with e'er a captain in the county!—but these outlandish heathen allemandes and cotillons are quite beyond me!—I shall never prosper at 'em, that's sure—mine are true-born English legs—they don't understand their curst French lingo! —their *pas* this, and *pas* that, and *pas* t'other!—damn me!—my feet don't like to be called paws! no, 'tis certain I have most Anti-gallican toes!

Enter SERVANT.

Servant. Here is Sir Lucius O'Trigger to wait on you, sir.

Acres. Show him in.   [*Exit* SERVANT.

Enter SIR LUCIUS O'TRIGGER.

Sir Lucius. Mr. Acres, I am delighted to embrace you.

Acres. My dear Sir Lucius, I kiss your hands.

Sir Lucius. Pray, my friend, what has brought you so suddenly to Bath?

Acres. Faith! I have followed Cupid's Jack-a-lantern, and find myself in a quagmire at last.—In short, I have been very ill-used, Sir Lucius.—I don't choose to mention names, but look on me as on a very ill-used gentleman.

Sir Lucius. Pray what is the case?—I ask no names.

Acres. Mark me, Sir Lucius, I fall as deep as need be in love with a young lady—her friends take my part—I follow her to Bath—send word of my arrival; and receive answer, that the lady is to be otherwise disposed of.— This, Sir Lucius, I call being ill-used.

Sir Lucius. Very ill, upon my conscience.—Pray, can you divine the cause of it?

Acres. Why, there's the matter; she has another lover, one Beverley, who, I am told, is now in Bath.—Odds slanders and lies! he must be at the bottom of it.

Sir Lucius. A rival in the case, is there?—and you think he has supplanted you unfairly?

Acres. Unfairly! to be sure he has. He never could have done it fairly.

Sir Lucius. Then sure you know what is to be done!

Acres. Not I, upon my soul!

Sir Lucius. We wear no swords here, but you understand me.

Acres. What! fight him.

Sir Lucius. Ay, to be sure: what can I mean else?

Acres. But he has given me no provocation.

Sir Lucius. Now, I think he has given you the greatest provocation in the world. Can a man commit a more heinous offence against another man than to fall in love with the same woman? Oh, by my soul! it is the most unpardonable breach of friendship.

Acres. Breach of friendship! ay, ay; but I have no acquaintance with this man. I never saw him in my life.

Sir Lucius. That's no argument at all—he has the less right than to take such a liberty.

Acres. Gad, that's true—I grow full of anger, Sir Lucius! —I fire apace! Odds hilts and blades! I find a man may have a deal of valour in him, and not know it! But couldn't I contrive to have a little right on my side?

Sir Lucius. What the devil signifies right, when your honour is concerned? Do you think Achilles, or my little Alexander the Great, ever inquired where the right lay? No, by my soul, they drew their broad-swords, and left the lazy sons of peace to settle the justice of it.

Acres. Your words are a grenadier's march to my heart! I believe courage must be catching! I certainly do feel a kind of valour rising as it were—a kind of courage, as I may say.—Odds flints, pans, and triggers! I'll challenge him directly.

Sir Lucius. Ah, my little friend, if I had Blunderbuss Hall here, I could show you a range of ancestry, in the old O'Trigger line, that would furnish the new room; every one of whom had killed his man!—For though the mansion-house and dirty acres have slipped through my

fingers, I thank heaven our honour and the family-pictures
are as fresh as ever.

Acres. O, Sir Lucius! I have had ancestors too!—every
man of 'em colonel or captain in the militia!—Odds balls
and barrels! say no more—I'm braced for it. The thunder
of your words has soured the milk of human kindness in
my breast:—Zounds! as the man in the plays says, *I
could do such deeds!*

Sir Lucius. Come, come, there must be no passion at all
in the case—these things should always be done civilly.

Acres. I must be in a passion, Sir Lucius—I must be
in a rage.—Dear Sir Lucius, let me be in a rage, if you
love me. Come, here's pen and paper.—[*Sits down to
write.*] I would the ink were red!—Indite, I say, indite!
—How shall I begin? Odds bullets and blades! I'll write
a good bold hand, however.

Sir Lucius. Pray compose yourself.

Acres. Come—now, shall I begin with an oath? Do, Sir
Lucius, let me begin with a damme.

Sir Lucius. Pho! pho! do the thing decently, and like a
Christian. Begin now—Sir——

Acres. That's too civil by half.

*Sir Lucius. To prevent the confusion that might
arise——*

Acres. Well—

Sir Lucius. From our both addressing the same lady——

Acres. Ay, there's the reason—*same lady*—well——

*Sir Lucius. I shall expect the honour of your com-
pany——*

Acres. Zounds! I'm not asking him to dinner.

Sir Lucius. Pray be easy.

Acres. Well, then, *honour of your company——*

Sir Lucius. To settle our pretensions——

Acres. Well.

Sir Lucius. Let me see, ay, King's-Mead-Fields will do—
in King's-Mead-Fields.

Acres. So, that's done—Well, I'll fold it up presently;
my own crest—a hand and dagger shall be the seal.

Sir Lucius. You see now this little explanation will put
a stop at once to all confusion or misunderstanding that
might arise between you.

Acres. Ay, we fight to prevent any misunderstanding.

Sir Lucius. Now, I'll leave you to fix your own time.—
Take my advice, and you'll decide it this evening if you

can; then let the worst come of it, 'twill be off your mind to-morrow.

Acres. Very true.

Sir Lucius. So I shall see nothing of you, unless it be by letter, till the evening.—I would do myself the honour to carry your message; but, to tell you a secret, I believe I shall have just such another affair on my own hands. There is a gay captain here, who put a jest on me lately, at the expense of my country, and I only want to fall in with the gentleman, to call him out.

Acres. By my valour, I should like to see you fight first! Odds life! I should like to see you kill him, if it was only to get a little lesson.

Sir Lucius. I shall be very proud of instructing you. Well for the present—but remember now, when you meet your antagonist, do every thing in a mild and agreeable manner. —Let your courage be as keen, but at the same time as polished, as your sword.   [*Exeunt severally.*

ACT FOUR

SCENE I—ACRES' *Lodgings*

ACRES *and* DAVID.

David. Then, by the mass, sir! I would do no such thing —ne'er a St. Lucius O'Trigger in the kingdom should make me fight, when I wasn't so minded. Oons! what will the old lady say, when she hears o't?

Acres. Ah! David, if you had heard Sir Lucius!—Odds sparks and flames! he would have roused your valour.

David. Not he, indeed. I hates such bloodthirsty cormorants. Look'ee, master, if you wanted a bout at boxing, quarter-staff, or short-staff, I should never be the man to bid you cry off: but for your curst sharps and snaps, I never knew any good come of 'em.

Acres. But my honour, David, my honour! I must be very careful of my honour.

David. Ay, by the mass! and I would be very careful of it; and I think in return my honour couldn't do less than to be very careful of me.

Acres. Odds blades! David, no gentleman will ever risk the loss of his honour!

David. I say then, it would be but civil in honour never to risk the loss of a gentleman.—Look'ee, master, this honour seems to me to be a marvellous false friend: ay, truly, a very courtier-like servant.—Put the case, I was a gentleman (which, thank God, no one can say of me); well —my honour makes me quarrel with another gentleman of my acquaintance.—So—we fight. (Pleasant enough that!) Boh;—I kill him—(the more's my luck!) now, pray who gets the profit of it?—Why, my honour. But put the case that he kills me!—by the mass! I go to the worms, and my honour whips over to my enemy.

Acres. No, David—in that case!—odds crowns and laurels! your honour follows you to the grave.

David. Now, that's just the place where I could make a shift to do without it.

Acres. Zounds! David, you are a coward!—It doesn't become my valour to listen to you.—What, shall I disgrace my ancestors?—Think of that, David—think what it would be to disgrace my ancestors!

David. Under favour, the surest way of not disgracing them, is to keep as long as you can out of their company. Look'ee now, master, to go to them in such haste—with an ounce of lead in your brains—I should think might as well be let alone. Our ancestors are very good kind of folks; but they are the last people I should choose to have a visiting acquaintance with.

Acres. But, David, now, you don't think there is such very, very, very great danger, hey?—Odds life! people often fight without any mischief done!

David. By the mass, I think 'tis ten to one against you! —Oons! here to meet some lion-hearted fellow, I warrant, with his damned double-barrelled swords, and cut-and-thrust pistols! Lord bless us! it makes me tremble to think o't—Those be such desperate bloody-minded weapons! Well, I never could abide 'em!—from a child I never could fancy 'em!—I suppose there an't been so merciless a beast in the world as your loaded pistol!

Acres. Zounds! I won't be afraid!—Odds fire and fury! you shan't make me afraid.—Here is the challenge, and I have sent for my dear friend Jack Absolute to carry it for me.

David. Ay, i' the name of mischief, let him be the messenger.—For my part I wouldn't lend a hand to it for the best horse in your stable. By the mass! it don't look like another letter! It is, as I may say, a designing and malicious-looking letter; and I warrant smells of gunpowder like a soldier's pouch!—Oons! I wouldn't swear it mayn't go off!

Acres. Out, you poltroon! you han't the valour of a grasshopper.

David. Well, I say no more—'twill be sad news, to be sure, at Clod Hall! but I ha' done. How Phillis will howl when she hears of it!—Ah, poor bitch, she little thinks what shooting her master's going after! And I warrant old Crop, who has carried your honour, field and road, these ten years, will curse the hour he was born.   [*Whimpering.*

Acres. It won't do, David—I am determined to fight—so get along, you coward, while I'm in the mind.

Enter SERVANT.

Servant. Captain Absolute, sir.

Acres. Oh! show him up.   [*Exit* SERVANT.

David. Well, Heaven send we be all alive this time tomorrow.

Acres. What's that?—Don't provoke me, David!

David. Good-bye, master.   [*Whimpering.*

Acres. Get along, you cowardly, dastardly, croaking raven!   [*Exit* DAVID.

Enter CAPTAIN ABSOLUTE.

Absolute. What's the matter, Bob?

Acres. A vile, sheep-hearted blockhead! If I hadn't the valour of St. George and the dragon to boot——

Absolute. But what did you want with me, Bob?

Acres. Oh!—There——   [*Gives him the challenge.*

Absolute. [*Aside to* Ensign Beverley.] So, what's going on now?—[*Aloud.*] Well, what's this?

Acres. A challenge!

Absolute. Indeed! Why, you won't fight him; will you, Bob?

Acres. Egad, but I will, Jack. Sir Lucius has wrought me to it. He has left me full of rage—and I'll fight this evening, that so much good passion mayn't be wasted.

Absolute. But what have I to do with this?

Acres. Why, as I think you know something of this fellow, I want you to find him out for me, and give him this mortal defiance.

Absolute. Well, give it to me, and trust me he gets it.

Acres. Thank you, my dear friend, my dear Jack; but it is giving you a great deal of trouble.

Absolute. Not in the least—I beg you won't mention it. —No trouble in the world, I assure you.

Acres. You are very kind.—What it is to have a friend! —You couldn't be my second, could you, Jack?

Absolute. Why no, Bob—not in this affair—it would not be quite so proper.

Acres. Well, then, I must get my friend Sir Lucius. I shall have your good wishes, however, Jack?

Absolute. Whenever he meets you, believe me.

Re-enter SERVANT.

Servant. Sir Anthony Absolute is below, inquiring for the captain.

Absolute. I'll come instantly.—[*Exit* SERVANT.] Well, my little hero, success attend you.   [*Going.*

Acres. Stay—stay, Jack.—If Beverley should ask you what kind of a man your friend Acres is, do tell him I am a devil of a fellow—will you, Jack?

Absolute. To be sure I shall. I'll say you are a determined dog—hey, Bob?

Acres. Ah, do, do—and if that frightens him, egad, perhaps he mayn't come. So tell him I generally kill a man a week; will you, Jack?

Absolute. I will, I will; I'll say you are called in the country Fighting Bob.

Acres. Right—right—'tis all to prevent mischief; for I don't want to take his life if I clear my honour.

Absolute. No!—that's very kind of you.

Acres. Why, you don't wish me to kill him—do you, Jack?

Absolute. No, upon my soul, I do not. But a devil of a fellow, hey?   [*Going.*

Acres. True, true—but stay—stay, Jack,—you may add, that you never saw me in such a rage before—a most devouring rage!

Absolute. I will, I will.

Acres. Remember, Jack—a determined dog!

Absolute. Ay, ay, Fighting Bob!   [*Exeunt severally.*

SCENE II—Mrs. Malaprop's *Lodgings*

Mrs. Malaprop *and* Lydia.

Mrs. Malaprop. Why, thou perverse one!—tell me what you can object to him? Isn't he a handsome man?—tell me that. A genteel man? a pretty figure of a man?

Lydia. [*Aside.*] She little thinks whom she is praising! —[*Aloud.*] So is Beverley, ma'am.

Mrs. Malaprop. No caparisons, miss, if you please. Caparisons don't become a young woman. No! Captain Absolute is indeed a fine gentleman!

Lydia. Ay, the Captain Absolute you have seen. [*Aside.*

Mrs. Malaprop. Then he's so well bred;—so full of alacrity, and adulation!—and has so much to say for himself:—in such good language, too! His physiognomy so grammatical! Then his presence is so noble! I protest, when I saw him, I thought of what Hamlet says in the play:—

"Hesperian curls—the front of Job himself!—
    An eye, like March, to threaten at command!—
    A station, like Harry Mercury, new—"

Something about kissing—on a hill—however, the similitude struck me directly.

Lydia. How enraged she'll be presently, when she discovers her mistake!   [*Aside.*

Enter Servant.

Servant. Sir Anthony and Captain Absolute are below, ma'am.

Mrs. Malaprop. Show them up here.—[*Exit* Servant.] Now, Lydia, I insist on your behaving as becomes a young woman. Show your good breeding, at least, though you have forgot your duty.

Lydia. Madam, I have told you my resolution!—I shall not only give him no encouragement, but I won't even speak to, or look at him.

[*Flings herself into a chair, with her face from the door.*

Enter Sir Anthony Absolute *and* Captain Absolute.

Sir Anthony. Here we are, Mrs. Malaprop; come to mitigate the frowns of unrelenting beauty,—and difficulty enough I had to bring this fellow.—I don't know what's the matter; but if I had not held him by force, he'd have given me the slip.

Mrs. Malaprop. You have infinite trouble, Sir Anthony, in the affair. I am ashamed for the cause!—[*Aside to* LYDIA.] Lydia, Lydia, rise, I beseech you!—pay your respects!

Sir Anthony. I hope, madam, that Miss Languish has reflected on the worth of this gentleman, and the regard due to her aunt's choice, and my alliance.—[*Aside to* CAPTAIN ABSOLUTE.] Now, Jack, speak to her.

Absolute. [*Aside.*] What the devil shall I do!—[*Aside to* SIR ANTHONY.] You see, sir, she won't even look at me whilst you are here. I knew she wouldn't! I told you so. Let me entreat you, sir, to leave us together!

[*Seems to expostulate with his father.*

Lydia. [*Aside.*] I wonder I han't heard my aunt exclaim yet! sure she can't have looked at him!—perhaps the regimentals are alike, and she is something blind.

Sir Anthony. I say, sir, I won't stir a foot yet!

Mrs. Malaprop. I am sorry to say, Sir Anthony, that my affluence over my niece is very small.—[*Aside to* LYDIA.] Turn round, Lydia: I blush for you!

Sir Anthony. May I not flatter myself, that Miss Languish will assign what cause of dislike she can have to my son!—[*Aside to* CAPTAIN ABSOLUTE.] Why don't you begin, Jack?—Speak, you puppy—speak!

Mrs. Malaprop. It is impossible, Sir Anthony, she can have any. She will not say she has.—[*Aside to* LYDIA.] Answer, hussy! why don't you answer?

Sir Anthony. Then, madam, I trust that a childish and hasty predilection will be no bar to Jack's happiness.— [*Aside to* CAPTAIN ABSOLUTE.] Zounds! sirrah! why don't you speak?

Lydia. [*Aside.*] I think my lover seems as little inclined to conversation as myself.—How strangely blind my aunt must be!

Absolute. Hem! hem! madam—hem!—[*Attempts to speak, then returns to* SIR ANTHONY.] Faith! sir, I am so confounded!—and—so—so—confused!—I told you I should be so, sir—I knew it.—The—the—tremor of my passion entirely takes away my presence of mind.

Sir Anthony. But it don't take away your voice, fool, does it?—Go up, and speak to her directly!

[CAPTAIN ABSOLUTE *makes signs to* MRS. MALAPROP
to leave them together.

Mrs. Malaprop. Sir Anthony, shall we leave them together?—[*Aside to* LYDIA.] Ah! you stubborn little vixen!

Sir Anthony. Not yet, ma'am, not yet!—[*Aside to*
CAPTAIN ABSOLUTE.] What the devil are you at? unlock
your jaws, sirrah, or——

Absolute. [*Aside.*] Now Heaven send she may be too
sullen to look round!—I must disguise my voice.—[*Draws
near* LYDIA, *and speaks in a low hoarse tone.*] Will not
Miss Languish lend an ear to the mild accents of true love?
Will not——

Sir Anthony. What the devil ails the fellow? why don't
you speak out?—not stand croaking like a frog in a quinsy!

Absolute. The—the—excess of my awe, and my—my—
modesty quite choke me!

Sir Anthony. Ah! your modesty again!—I'll tell you
what, Jack, if you don't speak out directly, and glibly too,
I shall be in such a rage!—Mrs. Malaprop, I wish the lady
would favour us with something more than a side-front.

[MRS. MALAPROP *seems to chide* LYDIA.

Absolute. [*Aside.*] So all will out, I see!—[*Goes up to*
LYDIA, *speaks softly.*] Be not surprised, my Lydia, suppress
all surprise at present.

Lydia. [*Aside.*] Heavens! 'tis Beverley's voice! Sure he
can't have imposed on Sir Anthony too!—[*Looks round by
degrees, then starts up.*] Is this possible?—my Beverley!
—how can this be?—my Beverley?

Absolute. Ah! 'tis all over.   [*Aside.*

Sir Anthony. Beverley!—the devil—Beverley!—What
can the girl mean?—this is my son, Jack Absolute.

Mrs. Malaprop. For shame, hussy! for shame! your head
runs so on that fellow, that you have him always in your
eyes!—beg Captain Absolute's pardon directly.

Lydia. I see no Captain Absolute, but my loved Beverley!

Sir Anthony. Zounds! the girl's mad!—her brain's turned
by reading.

Mrs. Malaprop. O' my conscience, I believe so!—What
do you mean by Beverley, hussy?—You saw Captain Absolute before to-day; there he is—your husband that shall be.

Lydia. With all my soul, ma'am—when I refuse my
Beverley——

Sir Anthony. Oh! she's as mad as Bedlam!—or has this fellow been playing us a rogue's trick!—Come here, sirrah, who the devil are you?

Absolute. Faith, sir, I am not quite clear myself; but I'll endeavour to recollect.

Sir Anthony. Are you my son or not?—answer for your mother, you dog, if you won't for me.

Mrs. Malaprop. Ay, sir, who are you? O mercy! I begin to suspect!——

Absolute. [*Aside.*] Ye powers of impudence, befriend me!—[*Aloud.*] Sir Anthony, most assuredly I am your wife's son; and that I sincerely believe myself to be yours also, I hope my duty has always shown.—Mrs. Malaprop, I am your most respectful admirer, and shall be proud to add affectionate nephew.—I need not tell my Lydia, that she sees her faithful Beverley, who, knowing the singular generosity of her temper, assumed that name and station, which has proved a test of the most disinterested love, which he now hopes to enjoy in a more elevated character.

Lydia. So!—there will be no elopement after all!

[*Sullenly.*

Sir Anthony. Upon my soul, Jack, thou art a very impudent fellow! to do you justice, I think I never saw a piece of more consummate assurance!

Absolute. Oh, you flatter me, sir—you compliment—'tis my modesty, you know, sir—my modesty that has stood in my way.

Sir Anthony. Well, I am glad you are not the dull, insensible varlet you pretended to be, however!—I'm glad you have made a fool of your father, you dog—I am. So this was your *penitence,* your *duty* and *obedience!*—I thought it was damned sudden!—*You never heard their names before,* not you!—*what, the Languishes of Worcestershire,* hey?—*if you could please me in the affair it was all you desired!*—Ah! you dissembling villain!—What!—[*Pointing to* LYDIA.] *she squints don't she?*—*a little redhaired girl!*—hey?—Why, you hypocritical young rascal! —I wonder you a'n't ashamed to hold up your head!

Absolute. 'Tis with difficulty, sir.—I am confused—very much confused, as you must perceive.

Mrs. Malaprop. O Lud! Sir Anthony!—a new light breaks in upon me!—hey!—how! what! captain, did you write the letters then?—What—am I to thank you for the

elegant compilation of *an old weather-beaten she-dragon*
—hey?—O mercy!—was it you that reflected on my parts
of speech?

Absolute. Dear sir! my modesty will be overpowered at
last, if you don't assist me.—I shall certainly not be able to
stand it!

Sir Anthony. Come, come, Mrs. Malaprop, we must forget and forgive;—odds life! matters have taken so clever a
turn all of a sudden, that I could find in my heart to be
so good-humoured! and so gallant! hey! Mrs. Malaprop!

Mrs. Malaprop. Well, Sir Anthony, since you desire it,
we will not anticipate the past!—so mind, young people—
our retrospection will be all to the future.

Sir Anthony. Come, we must leave them together; Mrs.
Malaprop, they long to fly into each other's arms, I
warrant!—Jack, isn't the cheek as I said, hey?—and the
eye, you rogue?—and the lip—hey? Come, Mrs. Malaprop, we'll not disturb their tenderness—theirs is the time
of life for happiness!—*Youth's the season made for joy*—
[*Sings.*]—hey!—Odds life! I'm in such spirits,—I don't
know what I could not do!—Permit me, ma'am—[*Gives
his hand to* MRS. MALAPROP.] Tol-de-rol—'gad, I should
like to have a little fooling myself—Tol-de-rol! de-rol.

      [*Exit, singing and handing* MRS. MALAPROP.—LYDIA
        sits sullenly in her chair.

Absolute. [*Aside.*] So much thought bodes me no good.
—[*Aloud.*] So grave, Lydia!

Lydia. Sir!

Absolute. [*Aside.*] So!—egad! I thought as much!—that
damned monosyllable has froze me!—[*Aloud.*] What,
Lydia, now that we are as happy in our friends' consent,
as in our mutual vows——

Lydia. Friends' consent indeed!   [*Peevishly.*

Absolute. Come, come, we must lay aside some of our
romance—a little and comfort may be endured after all.
And for your fortune, the lawyers shall make such settle-
ments as——

Lydia. Lawyers! I hate lawyers!

Absolute. Nay, then, we will not wait for their lingering
forms, but instantly procure the license, and——

Lydia. The license!—I hate license!

Absolute. Oh, my love! be not so unkind!—thus let me
entreat——   [*Kneeling.*

Lydia. Psha!—what signifies kneeling, when you know I must have you?

Absolute. [*Rising.*] Nay, madam, there shall be no constraint upon your inclinations, I promise you.—If I have lost your heart—I resign the rest—[*Aside.*] 'Gad, I must try what a little spirit will do.

Lydia. [*Rising.*] Then, sir, let me tell you, the interest you had there was acquired by a mean, unmanly imposition, and deserves the punishment of fraud.—What, you have been treating me like a child!—humouring my romance! and laughing, I suppose, at your success!

Absolute. You wrong me, Lydia, you wrong me—only hear——

Lydia. So, while I fondly imagined we were deceiving my relations, and flattered myself that I should outwit and incense them all—behold my hopes are to be crushed at once, by my aunt's consent and approbation—and I am myself the only dupe at last!—[*Walking about in a heat.*] But here, sir, here is the picture—Beverley's picture! [*taking a miniature from her bosom*] which I have worn, night and day, in spite of threats and entreaties!—There, sir; [*Flings it to him.*] and be assured I throw the original from my heart as easily.

Absolute. Nay, nay, ma'am, we will not differ as to that. —Here, [*Taking out a picture.*] here is Miss Lydia Languish.—What a difference!—ay, there is the heavenly assenting smile that first gave soul and spirit to my hopes! —those are the lips which sealed a vow, as yet scarce dry in Cupid's calendar! and there the half-resentful blush, that would have checked the ardour of my thanks!—Well, all that's past?—all over indeed!—There, madam—in beauty, that copy is not equal to you, but in my mind its merit over the original, in being still the same, is such— that—I cannot find in my heart to part with it.

[*Puts it up again.*

Lydia. [*Softening.*] 'Tis your own doing, sir—I, I, I suppose you are perfectly satisfied.

Absolute. O, most certainly—sure, now, this is much better than being in love!—ha! ha! ha!—there's some spirit in this!—What signifies breaking some scores of solemn promises:—all that's of no consequence, you know. To be sure people will say, that miss don't know her own mind but never mind that! Or, perhaps, they may be ill-natured enough to hint, that the gentleman grew tired of the lady and forsook her—but don't let that fret you.

Lydia. There is no bearing his insolence.

[*Bursts into tears.*

Re-enter MRS. MALAPROP *and* SIR ANTHONY ABSOLUTE.

Mrs. Malaprop. Come, we must interrupt your billing and cooing awhile.

Lydia. This is worse than your treachery and deceit, you base ingrate! [*Sobbing.*

Sir Anthony. What the devil's the matter now?—Zounds! Mrs. Malaprop, this is the oddest billing and cooing I ever heard!—but what the deuce is the meaning of it?—I am quite astonished!

Absolute. Ask the lady, sir.

Mrs. Malaprop. O mercy!—I'm quite analyzed, for my part!—Why, Lydia, what is the reason of this?

Lydia. Ask the gentleman, ma'am.

Sir Anthony. Zounds! I shall be in a frenzy!—Why, Jack, you are not come out to be any one else, are you?

Mrs. Malaprop. Ay, sir, there's no more trick, is there?— you are not like Cerberus, three gentlemen at once, are you?

Absolute. You'll not let me speak—I say the lady can account for this much better than I can.

Lydia. Ma'am, you once commanded me never to think of Beverley again—there is the man—I now obey you: for, from this moment, I renounce him for ever. [*Exit.*

Mrs. Malaprop. O mercy! and miracles! what a turn here is—why, sure, captain, you haven't behaved disrespectfully to my niece?

Sir Anthony. Ha! ha! ha!—ha! ha! ha!—now I see it. Ha! ha! ha!—now I see it—you have been too lively, Jack.

Absolute. Nay, sir, upon my word——

Sir Anthony. Come, no lying, Jack—I'm sure 'twas so.

Mrs. Malaprop. O Lud! Sir Anthony!—O fy, captain!

Absolute. Upon my soul, ma'am——

Sir Anthony. Come, no excuse, Jack; why, your father, you rogue, was so before you!—the blood of the Absolutes was always impatient.—Ha! ha! ha! poor little Lydia! why, you've frightened her, you dog, you have.

Absolute. By all that's good, sir——

Sir Anthony. Zounds! say no more, I tell you, Mrs. Malaprop shall make your peace. You must make his peace, Mrs. Malaprop:—you must tell her 'tis Jack's way—tell her 'tis all our ways—it runs in the blood of our family! Come away, Jack. Ha! ha! ha!—Mrs. Malaprop—a young villain!   [*Pushing him out.*

Mrs. Malaprop. O! Sir Anthony!—O fy, captain!
                                        [*Exeunt severally.*

SCENE III—*The North Parade*

Enter SIR LUCIUS O'TRIGGER.

Lucius. I wonder where this Captain Absolute hides himself! Upon my conscience! these officers are always in one's way in love affairs:—I remember I might have married Lady Dorothy Carmine, if it had not been for a little rogue of a major, who ran away with her before she could get a sight of me! And I wonder too what it is the ladies can see in them to be so fond of them—unless it be a touch of the old serpent in 'em, that makes the little creatures be caught, like vipers, with a bit of red cloth. Ha! isn't this the captain coming?—faith it is!—There is a probability of succeeding about that fellow, that is mighty provoking! Who the devil is he talking to?   [*Steps aside.*

Enter CAPTAIN ABSOLUTE.

Absolute. [*Aside.*] To what fine purpose I have been plotting! a noble reward for all my schemes, upon my soul!—a little gipsy!—I did not think her romance could have made her so damned absurd either. 'Sdeath, I never was in a worse humour in my life!—I could cut my own throat, or any other person's with the greatest pleasure in the world!

Sir Lucius. Oh, faith! I'm in the luck of it. I never could have found him in a sweeter temper for my purpose —to be sure I'm just come in the nick! Now to enter into conversation with him, and so quarrel genteelly.—[*Goes up to* CAPTAIN ABSOLUTE.] With regard to that matter, captain, I must beg leave to differ in opinion with you.

Absolute. Upon my word, then, you must be a very subtle disputant:—because, sir, I happened just then to be giving no opinion at all.

Sir Lucius. That's no reason. For give me leave to tell you, a man may think an untruth as well as speak one.

Absolute. Very true, sir; but if a man never utters his thoughts, I should think they might stand a chance of escaping controversy.

Sir Lucius. Then, sir, you differ in opinion with me, which amounts to the same thing.

Absolute. Hark'ee, Sir Lucius; if I had not before known you to be a gentleman, upon my soul, I should not have discovered it at this interview: for what you can drive at, unless you mean to quarrel with me, I cannot conceive!

Sir Lucius. I humbly thank you, sir, for the quickness of your apprehension.—[*Bowing.*] You have named the very thing I would be at.

Absolute. Very well, sir; I shall certainly not balk your inclinations.—But I should be glad you would be pleased to explain your motives.

Sir Lucius. Pray, sir, be easy; the quarrel is a very pretty quarrel as it stands; we should only spoil it by trying to explain it. However, your memory is very short, or you could not have forgot an affront you passed on me within this week. So, no more, but name your time and place.

Absolute. Well, sir, since you are so bent on it, the sooner the better; let it be this evening—here, by the Spring Gardens. We shall scarcely be interrupted.

Sir Lucius. Faith! that same interruption in affairs of this nature shows very great ill-breeding. I don't know what's the reason, but in England if a thing of this kind gets wind, people make such a pother, that a gentleman can never fight in peace and quietness. However, if it's the same to you, I should take it as a particular kindness if you'd let us meet in King's-Mead-Fields, as a little business will call me there about six o'clock, and I may despatch both matters at once.

Absolute. 'Tis the same to me exactly. A little after six, then, we will discuss this matter more seriously.

Sir Lucius. If you please, sir; there will be very pretty small-sword light, though it won't do for a long shot. So that matter's settled, and my mind's at ease!   [*Exit.*

Enter FAULKLAND.

Absolute. Well met! I was going to look for you. O Faulkland! all the demons of spite and disappointment have conspired against me! I'm so vex'd, that if I had not the prospect of a resource in being knocked o' the head by-and-by, I should scarce have spirits to tell you the cause.

Faulkland. What can you mean?—Has Lydia changed her mind?—I should have thought her duty and inclination would now have pointed to the same object.

Absolute. Ay, just as the eyes do of a person who squints: when her love-eye was fixed on me, t'other, her eye of duty, was finely obliqued: but when duty bid her point that the same way, off t'other turned on a swivel, and secured its retreat with a frown!

Faulkland. But what's the resource you——

Absolute. Oh, to wind up the whole, a good-natured Irishman here has—[*Mimicking* SIR LUCIUS.] begged leave to have the pleasure of cutting my throat; and I mean to indulge him—that's all.

Faulkland. Prithee, be serious!

Absolute. 'Tis fact, upon my soul! Sir Lucius O'Trigger —you know him by sight—for some affront, which I am sure I never intended, has obliged me to meet him this evening at six o'clock: 'tis on that account I wished to see you; you must go with me.

Faulkland. Nay, there must be some mistake, sure. Sir Lucius shall explain himself, and I dare say matters may be accommodated. But this evening did you say? I wish it had been any other time.

Absolute. Why? there will be light enough: there will (as Sir Lucius says) be very pretty small-sword light, though it will not do for a long shot. Confound his long shots.

Faulkland. But I am myself a good deal ruffled by a difference I have had with Julia. My vile tormenting temper has made me treat her so cruelly, that I shall not be myself till we are reconciled.

Absolute. By heavens! Faulkland, you don't deserve her!

Enter SERVANT, *gives* FAULKLAND *a letter, and exit.*

Faulkland. Oh, Jack! this is from Julia. I dread to open it! I fear it may be to take a last leave!—perhaps to bid me return her letters, and restore——Oh, how I suffer for my folly!

Absolute. Here, let me see.—[*Takes the letter and opens it.*] Ay, a final sentence, indeed!—'tis all over with you, faith!

Faulkland. Nay, Jack, don't keep me in suspense!

Absolute. Hear then—[Reads.] *As I am convinced that my dear Faulkland's own reflections have already up-*

*braided him for his last unkindness to me, I will not add a
word on the subject. I wish to speak with you as soon as
possible. Yours ever and truly,* JULIA. There's stubborn-
ness and resentment for you!—[*Gives him the letter.*] Why,
man, you don't seem one whit happier at this!

Faulkland. O yes, I am; but—but—

Absolute. Confound your buts! you never hear anything
that would make another man bless himself, but you immediately damn it with a but!

Faulkland. Now, Jack, as you are my friend, own
honestly—don't you think there is something forward,
something indelicate, in this haste to forgive? Women
should never sue for reconciliation: that should always
come from us. They should retain their coldness till wooed
to kindness; and their pardon, like their love, should "not
unsought be won."

Absolute. I have not patience to listen to you! thou'rt
incorrigible! so say no more on the subject. I must go to
settle a few matters. Let me see you before six, remember,
at my lodgings. A poor industrious devil like me, who have
toiled, and drudged, and plotted to gain my ends, and am
at last disappointed by other people's folly, may in pity
be allowed to swear and grumble a little; but a captious
sceptic in love, a slave to fretfulness and whim, who has
no difficulties but of his own creating, is a subject more
fit for ridicule than compassion!   [*Exit.*

Faulkland. I feel his reproaches; yet I would not change
this too exquisite nicety for the gross content with which
he tramples on the thorns of love! His engaging me in this
duel has started an idea in my head, which I will instantly
pursue. I'll use it as the touch-stone of Julia's sincerity and
disinterestedness. If her love proves pure and sterling ore,
my name will rest on it with honour; and once I've
stamped it there, I lay aside my doubts for ever! But if
the dross of selfishness, the alloy of pride, predominate,
'twill be best to leave her as a toy for some less cautious
fool to sigh for!   [*Exit.*

ACT FIVE

SCENE I—JULIA's *Dressing-Room*

JULIA *discovered alone.*

JULIA. How this message has alarmed me! what dreadful accident can he mean? why such charge to be alone?— O Faulkland!—how many unhappy moments—how many tears have you cost me.

Enter FAULKLAND.

Julia. What means this?—why this caution, Faulkland?

Faulkland. Alas! Julia, I am come to take a long farewell.

Julia. Heavens! what do you mean?

Faulkland. You see before you a wretch, whose life is forfeited. Nay, start not!—the infirmity of my temper has drawn all this misery on me. I left you fretful and passionate—an untoward accident drew me into a quarrel—the event is, that I must fly this kingdom instantly. O Julia, had I been so fortunate as to have called you mine entirely, before this mischance had fallen on me, I should not so deeply dread my banishment!

Julia. My soul is opprest with sorrow at the nature of your misfortune: had these adverse circumstances arisen from a less fatal cause I should have felt strong comfort in the thought that I could now chase from your bosom every doubt of the warm sincerity of my love. My heart has long known no other guardian—I now entrust my person to your honour—we will fly together. When safe from pursuit, my father's will may be fulfilled—and I receive a legal claim to be the partner of your sorrows, and tenderest comforter. Then on the bosom of your wedded Julia, you may lull your keen regret to slumbering, while virtuous love, with a cherub's hand, shall smoothe the brow of upbraiding thought, and pluck the thorn from compunction.

Faulkland. O Julia! I am bankrupt in gratitude! but the time is so pressing, it calls on you for so hasty a resolution. —Would you not wish some hours to weigh the advantages you forego, and what little compensation poor Faulkland can make you beside his solitary love?

Julia. I ask not a moment. No, Faulkland, I have loved you for yourself: and if I now, more than ever, prize the solemn engagement which so long has pledged us to each other, it is because it leaves no room for hard aspersions on my fame, and puts the seal of duty to an act of love. But let us not linger. Perhaps this delay——

Faulkland. 'Twill be better I should not venture out again till dark. Yet am I grieved to think what numberless distresses will press heavy on your gentle disposition!

Julia. Perhaps your fortune may be forfeited by this unhappy act.—I know not whether 'tis so; but sure that alone can never make us unhappy. The little I have will be sufficient to support us; and exile never should be splendid.

Faulkland. Ay, but in such an abject state of life, my wounded pride perhaps may increase the natural fretfulness of my temper, till I become a rude, morose companion, beyond your patience to endure. Perhaps the recollection of a deed my conscience cannot justify may haunt me in such gloomy and unsocial fits, that I shall hate the tenderness that would relieve me, break from your arms, and quarrel with your fondness!

Julia. If your thoughts should assume so unhappy a bent, you will the more want some mild and affectionate spirit to watch over and console you! one who, by bearing your infirmities with gentleness and resignation, may teach you so to bear the evils of your fortune.

Faulkland. Julia, I have proved you to the quick! and with this useless device I throw away all my doubts. How shall I plead to be forgiven this last unworthy effect of my restless, unsatisfied disposition?

Julia. Has no such disaster happened as you related?

Faulkland. I am ashamed to own that it was pretended; yet in pity, Julia, do not kill me with resenting a fault which never can be repeated: but sealing, this once, my pardon, let me to-morrow, in the face of Heaven, receive my future guide and monitress, and expiate my past folly by years of tender adoration.

Julia. Hold, Faulkland!—that you are free from a crime, which I before feared to name, Heaven knows how sincerely I rejoice! These are tears of thankfulness for that! But that your cruel doubts should have urged you to an imposition that has wrung my heart, gives me now a pang more keen than I can express.

Faulkland. By Heavens! Julia——

Julia. Yet hear me.—My father loved you, Faulkland! and you preserved the life that tender parent gave me; in his presence I pledged my hand—joyfully pledged it —where before I had given my heart. When, soon after, I lost that parent, it seemed to me that Providence had, in Faulkland, shown me whither to transfer without a pause, my grateful duty, as well as my affection; hence I have been content to bear from you what pride and delicacy would have forbid me from another. I will not upbraid you, by repeating how you have trifled with my sincerity——

Faulkland. I confess it all! yet hear——

Julia. After such a year of trial, I might have flattered myself that I should not have been insulted with a new probation of my sincerity, as cruel as unnecessary! I now see it is not in your nature to be content or confident in love. With this conviction—I never will be yours. While I had hopes that my persevering attention, and unreproaching kindness, might in time reform your temper, I should have been happy to have gained a dearer influence over you; but I will not furnish you with a licensed power to keep alive an incorrigible fault, at the expense of one who never would contend with you.

Faulkland. Nay, but, Julia, by my soul and honour, if after this——

Julia. But one word more.—As my faith has once been given to you, I never will barter it with another.—I shall pray for your happiness with the truest sincerity; and the dearest blessing I can ask of Heaven to send you will be to charm you from that unhappy temper, which alone has prevented the performance of our solemn engagement. All I request of you is, that you will yourself reflect upon this infirmity, and when you number up the many true delights it has deprived you of, let it not be your least regret, that it lost you the love of one who would have followed you in beggary through the world.   [*Exit.*

Faulkland. She's gone—for ever!—There was an awful resolution in her manner, that riveted me to my place.— O fool!—dolt!—barbarian! Cursed as I am, with more imperfections than my fellow-wretches, kind Fortune sent a heaven-gifted cherub to my aid, and, like a ruffian, I have driven her from my side!—I must now haste to my appointment. Well, my mind is tuned for such a scene. I shall wish only to become a principal in it, and reverse the

tale my cursed folly put me upon forging here.—O Love!
—tormentor!—fiend!—whose influence, like the moon's,
acting on men of dull souls, makes idiots of them, but
meeting subtler spirits, betrays their course, and urges
sensibility to madness!   [*Exit.*

Enter LYDIA *and* MAID.

Maid. My mistress, ma'am, I know, was here just now
—perhaps she is only in the next room.   [*Exit.*

Lydia. Heigh-ho! Though he has used me so, this fellow
runs strangely in my head. I believe one lecture from my
grave cousin will make me recall him. [*Re-enter* JULIA.]
O Julia, I have come to you with such an appetite for
consolation.—Lud! child, what's the matter with you? You
have been crying!—I'll be hanged if that Faulkland has
not been tormenting you.

Julia. You mistake the cause of my uneasiness!—Something has flurried me a little. Nothing that you can guess
at.—[*Aside.*] I would not accuse Faulkland to a sister!

Lydia. Ah! whatever vexations you may have, I can
assure you mine surpass them. You know who Beverley
proves to be?

Julia. I will now own to you, Lydia, that Mr. Faulkland
had before informed me of the whole affair. Had young
Absolute been the person you took him for, I should not
have accepted your confidence on the subject, without a
serious endeavour to counteract your caprice.

Lydia. So, then, I see I have been deceived by every
one! But I don't care—I'll never have him.

Julia. Nay, Lydia——

Lydia. Why, is it not provoking? when I thought we
were coming to the prettiest distress imaginable, to find
myself made a mere Smithfield bargain of at last! There,
had I projected one of the most sentimental elopements!—
so becoming a disguise!—so amiable a ladder of ropes!—
Conscious moon—four horses—Scotch parson—with such
surprise to Mrs. Malaprop—and such paragraphs in the
newspapers!—Oh, I shall die with disappointment!

Julia. I don't wonder at it!

Lydia. Now—sad reverse!—what have I to expect, but,
after a deal of flimsy preparation, with a bishop's license,
and my aunt's blessing, to go simpering up to the altar;
or perhaps be cried three times in a country church, and
have an unmannerly fat clerk ask the consent of every

butcher in the parish to join John Absolute and Lydia Languish, spinster! Oh that I should live to hear myself called spinster!

Julia. Melancholy, indeed!

Lydia. How mortifying, to remember the dear delicious shifts I used to be put to, to gain half a minute's conversation with this fellow! How often have I stole forth, in the coldest night in January, and found him in the garden, stuck like a dripping statue! There would he kneel to me in the snow, and sneeze and cough so pathetically! he shivering with cold and I with apprehension! and while the freezing blast numbed our joints, how warmly would he press me to pity his flame, and glow with mutual ardour!—Ah, Julia, that was something like being in love.

Julia. If I were in spirits, Lydia, I should chide you only by laughing heartily at you; but it suits more the situation of my mind, at present, earnestly to entreat you not to let a man, who loves you with sincerity, suffer that unhappiness from your caprice, which I know too well caprice can inflict.

Lydia. O Lud! what has brought my aunt here?

Enter MRS. MALAPROP, FAG, *and* DAVID.

Mrs. Malaprop. So! so! here's fine work!—here's fine suicide, parricide, and simulation, going on in the fields! and Sir Anthony not to be found to prevent the antistrophe!

Julia. For Heaven's sake, madam, what's the meaning of this?

Mrs. Malaprop. That gentleman can tell you—'twas he enveloped the affair to me.

Lydia. Do, sir, will you, inform us?   [*To* FAG.

Fag. Ma'am, I should hold myself very deficient in every requisite that forms the man of breeding, if I delayed a moment to give all the information in my power to a lady so deeply interested in the affair as you are.

Lydia. But quick! quick, sir!

Fag. True, ma'am, as you say, one should be quick in divulging matters of this nature; for should we be tedious, perhaps while we are flourishing on the subject, two or three lives may be lost!

Lydia. O patience!—do, ma'am, for Heaven's sake! tell us what is the matter?

Mrs. Malaprop. Why, murder's the matter! slaughter's

the matter! killing's the matter!—but he can tell you the perpendiculars.

Lydia. Then, prithee, sir, be brief.

Fag. Why, then, ma'am, as to murder—I cannot take upon me to say—and as to slaughter, or manslaughter, that will be as the jury finds it.

Lydia. But who, sir—who are engaged in this?

Fag. Faith, ma'am, one is a young gentleman whom I should be very sorry anything was to happen to—a very pretty behaved gentleman! We have lived much together, and always on terms.

Lydia. But who is this? who? who? who?

Fag. My master, ma'am—my master—I speak of my master.

Lydia. Heavens! What, Captain Absolute!

Mrs. Malaprop. Oh, to be sure, you are frightened now!

Julia. But who are with him, sir?

Fag. As to the rest, ma'am, this gentleman can inform you better than I?

Julia. Do speak, friend. [*To* DAVID.

David. Look'ee, my lady—by the mass! there's mischief going on. Folks don't use to meet for amusement with firearms, firelocks, fire-engines, fire-screens, fire-office, and the devil knows what other crackers beside!—This, my lady, I say, has an angry savour.

Julia. But who is there beside Captain Absolute, friend?

David. My poor master—under favour for mentioning him first. You know me, my lady—I am David—and my master of course is, or was, Squire Acres. Then comes Squire Faulkland.

Julia. Do, ma'am, let us instantly endeavour to prevent mischief.

Mrs. Malaprop. O fy! it would be very inelegant in us:—we should only participate things.

David. Ah! do, Mrs. Aunt, save a few lives—they are desperately given, believe me.—Above all, there is that bloodthirsty Philistine, Sir Lucius O'Trigger.

Mrs. Malaprop. Sir Lucius O'Trigger? O mercy! have they drawn poor little dear Sir Lucius into the scrape? Why how you stand, girl! you have no more feeling than one of the Derbyshire petrifactions!

Lydia. What are we to do, madam?

Mrs. Malaprop. Why, fly with the utmost felicity, to be

sure, to prevent mischief!—Here, friend, you can show us
the place?

Fag. If you please, ma'am, I will conduct you.—David,
do you look for Sir Anthony.   [*Exit* DAVID.

Mrs. Malaprop. Come, girls! this gentleman will exhort
us.—Come, sir, you're our envoy—lead the way, and we'll
precede.

Fag. Not a step before the ladies for the world!

Mrs. Malaprop. You're sure you know the spot?

Fag. I think I can find it, ma'am; and one good thing
is, we shall hear the report of the pistols as we draw near,
so we can't well miss them;—never fear, ma'am, never
fear.   [*Exeunt, he talking.*

SCENE II—*The South Parade*

Enter CAPTAIN ABSOLUTE, *putting his sword under his
great-coat.*

Absolute. A sword seen in the streets of Bath would
raise as great an alarm as a mad dog.—How provoking
this is in Faulkland!—never punctual! I shall be obliged to
go without him at last.—Oh, the devil! here's Sir Anthony!
how shall I escape him?

[*Muffles up his face, and takes a circle to go off.*

Enter SIR ANTHONY ABSOLUTE.

Sir Anthony. How one may be deceived at a little distance! Only that I see he don't know me, I could have
sworn that was Jack!—Hey! Gad's life! it is.—Why, Jack,
what are you afraid of? hey—sure I'm right. Why, Jack,
Jack Absolute!   [*Goes up to him.*

Absolute. Really, sir, you have the advantage of me:—I
don't remember ever to have had the honour—my name is
Saunderson, at your service.

Sir Anthony. Sir, I beg your pardon—I took you—hey?
—why, zounds! it is—Stay—[*Looks up to his face.*] So, so
—your humble servant, Mr. Saunderson! Why, you scoundrel, what tricks are you after now?

Absolute. Oh, a joke, sir, a joke! I came here on purpose
to look for you, sir.

Sir Anthony. You did! well, I am glad you were so lucky:
—but what are you muffled up so for?—what's this for?
—hey?

Absolute. 'Tis cool, sir, isn't it?—rather chilly somehow:
—but I shall be late—I have a particular engagement.

Sir Anthony. Stay!—Why, I thought you were looking
for me?—Pray, Jack, where is't you are going?

Absolute. Going, sir?

Sir Anthony. Ay, where are you going?

Absolute. Where am I going?

Sir Anthony. You unmannerly puppy!

Absolute. I was going, sir, to—to—to—to Lydia—sir, to
Lydia—to make matters up if I could; and I was looking
for you, sir, to—to—

Sir Anthony. To go with you, I suppose.—Well, come
along.

Absolute. Oh! zounds! no, sir, not for the world!—I
wished to meet with you, sir,—to—to—to—You find it
cool, I'm sure, sir—you'd better not stay out.

Sir Anthony. Cool!—not at all.—Well, Jack—and what
will you say to Lydia?

Absolute. Oh, sir, beg her pardon, humour her—promise
and vow: but I detain you, sir—consider the cold air on
your gout.

Sir Anthony. Oh, not at all!—not at all! I'm in no hurry.
—Ah! Jack, you youngsters, when once you are wounded
here [*Putting his hand to* CAPTAIN ABSOLUTE'S *breast.*]
Hey! what the deuce have you got here?

Absolute. Nothing, sir—nothing.

Sir Anthony. What's this?—here's something damned
hard.

Absolute. Oh, trinkets, sir! trinkets!—a bauble for Lydia.

Sir Anthony. Nay, let me see your taste.—[*Pulls his
coat open, the sword falls.*] Trinkets! a bauble for Lydia!—
Zounds! sirrah, you are not going to cut her throat, are
you?

Absolute. Ha! ha! ha!—I thought it would divert you,
sir, though I didn't mean to tell you till afterwards.

Sir Anthony. You didn't?—Yes, this is a very diverting
trinket, truly!

Absolute. Sir, I'll explain to you.—You know, sir, Lydia
is romantic, devilish romantic, and very absurd of course:
now, sir, I intend, if she refuses to forgive me, to unsheath
this sword, and swear—I'll fall upon its point, and expire
at her feet!

Sir Anthony. Fall upon a fiddlestick's end!—why, I suppose it is the very thing that would please her.—Get along, you fool!

Absolute. Well, sir, you shall hear of my success—you shall hear.—*O Lydia!—forgive me, or this pointed steel—* says I.

Sir Anthony. O, booby! *stay away and welcome—*says she.—Get along! and damn your trinkets!

[*Exit* CAPTAIN ABSOLUTE.

Enter DAVID, *running.*

David. Stop him! stop him! Murder! Thief! Fire!—Stop fire! Stop fire!—O Sir Anthony—call! call! bid'm stop! Murder! Fire!

Sir Anthony. Fire! Murder!—Where?

David. Oons! he's out of sight! and I'm out of breath for my part! O Sir Anthony, why didn't you stop him? why didn't you stop him?

Sir Anthony. Zounds! the fellow's mad!—Stop whom? stop Jack?

David. Ay, the captain, sir!—there's murder and slaughter——

Sir Anthony. Murder!

David. Ay, please you, Sir Anthony, there's all kinds of murder, all sorts of slaughter to be seen in the fields: there's fighting going on, sir—bloody sword-and-gun fighting!

Sir Anthony. Who are going to fight, dunce?

David. Everybody that I know of, Sir Anthony:—everybody is going to fight, my poor master, Sir Lucius O'Trigger, your son, the captain——

Sir Anthony. Oh, the dog! I see his tricks.—Do you know the place?

David. King's-Mead-Fields.

Sir Anthony. You know the way?

David. Not an inch; but I'll call the mayor—aldermen—constables—churchwardens—and beadles—we can't be too many to part them.

Sir Anthony. Come along—give me your shoulder! we'll get assistance as we go—the lying villain!—Well, I shall be in such a frenzy!—So—this was the history of his trinkets! I'll bauble him!　　　　　　　　　　　　[*Exeunt.*

SCENE III—*King's-Mead-Fields.*

Enter SIR LUCIUS O'TRIGGER *and* ACRES, *with pistols.*

Acres. By my valour! then, Sir Lucius, forty yards is a good distance. Odds levels and aims!—I say it is a good distance.

Sir Lucius. Is it for muskets or small field-pieces? Upon my conscience, Mr. Acres, you must leave those things to me.—Stay now—I'll show you.—[*Measures paces along the stage.*] There now, that is a very pretty distance—a pretty gentleman's distance.

Acres. Zounds! we might as well fight in a sentry-box! I tell you, Sir Lucius, the farther he is off, the cooler I shall take my aim.

Sir Lucius. Faith! then I suppose you would aim at him best of all if he was out of sight!

Acres. No, Sir Lucius; but I should think forty or eight and thirty yards——

Sir Lucius. Pho! pho! nonsense! three or four feet between the mouths of your pistols is as good as a mile.

Acres. Odds bullets, no!—by my valour! there is no merit in killing him so near; do, my dear Sir Lucius, let me bring him down at a long shot—a long shot, Sir Lucius, if you love me.

Sir Lucius. Well, the gentleman's friend and I must settle that.—But tell me now, Mr. Acres, in case of an accident, is there any little will or commission I could execute for you?

Acres. I am much obliged to you, Sir Lucius, but I don't understand——

Sir Lucius. Why, you may think there's no being shot at without a little risk—and if an unlucky bullet should carry a quietus with it—I say it will be no time then to be bothering you about family matters.

Acres. A quietus!

Sir Lucius. For instance, now—if that should be the case—would you choose to be pickled and sent home?—or would it be the same to you to lie here in the Abbey? I'm told there is very snug lying in the Abbey.

Acres. Pickled—Snug lying in the Abbey!—Odds tremors! Sir Lucius, don't talk so!

Sir Lucius. I suppose, Mr. Acres, you never were engaged in an affair of this kind before?

Acres. No, Sir Lucius, never before.

Sir Lucius. Ah! that's a pity!—there's nothing like being used to a thing. Pray now, how would you receive the gentleman's shot?

Acres. Odds files!—I've practised that—there, Sir Lucius —there. [*Puts himself in an attitude.*] A side-front, hey? Odd! I'll make myself small enough? I'll stand edgeways.

Sir Lucius. Now—you're quite out—for if you stand so when I take my aim——   [*Levelling at him.*

Acres. Zounds! Sir Lucius—are you sure it is not cocked?

Sir Lucius. Never fear.

Acres. But—but—you don't know—it may go off of its own head!

Sir Lucius. Pho! be easy.—Well, now if I hit you in the body, my bullet has a double chance—for if it misses a vital part of your right side, 'twill be very hard if it don't succeed on the left!

Acres. A vital part.

Sir Lucius. But, there—fix yourself so—[*Placing him.*] —let him see the broad-side of your full front—there— now a ball or two may pass clean through your body, and never do any harm at all.

Acres. Clean through me!—a ball or two clean through me!

Sir Lucius. Ay—may they—and it is much the genteelest attitude into the bargain.

Acres. Look'ee! Sir Lucius—I'd just as lieve be shot in an awkward posture as a genteel one; so, by my valour! I will stand edgeways.

Sir Lucius. [*Looking at his watch.*] Sure they don't mean to disappoint us—Hah!—no, faith—I think I see them coming.

Acres. Hey!—what!—coming!——

Sir Lucius. Ay.—Who are those yonder getting over the stile?

Acres. There are two of them indeed!—well—let them come—hey, Sir Lucius!—we—we—we—we—won't run.

Sir Lucius. Run!

Acres. No—I say—we won't run, by my valour!

Sir Lucius. What the devil's the matter with you?

Acres. Nothing—nothing—my dear friend—my dear Sir Lucius—but I—I—I don't feel quite so bold, somehow, as I did.

Sir Lucius. O fy!—consider your honour.

Acres. Ay—true—my honour. Do, Sir Lucius, edge in a word or two every now and then about my honour.

Sir Lucius. Well, here they're coming.   [*Looking.*

Acres. Sir Lucius—if I wa'n't with you, I should almost think I was afraid.—If my valour should leave me! Valour will come and go.

Sir Lucius. Then pray keep it fast, while you have it.

Acres. Sir Lucius—I doubt it is going—yes—my valour is certainly going!—it is sneaking off!—I feel it oozing out as it were at the palms of my hands!

Sir Lucius. Your honour—your honour.—Here they are.

Acres. O mercy!—now—that I was safe at Clod Hall! or could be shot before I was aware!

Enter FAULKLAND *and* CAPTAIN ABSOLUTE.

Sir Lucius. Gentlemen, your most obedient.—Hah!— what, Captain Absolute!—So, I suppose, sir, you are come here, just like myself—to do a kind office, first for your friend—then to proceed to business on your own account.

Acres. What, Jack!—my dear Jack!—my dear friend!

Absolute. Hark'ee, Bob, Beverley's at hand.

Sir Lucius. Well, Mr. Acres—I don't blame your saluting the gentleman civilly.—[*To* FAULKLAND.] So, Mr. Beverley, if you'll choose your weapons, the captain and I will measure the ground.

Faulkland. My weapons, sir!

Acres. Odds life! Sir Lucius, I'm not going to fight Mr. Faulkland; these are my particular friends.

Sir Lucius. What, sir, did you not come here to fight Mr. Acres?

Faulkland. Not I, upon my word, sir.

Sir Lucius. Well, now, that's mighty provoking! But I hope, Mr. Faulkland, as there are three of us come on purpose for the game, you won't be so cantankerous as to spoil the party by sitting out.

Absolute. O pray, Faulkland, fight to oblige Sir Lucius.

Faulkland. Nay, if Mr. Acres is so bent on the matter——

Acres. No, no, Mr. Faulkland;—I'll bear my disappointment like a Christian.—Look'ee, Sir Lucius, there's no occasion at all for me to fight; and if it is the same to you, I'd as lieve let it alone.

Sir Lucius. Observe me, Mr. Acres—I must not be trifled with. You have certainly challenged somebody—and you came here to fight him. Now, if that gentleman is willing to represent him—I can't see, for my soul, why it isn't just the same thing.

Acres. Why no—Sir Lucius—I tell you, 'tis one Beverley I've challenged—a fellow, you see, that dare not show his face!—if he were here, I'd make him give up his pretensions directly!

Absolute. Hold, Bob—let me set you right—there is no such man as Beverley in the case.—The person who assumed that name is before you; and as his pretensions are the same in both characters, he is ready to support them in whatever way you please.

Sir Lucius. Well, this is lucky.—Now you have an opportunity—

Acres. What, quarrel with my dear friend, Jack Absolute?—not if he were fifty Beverleys! Zounds! Sir Lucius, you would not have me so unnatural.

Sir Lucius. Upon my conscience, Mr. Acres, your valour has oozed away with a vengeance!

Acres. Not in the least! Odds backs and abettors! I'll be your second with all my heart—and if you should get a quietus, you may command me entirely. I'll get you snug lying in the Abbey here; or pickle you, and send you over to Blunderbuss-hall, or anything of the kind, with the greatest pleasure.

Sir Lucius. Pho! pho! you are little better than a coward.

Acres. Mind, gentlemen, he calls me a coward; coward was the word, by my valour!

Sir Lucius. Well, sir?

Acres. Look'ee, Sir Lucius, 'tisn't that I mind the word coward—coward may be said in joke.—But if you had called me a poltroon, odds daggers and balls——

Sir Lucius. Well, sir?

Acres. I should have thought you a very ill-bred man.

Sir Lucius. Pho! you are beneath my notice.

Absolute. Nay, Sir Lucius, you can't have a better second than my friend Acres.—He is a most determined dog—called in the country, Fighting Bob.—He generally kills a man a week—don't you, Bob?

Acres. Ay—at home!

Sir Lucius. Well, then, captain, 'tis we must begin—so come out, my little counsellor—[*Draws his sword.*]—and ask the gentleman, whether he will resign the lady, without forcing you to proceed against him?

Absolute. Come on them, sir—[*Draws.*]; since you won't let it be an amicable suit, here's my reply.

Enter SIR ANTHONY ABSOLUTE, DAVID, MRS. MALAPROP, LYDIA, *and* JULIA.

David. Knock 'em all down, sweet Sir Anthony; knock down my master in particular; and bind his hands over to their good behaviour!

Sir Anthony. Put up, Jack, put up, or I shall be in a frenzy—how came you in a duel, sir?

Absolute. Faith, sir, that gentleman can tell you better than I; 'twas he called on me, and you know, sir, I serve his majesty.

Sir Anthony. Here's a pretty fellow; I catch him going to cut a man's throat, and he tells me he serves his majesty!—Zounds! sirrah, then how durst you draw the king's sword against one of his subjects?

Absolute. Sir! I tell you, that gentleman called me out, without explaining his reasons.

Sir Anthony. Gad! sir, how came you to call my son out, without explaining your reasons?

Sir Lucius. Your son, sir, insulted me in a manner which my honour could not brook.

Sir Anthony. Zounds! Jack, how durst you insult the gentleman in a manner which his honour could not brook?

Mrs. Malaprop. Come, come, let's have no honour before ladies—Captain Absolute, come here—How could you intimidate us so?—Here's Lydia has been terrified to death for you.

Absolute. For fear I should be killed, or escape, ma'am?

Mrs. Malaprop. Nay, no delusions to the past—Lydia is convinced; speak, child.

Sir Lucius. With your leave, ma'am, I must put in a word, here: I believe I could interpret the young lady's silence. Now mark——

Lydia. What is it you mean, sir?

Sir Lucius. Come, come, Delia, we must be serious now —this is no time for trifling.

Lydia. 'Tis true, sir; and your reproof bids me offer this gentleman my hand, and solicit the return of his affections.

Absolute. O! my little angel, say you so?—Sir Lucius, I perceive there must be some mistake here, with regard to the affront which you affirm I have given you. I can only say that it could not have been intentional. And as you must be convinced, that I should not fear to support a real injury—you shall now see that I am not ashamed to atone for an inadvertency—I ask your pardon.—But for this lady, while honoured with her approbation, I will support my claim against any man whatever.

Sir Anthony. Well said, Jack, and I'll stand by you, my boy.

Acres. Mind, I give up all my claim—I make no pretensions to any thing in the world; and if I can't get a wife without fighting for her, by my valour! I'll live a bachelor.

Sir Lucius. Captain, give me your hand: an affront handsomely acknowledged becomes an obligation; and as for the lady, if she chooses to deny her own handwriting, here——   [*Takes out letters.*

Mrs. Malaprop. O, he will dissolve my mystery!—Sir Lucius, perhaps there's some mistake—perhaps I can illuminate——

Sir Lucius. Pray, old gentlewoman, don't interfere where you have no business.—Miss Languish, are you my Delia or not?

Lydia. Indeed, Sir Lucius, I am not.

          [*Walks aside with* CAPTAIN ABSOLUTE.

Mrs. Malaprop. Sir Lucius O'Trigger—ungrateful as you are—I own the soft impeachment—pardon my blushes, I am Delia.

Sir Lucius. You Delia—pho! pho! be easy.

Mrs. Malaprop. Why, thou barbarous vandyke—those letters are mine.—When you are more sensible of my benignity—perhaps I may be brought to encourage your addresses.

Sir Lucius. Mrs. Malaprop, I am extremely sensible of your condescension; and whether you or Lucy have put this trick on me, I am equally beholden to you.—And, to show you I am not ungrateful, Captain Absolute, since you have taken that lady from me, I'll give you my Delia into the bargain.

Absolute. I am much obliged to you, Sir Lucius; but here's my friend, Fighting Bob, unprovided for.

Sir Lucius. Hah! little Valour—here, will you make your fortune?

Acres. Odds wrinkles! No.—But give me your hand, Sir Lucius, forget and forgive; but if ever I give you a chance of pickling me again, say Bob Acres is a dunce, that's all.

Sir Anthony. Come, Mrs. Malaprop, don't be cast down —you are in your bloom yet.

Mrs. Malaprop. O Sir Anthony—men are all barbarians.
                                 [*All retire but* JULIA *and* FAULKLAND.

Julia. [*Aside.*] He seems dejected and unhappy—not sullen; there was some foundation, however, for the tale he told me—O woman! how true should be your judgment, when your resolution is so weak!

Faulkland. Julia!—how can I sue for what I so little deserve? I dare not presume—yet Hope is the child of Penitence.

Julia. Oh! Faulkland, you have not been more faulty in your unkind treatment of me than I am now in wanting inclination to resent it. As my heart honestly bids me place my weakness to the account of love, I should be ungenerous not to admit the same plea for yours.

Faulkland. Now I shall be blest indeed.

Sir Anthony. [*Coming forward.*] What's going on here? —So you have been quarrelling too, I warrant? Come, Julia, I never interfered before; but let me have a hand in the matter at last.—All the faults I have ever seen in my friend Faulkland seemed to proceed from what he calls the delicacy and warmth of his affection for you.—There, marry him directly, Julia; you'll find he'll mend surprisingly!   [*The rest come forward.*

Sir Lucius. Come, now, I hope there is no dissatisfied person, but what is content; for as I have been disappointed myself, it will be very hard if I have not the satisfaction of seeing other people succeed better.

Acres. You are right, Sir Lucius.—So, Jack, I wish you joy.—Mr. Faulkland the same.—Ladies,—come now, to show you I'm neither vexed nor angry, odds tabors and pipes! I'll order the fiddles in half an hour to the New Rooms—and I insist on your all meeting me there.

Sir Anthony. 'Gad! sir, I like your spirit; and at night we single lads will drink a health to the young couples, and a husband to Mrs. Malaprop.

Faulkland. Our partners are stolen from us, Jack—I

hope to be congratulated by each other—yours for having checked in time the errors of an ill-directed imagination, which might have betrayed an innocent heart; and mine, for having, by her gentleness and candour, reformed the unhappy temper of one, who by it made wretched whom he loved most, and tortured the heart he ought to have adored.

Absolute. Well, Jack, we have both tasted the bitters, as well as the sweets of love; with this difference only, that you always prepared the bitter cup for yourself, while I——

Lydia. Was always obliged to me for it, hey! Mr. Modesty?——But come, no more of that—our happiness is now as unalloyed as general.

Julia. Then let us study to preserve it so: and while Hope pictures to us a flattering scene of future bliss, let us deny its pencil those colours which are too bright to be lasting.—When hearts deserving happiness would unite their fortunes, Virtue would crown them with an unfading garland of modest hurtless flowers; but ill-judging Passion will force the gaudier rose into the wreath, whose thorn offends them when its leaves are dropped! [*Exeunt omnes.*

EPILOGUE

By the Author

SPOKEN BY MRS. BULKLEY

LADIES, for you—I heard our poet say—
He'd try to coax some moral from his play:
"One moral's plain," cried I, "without more fuss;
Man's social happiness all rests on us:
Through all the drama—whether damn'd or not—
Love gilds the scene, and women guide the plot.
From every rank obedience is our due—
D'ye doubt?—The world's great stage shall prove it true."
    The cit, well skill'd to shun domestic strife,
Will sup abroad; but first he'll ask his wife:
John Trot, his friend, for once will do the same,
But then—he'll just step home to tell his dame.
    The surly squire at noon resolves to rule,
And half the day—Zounds! madam is a fool!

Convinced at night, the vanquished victor says,
Ah, Kate! you women have such coaxing ways.
   The jolly toper chides each tardy blade,
Till reeling Bacchus calls on Love for aid:
Then with each toast he sees fair bumpers swim,
And kisses Chloe on the sparkling brim!
   Nay, I have heard that statesmen—great and wise—
Will sometimes counsel with a lady's eyes!
The servile suitors watch her various face,
She smiles preferment, or she frowns disgrace,
Curtsies a pension here—there nods a place.
   Nor with less awe, in scenes of humbler life,
Is view'd the mistress, or is heard the wife.
The poorest peasant of the poorest soil,
The child of poverty, and heir to toil,
Early from radiant Love's impartial light
Steals one small spark to cheer this world of night:
Dear spark! that oft through winter's chilling woes
Is all the warmth his little cottage knows!
   The wandering tar, who not for years has press'd,
The widow'd partner of his day of rest,
On the cold deck, far from her arms removed,
Still hums the ditty which his Susan loved;
And while around the cadence rude is blown,
The boatswain whistles in a softer tone.
   The soldier, fairly proud of wounds and toil,
Pants for the triumph of his Nancy's smile!
But ere the battle should he list her cries,
The lover trembles—and the hero dies!
That heart, by war and honour steel'd to fear,
Droops on a sigh, and sickens at a tear!
   But ye more cautious, ye nice-judging few,
Who give to beauty only beauty's due,
Though friends to love—ye view with deep regret
Our conquests marr'd, our triumphs incomplete,
Till polish'd wit more lasting charms disclose,
And judgment fix the darts which beauty throws!
In female breasts did sense and merit rule,
The lover's mind would ask no other school;
Shamed into sense, the scholars of our eyes,
Our beaux from gallantry would soon be wise;
Would gladly light, their homage to improve,
The lamp of knowledge at the torch of love!

ST. PATRICK'S DAY;
or, the scheming Lieutenant

A Farce

DRAMATIS PERSONÆ

AS ORIGINALLY ACTED AT COVENT-GARDEN THEATRE
ON MAY 2, 1775

LIEUTENANT O'CONNOR	Mr. Clinch
DOCTOR ROSY	Mr. Quick
JUSTICE CREDULOUS	Mr. Lee Lewis
SERJEANT TROUNCE	Mr. Booth
CORPORAL FLINT	
LAURETTA	Mrs. Cargill
MRS. BRIDGET CREDULOUS	Mrs. Pitt

Drummer, Soldiers, Countrymen, *and* Servant.

SCENE—A TOWN IN ENGLAND

ST. PATRICK'S DAY

ACT ONE

SCENE I—LIEUTENANT O'CONNOR'S *Lodgings*

Enter SERJEANT TROUNCE, CORPORAL FLINT, *and four*
SOLDIERS.

FIRST SOLDIER. I say you are wrong; we should all speak
together, each for himself, and all at once, that we may be
heard the better.

2 Soldier. Right, Jack, we'll argue in platoons.

3 Soldier. Ay, ay, let him have our grievances in a volley,
and if we be to have a spokesman, there's the corporal is
the lieutenant's countryman, and knows his humour.

Flint. Let me alone for that. I served three years, within
a bit, under his honour, in the Royal Inniskillions, and I
never will see a sweeter tempered gentleman, nor one more
free with his purse. I put a great shamrock in his hat
this morning, and I'll be bound for him he'll wear it, was
it as big as Steven's Green.

4 Soldier. I say again then you talk like youngsters, like
militia striplings: there's a discipline, look'ee in all things,
whereof the serjeant must be our guide; he's a gentleman
of words; he understands your foreign lingo, your figures,
and such like auxiliaries in scoring. Confess now for a
reckoning, whether in chalk or writing, ben't he your only
man?

Flint. Why the serjeant is a scholar to be sure, and has
the gift of reading.

Trounce. Good soldiers, and fellow-gentlemen, if you
make me your spokesman, you will show the more judgment; and let me alone for the argument. I'll be as loud
as a drum, and point blank from the purpose.

All. Agreed, agreed.

Flint. Oh, faith! here comes the lieutenant.—Now,
Serjeant.

87

Trounce. So then, to order.—Put on your mutiny looks; every man grumble a little to himself, and some of you hum the Deserter's March.

Enter LIEUTENANT O'CONNOR.

O'Connor. Well, honest lads, what is it you have to complain of?

Soldier. Ahem! hem!

Trounce. So please your honour, the very grievance of the matter is this:—ever since your honour differed with Justice Credulous, our inn-keepers use us most scurvily. By my halbert, their treatment is such, that if your spirit was willing to put up with it, flesh and blood could by no means agree; so we humbly petition that your honour would make an end of the matter at once, by running away with the justice's daughter, or else get us fresh quarters,— hem! hem!

O'Connor. Indeed! Pray which of the houses use you ill?

1 Soldier. There's the Red Lion an't half the civility of the old Red Lion.

2 Soldier. There's the White Horse, if he wasn't casehardened, ought to be ashamed to show his face.

O'Connor. Very well; the Horse and the Lion shall answer for it at the quarter sessions.

Trounce. The two Magpies are civil enough; but the Angel uses us like devils, and the Rising Sun refuses us light to go to bed by.

O'Connor. Then, upon my word, I'll have the Rising Sun put down, and the Angel shall give security for his good behaviour; but are you sure you do nothing to quit scores with them?

Flint. Nothing at all, your honour, unless now and then we happen to fling a cartridge into the kitchen fire, or put a spatterdash or so into the soup; and sometimes Ned drums up and down stairs a little of a night.

O'Connor. Oh, all that's fair; but hark'ee, lads, I must have no grumbling on St. Patrick's Day; so here, take this, and divide it amongst you. But observe me now,—show yourselves men of spirit, and don't spend sixpence of it in drink.

Trounce. Nay, hang it, your honour, soldiers should never bear malice; we must drink St. Patrick's and your honour's health.

All. Oh, damn malice! St. Patrick's and his honour's by all means.

Flint. Come away, then, lads, and first we'll parade round the Market-cross, for the honour of King George.

1 Soldier. Thank your honour.—Come along; St. Patrick, his honour, and strong beer for ever!   [*Exeunt* SOLDIERS.

O'Connor. Get along, you thoughtless vagabonds! yet, upon my conscience, 'tis very hard these poor fellows should scarcely have bread from the soil they would die to defend.

Enter DOCTOR ROSY.

Ah, my little Dr. Rosy, my Galen a-bridge, what's the news?

Rosy. All things are as they were, my Alexander; the justice is as violent as ever: I felt his pulse on the matter again, and, thinking his rage began to intermit, I wanted to throw in the bark of good advice, but it would not do. He says you and your cut-throats have a plot upon his life, and swears he had rather see his daughter in a scarlet fever than in the arms of a soldier.

O'Connor. Upon my word the army is very much obliged to him. Well, then, I must marry the girl first, and ask his consent afterwards.

Rosy. So, then, the case of her fortune is desperate, hey?

O'Connor. Oh, hang fortune,—let that take its chance; there is a beauty in Lauretta's simplicity, so pure a bloom upon her charms.

Rosy. So there is, so there is. You are for beauty as nature made her, hey! No artificial graces, no cosmetic varnish, no beauty in grey, hey!

O'Connor. Upon my word, doctor, you are right; the London ladies were always too handsome for me; then they are so defended, such a circumvallation of hoop, with a breastwork of whale-bone that would turn a pistol-bullet, much less Cupid's arrows,—then turret on turret on top, with stores of concealed weapons, under pretence of black pins,—and above all, a standard of feathers that would do honour to a knight of the Bath. Upon my conscience, I could as soon embrace an Amazon, armed at all points.

Rosy. Right, right, my Alexander! my taste to a tittle.

O'Connor. Then, doctor, though I admire modesty in women, I like to see their faces. I am for the changeable rose; but with one of these quality Amazons, if their mid-night dissipations had left them blood enough to raise a blush, they have not room enough in their cheeks to show it. To be sure, bashfulness is a very pretty thing; but, in my mind, there is nothing on earth so impudent as an everlasting blush.

Rosy. My taste, my taste!—Well, Lauretta is none of these. Ah! I never see her but she put me in mind of my poor dear wife.

O'Connor. Ay, faith; in my opinion she can't do a worse thing. Now he is going to bother me about an old hag that has been dead these six years.   [*Aside.*

Rosy. Oh, poor Dolly! I never shall see her like again; such an arm for a bandage—veins that seemed to invite the lancet. Then her skin, smooth and white as a gallipot; her mouth as large and not larger than the mouth of a penny phial; her lips conserve of roses; and then her teeth —none of your sturdy fixtures—ache as they would, it was but a small pull, and out they came. I believe I have drawn half a score of her poor dear pearls—[*Weeps.*]— But what avails her beauty? Death has no consideration —one must die as well as another.

O'Connor. [*Aside.*] Oh, if he begins to moralize——
[*Takes out his snuff-box.*

Rosy. Fair and ugly, crooked or straight, rich or poor —flesh is grass—flowers fade!

O'Connor. Here, doctor, take a pinch, and keep up your spirits.

Rosy. True, true, my friend; grief can't mend the matter —all's for the best; but such a woman was a great loss, lieutenant.

O'Connor. To be sure, for doubtless she had mental accomplishments equal to her beauty.

Rosy. Mental accomplishments! she would have stuffed an alligator, or pickled a lizard, with any apothecary's wife in the kingdom. Why, she could decipher a prescription, and invent the ingredients, almost as well as myself: then she was such a hand at making foreign waters!—for Seltzer, Pyrmont, Islington, or Chalybeate, she never had her equal; and her Bath and Bristol springs exceeded the originals.—Ah, poor Dolly! she fell a martyr to her own discoveries.

O'Connor. How so, pray?

Rosy. Poor soul! her illness was occasioned by her zeal

in trying an improvement on the Spa-water by an infusion
of rum and acid.

O'Connor. Ay, ay, spirits never agree with water-
drinkers.

Rosy. No, no, you mistake. Rum agreed with her well
enough; it was not the rum that killed the poor dear creature, for she died of a dropsy. Well, she is gone, never
to return, and has left no pledge of our loves behind. No
little babe, to hang like a label round papa's neck. Well,
well, we are all mortal—sooner or later—flesh is grass—
flowers fade.

O'Connor. Oh, the devil!—again!　　　　　　　[*Aside.*

Rosy. Life's a shadow—the world a stage—we strut an
hour.

O'Connor. Here, doctor.　　　　　　　[*Offers snuff.*

Rosy. True, true, my friend: well, high grief can't cure
it. All's for the best, hey! my little Alexander?

O'Connor. Right, right; an apothecary should never be
out of spirits. But come, faith, 'tis time honest Humphrey
should wait on the justice; that must be our first scheme.

Rosy. True, true; you should be ready: the clothes are
at my house, and I have given you such a character, that
he is impatient to have you: he swears you shall be his
body-guard. Well, I honour the army, or I should never
do so much to serve you.

O'Connor. Indeed I am bound to you for ever, doctor;
and when once I'm possessed of my dear Lauretta, I will
endeavour to make work for you as fast as possible.

Rosy. Now you put me in mind of my poor wife again.

O'Connor. Ah, pray forget her a little: we shall be too
late.

Rosy. Poor Dolly!

O'Connor. 'Tis past twelve.

Rosy. Inhuman dropsy!

O'Connor. The justice will wait.

Rosy. Cropped in her prime!

O'Connor. For heaven's sake, come!

Rosy. Well, flesh is grass.

O'Connor. O, the devil!

Rosy. We must all die——

O'Connor. Doctor!

Rosy. Kings, lords, and common whores——

　　　　[*Exeunt* LIEUTENANT O'CONNOR *forcing* ROSY *off.*

SCENE II—*A Room in* JUSTICE CREDULOUS' *House*

Enter LAURETTA *and* MRS. BRIDGET CREDULOUS.

Lauretta. I repeat it again, mamma, officers are the prettiest men in the world, and Lieutenant O'Connor is the prettiest officer I ever saw.

Mrs. Bridget. For shame, Laura! how can you talk so?—or if you must have a military man, there's Lieutenant Plow, or Captain Haycock, or Major Dray, the brewer, are all your admirers; and though they are peaceable, good kind of men, they have as large cockades, and become scarlet, as well as the fighting folks.

Lauretta. Psha! you know, mamma, I hate militia officers; a set of dunghill cocks with spurs on—heroes scratched off a church door—clowns in military masquerade, wearing the dress without supporting the character. No, give me the bold upright youth, who makes love to-day, and his head shot off to-morrow. Dear! to think how the sweet fellows sleep on the ground, and fight in silk stockings and lace ruffles.

Mrs. Bridget. Oh, barbarous! to want a husband that may wed you to-day, and be sent the Lord knows where before night; then in a twelvemonth perhaps to have him come like a Colossus, with one leg at New York, and the other at Chelsea Hospital.

Lauretta. Then I'll be his crutch, mamma.

Mrs. Bridget. No, give me a husband that knows where his limbs are, though he want the use of them:—and if he should take you with him, to sleep in a baggage-cart, and stroll about the camp like a gipsy, with a knapsack and two children at your back; then, by way of entertainment in the evening, to make a party with the serjeant's wife to drink bohea tea, and play at all-fours on a drum-head:—'tis a precious life, to be sure!

Lauretta. Nay, mamma, you shouldn't be against my lieutenant, for I heard him say you were the best natured and best looking woman in the world.

Mrs. Bridget. Why, child, I never said but that Lieutenant O'Connor was a very well-bred and discerning young man; 'tis your papa is so violent against him.

Lauretta. Why, Cousin Sophy married an officer.

Mrs. Bridget. Ay, Laura, an officer of the militia.

Lauretta. No, indeed, ma'am, a marching regiment.

Mrs. Bridget. No, child, I tell you he was a major of militia.

Lauretta. Indeed, mamma, it wasn't.

Enter JUSTICE CREDULOUS.

Justice. Bridget, my love, I have had a message.

Lauretta. It was cousin Sophy told me so.

Justice. I have had a message, love——

Mrs. Bridget. No, child, she would say no such thing.

Justice. A message, I say.

Lauretta. How could he be in the militia when he was ordered abroad?

Mrs. Bridget. Ay, girl, hold your tongue!—Well, my dear.

Justice. I have had a message from Doctor Rosy.

Mrs. Bridget. He ordered abroad! He went abroad for his health.

Justice. Why, Bridget!——

Mrs. Bridget. Well, deary.—Now hold your tongue, miss.

Justice. A message from Dr. Rosy, and Dr. Rosy says—

Lauretta. I'm sure, mamma, his regimentals——

Justice. Damn his regimentals!—Why don't you listen?

Mrs. Bridget. Ay, girl, how durst you interrupt your papa?

Lauretta. Well, papa.

Justice. Dr. Rosy says he'll bring——

Lauretta. Were blue turned up with red, mamma.

Justice. Laury!—says he will bring the young man——

Mrs. Bridget. Red! yellow, if you please, miss.

Justice. Bridget!—the young man that is to be hired——

Mrs. Bridget. Besides, miss, it is very unbecoming in you to want to have the last word with your mamma; you should know——

Justice. Why, zounds! will you hear me or no?

Mrs. Bridget. I am listening, my love, I am listening!—But what signifies my silence, what good is my not speaking a word, if this girl will interrupt and let nobody speak but herself?—Ay, I don't wonder, my life, at your impatience; your poor dear lips quiver to speak; but I suppose she'll run on, and not let you put in a word.—You may very well be angry; there is nothing, sure, so provoking as a chattering, talking——

Lauretta. Nay, I'm sure, mamma, it is you will not let papa speak now.

Mrs. Bridget. Why, you little provoking minx——

Justice. Get out of the room directly, both of you—get out!

Mrs. Bridget. Ay, go, girl.

Justice. Go, Bridget, you are worse than she, you old hag. I wish you were both up to the neck in the canal, to argue there till I took you out.

Enter SERVANT.

Servant. Doctor Rosy, sir.

Justice. Show him up.   [*Exit* SERVANT.

Lauretta. Then you own, mamma, it was a marching regiment?

Mrs. Bridget. You're a obstinate fool, I tell you; for if that had been the case——

Justice. You won't go?

Mrs. Bridget. We are going, Mr. Surly.—If that had been the case, I say, how could——

Lauretta. Nay, mamma, one proof——

Mrs. Bridget. How could Major——

Lauretta. And a full proof——

[JUSTICE CREDULOUS *drives them off.*

Justice. There they go, ding dong in for the day. Good lack! a fluent tongue is the only thing a mother don't like her daughter to resemble her in.

Enter DOCTOR ROSY.

Well, doctor, where's the lad—where's Trusty?

Rosy. At hand; he'll be here in a minute, I'll answer for't. He's such a one as you an't met with,—brave as a lion, gentle as a saline draught.

Justice. Ah, he comes in the place of a rogue, a dog that was corrupted by the lieutenant. But this is a sturdy fellow, is he, doctor?

Rosy. As Hercules; and the best back-sword in the country. Egad, he'll make the red coats keep their distance.

Justice. O the villains; this is St. Patrick's day, and the rascals have been parading my house all the morning. I know they have a design upon me; but I have taken all precautions: I have magazines of arms, and if this fellow does but prove faithful, I shall be more at ease.

Rosy. Doubtless he'll be a comfort to you.

Re-enter SERVANT.

Servant. There is a man below, inquires for Doctor Rosy.

Rosy. Show him up.

Justice. Hold! a little caution—how does he look?

Servant. A country-looking fellow, your worship.

Justice. Oh, well, well, for Doctor Rosy; these rascals try all ways to get in here.

Servant. Yes, please your worship; there was one here this morning wanted to speak to you; he said his name was Corporal Breakbones.

Justice. Corporal Breakbones!

Servant. And Drummer Crackskull came again.

Justice. Ay, did you ever hear of such a damned confounded crew? Well, show the lad in here!

[*Exit* SERVANT.

Rosy. Ay, he'll be your porter; he'll give the rogues an answer.

Enter LIEUTENANT O'CONNOR, *disguised.*

Justice. So, a tall—Efacks! what! has lost an eye?

Rosy. Only a bruise he got in taking seven or eight highwaymen.

Justice. He has a damned wicked leer somehow with the other.

Rosy. Oh, no, he's bashful—a sheepish look——

Justice. Well, my lad, what's your name?

O'Connor. Humphrey Hum.

Justice. Hum—I don't like Hum!

O'Connor. But I be mostly called honest Humphrey——

Rosy. There, I told you so, of noted honesty.

Justice. Well, honest Humphrey, the doctor has told you my terms, and you are willing to serve, hey?

O'Connor. And please your worship I shall be well content.

Justice. Well, then, hark'ye, honest Humphrey,—you are sure now, you will never be a rogue—never take a bribe hey, honest Humphrey?

O'Connor. A bribe! what's that?

Justice. A very ignorant fellow indeed!

Rosy. His worship hopes you will not part with your honesty for money.

O'Connor. Noa, noa.

Justice. Well said, Humphrey—my chief business with you is to watch the motions of a rake-helly fellow here, one Lieutenant O'Connor.

Rosy. Ay, you don't value the soldiers, do you, Humphrey?

O'Connor. Not I; they are but zwaggerers, and you'll see they'll be as much afraid of me as they would of their captain.

Justice. And i'faith, Humphrey, you have a pretty cudgel there!

O'Connor. Ay, the zwitch is better than nothing, but I should be glad of a stouter: ha' you got such a thing in the house as an old coach-pole, or a spare bed-post?

Justice. Oons, what a dragon it is!—Well, Humphrey, come with me.—I'll just show him to Bridget, doctor, and we'll agree.—Come along, honest Humphrey.   [*Exit.*

O'Connor. My dear doctor, now remember to bring the Justice presently to the walk: I have a scheme to get into his confidence at once.

Rosy. I will, I will.   [*They shake hands.*

Re-enter JUSTICE CREDULOUS.

Justice. Why, honest Humphrey, hey! what the devil are you at?

Rosy. I was just giving him a little advice.—Well I must go for the present.—Good-morning to your worship —you need not fear the lieutenant while he is in your house.

Justice. Well, get in, Humphrey. Good-morning to you, doctor.—[*Exit* DOCTOR ROSY.] Come along, Humphrey. —Now I think I am a match for the lieutenant and all his gang.   [*Exeunt.*

ACT TWO

SCENE I—*A Street*

Enter SERJEANT TROUNCE, DRUMMER, *and* SOLDIERS.

TROUNCE. Come, silence your drum—there is no valour stirring to-day. I thought St. Patrick would have given us a recruit or two to-day.

Soldier. Mark, serjeant!

Enter two COUNTRYMEN.

Trounce. Oh! these are the lads I was looking for; they have the look of gentlemen.—An't you single, my lads?

1 Countryman. Yes, an please you, I be quite single: my relations be all dead, thank heavens, more or less. I have but one poor mother left in the world, and she's an helpless woman.

Trounce. Indeed! a very extraordinary case—quite your own master then—the fitter to serve his Majesty.—Can you read?

1 Countryman. Noa, I was always too lively to take to learning; but John here is main clever at it.

Trounce. So, what you're a scholar, friend?

2 Countryman. I was born so, measter. Feyther kept grammar-school.

Trounce. Lucky man—in a campaign or two put yourself down chaplain to the regiment. And I warrant you have read of warriors and heroes?

2 Countryman. Yes, that I have: I have read of Jack the Giant Killer, and the Dragon of Wantly, and the—Noa, I believe that's all in the hero way, except once about a comet.

Trounce. Wonderful knowledge!—Well, my heroes, I'll write word to the king of your good intentions, and meet me half an hour hence at the Two Magpies.

Countrymen. We will, your honour, we will.

Trounce. But stay; for fear I shouldn't see you again in the crowd, clap these little bits of ribbon into your hats.

1 Countryman. Our hats are none of the best.

Trounce. Well, meet me at the Magpies, and I'll give you money to buy new ones.

Countryman. Bless your honour, thank your honour.

            [*Exeunt.*

Trounce. [*Winking at* SOLDIERS.] Jack!

           [*Exeunt* SOLDIERS.

Enter LIEUTENANT O'CONNOR.

So, here comes one would make a grenadier—Stop, friend, will you list?

O'Connor. Who shall I serve under?

Trounce. Under me, to be sure.

O'Connor. Isn't Lieutenant O'Connor your officer?

Trounce. He is, and I am commander over him.

O'Connor. What! be your serjeants greater than your captains?

Trounce. To be sure we are; 'tis our business to keep them in order. For instance, now, the general writes to me, dear Serjeant, or dear Trounce, or dear Serjeant Trounce, according to his hurry, if your lieutenant does not demean himself accordingly, let me know.—Yours, General Deluge.

O'Connor. And do you complain of him often?

Trounce. No, hang him, the lad is good-natured at the bottom, so I pass over small things. But hark'ee, between ourselves, he is most confoundedly given to wenching.

Enter CORPORAL FLINT.

Flint. Please your honour, the doctor is coming this way with his worship—We are all ready, and have our cues.
                                                                    [*Exit.*

O'Connor. Then, my dear Trounce, or my dear Serjeant, or my dear Serjeant Trounce, take yourself away.

Trounce. Zounds! the lieutenant—I smell of the black hole already.   [*Exit.*

Enter JUSTICE CREDULOUS *and* DOCTOR ROSY.

Justice. I thought I saw some of the cut-throats.

Rosy. I fancy not; there's no one but honest Humphrey. Ha! Odds life, here comes some of them—we'll stay by these trees, and let them pass.

Justice. Oh, the bloody-looking dogs!
                                          [*Walks aside with* DOCTOR ROSY.

Re-enter CORPORAL FLINT *and two* SOLDIERS.

Flint. Halloa, friend! do you serve Justice Credulous?

O'Connor. I do.

Flint. Are you rich?

O'Connor. Noa.

Flint. Nor ever will be with that old stingy booby. Look here—take it.   [*Gives him a purse.*

O'Connor. What must I do for this?

Flint. Mark me, our lieutenant is in love with the old rogue's daughter: help us to break his worship's bones, and carry off the girl, and you are a made man.

O'Connor. I'll see you hanged first, you pack of skurry villains!   [*Throws away the purse.*

Flint. What, sirrah, do you mutiny? Lay hold of him.

O'Connor. Nay, then, I'll try your armour for you.

[*Beats them.*

All. Oh! oh!—quarter! quarter!

[*Exeunt* CORPORAL FLINT *and* SOLDIERS.

Justice. [*Coming forward.*] Trim them, trounce them, break their bones, honest Humphrey—What a spirit he has!

Rosy. Aquafortis.

O'Connor. Betray your master!

Rosy. What a miracle of fidelity!

Justice. Ay, and it shall not go unrewarded—I'll give him sixpence on the spot. Here, honest Humphrey, there's for yourself: as for this bribe, [*takes up the purse,*] such trash is best in the hands of justice. Now, then, doctor, I think I may trust him to guard the women: while he is with them I may go out with safety.

Rosy. Doubtless you may—I'll answer for the lieutenant's behaviour whilst honest Humphrey is with your daughter.

Justice. Ay, ay, she shall go nowhere without him. Come along, honest Humphrey. How rare it is to meet with such a servant!   [*Exeunt.*

SCENE II—*A Garden*

LAURETTA *discovered. Enter* JUSTICE CREDULOUS *and* LIEUTENANT O'CONNOR.

Justice. Why, you little truant, how durst you wander so far from the house without my leave? Do you want to invite that scoundrel lieutenant to scale the walls and carry you off?

Lauretta. Lud, papa, you are so apprehensive for nothing.

Justice. Why, hussy——

Lauretta. Well, then, I can't bear to be shut up all day so like a nun. I am sure it is enough to make one wish to be run away with—and I wish I was run away with—I do —and I wish the lieutenant knew it.

Justice. You do, do you, hussy? Well, I think I'll take pretty good care of you. Here, Humphrey, I leave this lady in your care. Now you may walk about the garden, Miss Pert; but Humphrey shall go with you wherever you

go. So mind, honest Humphrey, I am obliged to go abroad
for a little while; let no one but yourself come near her;
don't be shame-faced, you booby, but keep close to her.
And now, miss, let your lieutenant or any of his crew come
near you if they can.   [*Exit*.

Lauretta. How this booby stares after him!
                                    [*Sits down and sings*.

O'Connor. Lauretta!
Lauretta. Not so free, fellow!   [*Sings*.
O'Connor. Lauretta! look on me.
Lauretta. Not so free, fellow!
O'Connor. No recollection!
Lauretta. Honest Humphrey, be quiet.
O'Connor. Have you forgot your faithful soldier?
Lauretta. Ah! Oh preserve me!
O'Connor. 'Tis, my soul! your truest slave, passing on
your father in this disguise.
Lauretta. Well now, I declare this is charming—you are
so disguised, my dear lieutenant, and you look so delight-
fully ugly. I am sure no one will find you out, ha! ha! ha!
—You know I am under your protection; papa charged
you to keep close to me.
O'Connor. True, my angel, and thus let me fulfil——
Lauretta. O pray now, dear Humphrey——
O'Connor. Nay, 'tis but what old Mittimus commanded.
                                    [*Offers to kiss her*.

Re-enter JUSTICE CREDULOUS.

Justice. Laury, my—hey! what the devil's here?
Lauretta. Well now, one kiss, and be quiet.
Justice. Your very humble servant, honest Humphrey!
Don't let me—pray don't let me interrupt you!
Lauretta. Lud, papa! Now that's so good-natured—indeed there's no harm. You did not mean any rudeness, did
you, Humphrey?
O'Connor. No, indeed, miss; his worship knows it is not
in me.
Justice. I know that you are a lying, canting, hypocritical scoundrel; and if you don't take yourself out of my
sight——
Lauretta. Indeed, papa, now I'll tell you how it was. I
was sometime taken with a sudden giddiness, and Humphrey seeing me beginning to totter, ran to my assistance,
quite frightened, poor fellow, and took me in his arms.

Justice. Oh! was that all—nothing but a little giddiness, hey!

O'Connor. That's all, indeed, your worship; for seeing miss change colour, I ran up instantly.

Justice. Oh, 'twas very kind in you!

O'Connor. And luckily recovered her.

Justice. And who made you a doctor, you impudent rascal, hey? Get out of my sight, I say, this instant, or by all the statutes——

Lauretta. Oh now, papa, you frighten me, and I am giddy again!—Oh, help!

O'Connor. O dear lady, she'll fall!

[*Takes her into his arms.*

Justice. Zounds! what before my face—why then, thou miracle of impudence!—[*Lays hold of him and discovers him.*]—Mercy on me, who have we here?—Murder! Robbery! Fire! Rape! Gunpowder! Soldiers! John! Susan! Bridget!

O'Connor. Good sir, don't be alarmed; I mean you no harm.

Justice. Thieves! Robbers! Soldiers!

O'Connor. You know my love for your daughter——

Justice. Fire! Cut-throats!

O'Connor. And that alone——

Justice. Treason! Gunpowder!

Enter a SERVANT *with a blunderbuss.*

Now, scoundrel! let her go this instant.

Lauretta. O papa, you'll kill me!

Justice. Honest Humphrey, be advised. Ay, miss, this way, if you please.

O'Connor. Nay, sir, but hear me——

Justice. I'll shoot.

O'Connor. And you'll be convinced——

Justice. I'll shoot.

O'Connor. How injurious——

Justice. I'll shoot—and so your very humble servant, honest Humphrey Hum.   [*Exeunt separately.*

SCENE III—*A Walk*

Enter DOCTOR ROSY.

Rosy. Well, I think my friend is now in a fair way of

succeeding. Ah! I warrant he is full of hope and fear, doubt and anxiety; truly he has the fever of love strong upon him: faint, peevish, languishing all day, with burning, restless nights. Ah! just my case when I pined for my poor dear Dolly! when she used to have her daily colics, and her little doctor be sent for. Then would I interpret the language of her pulse—declare my own sufferings in my receipt for her—send her a pearl necklace in a pillbox, or a cordial draught with an acrostic on the label. Well, those days are over: no happiness lasting: all is vanity—now sunshine, now cloudy—we are, as it were, king and beggar—then what avails——

Enter LIEUTENANT O'CONNOR.

O'Connor. O doctor! ruined and undone.

Rosy. The pride of beauty——

O'Connor. I am discovered, and——

Rosy. The gaudy palace——

O'Connor. The justice is——

Rosy. The pompous wig——

O'Connor. Is more enraged than ever.

Rosy. The gilded cane——

O'Connor. Why, doctor! [*Slapping him on the shoulder.*

Rosy. Hey!

O'Connor. Confound your morals! I tell you I am discovered, discomfited, disappointed.

Rosy. Indeed! Good lack, good lack, to think of the instability of human affairs! Nothing certain in this world—most deceived when most confident—fools of fortune all.

O'Connor. My dear doctor, I want at present a little practical wisdom. I am resolved this instant to try the scheme we were going to put into execution last week. I have the letter ready, and only want your assistance to recover my ground.

Rosy. With all my heart—I'll warrant you I'll bear a part in it: but how the deuce were you discovered?

O'Connor. I'll tell you as we go; there's not a moment to be lost.

Rosy. Heaven send we succeed better!—but there's no knowing.

O'Connor. Very true.

Rosy. We may and we may not.

O'Connor. Right.

Rosy. Time must show.

O'Connor. Certainly.

Rosy. We are but blind guessers.

O'Connor. Nothing more.

Rosy. Thick-sighted mortals.

O'Connor. Remarkably.

Rosy. Wandering in error.

O'Connor. Even so.

Rosy. Futurity is dark.

O'Connor. As a cellar.

Rosy. Men are moles.

[*Exeunt* LIEUTENANT O'CONNOR *forcing out* ROSY.

SCENE IV—*A Room in* JUSTICE CREDULOUS' *House*

Enter JUSTICE CREDULOUS *and* MRS. BRIDGET CREDULOUS.

Justice. Odds life, Bridget, you are enough to make one mad! I tell you he would have deceived a chief justice: the dog seemed as ignorant as my clerk, and talked of honesty as if he had been a churchwarden.

Mrs. Bridget. Pho! nonsense, honesty!—what had you to do, pray, with honesty? A fine business you have made of it with your Humphrey Hum: and miss, too, she must have been privy to it. Lauretta! ay, you would have her called so; but for my part I never knew any good come of giving girls these heathen Christian names: if you had called her Deborah, or Tabitha, or Ruth, or Rebecca, or Joan, nothing of this had ever happened; but I always knew Lauretta was a runaway name.

Justice. Psha, you're a fool!

Mrs. Bridget. No, Mr. Credulous, it is you who are a fool, and no one but such a simpleton would be so imposed on.

Justice. Why zounds, madam, how durst you talk so? If you have no respect for your husband, I should think *unus quorum* might command a little deference.

Mrs. Bridget. Don't tell me!—Unus fiddlestick! you ought to be ashamed to show your face at the sessions: you'll be a laughing-stock to the whole bench, and a by-word with all the pig-tailed lawyers and bag-wigged attorneys about town.

Justice. Is this language for his majesty's representative? By the statutes, it's high treason and petty treason, both at once!

Enter SERVANT.

Servant. A letter for your worship.

Justice. Who brought it?

Servant. A soldier.

Justice. Take it away and burn it.

Mrs. Bridget. Stay!—Now you're in such a hurry—it is some canting scrawl from the lieutenant, I suppose.— [*Takes the letter.—Exit* SERVANT.] Let me see:—ay, 'tis signed O'Connor.

Justice. Well, come read it out.

Mrs. Bridget. [Reads.] *Revenge is sweet.*

Justice. It begins so, does it? I'm glad of that; I'll let the dog know I'm of his opinion.

Mrs. Bridget. [Reads.] *And though disappointed of my designs upon your daughter, I have still the satisfaction of knowing I am revenged on her unnatural father; for this morning, in your chocolate, I had the pleasure to administer to you a dose of poison!*—Mercy on us!

Justice. No tricks, Bridget; come, you know it is not so; you know it is a lie.

Mrs. Bridget. Read it yourself.

Justice. [Reads.] *Pleasure to administer a dose of poison!* —Oh, horrible! Cut-throat villain!—Bridget!

Mrs. Bridget. Lovee, stay, here's a postscript.—[Reads.] *N.B. 'Tis not in the power of medicine to save you.*

Justice. Odds my life, Bridget! why don't you call for help? I've lost my voice.—My brain is giddy—I shall burst, and no assistance.—John!—Laury!—John!

Mrs. Bridget. You see, lovee, what you have brought on yourself.

Re-enter SERVANT.

Servant. Your worship!

Justice. Stay, John; did you perceive anything in my chocolate cup this morning?

Servant. Nothing, your worship, unless it was a little grounds.

Justice. What colour were they?

Servant. Blackish, your worship.

Justice. Ay, arsenic, black arsenic!—Why don't you run for Dr. Rosy, you rascal?

Servant. Now, sir?

Mrs. Bridget. Oh, lovee, you may be sure it is in vain; let him run for the lawyer to witness your will, my life.

Justice. Zounds! go for the doctor, you scoundrel. You are all confederate murderers.

Servant. Oh, here he is, your worship.　　　　　[*Exit.*

Justice. Now, Bridget, hold your tongue, and let me see if my horrid situation be apparent.

Enter DOCTOR ROSY.

Rosy. I have but just called to inform—hey! bless me, what's the matter with your worship?

Justice. There, he sees it already!—Poison in my face, in capitals! Yes, yes, I'm a sure job for the undertakers indeed!

Mrs. Bridget. Oh! oh! alas, doctor!

Justice. Peace, Bridget!—Why, doctor, my dear old friend, do you really see any change in me?

Rosy. Change! never was a man so altered: how came these black spots on your nose?

Justice. Spots on my nose!

Rosy. And that wild stare in your right eye!

Justice. In my right eye?

Rosy. Ay, and, alack, alack, how you are swelled!

Justice. Swelled!

Rosy. Ay, don't you think he is, madam?

Mrs. Bridget. Oh! 'tis in vain to conceal it!—Indeed, lovee, you are as big again as you were this morning.

Justice. Yes, I feel it now—I'm poisoned!—Doctor, help me, for the love of justice! Give me life to see my murderer hanged.

Rosy. What?

Justice. I'm poisoned, I say!

Rosy. Speak out!

Justice. What! can't you hear me?

Rosy. Your voice is so low and hollow, as it were, I can't hear a word you say.

Justice. I'm gone then!—*Hic jacet,* many years one of his majesty's justices!

Mrs. Bridget. Read, doctor!—Ah, lovee, the will!—Consider, my life, how soon you will be dead.

Justice. No, Bridget, I shall die by inches.

Rosy. I never heard such monstrous iniquity.—Oh, you are gone indeed, my friend! the mortgage of your little bit of clay is out, and the sexton has nothing to do but to close. We must all go, sooner or later—high and low—Death's a debt; his mandamus binds all alike—no bail, no demurrer.

Justice. Silence, Dr. Croaker! will you cure me or will you not?

Rosy. Alas! my dear friend, it is not in my power; but I'll certainly see justice done on your murderer.

Justice. I thank you, my dear friend, but I had rather see it myself.

Rosy. Ay, but if you recover, the villain will escape.

Mrs. Bridget. Will he? then indeed it would be a pity you should recover. I am so enraged against the villain, I can't bear the thought of his escaping the halter.

Justice. That's very kind in you, my dear; but if it's the same thing to you, my dear, I had as soon recover, notwithstanding.—What, doctor, no assistance!

Rosy. Efacks, I can do nothing, but there's the German quack, whom you wanted to send from town; I met him at the next door, and I know he has antidotes for all poisons.

Justice. Fetch him, my dear friend, fetch him! I'll get him a diploma if he cures me.

Rosy. Well, there's no time to be lost; you continue to swell immensely.   [*Exit.*

Mrs. Bridget. What, my dear, will you submit to be cured by a quack nostrum-monger? For my part, as much as I love you, I had rather follow you to your grave than see you owe your life to any but a regular-bred physician.

Justice. I'm sensible of your affection, dearest; and be assured nothing consoles me in my melancholy situation so much as the thoughts of leaving you behind.

Re-enter DOCTOR ROSY, *with* LIEUTENANT O'CONNOR *disguised.*

Rosy. Great luck; met him passing by the door.

O'Connor. Metto dowsei pulsum.

Rosy. He desires me to feel your pulse.

Justice. Can't he speak English?

Rosy. Not a word.

O'Connor. Palio vivem mortem soonem.

Rosy. He says you have not six hours to live.

Justice. O mercy! does he know my distemper?

Rosy. I believe not.

Justice. Tell him 'tis black arsenic they have given me.

Rosy. Geneable illi arsnecca.

O'Connor. Pisonatus.

Justice. What does he say?

Rosy. He says you are poisoned.

Justice. We know that; but what will be the effect?

Rosy. Quid effectum?

O'Connor. Diable tutellum.

Rosy. He says you'll die presently.

Justice. Oh, horrible! What, no antidote?

O'Connor. Curum benakere bono fullum.

Justice. What, does he say I must row in a boat to Fulham?

Rosy. He says he'll undertake to cure you for three thousand pounds.

Mrs. Bridget. Three thousand pounds! three thousand halters!—No, lovee, you shall never submit to such impositions; die at once, and be a customer to none of them.

Justice. I won't die, Bridget—I don't like death.

Mrs. Bridget. Psha! there is nothing in it: a moment, and it is over.

Justice. Ay, but it leaves a numbness behind that lasts a plaguy long time.

Mrs. Bridget. O my dear, pray consider the will.

Enter LAURETTA.

Lauretta. O my father, what is this I hear?

O'Connor. Quiddam seomriam deos tollam rosam.

Rosy. The doctor is astonished at the sight of your fair daughter.

Justice. How so?

O'Connor. Damsellum livivum suvum rislibani.

Rosy. He says that he has lost his heart to her, and that if you will give him leave to pay his addresses to the young lady, and promise your consent to the union, if he should gain her affections, he will, on those conditions, cure you instantly, without fee or reward.

Justice. The devil! did he say all that in so few words? What a fine language it is! Well, I agree, if he can prevail on the girl.—[*Aside.*] And that I am sure he never will.

Rosy. Greal.

O'Connor. Writhum bothum.

Rosy. He says you must give this under your hand, while he writes you a miraculous receipt.

[*Both sit down to write.*

Lauretta. Do, mamma, tell me the meaning of this.

Mrs. Bridget. Don't speak to me, girl.—Unnatural parent!

Justice. There, doctor; there's what he requires.

Rosy. And here's your receipt: read it yourself.

Justice. Hey! what's here? plain English!

Rosy. Read it out; a wondrous nostrum, I'll answer for it.

Justice. [Reads.] *In reading this you are cured, by your affectionate son-in-law,* O'CONNOR.—Who in the name of Beelzebub, sirrah, who are you?

O'Connor. Your affectionate son-in-law, O'Connor, and your very humble servant, Humphrey Hum.

Justice. 'Tis false, you dog! you are not my son-in-law; for I'll be poisoned again, and you shall be hanged.—I'll die, sirrah, and leave Bridget my estate.

Mrs. Bridget. Ay, pray do, my dear, leave me your estate; I'm sure he deserves to be hanged.

Justice. He does, you say!—Hark'ee, Bridget, you showed such a tender concern for me when you thought me poisoned, that, for the future, I am resolved never to take your advice again in anything.—[*To* LIEUTENANT O'CONNOR.] So, do you hear, sir, you are an Irishman and a soldier, ain't you?

O'Connor. I am, sir, and proud of both.

Justice. The two things on earth I most hate; so I tell you what—renounce your country and sell your commission, and I'll forgive you.

O'Connor. Hark'ee, Mr. Justice—if you were not the father of my Lauretta, I would pull your nose for asking the first, and break your bones for desiring the second.

Rosy. Ay, ay, you're right.

Justice. Is he? then I'm sure I must be wrong.—Here, sir, I give my daughter to you, who are the most impudent dog I ever saw in my life.

O'Connor. Oh, sir, say what you please; with such a gift as Lauretta, every word is a compliment.

Mrs. Bridget. Well, my lovee, I think this will be a good subject for us to quarrel about the rest of our lives.

Justice. Why, truly, my dear, I think so, though we are seldom at a loss for that.

Rosy. This is all as it should be.—My Alexander, I give you joy, and you, my little god-daughter; and now my sincere wish is, that you may make just such a wife as my poor dear Dolly.   [*Exeunt omnes.*

THE DUENNA

A Comic Opera

DRAMATIS PERSONÆ

AS ORIGINALLY ACTED AT COVENT-GARDEN THEATRE,
NOVEMBER 21, 1775

Don Ferdinand	*Mr. Mattocks*
Don Jerome	*Mr. Wilson*
Don Antonio	*Mr. Du Bellamy*
Don Carlos	*Mr. Leoni*
Isaac Mendoza	*Mr. Quick*
Father Paul	*Mr. Mahon*
Father Francis	*Mr. Fox*
Father Augustine	*Mr. Baker*
Lopez	*Mr. Wewitzer*
Donna Louisa	*Mrs. Mattocks*
Donna Clara	*Mrs. Cargill*
The Duenna	*Mrs. Green*

Masqueraders, Friars, Porter, Maid, *and* Servants.

SCENE—Seville

THE DUENNA

ACT ONE

SCENE I—*The Street before* JEROME'S *House*

Enter LOPEZ, *with a dark lantern.*

LOPEZ. Past three o'clock!—Soh! a notable hour for one of my regular disposition, to be strolling like a bravo through the streets of Seville! Well, of all services, to serve a young lover is the hardest.—Not that I am an enemy to love; but my love and my master's differ strangely.—Don Ferdinand is much too gallant to eat, drink, or sleep:—now my love gives me an appetite—then I am fond of dreaming of my mistress, and I love dearly to toast her.—This cannot be done without good sleep and good liquor: hence my partiality to a feather-bed and a bottle. What a pity, now, that I have not further time for reflections! but my master expects thee, honest Lopez, to secure his retreat from Donna Clara's window, as I guess.—[*Music without.*] Hey! sure, I heard music! So, so! Who have we here? Oh, Don Antonio, my master's friend, come from the masquerade, to serenade my young mistress, Donna Louisa, I suppose: so! we shall have the old gentleman up presently.—Lest he should miss his son, I had best lose no time in getting to my post.   [*Exit.*

Enter ANTONIO, *with* MASQUERADERS *and music.*
SONG.—*Antonio.*

> Tell me, my lute, can thy soft strain
>   So gently speak thy master's pain?
> So softly sing, so humbly sigh,
>   That, though my sleeping love shall know
>   Who sings—who sighs below,
> Her rosy slumbers shall not fly?
>   Thus, may some vision whisper more
>   Than ever I dare speak before.

111

First Masquerader. Antonio, your mistress will never wake, while you sing so dolefully; love, like a cradled infant, is lulled by a sad melody.

Antonio. I do not wish to disturb her rest.

1. *Masquerader*. The reason is, because you know she does not regard you enough to appear, if you awaked her.

Antonio. Nay, then, I'll convince you.   [*Sings*.

The breath of morn bids hence the night,
Unveil those beauteous eyes, my fair;
For till the dawn of love is there,
I feel no day, I own no light.

LOUISA—*replies from a window*.

Waking, I heard thy numbers chide,
Waking, the dawn did bless my sight;
'Tis Phœbus sure that woos, I cried,
Who speaks in song, who moves in light.

JEROME—*from a window*.

What vagabonds are these I hear,
Fiddling, fluting, rhyming, ranting,
Piping, scraping, whining, canting?
Fly, scurvy minstrels, fly!

TRIO.

Louisa.	Nay, prithee, father, why so rough?
Antonio.	An humble lover I.
Jerome.	How durst you, daughter, lend an ear
	To such deceitful stuff?
	Quick, from the window fly!
Louisa.	Adieu, Antonio!
Antonio.	Must you go?
Louisa.	We soon, perhaps, may meet again.
Antonio.	For though hard fortune is our foe,
	The God of love will fight for us.
Jerome.	Reach me the blunderbuss.
Antonio. *Louisa.*	The god of love, who knows our pain—
Jerome.	Hence, or these slugs are through your brain.

[*Exeunt severally*.

SCENE II—*A Piazza*

Enter FERDINAND *and* LOPEZ.

Lopez. Truly, sir, I think that a little sleep once in a week or so——

Ferdinand. Peace, fool! don't mention sleep to me.

Lopez. No, no, sir, I don't mention your lowbred, vulgar, sound sleep; but I can't help thinking that a gentle slumber, or half an hour's dozing, if it were only for the novelty of the thing——

Ferdinand. Peace, booby, I say!—Oh, Clara dear, cruel disturber of my rest!

Lopez. And of mine too.   [*Aside.*

Ferdinand. 'Sdeath, to trifle with me at such a juncture as this!—now to stand on punctilios!—Love me! I don't believe she ever did.

Lopez. Nor I either.   [*Aside.*

Ferdinand. Or is it, that her sex never know their desires for an hour together?

Lopez. Ah, they know them oftener than they'll own them.   [*Aside.*

Ferdinand. Is there, in the world, so inconsistent a creature as Clara?

Lopez. I could name one.   [*Aside.*

Ferdinand. Yes; the tame fool who submits to her caprice.

Lopez. I thought he couldn't miss it.   [*Aside.*

Ferdinand. Is she not capricious, teasing, tyrannical, obstinate, perverse, absurd? ay, a wilderness of faults and follies; her looks are scorn, and her very smiles—'Sdeath! I wish I hadn't mentioned her smiles; for she does smile such beaming loveliness, such fascinating brightness—Oh, death and madness! I shall die if I lose her.

Lopez. Oh, those damned smiles have undone all!

[*Aside.*

AIR—*Ferdinand.*

Could I her faults remember,
    Forgetting every charm,
Soon would impartial reason
    The tyrant love disarm:
But when enraged I number

Each failing of her mind,
Love still suggests each beauty,
And sees—while reason's blind.

Lopez. Here comes Don Antonio, sir.

Ferdinand. Well, go you home—I shall be there presently.

Lopez. Ah, those cursed smiles!   [*Exit.*

Enter ANTONIO.

Ferdinand. Antonio, Lopez tells me he left you chanting before our door—was my father waked?

Antonio. Yes, yes; he has a singular affection for music; so I left him roaring at his barred window, like the print of Bajazet in the cage. And what brings you out so early?

Ferdinand. I believe I told you, that to-morrow was the day fixed by Don Pedro and Clara's unnatural step-mother, for her to enter a convent, in order that her brat might possess her fortune: made desperate by this, I procured a key to the door, and bribed Clara's maid to leave it unbolted; at two this morning, I entered unperceived, and stole to her chamber—I found her waking and weeping.

Antonio. Happy Ferdinand!

Ferdinand. 'Sdeath! hear the conclusion.—I was rated as the most confident ruffian, for daring to approach her room at that hour of the night.

Antonio. Ay, ay, this was at first.

Ferdinand. No such thing! she would not hear a word from me, but threatened to raise her mother, if I did not instantly leave her.

Antonio. Well, but at last?

Ferdinand. At last! why I was forced to leave the house as I came in.

Antonio. And did you do nothing to offend her?

Ferdinand. Nothing, as I hope to be saved!—I believe, I might snatch a dozen or two of kisses.

Antonio. Was that all? well, I think, I never heard of such assurance!

Ferdinand. Zounds! I tell you I behaved with the utmost respect.

Antonio. O Lord! I don't mean you, but in her. But, hark ye, Ferdinand, did you leave your key with them?

Ferdinand. Yes; the maid who saw me out, took it from the door.

Antonio. Then, my life for it, her mistress elopes after you.

Ferdinand. Ay, to bless my rival, perhaps. I am in a humour to suspect everybody.—You loved her once, and thought her an angel, as I do now.

Antonio. Yes, I loved her, till I found she wouldn't love me, and then I discovered that she hadn't a good feature in her face.

AIR.

I ne'er could any lustre see
In eyes that would not look on me;
I ne'er saw nectar on a lip,
But where my own did hope to sip.
Has the maid who seeks my heart
Cheeks of rose, untouch'd by art?
I will own the colour true,
When yielding blushes aid their hue.

Is her hand so soft and pure?
I must press it, to be sure;
Nor can I be certain then,
Till it, grateful, press again.
Must I, with attentive eye,
Watch her heaving bosom sigh?
I will do so, when I see
That heaving bosom sigh for me.

Besides, Ferdinand, you have full security in my love for your sister; help me there, and I can never disturb you with Clara.

Ferdinand. As far as I can, consistently with the honour of our family, you know I will; but there must be no eloping.

Antonio. And yet, now, you would carry off Clara?

Ferdinand. Ay, that's a different case!—we never mean that others should act to our sisters and wives as we do to others'.—But, to-morrow, Clara is to be forced into a convent.

Antonio. Well, and am not I so unfortunately circumstanced? To-morrow, your father forces Louisa to marry Isaac, the Portuguese—but come with me, and we'll devise something I warrant.

Ferdinand. I must go home.

Antonio. Well, adieu!

Ferdinand. But, Don Antonio, if you did not love my sister, you have too much honour and friendship to supplant me with Clara——

AIR—*Antonio.*

Friendship is the bond of reason;
    But if beauty disapprove,
Heaven dissolves all other treason
    In the heart that's true to love.

The faith which to my friend I swore,
    As a civil oath I view;
But to the charms which I adore,
    'Tis religion to be true.   [*Exit.*

Ferdinand. There is always a levity in Antonio's manner of replying to me on this subject that is very alarming.—'Sdeath, if Clara should love him after all.

SONG.

Though cause for suspicion appears,
    Yet proofs of her love, too, are strong;
I'm a wretch if I'm right in my fears,
    And unworthy of bliss if I'm wrong.
What heart-breaking torments from jealousy flow,
Ah! none but the jealous—the jealous can know!

When blest with the smiles of my fair,
    I know not how much I adore:
Those smiles let another but share,
    And I wonder I prized them no more!
Then whence can I hope a relief from my woe,
When the falser she seems, still the fonder I grow?
                                                [*Exit.*

SCENE III—*A Room in* JEROME'S *House*

Enter LOUISA *and* DUENNA.

Louisa. But, my dear Margaret, my charming Duenna, do you think we shall succeed?

Duenna. I tell you again, I have no doubt on't; but it must be instantly put to the trial. Everything is prepared in your room, and for the rest we must trust to fortune.

Louisa. My father's oath was, never to see me till I had consented to——

Duenna. 'Twas thus I overheard him say to his friend, Don Guzman,—*I will demand of her to-morrow, once for all, whether she will consent to marry Isaac Mendoza; if she hesitates, I will make a solemn oath never to see or speak to her till she returns to her duty.*—These were his words.

Louisa. And on his known obstinate adherence to what he has once said, you have formed this plan for my escape.——But have you secured my maid in our interest?

Duenna. She is a party in the whole; but remember, if we succeed, you resign all right and title in little Isaac, the Jew, over to me.

Louisa. That I do with all my soul; get him if you can, and I shall wish you joy most heartily. He is twenty times as rich as my poor Antonio.

AIR.

Thou canst not boast of fortune's store,
    My love, while me they wealthy call:
But I was glad to find thee poor—
    For with my heart I'd give thee all.
      And then the grateful youth shall own
      I loved him for himself alone.

But when his worth my hand shall gain,
    No word or look of mine shall show
That I the smallest thought retain
    Of what my bounty did bestow;
      Yet still his grateful heart shall own
      I loved him for himself alone.

Duenna. I hear Don Jerome coming.—Quick, give me the last letter I brought you from Antonio—you know that is to be the ground of my dismission.—I must slip out to seal it up, as undelivered.   [*Exit.*

Enter JEROME *and* FERDINAND.

Jerome. What, I suppose you have been serenading too! Eh, disturbing some peaceable neighbourhood with villainous catgut and lascivious piping! Out on't! you set your sister, here, a vile example; but I come to tell you, madam, that I'll suffer no more of these midnight incantations—these amorous orgies, that steal the senses in the hearing; as, they say, Egyptian embalmers serve mummies, extracting the brain through the ears. However, there's an end of your frolics.—Isaac Mendoza will be here presently, and to-morrow you shall marry him.

Louisa. Never, while I have life!

Ferdinand. Indeed, sir, I wonder how you can think of such a man for a son-in-law.

Jerome. Sir, you are very kind to favour me with your sentiments—and pray, what is your objection to him?

Ferdinand. He is a Portuguese, in the first place.

Jerome. No such thing, boy; he has forsworn his country.

Louisa. He is a Jew.

Jerome. Another mistake: he has been a Christian these six weeks.

Ferdinand. Ay, he left his old religion for an estate, and has not had time to get a new one.

Louisa. But stands like a dead wall between church and synagogue, or like the blank leaves between the Old and New Testament.

Jerome. Anything more?

Ferdinand. But the most remarkable part of his character is his passion for deceit and tricks of cunning.

Louisa. Though at the same time the fool predominates so much over the knave, that I am told he is generally the dupe of his own art.

Ferdinand. True; like an unskilful gunner, he usually misses his aim, and is hurt by the recoil of his own piece.

Jerome. Anything more?

Louisa. To sum up all, he has the worst fault a husband can have—he's not my choice.

Jerome. But you are his; and choice on one side is sufficient—two lovers should never meet in marriage—be you sour as you please, he is sweet-tempered; and for your good fruit, there's nothing like ingrafting on a crab.

Louisa. I detest him as a lover, and shall ten times more as a husband.

Jerome. I don't know that—marriage generally makes a great change—but, to cut the matter short, will you have him or not?

Louisa. There is nothing else I could disobey you in.

Jerome. Do you value your father's peace?

Louisa. So much, that I will not fasten on him the regret of making an only daughter wretched.

Jerome. Very well, ma'am, then mark me—never more will I see or converse with you till you return to your duty —no reply—this and your chamber shall be your apartments; I never will stir out without leaving you under lock and key, and when I'm at home no creature can approach you but through my library: we'll try who can be most obstinate. Out of my sight!—there remain till you know your duty.   [*Pushes her out.*

Ferdinand. Surely, sir, my sister's inclinations should be consulted in a matter of this kind, and some regard paid to Don Antonio, being my particular friend.

Jerome. That, doubtless, is a very great recommendation!—I certainly have not paid sufficient respect to it.

Ferdinand. There is not a man living I would sooner choose for a brother-in-law.

Jerome. Very possible; and if you happen to have e'er a sister, who is not at the same time a daughter of mine, I'm sure I shall have no objection to the relationship; but at present, if you please, we'll drop the subject.

Ferdinand. Nay, sir, 'tis only my regard for my sister makes me speak.

Jerome. Then, pray sir, in future, let your regard for your father make you hold your tongue.

Ferdinand. I have done, sir. I shall only add a wish that you would reflect what at our age you would have felt, had you been crossed in your affection for the mother of her you are so severe to.

Jerome. Why, I must confess I had a great affection for your mother's ducats, but that was all, boy. I married her for her fortune, and she took me in obedience to her father, and a very happy couple we were. We never expected any love from one another, and so we were never disappointed. If we grumbled a little now and then, it was soon over, for we were never fond enough to quarrel; and when the good woman died, why, why,—I had as lieve she had lived, and I wish every widower in Seville could say the same. I shall now go and get the key of this dressing-room—so, good son, if you have any lecture in support of disobedience to give your sister, it must be brief; so make the best of your time, d'ye hear?   [*Exit.*

Ferdinand. I fear, indeed, my friend Antonio has little to hope for; however, Louisa has firmness, and my father's anger will probably only increase her affection.—In our intercourse with the world, it is natural for us to dislike those who are innocently the cause of our distress; but in the heart's attachment a woman never likes a man with ardour till she has suffered for his sake.—[*Noise.*] So! what bustle is here—between my father and the Duenna too, I'll e'en get out of the way.   [*Exit.*

Re-enter JEROME *with a letter, pulling in* DUENNA.

Jerome. I'm astonished! I'm thunderstruck! here's treachery with a vengeance! You, Antonio's creature, and chief manager of this plot for my daughter's eloping!—you, that I placed here as a scarecrow?

Duenna. What?

Jerome. A scarecrow—to prove a decoy-duck! What have you to say for yourself?

Duenna. Well, sir, since you have forced that letter from me, and discovered my real sentiments, I scorn to renounce them.—I am Antonio's friend, and it was my intention that your daughter should have served you as all such old tyrannical sots should be served—I delight in the tender passions and would befriend all under their influence.

Jerome. The tender passions! yes, they would become those impenetrable features! Why, thou deceitful hag! I placed thee as a guard to the rich blossoms of my daughter's beauty. I thought that dragon's front of thine would cry aloof to the sons of gallantry: steel traps and spring guns seemed writ in every wrinkle of it.—But you shall quit my house this instant. The tender passions, indeed! go, thou wanton sibyl, thou amorous woman of Endor, go!

Duenna. You base, scurrilous, old—but I won't demean myself by naming what you are.—Yes, savage, I'll leave your den; but I suppose you don't mean to detain my apparel—I may have my things, I presume?

Jerome. I took you, mistress, with your wardrobe on—what have you pilfered, eh?

Duenna. Sir, I must take leave of my mistress; she has valuables of mine: besides, my cardinal and veil are in her room.

Jerome. Your veil, forsooth! what, do you dread being gazed at? or are you afraid of your complexion? Well, go take your leave, and get your veil and cardinal! so! you

quit the house within these five minutes.—In—in—quick!
—[*Exit* DUENNA.] Here was a precious plot of mischief!—
these are the comforts daughters bring us!

AIR.

If a daughter you have, she's the plague of your life,
No peace shall you know, though you've buried your wife!
At twenty she mocks at the duty you taught her—
Oh, what a plague is an obstinate daughter!
      Sighing and whining,
      Dying and pining,
Oh, what a plague is an obstinate daughter!

When scarce in their teens they have wit to perplex us,
With letters and lovers for ever they vex us;
While each still rejects the fair suitor you've brought her;
Oh, what a plague is an obstinate daughter!
      Wrangling and jangling,
      Flouting and pouting,
Oh, what a plague is an obstinate daughter!

Re-enter LOUISA, *dressed as* DUENNA, *with cardinal
and veil, seeming to cry.*

This way, mistress, this way.—What, I warrant a tender
parting; so! tears of turpentine down those deal cheeks.
—Ay, you may well hide your head—yes, whine till your
heart breaks! but I'll not hear one word of excuse—so
you are right to be dumb. This way, this way.   [*Exeunt.*

Re-enter DUENNA.

Duenna. So, speed you well, sagacious Don Jerome! Oh
rare effects of passion and obstinacy! Now shall I try
whether I can't play the fine lady as well as my mistress,
and if I succeed, I may be a fine lady for the rest of
my life—I'll lose no time to equip myself.   [*Exit.*

SCENE IV—*The Court before* JEROME'S *House*

Enter JEROME *and* LOUISA.

Jerome. Come, mistress, there is your way—the world
lies before you, so troop, thou antiquated Eve, thou original
sin! Hold, yonder is some fellow skulking; perhaps it is
Antonio—go to him, d'ye hear, and tell him to make you
amends, and as he has got you turned away, tell him I say

it is but just he should take you himself; go—[*Exit*
LOUISA.] So! I am rid of her, thank heaven! and now I
shall be able to keep my oath, and confine my daughter
with better security.   [*Exit.*

SCENE V—*The Piazza.*

Enter CLARA *and* MAID.

Maid. But where, madam, is it you intend to go?

Clara. Anywhere to avoid the selfish violence of my
mother-in-law, and Ferdinand's insolent importunity.

Maid. Indeed, ma'am, since we have profited by Don
Ferdinand's key, in making our escape, I think we had
best find him, if it were only to thank him.

Clara. No—he has offended me exceedingly.   [*Retires.*

Enter LOUISA.

Louisa. So I have succeeded in being turned out of
doors—but how shall I find Antonio? I dare not inquire
for him, for fear of being discovered; I would send to
my friend Clara, but then I doubt her prudery would
condemn me.

Maid. Then suppose, ma'am, you were to try if your
friend Donna Louisa would not receive you?

Clara. No, her notions of filial duty are so severe, she
would certainly betray me.

Louisa. Clara is of a cold temper, and would think
this step of mine highly forward.

Clara. Louisa's respect for her father is so great, she
would not credit the unkindness of mine.

             [LOUISA *turns and sees* CLARA *and* MAID.

Louisa. Ha! who are those? sure one is Clara—if it be,
I'll trust her. Clara!   [*Advances.*

Clara. Louisa! and in masquerade too!

Louisa. You will be more surprised when I tell you,
that I have run away from my father.

Clara. Surprised indeed! and I should certainly chide
you most horridly, only that I have just run away from
mine.

Louisa. My dear Clara!   [*Embrace.*

Clara. Dear sister truant! and whither are you going?

Louisa. To find the man I love, to be sure; and, I

presume, you would have no aversion to meet with my
brother?

Clara. Indeed I should: he has behaved so ill to me,
I don't believe I shall ever forgive him.

AIR.

When sable night, each drooping plant restoring,
    Wept o'er the flowers her breath did cheer,
As some sad widow o'er her babe deploring,
    Wakes its beauty with a tear;
When all did sleep whose weary hearts did borrow
    One hour from love and care to rest,
Lo! as I press'd my couch in silent sorrow,
    My lover caught me to his breast!
      He vow'd he came to save me
      From those who would enslave me!
        Then kneeling,
        Kisses stealing,
    Endless faith he swore;
      But soon I chid him thence,
      For had his fond pretence
      Obtain'd one favour then,
      And he had press'd again,
I fear'd my treacherous heart might grant him more.

Louisa. Well, for all this, I would have sent him to
plead his pardon, but that I would not yet awhile have
him know of my flight. And where do you hope to find
protection?

Clara. The Lady Abbess of the convent of St. Catherine
is a relation and kind friend of mine—I shall be secure
with her, and you had best go thither with me.

Louisa. No; I am determined to find Antonio first; and,
as I live, here comes the very man I will employ to
seek him for me.

Clara. Who is he? he's a strange figure.

Louisa. Yes; that sweet creature is the man whom my
father has fixed on for my husband.

Clara. And will you speak to him? are you mad?

Louisa. He is the fittest man in the world for my
purpose; for, though I was to have married him to-morrow,
he is the only man in Seville who, I am sure, never saw
me in his life.

Clara. And how do you know him?

Louisa. He arrived but yesterday, and he was shown to me from the window, as he visited my father.

Clara. Well, I'll begone.

Louisa. Hold, my dear Clara—a thought has struck me: will you give me leave to borrow your name, as I see occasion?

Clara. It will but disgrace you; but use it as you please: I dare not stay.—[*Going.*]—But, Louisa, if you should see your brother, be sure you don't inform him that I have taken refuge with the Dame Prior of the convent of St. Catherine, on the left hand side of the piazza which leads to the church of St. Anthony.

Louisa. Ha! ha! ha! I'll be very particular in my directions where he may not find you.—[*Exeunt* CLARA *and* MAID.]—So! my swain, yonder, has done admiring himself, and draws nearer.   [*Retires.*

Enter ISAAC *and* CARLOS.

Isaac. [*Looking in a pocket-glass.*] I tell you, friend Carlos, I will please myself in that habit of my chin.

Carlos. But, my dear friend, how can you think to please a lady with such a face?

Isaac. Why, what's the matter with the face? I think it is a very engaging face; and, I am sure, a lady must have very little taste who could dislike my beard.—[*Sees* LOUISA.]—See now! I'll die if here is not a little damsel struck with it already.

Louisa. Signor, are you disposed to oblige a lady who greatly wants your assistance?   [*Unveils.*

Isaac. Egad, a very pretty black-eyed girl! she has certainly taken a fancy to me, Carlos. First, ma'am, I must beg the favour of your name.

Louisa. [*Aside.*] So! it's well I am provided.—[*Aloud.*] —My name, sir, is Donna Clara d'Almanza.

Isaac. What? Don Guzman's daughter? I'faith, I just now heard she was missing.

Louisa. But sure, sir, you have too much gallantry and honour to betray me, whose fault is love?

Isaac. So! a passion for me! poor girl! Why, ma'am, as for betraying you, I don't see how I could get anything by it; so, you may rely on my honour; but as for your love, I am sorry your case is so desperate.

Louisa. Why so, signor?

Isaac. Because I am positively engaged to another—an't I, Carlos?

Louisa. Nay, but hear me.

Isaac. No, no; what should I hear for? It is impossible for me to court you in an honourable way; and for anything else, if I were to comply now, I suppose you have some ungrateful brother, or cousin, who would want to cut my throat for my civility—so, truly, you had best go home again.

Louisa. [*Aside.*] Odious wretch!—[*Aloud.*]—But, good signor, it is Antonio d'Ercilla, on whose account I have eloped.

Isaac. How! what! it is not with me, then, that you are in love?

Louisa. No, indeed, it is not.

Isaac. Then you are a forward, impertinent simpleton! and I shall certainly acquaint your father.

Louisa. Is this your gallantry?

Isaac. Yet hold—Antonio d'Ercilla, did you say? egad, I may make something of this—Antonio d'Ercilla?

Louisa. Yes; and if ever you wish to prosper in love, you will bring me to him.

Isaac. By St. Iago and I will too!—Carlos, this Antonio is one who rivals me (as I have heard) with Louisa—now, if I could hamper him with this girl, I should have the field to myself; hey, Carlos! A lucky thought, isn't it?

Carlos. Yes, very good—very good!

Isaac. Ah! this little brain is never at a loss—cunning Isaac! cunning rogue! Donna Clara, will you trust yourself awhile to my friend's direction?

Louisa. May I rely on you, good signor?

Carlos. Lady, it is impossible I should deceive you.

AIR.

Had I a heart for falsehood framed,
   I ne'er could injure you;
For though your tongue no promise claim'd,
   Your charms would make me true.
To you no soul shall bear deceit,
   No stranger offer wrong;
But friends in all the aged you'll meet,
   And lovers in the young.

But when they learn that you have blest
   Another with your heart,

> They'll bid aspiring passion rest,
>   And act a brother's part:
> Then, lady, dread not here deceit,
>   Nor fear to suffer wrong;
> For friends in all the aged you'll meet,
>   And brothers in the young.

Isaac. Conduct the lady to my lodgings, Carlos; I must haste to Don Jerome. Perhaps you know Louisa, ma'am. She's divinely handsome, isn't she?

Louisa. You must excuse me not joining with you.

Isaac. Why I have heard it on all hands.

Louisa. Her father is uncommonly partial to her; but I believe you will find she has rather a matronly air.

Isaac. Carlos, this is all envy.—You pretty girls never speak well of one another.—[*To* CARLOS.] Hark ye, find out Antonio, and I'll saddle him with this scrape, I warrant. Oh, 'twas the luckiest thought! Donna Clara, your very obedient. Carlos, to your post.

DUET.

Isaac.   My mistress expects me, and I must go to her,
          Or how can I hope for a smile?

Louisa. Soon may you return a prosperous wooer,
          But think what I suffer the while.
          Alone, and away from the man whom I love,
            In strangers I'm forced to confide.

Isaac.   Dear lady, my friend you may trust, and he'll prove
          Your servant, protector, and guide.

AIR.

Carlos. Gentle maid, ah! why suspect me?
          Let me serve thee—then reject me.
          Canst thou trust, and I deceive thee?
          Art thou sad, and shall I grieve thee?
          Gentle maid, ah! why suspect me?
          Let me serve thee—then reject me.

TRIO.

Louisa. Never mayst thou happy be,
          If in aught thou'rt false to me.

Isaac.   Never may he happy be,
          If in aught he's false to thee.

Carlos.	Never may I happy be,
	If in aught I'm false to thee.
Louisa.	Never mayst thou, &c.
Isaac.	Never may he, &c.
Carlos.	Never may I, &c.	[*Exeunt.*

ACT TWO

SCENE I—A *Library in* JEROME's *House*

Enter JEROME and ISAAC.

Jerome. Ha! ha! ha! run away from her father! has she given him the slip? Ha! ha! ha! poor Don Guzman!

Isaac. Ay; and I am too conduct her to Antonio; by which means you see I shall hamper him so that he can give me no disturbance with your daughter—this is a trap, isn't it? a nice stroke of cunning, hey?

Jerome. Excellent! excellent! yes, yes, carry her to him, hamper him by all means, ha! ha! ha! Poor Don Guzman! an old fool! imposed on by a girl!

Isaac. Nay, they have the cunning of serpents, that's the truth on't.

Jerome. Psha! they are cunning only when they have fools to deal with. Why don't my girl play me such a trick? Let her cunning over-reach my caution, I say— hey, little Isaac!

Isaac. True, true; or let me see any of the sex make a fool of me!—No, no, egad! little Solomon (as my aunt used to call me) understands tricking a little too well.

Jerome. Ay, but such a driveller as Don Guzman!

Isaac. And such a dupe as Antonio!

Jerome. True; never were seen such a couple of credulous simpletons! But come, 'tis time you should see my daughter—you must carry on the siege by yourself, friend Isaac.

Isaac. Sir, you'll introduce——

Jerome. No—I have sworn a solemn oath not to see or to speak to her till she renounces her disobedience; win her to that, and she gains a father and a husband at once.

Isaac. Gad, I shall never be able to deal with her alone; nothing keeps me in such awe as perfect beauty—now there is something consoling and encouraging in ugliness.

Song.

Give Isaac the nymph who no beauty can boast,
But health and good humour to make her his toast;
If straight, I don't mind whether slender or fat,
And six feet or four—we'll ne'er quarrel for that.

Whate'er her complexion, I vow I don't care;
If brown, it is lasting—more pleasing, if fair:
And though in her face I no dimples should see,
Let her smile—and each dell is a dimple to me.

Let her locks be the reddest that ever were seen,
And her eyes may be e'en any colour but green;
For in eyes, though so various in lustre and hue,
I swear I've no choice—only let her have two.

'Tis true I'd dispense with a throne on her back,
And white teeth, I own, are genteeler than black;
A little round chin too's a beauty, I've heard;
But I only desire she mayn't have a beard.

Jerome. You will change your note, my friend, when you've seen Louisa.

Isaac. Oh, Don Jerome, the honour of your alliance——

Jerome. Ay, but her beauty will affect you—she is, though I say it who am her father, a very prodigy. There you will see features with an eye like mine—yes, i'faith, there is a kind of wicked sparkling—sometimes of a roguish brightness, that shows her to be my own.

Isaac. Pretty rogue!

Jerome. Then, when she smiles, you'll see a little dimple in one cheek only; a beauty it is certainly, yet, you shall not say which is prettiest, the cheek with the dimple, or the cheek without.

Isaac. Pretty rogue!

Jerome. Then the roses on those cheeks are shaded with a sort of velvet down, that gives a delicacy to the glow of health.

Isaac. Pretty rogue!

Jerome. Her skin pure dimity, yet more fair, being spangled here and there with a golden freckle.

Isaac. Charming pretty rogue! pray how is the tone of her voice?

Jerome. Remarkably pleasing—but if you could prevail on her to sing, you would be enchanted—she is a nightingale—a Virginia nightingale! But come, come; her maid shall conduct you to her antechamber.

Isaac. Well, egad, I'll pluck up resolution, and meet her frowns intrepidly.

Jerome. Ay! woo her briskly—win her, and give me a proof of your address, my little Solomon.

Isaac. But hold—I expect my friend Carlos to call on me here. If he comes, will you send him to me?

Jerome. I will. Lauretta!—[*Calls.*]—Come—she'll show you to the room. What! do you droop? here's a mournful face to make love with!   [*Exeunt.*

SCENE II—LOUISA's *Dressing-Room*

Enter ISAAC *and* MAID.

Maid. Sir, my mistress will wait on you presently.
                      [*Goes to the door.*

Isaac. When she's at leisure—don't hurry her.—[*Exit* MAID.]—I wish I had ever practised a love-scene—I doubt I shall make a poor figure—I couldn't be more afraid if I was going before the Inquisition. So, the door opens— yes, she's coming—the very rustling of her silk has a disdainful sound.

Enter DUENNA *dressed as* LOUISA.

Now dar'n't I look round, for the soul of me—her beauty will certainly strike me dumb if I do. I wish she'd speak first.

Duenna. Sir, I attend your pleasure.

Isaac. [*Aside.*] So! the ice is broke, and a pretty civil beginning too!—[*Aloud.*] Hem! madam—miss—I'm all attention.

Duenna. Nay, sir, 'tis I who should listen, and you propose.

Isaac. [*Aside.*] Egad, this isn't so disdainful neither—I believe I may venture to look. No—I dar'n't—one glance of those roguish sparklers would fix me again.

Duenna. You seem thoughtful, sir. Let me persuade you to sit down.

Isaac. [*Aside.*] So, so; she mollifies apace—she's struck with my figure! this attitude has had its effect.

Duenna. Come, sir, here's a chair.

Isaac. Madam, the greatness of your goodness over-

powers me—that a lady so lovely should deign to turn her
beauteous eyes on me so.

[*She takes his hand, he turns and sees her.*

Duenna. You seem surprised at my condescension.

Isaac. Why, yes, madam, I am a little surprised at it.—
[*Aside.*] Zounds! this can never be Louisa—she's as old
as my mother!

Duenna. But former prepossessions give way to my
father's commands.

Isaac. [*Aside.*] Her father! Yes, 'tis she then.—Lord,
Lord; how blind some parents are!

Duenna. Signor Isaac!

Isaac. [*Aside.*] Truly, the little damsel was right—she
has rather a matronly air, indeed! ah! 'tis well my affections are fixed on her fortune, and not her person.

Duenna. Signor, won't you sit?   [*She sits.*

Isaac. Pardon me, madam, I have scarce recovered my
astonishment at—your condescension, madam.—[*Aside.*]
She has the devil's own dimples, to be sure!

Duenna. I do not wonder, sir, that you are surprised at
my affability—I own, signor, that I was vastly prepos-
sessed against you, and, being teased by my father, I did
give some encouragement to Antonio; but then, sir, you
were described to me as quite a different person.

Isaac. Ay, and so you were to me, upon my soul,
madam.

Duenna. But when I saw you I was never more struck
in my life.

Isaac. That was just my case, too, madam: I was struck
all of a heap, for my part.

Duenna. Well, sir, I see our misapprehension has been
mutual—you expected to find me haughty and averse, and
I was taught to believe you a little black, snub-nosed
fellow, without person, manners, or address.

Isaac. Egad, I wish she had answered her picture as
well!   [*Aside.*

Duenna. But, sir, your air is noble—something so liberal
in your carriage, with so penetrating an eye, and so be-
witching a smile!

Isaac. Egad, now I look at her again, I don't think she
is so ugly!   [*Aside.*

Duenna. So little like a Jew, and so much like a gentleman!

Isaac. Well, certainly, there is something pleasing in the tone of her voice.   [*Aside.*

Duenna. You will pardon this breach of decorum in praising you thus, but my joy at being so agreeably deceived has given me such a flow of spirits!

Isaac. Oh, dear lady, may I thank those dear lips for this goodness?—[*Kisses her.*] Why she has a pretty sort of velvet down, that's the truth on't.   [*Aside.*

Duenna. O sir, you have the most insinuating manner, but indeed you should get rid of that odious beard—one might as well kiss a hedgehog.

Isaac. [*Aside.*] Yes, ma'am, the razor wouldn't be amiss —for either of us.—[*Aloud.*] Could you favour me with a song?

Duenna. Willingly, though I'm rather hoarse—ahem!
[*Begins to sing.*

Isaac. [*Aside.*] Very like a Virginia nightingale!—
[*Aloud.*] Ma'am, I perceive you're hoarse—I beg you will not distress——

Duenna. Oh, not in the least distressed. Now, sir.

SONG.

> When a tender maid
> Is first assay'd
> By some admiring swain.
> How her blushes rise
> If she meet his eyes,
> While he unfolds his pain!
> If he takes her hand, she trembles quite!
> Touch her lips, and she swoons outright!
> While a pit-a-pat, &c.
> Her heart avows her fright.
>
> But in time appear
> Fewer signs of fear;
> The youth she boldly views:
> If her hand he grasp,
> Or her bosom clasp,
> No mantling blush ensues!
> Then to church well pleased the lovers move,
> While her smiles her contentment prove;
> And a pit-a-pat, &c.
> Her heart avows her love.

Isaac. Charming, ma'am! enchanting! and, truly, your notes put me in mind of one that's very dear to me—a lady, indeed, whom you greatly resemble!

Duenna. How! is there, then, another so dear to you?

Isaac. Oh, no, ma'am, you mistake; it was my mother I meant.

Duenna. Come, sir, I see you are amazed and confounded at my condescension, and know not what to say.

Isaac. It is very true, indeed, ma'am; but it is a judgment, I look on it as a judgment on me, for delaying to urge the time when you'll permit me to complete my happiness, by acquainting Don Jerome with your condescension.

Duenna. Sir, I must frankly own to you, that I can never be yours with my father's consent.

Isaac. Good lack! how so?

Duenna. When my father, in his passion, swore he would never see me again till I acquiesced in his will, I also made a vow, that I would never take a husband from his hand; nothing shall make me break that oath: but if you have spirit and contrivance enough to carry me off without his knowledge, I'm yours.

Isaac. Hum!

Duenna. Nay, sir, if you hesitate——

Isaac. [*Aside.*] I'faith no bad whim this!—If I take her at her word, I shall secure her fortune, and avoid making any settlement in return; thus I shall not only cheat the lover, but the father too. Oh, cunning rogue, Isaac! ay, ay, let this little brain alone! Egad, I'll take her in the mind!

Duenna. Well, sir, what's your determination?

Isaac. Madam, I was dumb only from rapture—I applaud your spirit, and joyfully close with your proposal; for which thus let me, on this lily hand, express my gratitude.

Duenna. Well, sir, you must get my father's consent to walk with me in the garden. But by no means inform him of my kindness to you.

Isaac. No, to be sure, that would spoil all: but, trust me when tricking is the word—let me alone for a piece of cunning; this very day you shall be out of his power.

Duenna. Well, I leave the management of it all to you; I perceive plainly, sir, that you are not one that can be easily outwitted.

Isaac. Egad, you're right, madam—you're right, i'faith.

Re-enter MAID.

Maid. Here's a gentleman at the door, who begs permission to speak with Signor Isaac.

Isaac. A friend of mine, ma'am, and a trusty friend—let him come in—[*Exit* MAID.] He's one to be depended on, ma'am.

Enter CARLOS.

So coz.   [*Talks apart with* CARLOS.

Carlos. I have left Donna Clara at your lodgings, but can nowhere find Antonio.

Isaac. Well, I will search him out myself. Carlos, you rogue, I thrive, I prosper!

Carlos. Where is your mistress?

Isaac. There, you booby, there she stands.

Carlos. Why, she's damned ugly!

Isaac. Hush!   [*Stops his mouth.*

Duenna. What is your friend saying, signor?

Isaac. Oh, ma'am, he is expressing his raptures at such charms as he never saw before. Eh, Carlos?

Carlos. Ay, such as I never saw before, indeed!

Duenna. You are a very obliging gentleman. Well, Signor Isaac, I believe we had better part for the present. Remember our plan.

Isaac. Oh, ma'am, it is written in my heart, fixed as the image of those divine beauties. Adieu, idol of my soul!—yet once more permit me——   [*Kisses her.*

Duenna. Sweet, courteous sir, adieu!

Isaac. Your slave eternally! Come, Carlos, say something civil at taking leave.

Carlos. I'faith, Isaac, she is the hardest woman to compliment I ever saw; however, I'll try something I had studied for the occasion.

SONG.

Ah! sure a pair was never seen
    So justly form'd to meet by nature!
The youth excelling so in mien,
    The maid in ev'ry grace of feature.
Oh, how happy are such lovers,
    When kindred beauties each discovers;
        For surely she
        Was made for thee,
And thou to bless this lovely creature!

So mild your looks, your children thence
Will early learn the task of duty—
The boys with all their father's sense,
The girls with all their mother's beauty!
Oh, how happy to inherit
At once such graces and such spirit!
Thus while you live
May fortune give
Each blessing equal to your merit!   [*Exeunt.*

SCENE III—*A Library in* JEROME'S *House*

JEROME *and* FERDINAND *discovered.*

Jerome. Object to Antonio! I have said it. His poverty, can you acquit him of that?

Ferdinand. Sir, I own he is not over rich; but he is of as ancient and honourable a family as any in the kingdom.

Jerome. Yes, I know the beggars are a very ancient family in most kingdoms; but never in great repute, boy.

Ferdinand. Antonio, sir, has many amiable qualities.

Jerome. But he is poor; can you clear him of that, I say? Is he not a gay, dissipated rake, who has squandered his patrimony?

Ferdinand. Sir, he inherited but little; and that his generosity, more than his profuseness, has stripped him of; but he has never sullied his honour, which, with his title, has outlived his means.

Jerome. Psha! you talk like a blockhead! nobility, without an estate, is as ridiculous as gold lace on a frieze coat.

Ferdinand. This language, sir, would better become a Dutch or English trader than a Spaniard.

Jerome. Yes; and those Dutch and English traders, as you call them, are the wiser people. Why, booby, in England they were formerly as nice, as to birth and family, as we are: but they have long discovered what a wonderful purifier gold is; and now, no one there regards pedigree in anything but a horse. Oh, here comes Isaac! I hope he has prospered in his suit.

Ferdinand. Doubtless, that agreeable figure of his must have helped his suit surprisingly.

Jerome. How now?   [FERDINAND *walks aside.*

Enter ISAAC.

Well, my friend, have you softened her?

Isaac. Oh, yes; I have softened her.

Jerome. What, does she come to?

Isaac. Why, truly, she was kinder than I expected to find her.

Jerome. And the dear little angel was civil, eh?

Isaac. Yes, the pretty little angel was very civil.

Jerome. I'm transported to hear it! Well, and you were astonished at her beauty, hey?

Isaac. I was astonished, indeed! Pray, how old is Miss?

Jerome. How old? let me see—eight and twelve—she is twenty.

Isaac. Twenty?

Jerome. Ay, to a month.

Isaac. Then, upon my soul, she is the oldest-looking girl of her age in Christendom!

Jerome. Do you think so? But, I believe, you will not see a prettier girl.

Isaac. Here and there one.

Jerome. Louisa has the family face.

Isaac. Yes, egad, I should have taken it for a family face, and one that has been in the family some time, too.
[*Aside.*

Jerome. She has her father's eyes.

Isaac. Truly, I should have guessed them to have been so! If she had her mother's spectacles, I believe she would not see the worse.   [*Aside.*

Jerome. Her aunt Ursula's nose, and her grandmother's forehead, to a hair.

Isaac. Ay, 'faith, and her grandfather's chin, to a hair.
[*Aside.*

Jerome. Well, if she was but as dutiful as she's handsome—and hark ye, friend Isaac, she is none of your made-up beauties—her charms are of the lasting kind.

Isaac. I'faith, so they should—for if she be but twenty now, she may double her age before her years will overtake her face.

Jerome. Why, zounds, Master Isaac! you are not sneering, are you?

Isaac. Why now, seriously, Don Jerome, do you think your daughter handsome?

Jerome. By this light, she's as handsome a girl as any in Seville.

Isaac. Then, by these eyes, I think her as plain a woman as ever I beheld.

Jerome. By St. Iago! you must be blind.

Isaac. No, no; 'tis you are partial.

Jerome. How! have I neither sense nor taste? If a fair skin, fine eyes, teeth of ivory, with a lovely bloom, and a delicate shape,—if these, with a heavenly voice and a world of grace, are not charms, I know not what you call beautiful.

Isaac. Good lack, with what eyes a father sees! As I have life, she is the very reverse of all this: as for the dimity skin you told me of, I swear 'tis a thorough nankeen as ever I saw! for her eyes, their utmost merit is not squinting—for her teeth, where there is one of ivory, its neighbour is pure ebony, black and white alternately, just like the keys of a harpsichord. Then, as to her singing, and heavenly voice—by this hand, she has a shrill, cracked pipe, that sounds for all the world like a child's trumpet.

Jerome. Why, you little Hebrew scoundrel, do you mean to insult me? Out of my house, I say!

Ferdinand. [*Coming forward.*] Dear sir, what's the matter?

Jerome. Why, this Israelite here has the impudence to say your sister's ugly.

Ferdinand. He must be either blind or insolent.

Isaac. So, I find they are all in a story. Egad, I believe I have gone too far!   [*Aside.*

Ferdinand. Sure, sir, there must be some mistake; it can't be my sister whom he has seen.

Jerome. 'Sdeath! you are as great a fool as he! What mistake can there be? Did not I lock up Louisa, and haven't I the key in my own pocket? and didn't her maid show him into the dressing-room? and yet you talk of a mistake! No, the Portuguese meant to insult me—and, but that this roof protects him, old as I am, this sword should do me justice.

Isaac. I must get off as well as I can—her fortune is not the less handsome.   [*Aside.*

Duet.

Isaac.   Believe me, good sir, I ne'er meant to offend;
My mistress I love, and I value my friend:
To win her and wed her is still my request,
For better for worse—and I swear I don't jest.

Jerome. Zounds! you'd best not provoke me, my rage is
　　　　　so high!

Isaac.　Hold him fast, I beseech you, his rage is so
　　　　　high!

　　　　　Good sir, you're too hot, and this place I must
　　　　　fly.

Jerome. You're a knave and a sot, and this place you'd
　　　　　best fly.

Isaac. Don Jerome, come now, let us lay aside all joking,
and be serious.

Jerome. How?

Isaac. Ha! ha! ha! I'll be hanged if you haven't taken
my abuse of your daughter seriously.

Jerome. You meant it so, did not you?

Isaac. O mercy, no! a joke—just to try how angry it
would make you.

Jerome. Was that all, i'faith? I didn't know you had been
such a wag. Ha! ha! ha! By St. Iago! you made me very
angry, though. Well, and you do think Louisa handsome?

Isaac. Handsome! Venus de Medicis was a sybil to her.

Jerome. Give me your hand, you little jocose rogue!
Egad, I thought we had been all off.

Ferdinand. So! I was in hopes this would have been a
quarrel; but I find the Jew is too cunning.　　　[*Aside.*

Jerome. Ay, this gust of passion has made me dry—I
am seldom ruffled. Order some wine in the next room—
let us drink the poor girl's health. Poor Louisa! ugly, eh!
ha! ha! ha! 'twas a very good joke, indeed!

Isaac. And a very true one, for all that.　　　[*Aside.*

Jerome. And, Ferdinand, I insist upon your drinking
success to my friend.

Ferdinand. Sir, I will drink success to my friend with
all my heart.

Jerome. Come, little Solomon, if any sparks of anger
had remained, this would be the only way to quench them.

Trio.

A bumper of good liquor
Will end a contest quicker
Than justice, judge, or vicar;
　So fill a cheerful glass,
　And let good humour pass.
But if more deep the quarrel,

Why, sooner drain the barrel
Than be the hateful fellow
That's crabbed when he's mellow.
     A bumper, &c.   [*Exeunt.*

SCENE IV—Isaac's *Lodgings*

Enter LOUISA.

Louisa. Was ever truant daughter so whimsically circumstanced as I am? I have sent my intended husband
to look after my lover—the man of my father's choice is
gone to bring me the man of my own: but how dispiriting
is this interval of expectation!

SONG.

What bard, O Time, discover,
     With wings first made thee move?
Ah! sure it was some lover
     Who ne'er had left his love!
For who that once did prove
The pangs which absence brings,
     Though but one day
     He were away,
Could picture thee with wings?
     What bard, &c.

Enter CARLOS.

So, friend, is Antonio found?

Carlos. I could not meet with him, lady; but I doubt
not my friend Isaac will be here with him presently.

Louisa. Oh, shame! you have used no diligence. Is this
your courtesy to a lady, who has trusted herself to your
protection?

Carlos. Indeed, madam, I have not been remiss.

Louisa. Well, well; but if either of you had known how
each moment of delay weighs upon the heart of her who
loves, and waits the object of her love, oh, ye would not
then have trifled thus!

Carlos. Alas, I know it well!

Louisa. Were you ever in love, then?

Carlos. I was, lady; but, while I have life, I will never
be again.

Louisa. Was your mistress so cruel?

Carlos. If she had always been so, I should have been happier.

SONG.

Oh, had my love ne'er smiled on me,
      I ne'er had known such anguish;
But think how false, how cruel she,
      To bid me cease to languish;
To bid me hope her hand to gain,
      Breathe on a flame half perish'd;
And then with cold and fixed disdain,
      To kill the hope she cherish'd.

Not worse his fate, who on a wreck,
      That drove as winds did blow it,
Silent had left the shatter'd deck,
      To find a grave below it.
Then land was cried—no more resign'd,
      He glow'd with joy to hear it;
Not worse his fate, his woe, to find
      The wreck must sink ere near it!

Louisa. As I live, here is your friend coming with Antonio! I'll retire for a moment to surprise him.   [*Exit.*

Enter ISAAC *and* ANTONIO.

Antonio. Indeed, my good friend, you must be mistaken. Clara d'Almanza in love with me, and employ you to bring me to meet her! It is impossible!

Isaac. That you shall see in an instant. Carlos, where is the lady?—[CARLOS *points to the door.*] In the next room, is she?

Antonio. Nay, if that lady is really here, she certainly wants me to conduct her to a dear friend of mine, who has long been her lover.

Isaac. Psha! I tell you 'tis no such thing—you are the man she wants, and nobody but you. Here's ado to persuade you to take a pretty girl that's dying for you!

Antonio. But I have no affection for this lady.

Isaac. And you have for Louisa, hey? But take my word for it, Antonio, you have no chance there—so you may as well secure the good that offers itself to you.

Antonio. And could you reconcile it to your conscience to supplant your friend?

Isaac. Pish! Conscience has no more to do with gallantry than it has with politics. Why, you are no honest fellow if love can't make a rogue of you; so come—do go in and speak to her, at least.

Antonio. Well, I have no objection to that.

Isaac. [*Opens the door.*] There—there she is—yonder by the window—get in, do.—[*Pushes him in, and half shuts the door.*] Now, Carlos, now I shall hamper him, I warrant! Stay, I'll peep how they go on. Egad, he looks confoundedly posed! Now she's coaxing him. See, Carlos, he begins to come to—ay, ay, he'll soon forget his conscience.

Carlos. Look—now they are both laughing!

Isaac. Ay, so they are—yes, yes, they are laughing at that dear friend he talked of—ay, poor devil, they have outwitted him.

Carlos. Now he's kissing her hand.

Isaac. Yes, yes, faith, they're agreed—he's caught, he's entangled. My dear Carlos, we have brought it about. Oh, this little cuunning head! I'm a Machiavel—a very Machiavel!

Carlos. I hear somebody inquiring for you—I'll see who it is.   [*Exit.*

Re-enter ANTONIO *and* LOUISA.

Antonio. Well, my good friend, this lady has so entirely convinced me of the certainty of your success at Don Jerome's, that I now resign my pretensions there.

Isaac. You never did a wiser thing, believe me; and, as for deceiving your friend, that's nothing at all—tricking is all fair in love, isn't it, ma'am?

Louisa. Certainly, sir; and I am particularly glad to find you are of that opinion.

Isaac. O Lud! yes, ma'am—let any one outwit me that can, I say! But here, let me join your hands. There you lucky rogue! I wish you happily married from the bottom of my soul!

Louisa. And I am sure, if you wish it, no one else should prevent it.

Isaac. Now, Antonio, we are rivals no more; so let us be friends, will you?

Antonio. With all my heart, Isaac.

Isaac. It is not every man, let me tell you, that would have taken such pains, or been so generous to a rival.

Antonio. No, 'faith, I don't believe there's another beside yourself in all Spain.

Isaac. Well, but you resign all pretensions to the other lady?

Antonio. That I do, most sincerely.

Isaac. I doubt you have a little hankering there still.

Antonio. None in the least, upon my soul.

Isaac. I mean after her fortune.

Antonio. No, believe me. You are heartily welcome to every thing she has.

Isaac. Well, i'faith, you have the best of the bargain, as to beauty, twenty to one. Now I'll tell you a secret— I am to carry off Louisa this very evening.

Louisa. Indeed!

Isaac. Yes, she has sworn not to take a husband from her father's hand—so I've persuaded him to trust her to walk with me in the garden, and then we shall give him the slip.

Louisa. And is Don Jerome to know nothing of this?

Isaac. O Lud, no! there lies the jest. Don't you see that, by this step, I over-reach him? I shall be entitled to the girl's fortune, without settling a ducat on her. Ha! ha! ha! I'm a cunning dog, an't I? a sly little villain, eh?

Antonio. Ha! ha! ha! you are indeed!

Isaac. Roguish, you'll say, but keen, eh? devilish keen?

Antonio. So you are indeed—keen—very keen.

Isaac. And what a laugh we shall have at Don Jerome's when the truth comes out! hey?

Louisa. Yes, I'll answer for it, we shall have a good laugh, when the truth comes out. Ha! ha! ha!

Re-enter CARLOS.

Carlos. Here are the dancers come to practise the fandango you intended to have honoured Donna Louisa with.

Isaac. Oh, I shan't want them; but, as I must pay them, I'll see a caper for my money. Will you excuse me?

Louisa. Willingly.

Isaac. Here's my friend, whom you may command for any service. Madam, your most obedient—Antonio, I wish you all happiness.—[*Aside.*] Oh, the easy blockhead! what a tool I have made of him!—This was a masterpiece!
[*Exit.*

Louisa. Carlos, will you be my guard again, and convey me to the convent of St. Catherine?

Antonio. Why, Louisa—why should you go there?

Louisa. I have my reasons, and you must not be seen to go with me; I shall write from thence to my father; perhaps, when he finds what he has driven me to, he may relent.

Antonio. I have no hope from him. O Louisa! in these arms should be your sanctuary.

Louisa. Be patient but for a little while—my father cannot force me from thence. But let me see you there before evening, and I will explain myself.

Antonio. I shall obey.

Louisa. Come, friend. Antonio, Carlos has been a lover himself.

Antonio. Then he knows the value of his trust.

Carlos. You shall not find me unfaithful.

TRIO.

Soft pity never leaves the gentle breast
Where love has been received a welcome guest;
As wandering saints poor huts have sacred made,
He hallows every heart he once has sway'd,
And, when his presence we no longer share,
Still leaves compassion as a relic there.   [*Exeunt.*

ACT THREE

SCENE I—*A Library in* JEROME's *House*

Enter JEROME *and* SERVANT.

Jerome. Why, I never was so amazed in my life! Louisa gone off with Isaac Mendoza! What! steal away with the very man whom I wanted her to marry—elope with her own husband, as it were—it is impossible!

Servant. Her maid says, sir, they had your leave to walk in the garden, while you were abroad. The door by the shrubbery was found open, and they have not been heard of since.   [*Exit.*

Jerome. Well, it is the most unaccountable affair! 'sdeath! there is certainly some infernal mystery in it I can't comprehend!

Enter SECOND SERVANT, *with a letter.*

Servant. Here is a letter, sir, from Signor Isaac.   [*Exit.*

Jerome. So, so, this will explain—ay, Isaac Mendoza —let me see——   [*Reads.*

> *Dearest Sir,*
>
> *You must, doubtless, be much surprised at my flight with your daughter!*—yes, 'faith, and well I may—*I had the happiness to gain her heart at our first interview*—The devil you had!—*But, she having unfortunately made a vow not to receive a husband from your hands, I was obliged to comply with her whim!*—So, so!—*We shall shortly throw ourselves at your feet, and I hope you will have a blessing ready for one, who will then be your son-in-law.*
>
> ISAAC MENDOZA.

A whim, hey? Why, the devil's in the girl, I think! This morning, she would die sooner than have him, and before evening she runs away with him! Well, well, my will's accomplished—let the motive be what it will—and the Portuguese, sure, will never deny to fulfil the rest of the article.

Re-enter SERVANT, *with another letter.*

Servant. Sir, here's a man below, who says he brought this from my young lady, Donna Louisa.   [*Exit.*

Jerome. How! yes, it's my daughter's hand, indeed! Lord, there was no occasion for them both to write; well, let's see what she says——   [*Reads.*

> *My dearest father,*
>
> *How shall I entreat your pardon for the rash step I have taken—how confess the motive?*—Pish! hasn't Isaac just told me the motive?—one would think they weren't together when they wrote.—*If I have a spirit too resentful of ill usage, I have also a heart as easily affected by kindness.*—So, so, here the whole matter comes out; her resentment for Antonio's ill usage has made her sensible of Isaac's kindness—yes, yes, it is all plain enough. Well. *I am not married yet, though with a man who, I am convinced, adores me.*—Yes, yes, I dare say Isaac is very fond of her. *But I shall anxiously expect your answer, in which, should I be so fortunate as to receive your consent, you will make completely happy your ever affectionate daughter,*
>
> LOUISA.

My consent! to be sure she shall have it! Egad, I was never better pleased—I have fulfilled my resolution—I knew I should. Oh, there's nothing like obstinacy! Lewis!

[*Calls.*

Re-enter SERVANT.

Let the man who brought the last letter, wait; and get me a pen and ink below.—[*Exit* SERVANT.] I am impatient to set poor Louisa's heart at rest. Holloa! Lewis! Sancho!

[*Calls.*

Enter SERVANTS.

See that there be a noble supper provided in the saloon to-night; serve up my best wines, and let me have music, d'ye hear?

Servant. Yes, sir.

Jerome. And order all my doors to be thrown open; admit all guests, with masks or without masks.—[*Exeunt* SERVANTS.] I'faith, we'll have a night of it! and I'll let them see how merry an old man can be.

SONG.

Oh, the days when I was young.
    When I laugh'd in fortune's spite;
Talk'd of love the whole day long,
    And with nectar crown'd the night!
Then it was, old Father Care,
    Little reck'd I of thy frown;
Half thy malice youth could bear,
    And the rest a bumper drown.

Truth, they say, lies in a well,
    Why, I vow I ne'er could see;
Let the water-drinkers tell,
    There it always lay for me.
For when sparkling wine went round,
    Never saw I falsehood's mask;
But still honest truth I found
    In the bottom of each flask.

True, at length my vigour's flown,
    I have years to bring decay;
Few the locks that now I own,
    And the few I have are grey.

Yet, old Jerome, thou mayst boast,
    While thy spirits do not tire;
Still beneath thy age's frost
    Glows a spark of youthful fire.   [*Exit.*

SCENE II—*The New Piazza*

Enter FERDINAND *and* LOPEZ.

Ferdinand. What, could you gather no tidings of her? nor guess where she was gone? O Clara! Clara!

Lopez. In truth, sir, I could not. That she was run away from her father, was in everybody's mouth; and that Don Guzman was in pursuit of her, was also a very common report. Where she was gone, or what was become of her, no one could take upon them to say.

Ferdinand. 'Sdeath and fury, you blockhead! she can't be out of Seville.

Lopez. So I said to myself, sir. 'Sdeath and fury, you blockhead, says I, she can't be out of Seville. Then some said, she had hanged herself for love; and others have it, Don Antonio had carried her off.

Ferdinand. 'Tis false, scoundrel! no one said that.

Lopez. Then I misunderstood them, sir.

Ferdinand. Go, fool, get home! and never let me see you again till you bring me news of her.—[*Exit* LOPEZ.] Oh, how my fondness for this ungrateful girl has hurt my disposition.

Enter ISAAC.

Isaac. So, I have her safe, and have only to find a priest to marry us. Antonio now may marry Clara, or not, if he pleases.

Ferdinand. What! what was that you said of Clara?

Isaac. Oh, Ferdinand! my brother-in-law that shall be, who thought of meeting you?

Ferdinand. But what of Clara?

Isaac. I'faith, you shall hear. This morning, as I was coming down, I met a pretty damsel, who told me her name was Clara d'Almanza, and begged my protection.

Ferdinand. How!

Isaac. She said she had eloped from her father, Don Guzman, but that love for a young gentleman in Seville was the cause.

Ferdinand. Oh, Heavens! did she confess it?

Isaac. Oh, yes, she confessed at once. But then, says she, my lover is not informed of my flight, nor suspects my intention.

Ferdinand. [*Aside.*] Dear creature! no more I did indeed! Oh, I am the happiest fellow!—[*Aloud.*] Well, Isaac?

Isaac. Why then she entreated me to find him out for her, and bring him to her.

Ferdinand. Good Heavens, how lucky! Well, come along, let's lose no time.   [*Pulling him.*

Isaac. Zooks! where are we to go?

Ferdinand. Why, did anything more pass?

Isaac. Anything more! yes; the end on't was, that I was moved with her speeches, and complied with her desires.

Ferdinand. Well and where is she?

Isaac. Where is she? why, don't I tell you? I complied with her request, and left her safe in the arms of her lover.

Ferdinand. 'Sdeath, you trifle with me!—I have never seen her.

Isaac. You! O Lud no! how the devil should you? 'Twas Antonio she wanted; and with Antonio I left her.

Ferdinand. [*Aside.*] Hell and madness!—[*Aloud.*] What, Antonio d'Ercilla?

Isaac. Ay, ay, the very man; and the best part of it was, he was shy of taking her at first. He talked a good deal about honour, and conscience, and deceiving some dear friend; but, Lord, we soon overruled that!

Ferdinand. You did!

Isaac. Oh, yes, presently.—Such deceit! says he.—Pish! says the lady, tricking is all fair in love. But then, my friend, says he.—Psha! damn your friend, says I. So, poor wretch, he has no chance.—No, no; he may hang himself as soon as he pleases.

Ferdinand. I must go, or I shall betray myself.   [*Aside.*

Isaac. But stay, Ferdinand, you han't heard the best of the joke.

Ferdinand. Curse on your joke!

Isaac. Good lack! what's the matter now? I thought to have diverted you.

Ferdinand. Be racked! tortured! damned!

Isaac. Why, sure you are not the poor devil of a lover,

are you?—I'faith, as sure as can be, he is! This is a better joke than t'other. Ha! ha! ha!

Ferdinand. What! do you laugh? you vile, mischievous varlet!—[*Collars him.*] But that you're beneath my anger, I'd tear your heart out!　　　　　[*Throws him from him.*

Isaac. O mercy! here's usage for a brother-in-law!

Ferdinand. But, hark ye, rascal! tell me directly where these false friends are gone, or, by my soul——　　[*Draws.*

Isaac. For Heaven's sake, now, my dear brother-in-law, don't be in a rage! I'll recollect as well as I can.

Ferdinand. Be quick, then!

Isaac. I will, I will!—but people's memories differ; some have a treacherous memory: now mine is a cowardly memory—it takes to its heels at sight of a drawn sword—it does i'faith; and I could as soon fight as recollect.

Ferdinand. Zounds! tell me the truth, and I won't hurt you.

Isaac. No, no, I know you won't, my dear brother-in-law; but that ill-looking thing there——

Ferdinand. What, then, you won't tell me?

Isaac. Yes, yes, I will; I'll tell you all, upon my soul! —but why need you listen, sword in hand?

Ferdinand. Why, there.—[*Puts up.*] Now.

Isaac. Why, then, I believe they are gone to—that is, my friend Carlos told me he had left Donna Clara—dear Ferdinand, keep your hands off—at the convent of St. Catherine.

Ferdinand. St. Catherine!

Isaac. Yes; and that Antonio was to come to her there.

Ferdinand. Is this the truth?

Isaac. It is indeed; and all I know, as I hope for life!

Ferdinand. Well, coward, take your life; 'tis that false, dishonourable Antonio, who shall feel my vengeance.

Isaac. Ay, ay, kill him; cut his throat, and welcome.

Ferdinand. But, for Clara! infamy on her! she is not worth my resentment.

Isaac. No more she is, my dear brother-in-law. I'faith I would not be angry about her; she is not worth it, indeed.

Ferdinand. 'Tis false! she is worth the enmity of princes!

Isaac. True, true, so she is; and I pity you exceedingly for having lost her.

Ferdinand. 'Sdeath, you rascal! how durst you talk of pitying me?

Isaac. Oh, dear brother-in-law, I beg pardon! I don't pity you in the least, upon my soul!

Ferdinand. Get hence, fool, and provoke me no further; nothing but your insignificance saves you!

Isaac. [*Aside.*] I'faith, then, my insignificance is the best friend I have.—[*Aloud.*] I'm going, dear Ferdinand. [*Aside.*] What a curst hot-headed bully it is!

[*Exeunt severally.*

SCENE III—*The Garden of the Convent*

Enter LOUISA *and* CLARA.

Louisa. And you really wish my brother may not find you out?

Clara. Why else have I concealed myself under this disguise?

Louisa. Why, perhaps because the dress becomes you: for you certainly don't intend to be a nun for life.

Clara. If, indeed, Ferdinand had not offended me so last night——

Louisa. Come, come, it was his fear of losing you made him so rash.

Clara. Well, you may think me cruel, but I swear, if he were here this instant, I believe I should forgive him.

SONG.

By him we 'love offended,
    How soon our anger flies
One day apart, 'tis ended;
    Behold him, and it dies.

Last night, your roving brother,
    Enraged, I bade depart;
And sure his rude presumption
    Deserved to lose my heart.

Yet, were he now before me,
    In spite of injured pride,
I fear my eyes would pardon
    Before my tongue could chide.

Louisa. I protest, Clara, I shall begin to think you are seriously resolved to enter on your probation.

Clara. And, seriously, I very much doubt whether the character of a nun would not become me best.

Louisa. Why, to be sure, the character of a nun is a very becoming one at a masquerade: but no pretty woman, in her senses, ever thought of taking the veil for above a night.

Clara. Yonder I see your Antonio is returned—I shall only interrupt you; ah, Louisa, with what happy eagerness you turn to look for him!   [*Exit.*

Enter ANTONIO.

Antonio. Well, my Louisa, any news since I left you?

Louisa. None. The messenger is not yet returned from my father.

Antonio. Well, I confess, I do not perceive what we are to expect from him.

Louisa. I shall be easier, however, in having made the trial: I do not doubt your sincerity, Antonio; but there is a chilling air around poverty, that often kills affection, that was not nursed in it. If we would make love our household god, we had best secure him a comfortable roof.

SONG.—*Antonio.*

How oft, Louisa, hast thou told,
   (Nor wilt thou the fond boast disown,)
Thou wouldst not lose Antonio's love
   To reign the partner of a throne!
And by those lips that spoke so kind,
   And by that hand I've press'd to mine,
To be the lord of wealth and power,
   By heavens, I would not part with thine!

Then how, my soul, can we be poor,
   Who own what kingdoms could not buy?
Of this true heart thou shalt be queen,
   In serving thee, a monarch I.
Thus uncontroll'd, in mutual bliss,
   I rich in love's exhaustless mine,
Do thou snatch treasures from my lips,
   And I'll take kingdoms back from thine!

Enter MAID *with a letter.*

Louisa. My father's answer, I suppose.

Antonio. My dearest Louisa, you may be assured that it contains nothing but threats and reproaches.

Louisa. Let us see, however.—[*Reads.*] *Dearest daughter, make your lover happy: you have my full consent to marry as your whim has chosen, but be sure come home and sup with your affectionate father.*

Antonio. You jest, Louisa!

Louisa. [*Gives him the letter.*] Read! read!

Antonio. 'Tis so, by heavens! Sure there must be some mistake; but that's none of our business.——Now, Louisa, you have no excuse for delay.

Louisa. Shall we not then return and thank my father?

Antonio. But first let the priest put it out of his power to recall his word.—I'll fly to procure one.

Louisa. Nay, if you part with me again, perhaps you may lose me.

Antonio. Come, then—there is a friar of a neighbouring convent is my friend; you have already been diverted by the manners of a nunnery; let us see whether there is less hypocrisy among the holy fathers.

Louisa. I'm afraid not, Antonio—for in religion, as in friendship, they who profess most are the least sincere.
                                                              [*Exeunt.*

Re-enter CLARA.

Clara. So, yonder they go, as happy as a mutual and confessed affection can make them, while I am left in solitude. Heigho! love may perhaps excuse the rashness of an elopement from one's friend, but I am sure nothing but the presence of the man we love can support it. Ha! what do I see! Ferdinand, as I live! How could he gain admission? By potent gold, I suppose, as Antonio did. How eager and disturbed he seems! He shall not know me as yet.   [*Lets down her veil.*

Enter FERDINAND.

Ferdinand. Yes, those were certainly they—my information was right.   [*Going.*

Clara. [*Stops him.*] Pray, signor, what is your business here?

Ferdinand. No matter—no matter! Oh! they stop.— [*Looks out.*] Yes, that is the perfidious Clara indeed!

Clara. So, a jealous error—I'm glad to see him so moved.   [*Aside.*

Ferdinand. Her disguise can't conceal her—no, no, I know her too well.

Clara. [*Aside.*] Wonderful discernment!—[*Aloud.*] But, signor——

Ferdinand. Be quiet, good nun; don't tease me!—By heavens, she leans upon his arm, hangs fondly on it! O woman, woman!

Clara. But, signor, who is it you want?

Ferdinand. Not you, not you, so prythee don't tease me. Yet pray stay—gentle nun, was it not Donna Clara d'Almanza just parted from you?

Clara. Clara d'Almanza, signor, is not yet out of the garden.

Ferdinand. Ay, ay, I knew I was right! And pray is not that gentleman, now at the porch with her, Antonio d'Ercilla?

Clara. It is indeed, signor.

Ferdinand. So, so; but now one question more—can you inform me for what purpose they have gone away?

Clara. They are gone to be married, I believe.

Ferdinand. Very well—enough. Now if I don't mar their wedding!   [*Exit.*

Clara. [*Unveils.*] I thought jealousy had made lovers quick-sighted, but it has made mine blind. Louisa's story accounts to me for this error, and I am glad to find I have power enough over him to make him so unhappy. But why should not I be present at his surprise when undeceived? When he's through the porch, I'll follow him; and, perhaps, Louisa shall not singly be a bride.

SONG.

Adieu, thou dreary pile, where never dies
The sullen echo of repentant sighs!
Ye sister mourners of each lonely cell
Inured to hymns and sorrow, fare ye well!
For happier scenes I fly this darksome grove,
To saints a prison, but a tomb to love!   [*Exit.*

SCENE IV—*A Court before the Priory*

Enter ISAAC, *crossing the stage,* ANTONIO *following.*

Antonio. What, my friend Isaac!

Isaac. What, Antonio! wish me joy! I have Louisa safe.

Antonio. Have you? I wish you joy with all my soul.

Isaac. Yes, I come here to procure a priest to marry us.

Antonio. So, then, we are both on the same errand; I am come to look for Father Paul.

Isaac. Ha! I'm glad on't—but, i'faith, he must tack me first; my love is waiting.

Antonio. So is mine—I left her in the porch.

Isaac. Ay, but I'm in haste to go back to Don Jerome.

Antonio. And so am I too.

Isaac. Well, perhaps he'll save time, and marry us both together—or I'll be your father, and you shall be mine. Come along—but you are obliged to me for all this.

Antonio. Yes, yes.   [*Exeunt.*

SCENE V—*A Room in the Priory*

Father Paul, Father Francis, Father Augustine, *and other* Friars, *discovered at a table drinking.*

Glee and Chorus.

This bottle's the sun of our table,
    His beams are rosy wine:
We, planets, that are not able
    Without his help to shine.
Let mirth and glee abound!
    You'll soon grow bright
    With borrow'd light,
And shine as he goes round.

Paul. Brother Francis, toss the bottle about, and give me your toast.

Francis. Have we drunk the Abbess of St. Ursuline?

Paul. Yes, yes; she was the last.

Francis. Then I'll give you the blue-eyed nun of St. Catherine's.

Paul. With all my heart.—[*Drinks.*] Pray, brother Augustine, were there any benefactions left in my absence?

Augustine. Don Juan Corduba has left a hundred ducats, to remember him in our masses.

Paul. Has he? let them be paid to our wine-merchant, and we'll remember him in our cups, which will do just as well. Anything more?

Augustine. Yes; Baptista, the rich miser, who died last week, has bequeathed us a thousand pistoles, and the silver lamp he used in his own chamber, to burn before the image of St. Anthony.

Paul. 'Twas well meant, but we'll employ his money better—Baptista's bounty shall light the living, not the dead. St. Anthony is not afraid to be left in the dark, though he was.—[*Knocking.*] See who's there.

[FATHER FRANCIS *goes to the door and opens it.*

Enter PORTER.

Porter. Here's one without, in pressing haste to speak with Father Paul.

Francis. Brother Paul!

[FATHER PAUL *comes from behind a curtain with a glass of wine, and in his hand a piece of cake.*

Paul. Here! how durst you, fellow, thus abruptly break in upon our devotions?

Porter. I thought they were finished.

Paul. No, they were not—were they, brother Francis?

Francis. Not by a bottle each.

Paul. But neither you nor your fellows mark how the hours go; no, you mind nothing but the gratifying of your appetites; ye eat, and swill, and sleep, and gourmandise, and thrive, while we are wasting in mortification.

Porter. We ask no more than nature craves.

Paul. 'Tis false, ye have more appetites than hairs! and your flushed, sleek, and pampered appearance is the disgrace of our order—out on't! If you are hungry, can't you be content with the wholesome roots of the earth? and if you are dry, isn't there the crystal spring?—[*Drinks.*] Put this away,—[*Gives the glass.*] and show me where I am wanted.—[PORTER *drains the glass.*—PAUL, *going, turns.*] So you would have drunk it if there had been any left! Ah, glutton! glutton!   [*Exeunt.*

SCENE VI—*The Court before the Priory*

Enter ISAAC *and* ANTONIO.

Isaac. A plaguy while coming, this same father Paul. —He's detained at vespers, I suppose, poor fellow.

Antonio. No, here he comes.

Enter FATHER PAUL.

Good father Paul, I crave your blessing.

Isaac. Yes, good father Paul, we are come to beg a favour.

Paul. What is it, pray?

Isaac. To marry us, good father Paul; and in truth thou dost look like the priest of Hymen.

Paul. In short, I may be called so; for I deal in repentance and mortification.

Isaac. No, no, thou seemest an officer of Hymen, because thy presence speaks content and good humour.

Paul. Alas, my appearance is deceitful. Bloated I am, indeed! for fasting is a windy recreation, and it hath swollen me like a bladder.

Antonio. But thou hast a good fresh colour in thy face, father; rosy, i'faith!

Paul. Yes, I have blushed for mankind, till the hue of my shame is as fixed as their vices.

Isaac. Good man!

Paul. And I have laboured, too, but to what purpose? they continue to sin under my very nose.

Isaac. Efecks, father, I should have guessed as much, for your nose seems to be put to the blush more than any other part of your face.

Paul. Go, you're a wag.

Antonio. But to the purpose, father—will you officiate for us?

Paul. To join young people thus clandestinely is not safe: and, indeed, I have in my heart many weighty reasons against it.

Antonio. And I have in my hand many weighty reasons for it. Isaac, haven't you an argument or two in our favour about you?

Isaac. Yes, yes; here is a most unanswerable purse.

Paul. For shame! you make me angry: you forget who I am, and when importunate people have forced their trash—ay, into this pocket here—or into this—why, then the sin was theirs.—[*They put money into his pockets.*] Fie, now how you distress me! I would return it, but that I must touch it that way, and so wrong my oath.

Antonio. Now then, come with us.

Isaac. Ay, now give us our title to joy and rapture.

Paul. Well, when your hour of repentance comes, don't blame me.

Antonio. [*Aside.*] No bad caution to my friend Isaac. —[*Aloud.*] Well, well, father, do you do your part, and I'll abide the consequences.

Isaac. Ay, and so will I.

Enter LOUISA, *running.*

Louisa. O Antonio, Ferdinand is at the porch, and inquiring for us.

Isaac. Who? Don Ferdinand! he's not inquiring for me, I hope.

Antonio. Fear not, my love; I'll soon pacify him.

Isaac. Egad, you won't. Antonio, take my advice, and run away; this Ferdinand is the most unmerciful dog, and has the cursedest long sword! and, upon my soul, he comes on purpose to cut your throat.

Antonio. Never fear, never fear.

Isaac. Well, you may stay if you will; but I'll get some one to marry me: for by St. Iago, he shall never meet me again, while I am master of a pair of heels.

[*Runs out.*—LOUISA *lets down her veil.*

Enter FERDINAND.

Ferdinand. So, sir, I have met with you at last.

Antonio. Well, sir.

Ferdinand. Base, treacherous man! whence can a false, deceitful soul, like yours, borrow confidence, to look so steadily on the man you've injured!

Antonio. Ferdinand, you are too warm: 'tis true you find me on the point of wedding one I loved beyond my life; but no argument of mine prevailed on her to elope. —I scorn deceit, as much as you. By heaven I knew not that she had left her father's till I saw her!

Ferdinand. What a mean excuse! You have wronged your friend, then, for one, whose wanton forwardness anticipated your treachery—of this, indeed, your Jew pander informed me; but let your conduct be consistent, and since you have dared to do a wrong, follow me, and show you have a spirit to avow it.

Louisa. Antonio, I perceive his mistake—leave him to me.

Paul. Friend, you are rude, to interrupt the union of two willing hearts.

Ferdinand. No, meddling priest! the hand he seeks is mine.

Paul. If so, I'll proceed no further. Lady, did you ever promise this youth your hand?

[*To* LOUISA, *who shakes her head.*

Ferdinand. Clara, I thank you for your silence—I would not have heard your tongue avow such falsity; be't your punishment to remember that I have not reproached you.

Enter CLARA, *veiled.*

Clara. What mockery is this?

Ferdinand. Antonio, you are protected now, but we shall meet.   [*Going,* CLARA *holds one arm, and* LOUISA *the other.*

DUET.

Louisa.	Turn thee round, I pray thee,
	Calm awhile thy rage.
Clara.	I must help to stay thee,
	And thy wrath assuage.
Louisa.	Couldst thou not discover
	One so dear to thee?
Clara.	Canst thou be a lover,
	And thus fly from me? [*Both unveil.*

Ferdinand. How's this? My sister! Clara, too—I'm confounded.

Louisa. 'Tis even so, good brother.

Paul. How! what impiety? did the man want to marry his own sister?

Louisa. And ar'n't you ashamed of yourself not to know your own sister?

Clara. To drive away your own mistress——

Louisa. Don't you see how jealousy blinds people?

Clara. Ay, and will you ever be jealous again?

Ferdinand. Never—never!—You, sister, I know will forgive me—but how, Clara, shall I presume——

Clara. No, no; just now you told me not to tease you—"Who do you want, good signor?" "Not you, not you!" Oh you blind wretch! but swear never to be jealous again, and I'll forgive you.

Ferdinand. By all——

Clara. There, that will do—you'll keep the oath just as well.   [*Gives her hand.*

Louisa. But, brother, here is one to whom some apology is due.

Ferdinand. Antonio, I am ashamed to think——

Antonio. Not a word of excuse, Ferdinand—I have not been in love myself without learning that a lover's anger should never be resented. But come—let us retire, with this good father, and we'll explain to you the cause of this error.

GLEE AND CHORUS.

Oft does Hymen smile to hear
    Wordy vows of feign'd regard;
Well, he knows when they're sincere,
    Never slow to give reward:
For his glory is to prove
Kind to those who wed for love.   [*Exeunt.*

SCENE VII—*A Grand Saloon in* JEROME'S *House*

Enter JEROME, LOPEZ, *and* SERVANTS.

Jerome. Be sure, now, let everything be in the best order—let all my servants have on their merriest faces: but tell them to get as little drunk as possible, till after supper.—[*Exeunt* SERVANTS.] So, Lopez, where's your master? shan't we have him at supper?

Lopez. Indeed, I believe not, sir—he's mad, I doubt! I'm sure he has frighted me from him.

Jerome. Ay, ay, he's after some wench, I suppose: a young rake! Well, well, we'll be merry without him.

[*Exit* LOPEZ.

Enter a SERVANT.

Servant. Sir, here is Signor Isaac.   [*Exit.*

Enter ISAAC.

Jerome. So, my dear son-in-law—there, take my blessing and forgiveness. But where's my daughter? where's Louisa?

Isaac. She's without, impatient for a blessing, but almost afraid to enter.

Jerome. Oh, fly and bring her in.—[*Exit* ISAAC.] Poor girl, I long to see her pretty face.

Isaac. [*Without.*] Come, my charmer! my trembling angel!

Re-enter ISAAC *with* DUENNA; JEROME *runs to meet them; she kneels.*

Jerome. Come to my arms, my—[*Starts back.*] Why, who the devil have we here?

Isaac. Nay, Don Jerome, you promised her forgiveness; see how the dear creature droops!

Jerome. Droops indeed! Why, Gad take me, this is old Margaret! But where's my daughter? where's Louisa?

Isaac. Why, here, before your eyes—nay, don't be abashed, my sweet wife!

Jerome. Wife with a vengeance! Why, zounds! you have not married the Duenna!

Duenna. [*Kneeling.*] Oh, dear papa! you'll not disown me, sure!

Jerome. Papa! papa! Why, zounds! your impudence is as great as your ugliness!

Isaac. Rise, my charmer, go throw your snowy arms about his neck, and convince him you are——

Duenna. Oh, sir, forgive me!   [*Embraces him.*
Jerome. Help! murder!

Enter SERVANTS.

Servant. What's the matter, sir?

Jerome. Why, here, this damned Jew has brought an old harridan to strangle me.

Isaac. Lord, it is his own daughter, and he is so hard-hearted he won't forgive her!

Enter ANTONIO and LOUISA; they kneel.

Jerome. Zounds and fury! what's here now? who sent for you, sir, and who the devil are you?

Antonio. This lady's husband, sir.

Isaac. Ay, that he is, I'll be sworn; for I left them with a priest, and was to have given her away.

Jerome. You were?

Isaac. Ay; that's my honest friend, Antonio; and that's the little girl I told you I had hampered him with.

Jerome. Why, you are either drunk or mad—this is my daughter.

Isaac. No, no; 'tis you are both drunk and mad, I think —here's your daughter.

Jerome. Hark ye, old iniquity! will you explain all this, or not?

Duenna. Come then, Don Jerome, I will—though our habits might inform you all. Look on your daughter, there, and on me.

Isaac. What's this I hear?

Duenna. The truth is, that in your passion this morning you made a small mistake; for you turned your daughter out of doors, and locked up your humble servant.

Isaac. O Lud! O Lud! here's a pretty fellow, to turn his daughter out of doors, instead of an old Duenna!

Jerome. And, O Lud! O Lud! here's a pretty fellow, to marry an old Duenna instead of my daughter! But how came the rest about?

Duenna. I have only to add, that I remained in your daughter's place, and had the good fortune to engage the affections of my sweet husband here.

Isaac. Her husband! why, you old witch, do you think I'll be your husband now? This is a trick, a cheat! and you ought all to be ashamed of yourselves.

Antonio. Hark ye, Isaac, do you dare to complain of tricking? Don Jerome, I give you my word, this cunning Portuguese has brought all this upon himself, by endeavouring to overreach you, by getting your daughter's fortune, without making any settlement in return.

Jerome. Overreach me!

Louisa. 'Tis so, indeed, sir, and we can prove it to you.

Jerome. Why, Gad, take me, it must be so, or he never could put up with such a face as Margaret's—so, little Solomon, I wish you joy of your wife, with all my soul.

Louisa. Isaac, tricking is all fair in love—let you alone for the plot!

Antonio. A cunning dog, ar'n't you? A sly little villain, eh?

Louisa. Roguish, perhaps; but keen, devilish keen!

Jerome. Yes, yes; his aunt always called him little Solomon.

Isaac. Why, the plagues of Egypt upon you all! but do you think I'll submit to such an imposition?

Antonio. Isaac, one serious word—you'd better be content as you are; for, believe me, you will find that, in the opinion of the world, there is not a fairer subject for contempt and ridicule than a knave become the dupe of his own art.

Isaac. I don't care—I'll not endure this. Don Jerome, 'tis you have done this—you would be so cursed positive about the beauty of her you locked up, and all the time I told you she was as old as my mother, and as ugly as the devil.

Duenna. Why, you little insignificant reptile!——

Jerome. That's right!—attack him, Margaret.

Duenna. Dare such a thing as you pretend to talk of beauty?—A walking rouleau?—a body that seems to owe all its consequence to the dropsy! a pair of eyes like two dead beetles in a wad of brown dough! a beard like an artichoke, with dry, shrivelled jaws that would disgrace the mummy of a monkey?

Jerome. Well done, Margaret!

Duenna. But you shall know that I have a brother who wears a sword—and, if you don't do me justice——

Isaac. Fire seize your brother, and you too! I'll fly to Jerusalem to avoid you!

Duenna. Fly where you will, I'll follow you.

Jerome. Throw your snowy arms about him, Margaret. —[*Exeunt* Isaac *and* Duenna.] But, Louisa, are you really married to this modest gentleman?

Louisa. Sir, in obedience to your commands, I gave him my hand within this hour.

Jerome. My commands!

Antonio. Yes, sir; here is your consent, under your own hand.

Jerome. How! would you rob me of my child by a trick, a false pretence? and do you think to get her fortune by the same means? Why, 'slife! you are as great a rogue as Isaac!

Antonio. No, Don Jerome; though I have profited by this paper in gaining your daughter's hand, I scorn to obtain her fortune by deceit. There, sir—[*Gives a letter.*] Now give her your blessing for a dower, and all the little I possess shall be settled on her in return. Had you wedded her to a prince, he could do no more.

Jerome. Why, Gad, take me, but you are a very extraordinary fellow! But have you the impudence to suppose no one can do a generous action but yourself? Here, Louisa, tell this proud fool of yours that he's the only man I know that would renounce your fortune; and, by my soul! he's the only man in Spain that's worthy of it. There, bless you both: I'm an obstinate old fellow when

I'm in the wrong; but you shall now find me as steady in the right.

Enter FERDINAND *and* CLARA.

Another wonder still! Why, sirrah! Ferdinand, you have not stole a nun, have you?

Ferdinand. She is a nun in nothing but her habit, sir —look nearer, and you will perceive 'tis Clara d'Almanza, Don Guzman's daughter; and, with pardon for stealing a wedding, she is also my wife.

Jerome. Gadsbud, and a great fortune! Ferdinand, you are a prudent young rogue, and I forgive you: and, ifecks, you are a pretty little damsel. Give your father-in-law a kiss, you smiling rogue!

Clara. There, old gentleman; and now mind you behave well to us.

Jerome. Ifecks, those lips ha'n't been chilled by kissing beads! Egad, I believe I shall grow the best-humoured fellow in Spain. Lewis! Sancho! Carlos! d'ye hear? are all my doors thrown open? Our children's weddings are the only holidays our age can boast; and then we drain, with pleasure, the little stock of spirits time has left us.— [*Music within.*] But, see, here come our friends and neighbours!

Enter MASQUERADERS.

And, i'faith, we'll make a night on't, with wine, and dance, and catches—then old and young shall join us.

FINALE.

Jerome.	Come now for jest and smiling,
	Both old and young beguiling,
	Let us laugh and play, so blithe and gay,
	Till we banish care away.

Louisa.	Thus crown'd with dance and song,
	The hours shall glide along,
	With a heart at ease, merry, merry glees
	Can never fail to please.

Ferdinand.	Each bride with blushes glowing,
	Our wine as rosy flowing,
	Let us laugh and play, so blithe and gay,
	Till we banish care away.

Antonio.   Then healths to every friend
              The night's repast shall end,
                  With a heart at ease, merry, merry glees
                  Can never fail to please.

Clara.   Nor, while we are so joyous,
              Shall anxious fear annoy us;
                  Let us laugh and play, so blithe and gay,
                  Till we banish care away.

Jerome.   For generous guests like these
              Accept the wish to please,
                  So we'll laugh and play, so blithe and gay,
                  Your smiles drive care away.

                                          [*Exeunt omnes.*

A TRIP TO SCARBOROUGH

A Comedy

DRAMATIS PERSONÆ

AS ACTED AT DRURY LANE THEATRE IN 1781 [1]

LORD FOPPINGTON	*Mr. Dodd*
SIR TUNBELLY CLUMSY	*Mr. Moody*
COLONEL TOWNLY	*Mr. Brereton*
LOVELESS	*Mr. Smith*
TOM FASHION	*Mr. J. Palmer*
LA VAROLE	*Mr. Burton*
LORY	*Mr. Baddeley*
PROBE	*Mr. Parsons*
MENDLEGS	*Mr. Norris*
JEWELLER	*Mr. Lamash*
SHOEMAKER	*Mr. Carpenter*
TAILOR	*Mr. Parker*
AMANDA	*Mrs. Robinson*
BERINTHIA	*Miss Farren*
MISS HOYDEN	*Mrs. Abington*
MRS. COUPLER	*Mrs. Booth*
NURSE	*Mrs. Bradshaw*

Sempstress, Postilion, Maid, *and* Servants.

SCENE—SCARBOROUGH AND ITS NEIGHBOURHOOD

---

[1] The play was first performed on February 24, 1777.

PROLOGUE

WHAT various transformations we remark,
From east Whitechapel to the west Hyde Park!
Men, women, children, houses, signs, and fashions,
State, stage, trade, taste, the humours and the passions;
The Exchange, 'Change Alley, wheresoe'er you're ranging,
Court, city, country, all are changed or changing:
The streets, some time ago, were paved with stones,
Which, aided by a hackney-coach, half broke your bones.
The purest lovers then indulged in bliss;
They ran great hazard if they stole a kiss.
One chaste salute!—the damsel cried—Oh, fie!
As they approach'd—slap went the coach awry—
Poor Sylvia got a bump, and Damon a black eye.

But now weak nerves in hackney-coaches roam,
And the cramm'd glutton snores, unjolted, home;
Of former times, that polish'd thing a beau,
Is metamorphosed now from top to toe;
Then the full flaxen wig, spread o'er the shoulders,
Conceal'd the shallow head from the beholders.
But now the whole's reversed—each fop appears,
Cropp'd and trimm'd up, exposing head and ears:
The buckle then its modest limits knew,
Now, like the ocean, dreadful to the view,
Hath broke its bounds, and swallowed up the shoe:
The wearer's foot like his once fine estate,
Is almost lost, the encumbrance is so great.
Ladies may smile—are they not in the plot?
The bounds of nature have not they forgot?
Were they design'd to be, when put together,
Made up, like shuttlecocks, of cork and feather?
Their pale-faced grandmammas appeared with grace
When dawning blushes rose upon the face;
No blushes now their once-loved station seek;
The foe is in possession of the cheek!
No heads of old, too high in feather'd state,
Hinder'd the fair to pass the lowest gate;

165

A church to enter now, they must be bent,
If ever they should try the experiment.
    As change thus circulates throughout the nation,
Some plays may justly call for alteration;
At least to draw some slender covering o'er,
That *graceless wit* [1] which was too bare before:
Those writers well and wisely use their pens,
Who turn our wantons into Magdalens;
And howsoever wicked wits revile 'em,
We hope to find in you their stage asylum.

[1] "And *Van* wants grace, who never wanted wit."—POPE.

A TRIP TO SCARBOROUGH

ACT ONE

SCENE I—*The Hall of an Inn*

Enter TOM FASHION *and* LORY, POSTILION *following with a portmanteau.*

FASHION. Lory, pay the postboy, and take the portmanteau.

Lory. [*Aside to* TOM FASHION.] Faith, sir, we had better let the postboy take the portmanteau and pay himself.

Fashion. [*Aside to* LORY.] Why, sure, there's something left in it!

Lory. Not a rag, upon my honour, sir! We eat the last of your wardrobe at New Malton—and, if we had had twenty miles further to go, our next meal must have been of the cloak-bag.

Fashion. Why, 'sdeath, it appears full!

Lory. Yes, sir—I made bold to stuff it with hay, to save appearances, and look like baggage.

Fashion. [*Aside.*] What the devil shall I do?—[*Aloud.*] Hark'ee, boy, what's the chaise?

Postilion. Thirteen shillings, please your honour.

Fashion. Can you give me change for a guinea?

Postilion. Oh, yes, sir.

Lory. [*Aside.*] So, what will he do now?—[*Aloud.*] Lord, sir, you had better let the boy be paid below.

Fashion. Why, as you say, Lory, I believe it will be as well.

Lory. Yes, yes, I'll tell them to discharge you below, honest friend.

Postilion. Please your honour, there are the turnpikes too.

Fashion. Ay, ay, the turnpikes by all means.

Postilion. And I hope your honour will order me something for myself.

Fashion. To be sure; bid them give you a crown.

Lory. Yes, yes—my master doesn't care what you charge them—so get along, you——

Postilion. And there's the ostler, your honour.

Lory. Psha! damn the ostler!—would you impose upon the gentleman's generosity?—[*Pushes him out.*] A rascal, to be so cursed ready with his change!

Fashion. Why, faith, Lory, he had nearly posed me.

Lory. Well, sir, we are arrived at Scarborough, not worth a guinea! I hope you'll own yourself a happy man —you have outlived all your cares.

Fashion. How so, sir?

Lory. Why, you have nothing left to take care of.

Fashion. Yes, sirrah, I have myself and you to take care of still.

Lory. Sir, if you could prevail with somebody else to do that for you, I fancy we might both fare the better for it. But now, sir, for my Lord Foppington, your elder brother.

Fashion. Damn my eldest brother.

Lory. With all my heart; but get him to redeem your annuity, however. Look you, sir; you must wheedle him, or you must starve.

Fashion. Look you, sir; I would neither wheedle him, nor starve.

Lory. Why, what will you do, then?

Fashion. Cut his throat, or get someone to do it for me.

Lory. Gad so, sir, I'm glad to find I was not so well acquainted with the strength of your conscience as with the weakness of your purse.

Fashion. Why, art thou so impenetrable a blockhead as to believe he'll help me with a farthing?

Lory. Not if you treat him *de haut en bas,* as you used to do.

Fashion. Why, how wouldst have me treat him?

Lory. Like a trout—tickle him.

Fashion. I can't flatter.

Lory. Can you starve?

Fashion. Yes.

Lory. I can't. Good by t'ye, sir.

Fashion. Stay—thou'lt distract me. But who comes here? My old friend, Colonel Townley.

Enter COLONEL TOWNLY.

My dear Colonel, I am rejoiced to meet you here.

Colonel Townly. Dear Tom, this is an unexpected pleas-

ure! What, are you come to Scarborough to be present at
your brother's wedding?

Lory. Ah, sir, if it had been his funeral, we should have
come with pleasure.

Colonel Townly. What, honest Lory, are you with your
master still?

Lory. Yes, sir; I have been starving with him ever since
I saw your honour last.

Fashion. Why, Lory is an attached rogue; there's no getting rid of him.

Lory. True, sir, as my master says, there's no seducing
me from his service.—[*Aside.*] Till he's able to pay me my
wages.

Fashion. Go, go, sir, and take care of the baggage.

Lory. Yes, sir, the baggage!—O Lord! [*Takes up the
portmanteau.*] I suppose, sir, I must charge the landlord
to be very particular where he stows this?

Fashion. Get along, you rascal.—[*Exit* LORY *with the
portmanteau.*] But, Colonel, are you acquainted with my
proposed sister-in-law?

Colonel Townly. Only by character. Her father, Sir Tunbelly Clumsy, lives within a quarter of a mile of this place,
in a lonely old house, which nobody comes near. She never
goes abroad, nor sees company at home; to prevent all
misfortunes, she has her breeding within doors; the parson
of the parish teaches her to play upon the dulcimer, the
clerk to sing, her nurse to dress, and her father to dance;
—in short, nobody has free admission there but our old
acquaintance, Mother Coupler, who has procured your
brother this match, and is, I believe, a distant relation of
Sir Tunbelly's.

Fashion. But is her fortune so considerable?

Colonel Townly. Three thousand a year, and a good
sum of money, independent of her father, beside.

Fashion. 'Sdeath! that my old acquaintance, Dame
Coupler, could not have thought of me, as well as my
brother, for such a prize.

Colonel Townly. Egad, I wouldn't swear that you are
too late—his lordship, I know, hasn't yet seen the lady—
and, I believe, has quarrelled with his patroness.

Fashion. My dear Colonel, what an idea have you
started!

Colonel Townly. Pursue it, if you can, and I promise
you shall have my assistance; for, besides my natural con-

tempt for his lordship, I have at present the enmity of a rival towards him.

Fashion. What, has he been addressing your old flame, the widow Berinthia?

Colonel Townly. Faith, Tom, I am at present most whimsically circumstanced. I came here a month ago to meet the lady you mention; but she failing in her promise, I, partly from pique and partly from idleness, have been diverting my chagrin by offering up incense to the beauties of Amanda, our friend Loveless's wife.

Fashion. I never have seen her, but have heard her spoken of as a youthful wonder of beauty and prudence.

Colonel Townly. She is so indeed; and, Loveless being too careless and insensible of the treasure he possesses, my lodging in the same house has given me a thousand opportunities of making my assiduities acceptable; so that, in less than a fortnight, I began to bear my disappointment from the widow with the most Christian resignation.

Fashion. And Berinthia has never appeared?

Colonel Townly. Oh, there's the perplexity! for, just as I began not to care whether I ever saw her again or not, last night she arrived.

Fashion. And instantly resumed her empire.

Colonel Townly. No, faith—we met—but, the lady not condescending to give me any serious reasons for having fooled me for a month, I left her in a huff.

Fashion. Well, well, I'll answer for it she'll soon resume her power, especially as friendship will prevent your pursuing the other too far.—But my coxcomb of a brother is an admirer of Amanda's too, is he?

Colonel Townly. Yes, and I believe is most heartily despised by her. But come with me, and you shall see her and your old friend Loveless.

Fashion. I must pay my respects to his lordship—perhaps you can direct me to his lodgings.

Colonel Townly. Come with me; I shall pass by it.

Fashion. I wish you could pay this visit for me, or could tell me what I should say to him.

Colonel Townly. Say nothing to him—apply yourself to his bag, his sword, his feather, his snuff-box; and when you are well with them, desire him to lend you a thousand pounds, and I'll engage you prosper.

Fashion. 'Sdeath and furies! why was that coxcomb

thrust into the world before me? O Fortune, Fortune, thou
art a jilt, by Gad!   [*Exeunt.*

SCENE II—LORD FOPPINGTON'S *Dressing-room*

Enter LORD FOPPINGTON *in his dressing-gown, and*
LA VAROLE.

Lord Foppington. [*Aside.*] Well, 'tis an unspeakable
pleasure to be a man of quality—strike me dumb! Even
the boors of this northern spa have learned the respect due
to a title.—[*Aloud.*] La Varole!

La Varole. Milor——

Lord Foppington. You ha'n't yet been at Muddymoat
Hall, to announce my arrival, have you?

La Varole. Not yet, milor.

Lord Foppington. Then you need not go till Saturday—
[*Exit* LA VAROLE] as I am in no particular haste to view
my intended sposa. I shall sacrifice a day or two more to
the pursuit of my friend Loveless's wife. Amanda is a
charming creature—strike me ugly! and, if I have any discernment in the world, she thinks no less of my Lord
Foppington.

Re-enter LA VAROLE.

La Varole. Milor, de shoemaker, de tailor, de hosier, de
sempstress, de peru, be all ready, if your lordship please
to dress.

Lord Foppington. 'Tis well, admit them.

La Varole. Hey, messieurs, entrez!

Enter TAILOR, SHOEMAKER, SEMPSTRESS, JEWELLER,
and MENDLEGS.

Lord Foppington. So, gentlemen, I hope you have all
taken pains to show yourselves masters in your professions?

Tailor. I think I may presume, sir——

La Varole. Milor, you clown, you!

Tailor. My lord—I ask your lordship's pardon, my lord.
I hope, my lord, your lordship will be pleased to own I
have brought your lordship as accomplished a suit of
clothes as ever peer of England wore, my lord—will your
lordship please to view 'em now?

Lord Foppington. Ay; but let my people dispose the glasses so that I may see myself before and behind; for I love to see myself all round.   [*Puts on his clothes.*

Enter TOM FASHION *and* LORY. *They remain behind, conversing apart.*

Fashion. Heyday! what the devil have we here? Sure my gentleman's grown a favourite at court, he has got so many people at his levee.

Lory. Sir, these people come in order to make him a favourite at court—they are to establish him with the ladies.

Fashion. Good Heaven! to what an ebb of taste are women fallen, that it should be in the power of a laced coat to recommend a gallant to them?

Lory. Sir, tailors and hair-dressers debauch all the women.

Fashion. Thou sayest true. But now for my reception.

Lord Foppington. [*To* TAILOR.] Death and eternal tortures! Sir—I say the coat is too wide here by a foot.

Tailor. My lord, if it had been tighter, 'twould neither have hooked nor buttoned.

Lord Foppington. Rat the hooks and buttons, sir! Can any thing be worse than this? As Gad shall jedge me, it hangs on my shoulders like a chairman's surtout.

Tailor. 'Tis not for me to dispute your lordship's fancy.

Lory. There, sir, observe what respect does.

Fashion. Respect! damn him for a coxcomb!—But let's accost him.—[*Coming forward.*] Brother, I'm your humble servant.

Lord Foppington. O Lard, Tam! I did not expect you in England.—Brother, I'm glad to see you.—But what has brought you to Scarborough, Tam!—[*To the* TAILOR.] Look you, sir, I shall never be reconciled to this nauseous wrapping-gown, therefore pray get me another suit with all possible expedition; for this is my eternal aversion.— [*Exit* TAILOR.] Well but, Tam, you don't tell me what has driven you to Scarborough.—Mrs. Calico, are not you of my mind?

Sempstress. Directly, my lord.—I hope your lordship is pleased with your ruffles?

Lord Foppington. In love with them, stap my vitals!— Bring my bill, you shall be paid to-morrow.

Sempstress. I humbly thank your worship.   [*Exit.*

Lord Foppington. Hark thee, shoemaker, these shoes aren't ugly, but they don't fit me.

Shoemaker. My lord, I think they fit you very well.

Lord Foppington. They hurt me just below the instep.

Shoemaker. [*Feels his foot.*] No, my lord, they don't hurt you there.

Lord Foppington. I tell thee they pinch me execrably.

Shoemaker. Why then, my lord, if those shoes pinch you, I'll be damned.

Lord Foppington. Why, will thou undertake to persuade me I cannot feel?

Shoemaker. Your lordship may please to feel what you think fit, but that shoe does not hurt you—I think I understand my trade.

Lord Foppington. Now, by all that's good and powerful, thou art an incomprehensive coxcomb!—but thou makest good shoes, and so I'll bear with thee.

Shoemaker. My lord, I have worked for half the people of quality in this town these twenty years, and 'tis very hard I shouldn't know when a shoe hurts, and when it don't.

Lord Foppington. Well, pr'ythee be gone about thy business.—[*Exit* SHOEMAKER.] Mr. Mendlegs, a word with you.—The calves of these stockings are thickened a little too much; they make my legs look like a porter's.

Mendlegs. My lord, methinks they look mighty well.

Lord Foppington. Ay, but you are not so good a judge of those things as I am—I have studied them all my life— therefore pray let the next be the thickness of a crown-piece less.

Mendlegs. Indeed, my lord, they are the same kind I had the honour to furnish your lordship with in town.

Lord Foppington. Very possibly, Mr. Mendlegs; but that was in the beginning of the winter, and you should always remember, Mr. Hosier, that if you make a nobleman's spring legs as robust as his autumnal calves, you commit a monstrous impropriety, and make no allowance for the fatigues of the winter.   [*Exit* MENDLEGS.

Jeweller. I hope, my lord, these buckles have had the unspeakable satisfaction of being honoured with your lordship's approbation?

Lord Foppington. Why, they are of a pretty fancy; but don't you think them rather of the smallest?

Jeweller. My lord, they could not well be larger, to keep on your lordship's shoe.

Lord Foppington. My good sir, you forget that these matters are not as they used to be; formerly, indeed, the buckle was a sort of machine, intended to keep on the shoe; but the case is now quite reversed, and the shoe is of no earthly use, but to keep on the buckle.—Now give me my watches, [SERVANT *fetches the watches.*] my chapeau, [SERVANT *brings a dress hat.*] my handkerchief, [SERVANT *pours some scented liquor on a handkerchief and brings it.*] my snuff-box. [SERVANT *brings snuff-box.*] There, now the business of the morning is pretty well over.
[*Exit* JEWELLER.

Fashion. [*Aside to* LORY.] Well, Lory, what dost think on't?—a very friendly reception from a brother, after three years' absence!

Lory. [*Aside to* TOM FASHION.] Why, sir, 'tis your own fault—here you have stood ever since you came in, and have not commended any one thing that belongs to him.
[SERVANTS *all go off.*

Fashion. [*Aside to* LORY.] Nor ever shall, while they belong to a coxcomb.—[*To* LORD FOPPINGTON.] Now your people of business are gone, brother, I hope I may obtain a quarter of an hour's audience of you?

Lord Foppington. Faith, Tam, I must beg you'll excuse me at this time, for I have an engagement which I would not break for the salvation of mankind.—Hey!—there!—is my carriage at the door?—You'll excuse me, brother.
[*Going.*

Fashion. Shall you be back to dinner?

Lord Foppington. As Gad shall jedge me, I can't tell; for it is passible I may dine with some friends at Donner's.

Fashion. Shall I meet you there? For I must needs talk with you.

Lord Foppington. That I'm afraid mayn't be quite so praper; for those I commonly eat with are people of nice conversation; and you know, Tam, your education has been a little at large.—But there are other ordinaries in town—very good beef ordinaries—I suppose, Tam, you can eat beef?—However, dear Tam, I'm glad to see thee in England, stap my vitals! [*Exit,* LA VAROLE *following.*

Fashion. Hell and furies! is this to be borne?

Lory. Faith, sir, I could almost have given him a knock o' the pate myself.

Fashion. 'Tis enough; I will now show you the excess of my passion, by being very calm.—Come, Lory, lay your loggerhead to mine, and, in cold blood, let us contrive his destruction.

Lory. Here comes a head, sir, would contrive it better than both our loggerheads, if she would but join in the confederacy.

Fashion. By this light, Madam Coupler! she seems dissatisfied at something: let us observe her.

Enter MRS. COUPLER.

Mrs. Coupler. So! I am likely to be well rewarded for my services, truly; my suspicions, I find, were but too just. —What! refuse to advance me a petty sum, when I am upon the point of making him master of a galleon! but let him look to the consequences; an ungrateful, narrow-minded coxcomb.

Fashion. So he is, upon my soul, old lady; it must be my brother you speak of.

Mrs. Coupler. Ha! stripling, how came you here? What, hast spent all, eh? And art thou come to dun his lordship for assistance?

Fashion. No, I want somebody's assistance to cut his lordship's throat, without the risk of being hanged for him.

Mrs. Coupler. Egad, sirrah, I could help thee to do him almost as good a turn, without the danger of being burned in the hand for't.

Fashion. How—how, old Mischief?

Mrs. Coupler. Why, you must know I have done you the kindness to make up a match for your brother.

Fashion. I am very much beholden to you, truly!

Mrs. Coupler. You may be before the wedding-day, yet: the lady is a great heiress, the match is concluded, the writings are drawn, and his lordship is come hither to put the finishing hand to the business.

Fashion. I understand as much.

Mrs. Coupler. Now, you must know, stripling, your brother's a knave.

Fashion. Good.

Mrs. Coupler. He has given me a bond of a thousand pounds for helping him to this fortune, and has promised me as much more, in ready money, upon the day of the marriage; which, I understand by a friend, he never designs to pay me; and his just now refusing to pay me a part is a proof of it. If, therefore, you will be a generous young rogue, and secure me five thousand pounds, I'll help you to the lady.

Fashion. And how the devil wilt thou do that?

Mrs. Coupler. Without the devil's aid, I warrant thee. Thy brother's face not one of the family ever saw; the whole business has been managed by me, and all his letters go through my hands. Sir Tunbelly Clumsy, my relation—for that's the old gentleman's name—is apprised of his lordship's being down here, and expects him to-morrow to receive his daughter's hand; but the peer, I find, means to bait here a few days longer, to recover the fatigue of his journey, I suppose. Now you shall go to Muddymoat Hall in his place.—I'll give you a letter of introduction: and if you don't marry the girl before sunset, you deserve to be hanged before morning.

Fashion. Agreed! agreed! and for thy reward——

Mrs. Coupler. Well, well;—though I warrant thou hast not a farthing of money in thy pocket now—no—one may see it in thy face.

Fashion. Not a sous, by Jupiter!

Mrs. Coupler. Must I advance, then? Well, be at my lodgings, next door, this evening, and I'll see what may be done—we'll sign and seal, and when I have given thee some further instructions, thou shalt hoist sail and begone.
                                                            [*Exit.*

Fashion. So, Lory, Fortune, thou seest, at last takes care of merit! we are in a fair way to be great people.

Lory. Ay, sir, if the devil don't step between the cup and the lip, as he used to do.

Fashion. Why, faith, he has played me many a damned trick to spoil my fortune; and, egad, I am almost afraid he's at work about it again now; but if I should tell thee how, thou'dst wonder at me.

Lory. Indeed, sir, I should not.

Fashion. How dost know?

Lory. Because, sir, I have wondered at you so often, I can wonder at you no more.

Fashion. No! what wouldst thou say, if a qualm of conscience should spoil my design?

Lory. I would eat my words, and wonder more than ever.

Fashion. Why faith, Lory, though I have played many a

roguish trick, this is so full-grown a cheat, I find I must take pains to come up to't—I have scruples.

Lory. They are strong symptoms of death. If you find they increase, sir, pray make your will.

Fashion. No, my conscience shan't starve me neither: but thus far I'll listen to it. Before I execute this project, I'll try my brother to the bottom. If he has yet so much humanity about him as to assist me—though with a moderate aid—I'll drop my project at his feet, and show him how I can do for him much more than what I'd ask he'd do for me. This one conclusive trial of him I resolve to make.

> Succeed or fail, still victory is my lot;
> If I subdue his heart, 'tis well—if not,
> I will subdue my conscience to my plot. [*Exeunt.*

ACT TWO

SCENE I—LOVELESS's *Lodgings*

Enter LOVELESS *and* AMANDA.

LOVELESS. How do you like these lodgings, my dear? For my part, I am so pleased with them, I shall hardly remove whilst we stay here, if you are satisfied.

Amanda. I am satisfied with everything that pleases you, else I had not come to Scarborough at all.

Loveless. Oh, a little of the noise and folly of this place will sweeten the pleasures of our retreat; we shall find the charms of our retirement doubled when we return to it.

Amanda. That pleasing prospect will be my chiefest entertainment, whilst, much against my will, I engage in those empty pleasures which 'tis so much the fashion to be fond of.

Loveless. I own most of them are, indeed, but empty; yet there are delights of which a private life is destitute, which may divert an honest man, and be a harmless entertainment to a virtuous woman: good music is one; and truly (with some small allowance) the plays, I think, may be esteemed another.

Amanda. Plays, I must confess, have some small charms. What do you think of that you saw last night?

Loveless. To say truth, I did not mind it much—my attention was for some time taken off to admire the workmanship of Nature in the face of a young lady who sat at some distance from me, she was so exquisitely handsome.

Amanda. So exquisitely handsome!

Loveless. Why do you repeat my words, my dear?

Amanda. Because you seemed to speak them with such pleasure, I thought I might oblige you with their echo.

Loveless. Then you are alarmed, Amanda?

Amanda. It is my duty to be so when you are in danger.

Loveless. You are too quick in apprehending for me. I viewed her with a world of admiration, but not one glance of love.

Amanda. Take heed of trusting to such nice distinctions. But were your eyes the only things that were inquisitive? Had I been in your place, my tongue, I fancy, had been curious too. I should have asked her where she lived—yet still without design—who was she, pray?

Loveless. Indeed I cannot tell.

Amanda. You will not tell.

Loveless. Upon my honour, then, I did not ask.

Amanda. Nor do you know what company was with her?

Loveless. I do not. But why are you so earnest?

Amanda. I thought I had cause.

Loveless. But you thought wrong, Amanda; for turn the case, and let it be your story: should you come home and tell me you had seen a handsome man, should I grow jealous because you had eyes?

Amanda. But should I tell you he was exquisitely so, and that I had gazed on him with admiration, should you not think 'twere possible I might go one step further, and inquire his name?

Loveless. [*Aside.*] She has reason on her side; I have talked too much; but I must turn off another way.— [*Aloud.*] Will you then make no difference, Amanda, between the language of our sex and yours? There is a modesty restrains your tongues, which makes you speak by halves when you commend; but roving flattery gives a loose to ours, which makes us still speak double what we think.

Enter SERVANT.

Servant. Madam, there is a lady at the door in a chair desires to know whether your ladyship sees company; her name is Berinthia.

Amanda. Oh dear! 'tis a relation I have not seen these five years; pray her to walk in.—[*Exit* SERVANT.] Here's another beauty for you; she was, when I saw her last, reckoned extremely handsome.

Loveless. Don't be jealous now; for I shall gaze upon her too.

Enter BERINTHIA.

Ha! by heavens, the very woman!   [*Aside.*

Berinthia. [*Salutes* AMANDA.] Dear Amanda, I did not expect to meet you in Scarborough.

Amanda. Sweet cousin, I'm overjoyed to see you.—Mr. Loveless, here's a relation and a friend of mine, I desire you'll be better acquainted with.

Loveless. [*Salutes* BERINTHIA.] If my wife never desires a harder thing, madam, her request will be easily granted.

Re-enter SERVANT.

Servant. Sir, my Lord Foppington presents his humble service to you, and desires to know how you do. He's at the next door; and, if it be not inconvenient to you, he'll come and wait upon you.

Loveless. Give my compliments to his lordship, and I shall be glad to see him—[*Exit* SERVANT.] If you are not acquainted with his lordship, madam, you will be entertained with his character.

Amanda. Now it moves my pity more than my mirth to see a man whom nature has made no fool be so very industrious to pass for an ass.

Loveless. No, there you are wrong, Amanda; you should never bestow your pity upon those who take pains for your contempt: pity those whom nature abuses, never those who abuse nature.

Enter LORD FOPPINGTON.

Lord Foppington. Dear Loveless, I am your most humble servant.

Loveless. My lord, I'm yours.

Lord Foppington. Madam, your ladyship's very obedient slave.

Loveless. My lord, this lady is a relation of my wife's.

Lord Foppington. [*Salutes* BERINTHIA.] The beautifullest race of people upon earth, rat me! Dear Loveless, I am overjoyed that you think of continuing here: I am, stap my vitals!—[*To* AMANDA.] For Gad's sake, madam, how has your ladyship been able to subsist thus long, under the fatigue of a country life?

Amanda. My life has been very far from that, my lord; it has been a very quiet one.

Lord Foppington. Why, that's the fatigue I speak of, madam; for 'tis impossible to be quiet without thinking: now thinking is to me the greatest fatigue in the world.

Amanda. Does not your lordship love reading, then?

Lord Foppington. Oh, passionately, madam; but I never think of what I read. For example, madam, my life is a perpetual stream of pleasure, that glides through with such a variety of entertainments, I believe the wisest of our ancestors never had the least conception of any of 'em. I rise, madam, when in tawn, about twelve o'clock. I don't rise sooner, because it is the worst thing in the world for the complexion: nat that I pretend to be a beau; but a man must endeavour to look decent, lest he makes so odious a figure in the side-bax, the ladies should be compelled to turn their eyes upon the play. So at twelve o'clock, I say, I rise. Naw, if I find it is a good day, I resolve to take the exercise of riding; so drink my chocolate, and draw on my boots by two. On my return, I dress; and, after dinner, lounge perhaps to the opera.

Berinthia. Your lordship, I suppose, is fond of music?

Lord Foppington. Oh, passionately, on Tuesdays and Saturdays; for then there is always the best company, and one is not expected to undergo the fatigue of listening.

Amanda. Does your lordship think that the case at the opera?

Lord Foppington. Most certainly, madam. There is my Lady Tattle, my Lady Prate, my Lady Titter, my Lady Sneer, my Lady Giggle, and my Lady Grin—these have boxes in the front, and while any favourite air is singing, are the prettiest company in the waurld, stap my vitals!— Mayn't we hope for the honour to see you added to our society, madam?

Amanda. Alas! my lord, I am the worst company in the world at a concert, I'm so apt to attend to the music.

Lord Foppington. Why, madam, that is very pardonable in the country or at church, but a monstrous inattention in a polite assembly. But I am afraid I tire the company?

Loveless. Not at all. Pray go on.

Lord Foppington. Why then, ladies, there only remains

to add, that I generally conclude the evening at one or other of the clubs; nat that I ever play deep; indeed I have been for some time tied up from losing above five thousand paunds at a sitting.

Loveless. But isn't your lordship sometimes obliged to attend the weighty affairs of the nation?

Lord Foppington. Sir, as to weighty affairs, I leave them to weighty heads; I never intend mine shall be a burden to my body.

Berinthia. Nay, my lord, but you are a pillar of the state.

Lord Foppington. An ornamental pillar, madam; for sooner than undergo any part of the fatigue, rat me, but the whole building should fall plump to the ground!

Amanda. But, my lord, a fine gentleman spends a great deal of his time in his intrigues; you have given us no account of them yet.

Lord Foppington. [*Aside.*] So! she would inquire into my amours—that's jealousy, poor soul!—I see she's in love with me.—[*Aloud.*] O Lord, madam, I had like to have forgot a secret I must need tell your ladyship.—Ned, you must not be so jealous now as to listen.

Loveless. [*Leading* BERINTHIA *up the stage.*] Not I, my lord; I am too fashionable a husband to pry into the secrets of my wife.

Lord Foppington. [*Aside to* AMANDA *squeezing her hand.*] I am in love with you to desperation, strike me speechless!

Amanda. [*Strikes him on the ear.*] Then thus I return your passion.—An impudent fool!

Lord Foppington. God's curse, madam, I am a peer of the realm!

Loveless. [*Hastily returning.*] Hey! what the devil, do you affront my wife, sir? Nay, then——

[*Draws. They fight.*

Amanda. What has my folly done?—Help! murder! help! Part them for Heaven's sake.

Lord Foppington. [*Falls back and leans on his sword.*] Ah! quite through the body, stap my vitals!

Enter SERVANTS.

Loveless. [*Runs to* LORD FOPPINGTON.] I hope I ha'nt killed the fool, however. Bear him up.—Call a surgeon there.

Lord Foppington. Ay, pray make haste. [*Exit* SERVANT.

Loveless. This mischief you may thank yourself for.

Lord Foppington. I may say so; love's the devil indeed, Ned.

Re-enter SERVANT, *with* PROBE.

Servant. Here's Mr. Probe, sir, was just going by the door.

Lord Foppington. He's the welcomest man alive.

Probe. Stand by, stand by, stand by; pray, gentlemen, stand by. Lord have mercy upon us, did you never see a man run through the body before?—Pray stand by.

Lord Foppington. Ah, Mr. Probe, I'm a dead man.

Probe. A dead man, and I by! I should laugh to see that, egad.

Loveless. Pr'ythee don't stand prating, but look upon his wound.

Probe. Why, what if I don't look upon his wound this hour, sir?

Loveless. Why, then he'll bleed to death, sir.

Probe. Why, then I'll fetch him to life again, sir.

Loveless. 'Slife! he's run through the body, I tell thee.

Probe. I wish he was run through the heart, and I should get the more credit by his cure. Now I hope you are satisfied? Come, now let me come at him—now let me come at him.—[*Viewing his wound.*] Oons! what a gash is here! why, sir, a man may drive a coach and six horses into your body.

Lord Foppington. Oh!

Probe. Why, what the devil have you run the gentleman through with—a scythe?—[*Aside.*] A little scratch between the skin and the ribs, that's all.

Loveless. Let me see his wound.

Probe. Then you shall dress it, sir; for if anybody looks upon it I won't.

Loveless. Why, thou art the veriest coxcomb I ever saw!

Probe. Sir, I am not master of my trade for nothing.

Lord Foppington. Surgeon!

Probe. Sir.

Lord Foppington. Are there any hopes?

Probe. Hopes! I can't tell. What are you willing to give for a cure?

Lord Foppington. Five hundred paunds with pleasure.

Probe. Why then perhaps there may be hopes; but we must avoid further delay.—Here, help the gentleman into a chair, and carry him to my house presently—that's the properest place—[*Aside.*] to bubble him out of his money. —[*Aloud.*] Come, a chair—a chair quickly—there, in with him. [SERVANTS *put* LORD FOPPINGTON *into a chair.*

Lord Foppington. Dear Loveless, adieu; if I die, I forgive thee; and if I live, I hope thou wilt do as much by me. I am sorry you and I should quarrel, but I hope here's an end on't; for if you are satisfied, I am.

Loveless. I shall hardly think it worth my prosecuting any further, so you may be at rest, sir.

Lord Foppington. Thou art a generous fellow, strike me dumb!—[*Aside.*] But thou hast an impertinent wife, stap my vitals!

Probe. So—carry him off!—carry him off!—We shall have him into a fever by-and-by.—Carry him off!

[*Exit with* LORD FOPPINGTON.

Enter COLONEL TOWNLY.

Colonel Townly. So, so, I am glad to find you all alive. —I met a wounded peer carrying off. For heaven's sake what was the matter?

Loveless. Oh, a trifle! he would have made love to my wife before my face, so she obliged him with a box o' the ear, and I ran him through the body, that was all.

Colonel Townly. Bagatelle on all sides. But pray, madam, how long has this noble lord been an humble servant of yours?

Amanda. This is the first I have heard on't—so I suppose, 'tis his quality more than his love has brought him into this adventure. He thinks his title an authentic passport to every woman's heart below the degree of a peeress.

Colonel Townly. He's coxcomb enough to think anything: but I would not have you brought into trouble for him. I hope there's no danger of his life?

Loveless. None at all. He's fallen into the hands of a roguish surgeon, who, I perceive, designs to frighten a little money out of him: but I saw his wound—'tis nothing: he may go to the ball to-night if he pleases.

Colonel Townly. I am glad you have corrected him without further mischief, or you might have deprived me

of the pleasure of executing a plot against his lordship,
which I have been contriving with an old acquaintance
of yours.

Loveless. Explain.

Colonel Townly. His brother, Tom Fashion, is come
down here, and we have it in contemplation to save him
the trouble of his intended wedding; but we want your
assistance. Tom would have called but he is preparing for
his enterprise, so I promised to bring you to him—so, sir,
if these ladies can spare you——

Loveless. I'll go with you with all my heart.—[*Aside.*]
Though I could wish, methinks, to stay and gaze a little
longer on that creature. Good gods! how engaging she is!
—but what have I to do with beauty? I have already
had my portion, and must not covet more.

Amanda. Mr. Loveless, pray one word with you before
you go.   [*Exit* COLONEL TOWNLY.

Loveless. What would my dear?

Amanda. Only a woman's foolish question: how do you
like my cousin here?

Loveless. Jealous already, Amanda?

Amanda. Not at all: I ask you for another reason.

Loveless. [*Aside.*] Whate'er her reason be, I must not
tell her true.—[*Aloud.*] Why, I confess, she's handsome:
but you must not think I slight your kinswoman, if I own
to you, of all the women who may claim that character,
she is the last that would triumph in my heart.

Amanda. I'm satisfied.

Loveless. Now tell me why you asked?

Amanda. At night I will—adieu!

Loveless. I'm yours.   [*Kisses her and exits.*

Amanda. I'm glad to find he does not like her, for I
have a great mind to persuade her to come and live with
me.   [*Aside.*

Berinthia. So! I find my colonel continues in his airs;
there must be something more at the bottom of this than
the provocation he pretends from me.   [*Aside.*

Amanda. For Heaven's sake, Berinthia, tell me what way
I shall take to persuade you to come and live with me.

Berinthia. Why, one way in the world there is, and but
one.

Amanda. And pray what is that?

Berinthia. It is to assure me—I shall be very welcome.

Amanda. If that be all, you shall e'en sleep here to-night.

Berinthia. To-night!

Amanda. Yes, to-night.

Berinthia. Why, the people where I lodge will think me mad.

Amanda. Let 'em think what they please.

Berinthia. Say you so, Amanda? Why, then, they shall think what they please: for I'm a young widow, and I care not what anybody thinks.—Ah, Amanda, it's a delicious thing to be a young widow!

Amanda. You'll hardly make me think so.

Berinthia. Poh! because you are in love with your husband.

Amanda. Pray, 'tis with a world of innocence I would inquire whether you think those we call women of reputation do really escape all other men as they do those shadows of beaux.

Berinthia. Oh no, Amanda; there are a sort of men make dreadful work amongst 'em, men that may be called the beau's antipathy, for they agree in nothing but walking upon two legs. These have brains, the beau has none. These are in love with their mistress, the beau with himself. They take care of their reputation, the beau is industrious to destroy it. They are decent, he's a fop; in short, they are men, he's an ass.

Amanda. If this be their character, I fancy we had here, e'en now, a pattern of 'em both.

Berinthia. His lordship and Colonel Townly?

Amanda. The same.

Berinthia. As for the lord, he is eminently so; and for the other, I can assure you there's not a man in town who has a better interest with the women that are worth having an interest with.

Amanda. He answers the opinion I had ever of him. [*Takes her hand.*] I must acquaint you with a secret—'tis not that fool alone has talked to me of love; Townly has been tampering too.

Berinthia. [*Aside.*] So, so! here the mystery comes out! —[*Aloud.*] Colonel Townly! impossible, my dear!

Amanda. 'Tis true indeed; though he has done it in vain; nor do I think that all the merit of mankind combined could shake the tender love I bear my husband; yet I will own to you, Berinthia, I did not start at his addresses, as when they came from one whom I contemned.

Berinthia. [*Aside.*] Oh, this is better and better!—

[*Aloud.*] Well said, Innocence! and you really think, my dear, that nothing could abate your constancy and attachment to your husband?

Amanda. Nothing, I am convinced.

Berinthia. What, if you found he loved another woman better?

Amanda. Well!

Berinthia. Well!—why, were I that thing they call a slighted wife, somebody should run the risk of being that thing they call—a husband. Don't I talk madly?

Amanda. Madly indeed!

Berinthia. Yet I'm very innocent.

Amanda. That I dare swear you are. I know how to make allowances for your humour: but you resolve then never to marry again?

Berinthia. Oh no! I resolve I will.

Amanda. How so?

Berinthia. That I never may.

Amanda. You banter me.

Berinthia. Indeed I don't: but I consider I'm a woman, and form my resolutions accordingly.

Amanda. Well, my opinion is, form what resolutions you will, matrimony will be the end on't.

Berinthia. I doubt it—but a—Heavens! I have business at home, and am half an hour too late.

Amanda. As you are to return with me, I'll just give some orders, and walk with you.

Berinthia. Well, make haste, and we'll finish this subject as we go—[*Exit* AMANDA.]. Ah, poor Amanda! you have led a country life. Well, this discovery is lucky! Base Townly! at once false to me and treacherous to his friend! —And my innocent and demure cousin too! I have it in my power to be revenged on her, however. Her husband, if I have any skill in countenance, would be as happy in my smiles as Townly can hope to be in hers. I'll make the experiment, come what will on't. The woman who can forgive the being robbed of a favoured lover, must be either an idiot or a wanton.   [*Exit.*

ACT THREE

SCENE I—LORD FOPPINGTON'S *Lodgings*

Enter LORD FOPPINGTON, *and* LA VAROLE.

LORD FOPPINGTON. Hey, fellow, let thy vis-a-vis come to the door.

La Varole. Will your lordship venture so soon to expose yourself to the weather?

Lord Foppington. Sir, I will venture as soon as I can expose myself to the ladies.

La Varole. I wish your lordship would please to keep house a little longer; I'm afraid your honour does not well consider your wound.

Lord Foppington. My wound!—I would not be in eclipse another day, though I had as many wounds in my body as I have had in my heart. So mind, Varole, let these cards be left as directed; for this evening I shall wait on my future father-in-law, Sir Tunbelly, and I mean to commence my devoirs to the lady, by giving an entertainment at her father's expense; and hark thee, tell Mr. Loveless I request he and his company will honour me with their presence, or I shall think we are not friends.

La Varole. I will be sure, milor.   [*Exit.*

Enter TOM FASHION.

Fashion. Brother, your servant; how do you find yourself to-day?

Lord Foppington. So well that I have ardered my coach to the door—so there's no danger of death this baut, Tam.

Fashion. I'm very glad of it.

Lord Foppington. [*Aside.*] That I believe a lie.— [*Aloud.*] Pr'ythee, Tam, tell me one thing—did not your heart cut a caper up to your mauth, when you heard I was run through the bady?

Fashion. Why do you think it should?

Lord Foppington. Because I remember mine did so when I heard my uncle was shot through the head.

Fashion. It, then, did very ill.

Lord Foppington. Pr'ythee, why so?

Fashion. Because he used you very well.

Lord Foppington. Well!—Naw, strike me dumb! he starved me; he has let me want a thausand women for want of a thausand paund.

Fashion. Then he hindered you from making a great many ill bargains; for I think no woman worth money that will take money.

Lord Foppington. If I was a younger brother I should think so too.

Fashion. Then you are seldom much in love?

Lord Foppington. Never, stap my vitals!

Fashion. Why, then, did you make all this bustle about Amanda?

Lord Foppington. Because she's a woman of insolent virtue, and I thought myself piqued in honour to debauch her.

Fashion. Very well.—[*Aside.*] Here's a rare fellow for you, to have the spending of ten thousand pounds a year! But now for my business with him.—[*Aloud.*] Brother, though I know to talk of any business (especially of money) is a theme not quite so entertaining to you as that of the ladies, my necessities are such, I hope you'll have patience to hear me

Lord Foppington. The greatness of your necessities, Tam, is the worst argument in the waurld for your being patiently heard. I do believe you are going to make a very good speech, but, strike me dumb! it has the worst beginning of any speech I have heard this twelvemonth.

Fashion. I'm sorry you think so.

Lord Foppington. I do believe thou art: but, come, let's know the affair quickly.

Fashion. Why, then, my case, in a word, is this: the necessary expenses of my travels have so much exceeded the wretched income of my annuity, that I have been forced to mortgage it for five hundred pounds, which is spent. So unless you are so kind as to assist me in redeeming it, I know no remedy but to take a purse.

Lord Foppington. Why, faith, Tam, to give you my sense of the thing, I do think taking a purse the best remedy in the waurld; for if you succeed, you are relieved that way, if you are taken [*Drawing his hand round his neck.*], you are relieved t'other.

Fashion. I'm glad to see you are in so pleasant a humour; I hope I shall find the effects on't.

Lord Foppington. Why, do you then really think it a

reasonable thing, that I should give you five hundred paunds?

Fashion. I do not ask it as a due, brother; I am willing to receive it as a favour.

Lord Foppington. Then thou art willing to receive it anyhow, strike me speechless! But these are damned times to give money in; taxes are so great, repairs so exorbitant, tenants such rogues, and bouquets so dear, that the devil take me I'm reduced to that extremity in my cash, I have been forced to retrench in that one article of sweet pawder, till I have brought it down to five guineas a maunth—now judge, Tam, whether I can spare you five paunds.

Fashion. If you can't I must starve, that's all.—[*Aside.*] Damn him!

Lord Foppington. All I can say is, you should have been a better husband.

Fashion. Ouns! if you can't live upon ten thousand a year, how do you think I should do't upon two hundred?

Lord Foppington. Don't be in a passion, Tam, for passion is the most unbecoming thing in the waurld—to the face. Look you, I don't love to say anything to you to make you melancholy, but upon this occasion I must take leave to put you in mind that a running horse does require more attendance than a coach-horse. Nature has made some difference twixt you and me.

Fashion. Yes—she has made you older.—[*Aside.*] Plague take her.

Lord Foppington. That is not all, Tam.

Fashion. Why, what is there else?

Lord Foppington. [*Looks first on himself and then on his brother.*] Ask the ladies.

Fashion. Why, thou essence-bottle, thou musk-cat! dost thou then think thou hast any advantage over me but what Fortune has given thee?

Lord Foppington. I do, stap my vitals!

Fashion. Now, by all that's great and powerful, thou art the prince of coxcombs!

Lord Foppington. Sir, I am proud at being at the head of so prevailing a party.

Fashion. Will nothing provoke thee?—Draw, coward!

Lord Foppington. Look you, Tam, you know I have always taken you for a mighty dull fellow, and here is one of the foolishest plats broke out that I have seen a lang time. Your poverty makes life so burdensome to you, you would provoke me to a quarrel, in hopes either to slip through my lungs into my estate, or to get yourself run through the guts, to put an end to your pain. But I will disappoint you in both your designs; far, with the temper of a philasapher, and the discretion of a statesman—I shall leave the room with my sword in the scabbard.   [*Exit.*

Fashion. So! farewell, brother; and now, conscience, I defy thee. Lory!

Enter LORY.

Lory. Sir!

Fashion. Here's rare news, Lory; his lordship has given me a pill has purged off all my scruples.

Lory. Then my heart's at ease again: for I have been in a lamentable fright, sir, ever since your conscience had the impudence to intrude into your company.

Fashion. Be at peace; it will come there no more: my brother has given it a wring by the nose, and I have kicked it downstairs. So run away to the inn, get the chaise ready quickly, and bring it to Dame Coupler's without a moment's delay.

Lory. Then, sir, you are going straight about the fortune?

Fashion. I am.—Away—fly, Lory!

Lory. The happiest day I ever saw. I'm upon the wing already. Now then I shall get my wages.   [*Exeunt.*

SCENE II—*A Garden behind* LOVELESS's *Lodgings.*

Enter LOVELESS *and* SERVANT.

Loveless. Is my wife within?

Servant. No, sir, she has gone out this half-hour.

Loveless. Well, leave me.—[*Exit* SERVANT.] How strangely does my mind run on this widow!—Never was my heart so suddenly seized on before. That my wife should pick out her, of all womankind, to be her playfellow! But what fate does, let fate answer for: I sought it not. So! by Heavens! here she comes.

Enter BERINTHIA.

Berinthia. What makes you look so thoughtful, sir? I hope you are not ill.

Loveless. I was debating, madam, whether I was so or not, and that was it which made me look so thoughtful.

Berinthia. Is it then so hard a matter to decide? I thought all people were acquainted with their own bodies, though few people know their own minds.

Loveless. What if the distemper I suspect be in the mind?

Berinthia. Why then I'll undertake to prescribe you a cure.

Loveless. Alas! you undertake you know not what.

Berinthia. So far at least, then, you allow me to be a physician.

Loveless. Nay, I'll allow you to be so yet further: for I have reason to believe, should I put myself into your hands, you would increase my distemper.

Berinthia. How?

Loveless. Oh, you might betray me to my wife.

Berinthia. And so lose all my practice.

Loveless. Will you then keep my secret?

Berinthia. I will.

Loveless. Well—but swear it.

Berinthia. I swear by woman.

Loveless. Nay, that's swearing by my deity; swear by your own, and I shall believe you.

Berinthia. Well then, I swear by man!

Loveless. I'm satisfied. Now hear my symptoms, and give me your advice. The first were these; when I saw you at the play, a random glance you threw at first alarmed me. I could not turn my eyes from whence the danger came— I gazed upon you till my heart began to pant—nay, even now, on your approaching me, my illness is so increased that if you do not help me I shall, whilst you look on, consume to ashes.　　　　　　　　　　　　[*Takes her hand.*

Berinthia. O Lord, let me go! 'tis the plague, and we shall be infected.　　　　　　　　　　　　[*Breaking from him.*

Loveless. Then we'll die together, my charming angel.

Berinthia. O Gad! the devil's in you! Lord, let me go!— here's somebody coming.

Re-enter SERVANT.

Servant. Sir, my lady's come home, and desires to speak with you.

Loveless. Tell her I'm coming.—[*Exit* SERVANT.] But before I go, one glass of nectar to drink her health.

　　　　　　　　　　　　　　　　　　　　[*To* BERINTHIA.

Berinthia. Stand off, or I shall hate you, by Heavens!

Loveless. [*Kissing her.*] In matters of love, a woman's oath is no more to be minded than a man's.   [*Exit.*

Berinthia. Um!

Enter COLONEL TOWNLY.

Colonel Townly. [*Aside.*] So? what's here—Berinthia and Loveless—and in such close conversation!—I cannot now wonder at her indifference in excusing herself to me! —O rare woman!—Well then, let Loveless look to his wife, 'twill be but the retort courteous on both sides.—[*Aloud.*] Your servant, madam; I need not ask you how you do, you have got so good a colour.

Berinthia. No better than I used to have, I suppose.

Colonel Townly. A little more blood in your cheeks.

Berinthia. I have been walking!

Colonel Townly. Is that all? Pray was it Mr. Loveless went from here just now?

Berinthia. O yes—he has been walking with me.

Colonel Townly. He has!

Berinthia. Upon my word I think he is a very agreeable man; and there is certainly something particularly insinuating in his address.

Colonel Townly. [*Aside.*] So, so! she hasn't even the modesty to dissemble! [*Aloud.*] Pray, madam, may I, without impertinence, trouble you with a few serious questions?

Berinthia. As many as you please; but pray let them be as little serious as possible.

Colonel Townly. Is it not near two years since I have presumed to address you?

Berinthia. I don't know exactly—but it has been a tedious long time.

Colonel Townly. Have I not, during that period, had every reason to believe that my assiduities were far from being unacceptable?

Berinthia. Why, to do you justice, you have been extremely troublesome—and I confess I have been more civil to you than you deserved.

Colonel Townly. Did I not come to this place at your express desire, and for no purpose but the honour of meeting you?—and after waiting a month in disappointment, have you condescended to explain, or in the slightest way apologize for, your conduct?

Berinthia. O heavens! apologize for my conduct!—

apologize to you! O you barbarian! But pray now, my good
serious colonel, have you anything more to add?

Colonel Townly. Nothing, madam, but that after such
behaviour I am less surprised at what I saw just now; it
is not very wonderful that the woman who can trifle with
the delicate addresses of an honourable lover should be
found coquetting with the husband of her friend.

Berinthia. Very true: no more wonderful than it was
for this honourable lover to divert himself in the absence
of this coquette, with endeavouring to seduce his friend's
wife! O colonel, colonel, don't talk of honour or your
friend, for Heaven's sake!

Colonel Townly. [*Aside.*] 'Sdeath! how came she to suspect this!—[*Aloud.*] Really, madam, I don't understand
you.

Berinthia. Nay, nay, you saw I did not pretend to misunderstand you.—But here comes the lady; perhaps you
would be glad to be left with her for an explanation.

Colonel Townly. O madam, this recrimination is a poor
resource; and to convince you how much you are mistaken, I beg leave to decline the happiness you propose
me.—Madam, your servant.

Enter AMANDA. COLONEL TOWNLY *whispers to* AMANDA,
and exit.

Berinthia. [*Aside.*] He carries it off well, however; upon
my word, very well! How tenderly they part!—[*Aloud.*]
So, cousin; I hope you have not been chiding your admirer
for being with me? I assure you we have been talking of
you.

Amanda. Fy, Berinthia!—my admirer! will you never
learn to talk in earnest of anything?

Berinthia. Why this shall be in earnest, if you please;
for my part, I only tell you matter of fact.

Amanda. I'm sure there's so much jest and earnest in
what you say to me on this subject, I scarce know how to
take it. I have just parted with Mr. Loveless; perhaps it is
fancy, but I think there is an alteration in his manner
which alarms me.

Berinthia. And so you are jealous; is that all?

Amanda. That all! is jealousy, then, nothing?

Berinthia. It should be nothing, if I were in your case.

Amanda. Why, what would you do?

Berinthia. I'd cure myself.

Amanda. How?

Berinthia. Care as little for my husband as he did for me. Look you, Amanda, you may build castles in the air, and fume, and fret, and grow thin, and lean, and pale, and ugly, if you please; but I tell you, no man worth having is true to his wife, or ever was, or ever will be so.

Amanda. Do you then really think he's false to me? for I did not suspect him.

Berinthia. Think so? I am sure of it.

Amanda. You are sure on't?

Berinthia. Positively—he fell in love at the play.

Amanda. Right—the very same. But who could have told you this?

Berinthia. Um!—Oh, Townly! I suppose your husband has made him his confidant.

Amanda. O base Loveless! And what did Townly say on't?

Berinthia. [*Aside.*] So, so! why should she ask that?—[*Aloud.*] Say! why he abused Loveless extremely, and said all the tender things of you in the world.

Amanda. Did he?—Oh! my heart!—I'm very ill—dear Berinthia, don't leave me a moment. [*Exeunt.*

SCENE III—*Outside of* Sir Tunbelly Clumsy's *House*

Enter Tom Fashion *and* Lory.

Fashion. So here's our inheritance, Lory, if we can but get into possession. But methinks the seat of our family looks like Noah's ark, as if the chief part on't were designed for the fowls of the air, and the beasts of the field.

Lory. Pray, sir, don't let your head run upon the orders of building here: get but the heiress, let the devil take the house.

Fashion. Get but the house, let the devil take the heiress! I say.—But come, we have no time to squander; knock at the door.—[Lory *knocks two or three times at the gate.*] What the devil! have they got no ears in this house? —Knock harder.

Lory. Egad, sir, this will prove some enchanted castle; we shall have the giant come out by-and-by, with his club, and beat our brains out. [*Knocks again.*

Fashion. Hush, they come.

Servant. [*Within.*] Who is there?

Lory. Open the door and see: is that your country breeding?

Servant. Ay, but two words to that bargain.—Tummus, is the blunderbuss primed?

Fashion. Ouns! give 'em good words, Lory,—or we shall be shot here a fortune catching.

Lory. Egad, sir, I think you're in the right on't.—Ho! Mr. What-d'ye-call-'um, will you please to let us in? or are we to be left to grow like willows by your moat side?

SERVANT *appears at the window with a blunderbuss.*

Servant. Well naw, what's ya're business?

Fashion. Nothing, sir, but to wait upon Sir Tunbelly, with your leave.

Servant. To weat upon Sir Tunbelly! why, you'll find that's just as Sir Tunbelly pleases.

Fashion. But will you do me the favour, sir, to know whether Sir Tunbelly pleases or not?

Servant. Why, look you, d'ye see, with good words much may be done. Ralph, go thy ways, and ask Sir Tunbelly if he pleases to be waited upon—and dost hear, call to nurse, that she may lock up Miss Hoyden before the gates open.

Fashion. D'ye hear that, Lory?

Enter SIR TUNBELLY CLUMSY, *with* SERVANTS, *armed with guns, clubs, pitchforks, &c.*

Lory. Oh! [*Runs behind his master.*] O Lord! O Lord! Lord! we are both dead men!

Fashion. Fool! thy fear will ruin us. [*Aside to* LORY.

Lory. My fear, sir? 'sdeath, sir, I fear nothing.— [*Aside.*] Would I were well up to the chin in a horse-pond!

Sir Tunbelly. Who is it here hath any business with me?

Fashion. Sir, 'tis I, if your name be Sir Tunbelly Clumsy.

Sir Tunbelly. Sir, my name is Sir Tunbelly Clumsy, whether you have any business with me or not.—So you see I am not ashamed of my name, nor my face either.

Fashion. Sir, you have no cause that I know of.

Sir Tunbelly. Sir, if you have no cause either, I desire to know who you are; for, till I know your name, I shan't ask you to come into my house: and when I do know your name, 'tis six to four I don't ask you then.

Fashion. Sir, I hope you'll find this letter an authentic passport.   [*Gives him a letter.*

Sir Tunbelly. Cod's my life, from Mrs. Coupler!—I ask your lordship's pardon ten thousand times.—[*To a* SERVANT.] Here, run in a-doors quickly; get a Scotch coal fire in the parlour, set all the Turkey work chairs in their places, get the brass candlesticks out, and be sure stick the socket full of laurel—run!—[*Turns to* TOM FASHION.]— My lord, I ask your lordship's pardon.—[*To* SERVANT.] And, do you hear, run away to nurse; bid her let Miss Hoyden loose again.—[*Exit* SERVANT.] I hope your honour will excuse the disorder of my family. We are not used to receive men of your lordship's great quality every day. Pray, where are your coaches and servants, my lord?

Fashion. Sir, that I might give you and your daughter a proof how impatient I am to be nearer akin to you, I left my equipage to follow me, and came away post with only one servant.

Sir Tunbelly. Your lordship does me too much honour— it was exposing your person to too much fatigue and danger, I protest it was: but my daughter shall endeavour to make you what amends she can: and, though I say it that should not say it, Hoyden has charms.

Fashion. Sir, I am not a stranger to them, though I am to her; common fame has done her justice.

Sir Tunbelly. My lord, I am common fame's very grateful, humble servant. My lord, my girl's young—Hoyden is young, my lord: but this I must say for her, what she wants in art she has in breeding; and what's wanting in her age, is made good in her constitution.—So pray, my lord, walk in; pray, my lord, walk in.

Fashion. Sir, I wait upon you.   [*Exeunt.*

SCENE IV—*A Room in* SIR TUNBELLY CLUMSY'S *House*

MISS HOYDEN *discovered alone.*

Miss Hoyden. Sure, nobody was ever used as I am! I know well enough what other girls do, for all they think to make a fool o' me. It's well I have a husband a-coming, or ecod I'd marry the baker, I would so. Nobody can knock at the gate, but presently I must be locked up; and here's the young greyhound can run loose about the house all the day, so she can.—'Tis very well!

Nurse. [*Without opening the door.*] Miss Hoyden! miss, miss, miss! Miss Hoyden!

Enter Nurse.

Miss Hoyden. Well, what do you make such a noise for, eh? What do you din a body's ears for? Can't one be at quiet for you?

Nurse. What do I din your ears for? Here's one come will din your ears for you.

Miss Hoyden. What care I who's come? I care not a fig who comes, or who goes, so long as I must be locked up like the ale-cellar.

Nurse. That, miss, is for fear you should be drank before you are ripe.

Miss Hoyden. Oh, don't trouble your head about that; I'm as ripe as you, though not so mellow.

Nurse. Very well! Now I have a good mind to lock you up again, and not let you see my lord to-night.

Miss Hoyden. My lord: why, is my husband come?

Nurse. Yes, marry, is he; and a goodly person too.

Miss Hoyden. [*Hugs* Nurse.] Oh, my dear nurse, forgive me this once, and I'll never misuse you again; no, if I do, you shall give me three thumps on the back, and a great pinch by the cheek.

Nurse. Ah, the poor thing! see now it melts; it's as full of good-nature as an egg's full of meat.

Miss Hoyden. But, my dear nurse, don't lie now—is he come, by your troth?

Nurse. Yes, by my truly, is he.

Miss Hoyden. O Lord! I'll go and put on my laced tucker, though I'm locked up for a month for't.

[Exeunt. Miss Hoyden goes off capering,
and twirling her doll by its leg.

ACT FOUR

SCENE I—*A Room in* Sir Tunbelly Clumsy's *House*

Enter Miss Hoyden and Nurse.

Nurse. Well, miss, how do you like your husband that is to be?

Miss Hoyden. O Lord, nurse, I'm so overjoyed I can scarce contain myself!

Nurse. Oh, but you must have a care of being too fond; for men, nowadays, hate a woman that loves 'em.

Miss Hoyden. Love him! why, do you think I love him, nurse? Ecod I would not care if he was hanged, so I were but once married to him. No, that which pleases me is to think what work I'll make when I get to London; for when I am a wife and a lady both, ecod, I'll flaunt it with the best of 'em. Ay, and I shall have money enough to do so too, nurse.

Nurse. Ah, there's no knowing that, miss; for though these lords have a power of wealth indeed, yet, as I have heard say, they give it all to their sluts and their trulls, who joggle it about in their coaches, with a murrain to 'em, whilst poor madam sits sighing and wishing, and has not a spare half-crown to buy her a Practice of Piety.

Miss Hoyden. Oh, but for that, don't deceive yourself, nurse; for this I must say of my lord, he's as free as an open house at Christmas; for this very morning he told me I should have six hundred a year to buy pins. Now if he gives me six hundred a year to buy pins, what do you think he'll give me to buy petticoats?

Nurse. Ay, my dearest, he deceives thee foully, and he's no better than a rogue for his pains! These Londoners have got a gibberish with 'em would confound a gipsy. That which they call pin-money, is to buy everything in the versal world, down to their very shoe-knots. Nay, I have heard some folks say that some ladies, if they'll have gallants as they call 'em, are forced to find them out of their pin-money too.—But look, look, if his honour be not coming to you!—Now, if I were sure you would behave yourself handsomely, and not disgrace me that have brought you up, I'd leave you alone together.

Miss Hoyden. That's my best nurse; do as you'd be done by. Trust us together this once, and if I don't show my breeding, I wish I may never be married, but die an old maid.

Nurse. Well, this once I'll venture you. But if you disparage me——

Miss Hoyden. Never fear. [*Exit* NURSE.

Enter TOM FASHION.

Fashion. Your servant, madam; I'm glad to find you

alone, for I have something of importance to speak to you about.

Miss Hoyden. Sir (my lord, I meant), you may speak to me about what you please, I shall give you a civil answer.

Fashion. You give so obliging an one, it encourages me to tell you in a few words what I think, both for your interest and mine. Your father, I suppose you know, has resolved to make me happy in being your husband; and I hope I may obtain your consent to perform what he desires.

Miss Hoyden. Sir, I never disobey my father in anything but eating green gooseberries.

Fashion. So good a daughter must needs be an admirable wife. I am therefore impatient till you are mine, and hope you will so far consider the violence of my love, that you won't have the cruelty to defer my happiness so long as your father designs it.

Miss Hoyden. Pray, my lord, how long is that?

Fashion. Madam, a thousand years—a whole week.

Miss Hoyden. Why, I thought it was to be to-morrow morning, as soon as I was up. I'm sure nurse told me so.

Fashion. And it shall be to-morrow morning, if you'll consent.

Miss Hoyden. If I'll consent! Why I thought I was to obey you as my husband.

Fashion. That's when we are married. Till then, I'm to obey you.

Miss Hoyden. Why then, if we are to take it by turns, it's the same thing. I'll obey you now, and when we are married you shall obey me.

Fashion. With all my heart. But I doubt we must get nurse on our side, or we shall hardly prevail with the chaplain.

Miss Hoyden. No more we shan't, indeed; for he loves her better than he loves his pulpit, and would always be a-preaching to her by his good will.

Fashion. Why then, my dear, if you'll call her hither we'll persuade her presently.

Miss Hoyden. O Lud! I'll tell you a way how to persuade her to anything.

Fashion. How's that?

Miss Hoyden. Why tell her she's a handsome comely woman, and give her half a crown.

Fashion. Nay, if that will do, she shall have half a score of 'em.

Miss Hoyden. O gemini! for half that she'd marry you herself.—I'll run and call her.   [*Exit.*

Fashion. So! matters go on swimmingly. This is a rare girl, i'faith. I shall have a fine time on't with her at London.

Enter LORY.

So, Lory, what's the matter?

Lory. Here, sir—an intercepted packet from the enemy; your brother's postilion brought it. I knew the livery, pretended to be a servant of Sir Tunbelly's, and so got possession of the letter.

Fashion. [*Looks at the letter.*] Ouns! he tells Sir Tunbelly here that he will be with him this evening, with a large party to supper.—Egad, I must marry the girl directly.

Lory. Oh, zounds, sir, directly to be sure. Here she comes.   [*Exit.*

Fashion. And the old Jezebel with her.

Re-enter MISS HOYDEN *and* NURSE.

How do you do, good Mrs. Nurse? I desired your young lady would give me leave to see you, that I might thank you for your extraordinary care and kind conduct in her education: pray accept this small acknowledgment for it at present, and depend upon my further kindness when I shall be that happy thing, her husband. [*Gives her money.*

Nurse. [*Aside.*] Gold, by the maakins!—[*Aloud.*] Your honour's goodness is too great. Alas! all I can boast of is, I gave her pure and good milk, and so your honour would have said, an you had seen how the poor thing thrived, and how it would look up in my face, and crow and laugh, it would.

Miss Hoyden. [*To* NURSE, *taking her angrily aside.*] Pray, one word with you. Pr'ythee, nurse, don't stand ripping up old stories, to make one ashamed before one's love. Do you think such a fine proper gentleman as he is cares for a fiddlecome tale of a child? If you have a mind to make him have a good opinion of a woman, don't tell him what one did then, tell him what one can do now.— [*To* TOM FASHION.] I hope your honour will excuse my mis-manners to whisper before you. It was only to give some orders about the family.

Fashion. Oh, everything, madam, is to give way to business; besides, good housewifery is a very commendable quality in a young lady.

Miss Hoyden. Pray, sir, are young ladies good housewives at London-town? Do they darn their own linen?

Fashion. Oh no, they study how to spend money, not to save.

Miss Hoyden. Ecod, I don't know but that may be better sport, eh, nurse?

Fashion. Well, you have your choice, when you come there.

Miss Hoyden. Shall I? then, by my troth, I'll get there as fast as I can.—[*To* Nurse.] His honour desires you'll be so kind as to let us be married to-morrow.

Nurse. To-morrow, my dear madam?

Fashion. Ay, faith, nurse, you may well be surprised at miss's wanting to put it off so long. To-morrow! no, no; 'tis now, this very hour, I would have the ceremony performed.

Miss Hoyden. Ecod, with all my heart.

Nurse. O mercy! worse and worse!

Fashion. Yes, sweet nurse, now and privately; for all things being signed and sealed, why should Sir Tunbelly make us stay a week for a wedding-dinner?

Nurse. But if you should be married now, what will you do when Sir Tunbelly calls for you to be married?

Miss Hoyden. Why then we will be married again.

Nurse. What, twice, my child?

Miss Hoyden. Ecod, I don't care how often I'm married, not I.

Nurse. Well, I'm such a tender-hearted fool, I find I can refuse you nothing. So you shall e'en follow your own inventions.

Miss Hoyden. Shall I? O Lord, I could leap over the moon!

Fashion. Dear nurse, this goodness of yours shall be still more rewarded. But now you must employ your power with the chaplain, that he may do this friendly office too, and then we shall be all happy. Do you think you can prevail with him?

Nurse. Prevail with him! or he shall never prevail with me, I can tell him that.

Fashion. I'm glad to hear it; however, to strengthen your interest with him, you may let him know I have several fat livings in my gift, and that the first that falls shall be in your disposal.

Nurse. Nay, then, I'll make him marry more folks than one, I'll promise him!

Miss Hoyden. Faith, do, nurse, make him marry you too; I'm sure he'll do't for a fat living.

Fashion. Well, nurse, while you go and settle matters with him, your lady and I will go and take a walk in the garden.—[*Exit* Nurse.] Come, madam, dare you venture yourself alone with me? [*Takes* Miss Hoyden *by the hand.*

Miss Hoyden. Oh dear, yes, sir; I don't think you'll do anything to me, I need be afraid on.   [*Exeunt.*

SCENE II—Amanda's *Dressing-room*

Enter Amanda *followed by her* Maid.

Maid. If you please, madam, only to say whether you'll have me buy them or not?

Amanda. Yes—no—Go, teaser; I care not what you do. Pr'ythee, leave me.   [*Exit* Maid.

Enter Berinthia.

Berinthia. What, in the name of Jove, is the matter with you?

Amanda. The matter, Berinthia! I'm almost mad; I'm plagued to death.

Berinthia. Who is it that plagues you?

Amanda. Who do you think should plague a wife but her husband?

Berinthia. O, ho! is it come to that?—We shall have you wish yourself a widow, by-and-by.

Amanda. Would I were anything but what I am! A base, ungrateful man, to use me thus!

Berinthia. What, has he given you fresh reason to suspect his wandering?

Amanda. Every hour gives me reason.

Berinthia. And yet, Amanda, you perhaps at this moment cause in another's breast the same tormenting doubts and jealousies which you feel so sensibly yourself.

Amanda. Heaven knows I would not.

Berinthia. Why, you can't tell but there may be some one as tenderly attached to Townly, whom you boast of as your conquest, as you can be to your husband?

Amanda. I'm sure, I never encouraged his pretensions.

Berinthia. Psha! psha! no sensible man ever perseveres to love without encouragement. Why have you not treated him as you have Lord Foppington?

Amanda. Because he presumed not so far. But let us drop the subject. Men, not women, are riddles. Mr. Loveless now follows some flirt for variety, whom I'm sure he does not like so well as he does me.

Berinthia. That's more than you know, madam.

Amanda. Why, do you know the ugly thing?

Berinthia. I think I can guess at the person; but she's no such ugly thing neither.

Amanda. Is she very handsome?

Berinthia. Truly I think so.

Amanda. Whate'er she be, I'm sure he does not like her well enough to bestow anything more than a little outward gallantry upon her.

Berinthia. [*Aside.*] Outward gallantry! I can't bear this. —[*Aloud.*] Come, come, don't you be too secure, Amanda: while you suffer Townly to imagine that you do not detest him for his designs on you, you have no right to complain that your husband is engaged elsewhere. But here comes the person we were speaking of.

Enter COLONEL TOWNLY.

Colonel Townly. Ladies, as I come uninvited, I beg, if I intrude, you will use the same freedom in turning me out again.

Amanda. I believe it is near the time Loveless said he would be at home. He talked of accepting Lord Foppington's invitation to sup at Sir Tunbelly Clumsy's.

Colonel Townly. His lordship has done me the honour to invite me also. If you'll let me escort you, I'll let you into a mystery as we go, in which you must play a part when we arrive.

Amanda. But we have two hours yet to spare; the carriages are not ordered till eight, and it is not a five minutes' drive. So, cousin, let us keep the colonel to play at piquet with us, till Mr. Loveless comes home.

Berinthia. As you please, madam; but you know I have a letter to write.

Colonel Townly. Madam, you know you may command me, though I am a very wretched gamester.

Amanda. Oh, you play well enough to lose your money, and that's all the ladies require; and so, without any more ceremony, let us go into the next room, and call for cards and candles.   [*Exeunt.*

SCENE III—BERINTHIA'S *Dressing-room*

Enter LOVELESS.

Loveless. So, thus far all's well: I have got into her dressing-room, and it being dusk, I think nobody has perceived me steal into the house. I heard Berinthia tell my wife she had some particular letters to write this evening, before she went to Sir Tunbelly's, and here are the implements of correspondence.—How shall I muster up assurance to show myself when she comes? I think she has given me encouragement; and, to do my impudence justice, I have made the most of it.—I hear a door open, and some one coming. If it should be my wife, what the devil should I say? I believe she mistrusts me, and, by my life, I don't deserve her tenderness. However, I am determined to reform, though not yet. Ha! Berinthia!—So, I'll step in here, till I see what sort of humour she is in.

[*Goes into the closet.*

Enter BERINTHIA.

Berinthia. Was ever so provoking a situation! To think I should sit and hear him compliment Amanda to my face! I have lost all patience with them both! I would not for something have Loveless know what temper of mind they have piqued me into; yet I can't bear to leave them together. No, I'll put my papers away, and return, to disappoint them.—[*Goes to the closet.*]—O Lord! a ghost! a ghost! a ghost!

Re-enter LOVELESS.

Loveless. Peace, my angel; it's no ghost, but one worth a hundred spirits.

Berinthia. How, sir, have you had the insolence to presume to——run in again; here's somebody coming.

[LOVELESS *goes into the closet.*

Enter MAID.

Maid. O Lord, ma'am, what's the matter?

Berinthia. O Heavens! I'm almost frightened out of my wits! I thought verily I had seen a ghost, and 'twas nothing but a black hood pinned against the wall. You may go again; I am the fearfullest fool! [*Exit* MAID.

Re-enter LOVELESS.

Loveless. Is the coast clear?

Berinthia. The coast clear! Upon my word, I wonder at your assurance.

Loveless. Why, then, you wonder before I have given you a proof of it. But where's my wife?

Berinthia. At cards.

Loveless. With whom?

Berinthia. With Townly.

Loveless. Then we are safe enough.

Berinthia. You are so! Some husbands would be of another mind, were he at cards with their wives.

Loveless. And they'd be in the right on't, too; but I dare trust mine.

Berinthia. Indeed! and she, I doubt not, has the same confidence in you. Yet, do you think she'd be content to come and find you here?

Loveless. Egad, as you say, that's true!—Then for fear she should come, hadn't we better go into the next room, out of her way?

Berinthia. What, in the dark?

Loveless. Ay, or with a light, which you please.

Berinthia. You are certainly very impudent.

Loveless. Nay, then—let me conduct you, my angel!

Berinthia. Hold, hold! you are mistaken in your angel, I assure you.

Loveless. I hope not; for by this hand I swear——

Berinthia. Come, come, let go my hand, or I shall hate you!—I'll cry out, as I live!

Loveless. Impossible! you cannot be so cruel.

Berinthia. Ha! here's some one coming. Begone instantly.

Loveless. Will you promise to return, if I remain here?

Berinthia. Never trust myself in a room again with you while I live.

Loveless. But I have something particular to communicate to you.

Berinthia. Well, well, before we go to Sir Tunbelly's, I'll walk upon the lawn. If you are fond of a moonlight evening, you'll find me there.

Loveless. I'faith, they're coming here now! I take you at your word.   [*Exit into the closet.*

Berinthia. 'Tis Amanda, as I live! I hope she has not heard his voice; though I mean she should have her share of jealousy in her turn.

Enter AMANDA.

Amanda. Berinthia, why did you leave me?

Berinthia. I thought I only spoiled your party.

Amanda. Since you have been gone, Townly has attempted to renew his importunities. I must break with him, for I cannot venture to acquaint Mr. Loveless with his conduct.

Berinthia. Oh, no! Mr. Loveless mustn't know of it by any means.

Amanda. Oh, not for the world—I wish, Berinthia, you would undertake to speak to Townly on the subject.

Berinthia. Upon my word, it would be a very pleasant subject for me to talk upon! But, come, let us go back; and you may depend on't I'll not leave you together again, if I can help it.   [*Exeunt.*

Re-enter LOVELESS.

Loveless. So—so! a pretty piece of business I have overheard! Townly makes love to my wife, and I am not to know it for all the world. I must inquire into this—and, by Heaven, if I find that Amanda has, in the smallest degree—yet what have I been at here!—Oh, 'sdeath! that's no rule.

> That wife alone unsullied credit wins,
> Whose virtues can atone her husband's sins,
> Thus, while the man has other nymphs in view
> It suits the woman to be doubly true.   [*Exit.*

ACT FIVE

SCENE I—*The Garden behind* LOVELESS's *Lodgings*

Enter LOVELESS.

LOVELESS. Now, does she mean to make a fool of me, or not! I shan't wait much longer, for my wife will soon be inquiring for me to set out on our supping party. Suspense is at all times the devil, but of all modes of suspense, the watching for a loitering mistress is the worst.—But let me accuse her no longer; she approaches with one smile to o'erpay the anxieties of a year.

Enter BERINTHIA.

O Berinthia, what a world of kindness are you in my debt! had you stayed five minutes longer——

Berinthia. You would have gone, I suppose?

Loveless. Egad, she's right enough.   [*Aside.*

Berinthia. And I assure you 'twas ten to one that I came at all. In short, I begin to think you are too dangerous a being to trifle with; and as I shall probably only make a fool of you at last, I believe we had better let matters rest as they are.

Loveless. You cannot mean it, sure?

Berinthia. What more would you have me give to a married man?

Loveless. How doubly cruel to remind me of my misfortunes!

Berinthia. A misfortune to be married to so charming a woman as Amanda?

Loveless. I grant her all her merit, but——'sdeath! now see what you have done by talking of her—she's here, by all that's unlucky, and Townly with her.—I'll observe them.

Berinthia. O Gad, we had better get out of the way; for I should feel as awkward to meet her as you.

Loveless. Ay, if I mistake not, I see Townly coming this way also. I must see a little into this matter.   [*Steps aside.*

Berinthia. Oh, if that's your intention, I am no woman if I suffer myself to be outdone in curiosity.

[*Goes on the other side.*

Enter AMANDA.

Amanda. Mr. Loveless come home, and walking on the lawn! I will not suffer him to walk so late, though perhaps it is to show his neglect of me.—Mr. Loveless, I must speak with you.—Ha! Townly again!—How I am persecuted!

Enter COLONEL TOWNLY.

Colonel Townly. Madam, you seem disturbed.

Amanda. Sir, I have reason.

Colonel Townly. Whatever be the cause, I would to Heaven it were in my power to bear the pain, or to remove the malady.

Amanda. Your interference can only add to my distress.

Colonel Townly. Ah, madam, if it be the sting of unrequited love you suffer from, seek for your remedy in revenge: weigh well the strength and beauty of your charms, and rouse up that spirit a woman ought to bear. Disdain the false embraces of a husband. See at your feet a real lover; his zeal may give him title to your pity, although his merit cannot claim your love.

Loveless. So, so, very fine, i'faith!   [*Aside.*

Amanda. Why do you presume to talk to me thus? Is this your friendship to Mr. Loveless? I perceive you will compel me at last to acquaint him with your treachery.

Colonel Townly. He could not upbraid me if you were. —He deserves it from me; for he has not been more false to you than faithless to me.

Amanda. To you?

Colonel Townly. Yes, madam; the lady for whom he now deserts those charms which he was never worthy of, was mine by right; and, I imagine too, by inclination. Yes, madam, Berinthia, who now——

Amanda. Berinthia! Impossible!

Colonel Townly. 'Tis true, or may I never merit your attention. She is the deceitful sorceress who now holds your husband's heart in bondage.

Amanda. I will not believe it.

Colonel Townly. By the faith of a true lover, I speak from conviction. This very day I saw them together, and overheard——

Amanda. Peace, sir! I will not even listen to such slander—this is a poor device to work on my resentment, to listen to your insidious addresses. No, sir; though Mr. Loveless may be capable of error, I am convinced I cannot be deceived so grossly in him as to believe what you now report; and for Berinthia, you should have fixed on some more probable person for my rival than her who is my relation and my friend: for while I am myself free from guilt, I will never believe that love can beget injury, or confidence create ingratitude.

Colonel Townly. If I do not prove to you——

Amanda. You never shall have an opportunity. From the artful manner in which you first showed yourself to me, I might have been led, as far as virtue permitted, to have thought you less criminal than unhappy; but this last unmanly artifice merits at once my resentment and contempt.   [*Exit.*

Colonel Townly. Sure there's divinity about her; and she has dispensed some portion of honour's light to me: yet can I bear to lose Berinthia without revenge or compensation? Perhaps she is not so culpable as I thought her. I was mistaken when I began to think lightly of Amanda's virtue, and may be in my censure of my Berinthia. Surely I love her still, for I feel I should be happy to find myself in the wrong.   [*Exit.*

Re-enter LOVELESS *and* BERINTHIA.

Berinthia. Your servant, Mr. Loveless.

Loveless. Your servant, madam.

Berinthia. Pray what do you think of this?

Loveless. Truly, I don't know what to say.

Berinthia. Don't you think we steal forth two contemptible creatures?

Loveless. Why, tolerably so, I must confess.

Berinthia. And do you conceive it possible for you ever to give Amanda the least uneasiness again?

Loveless. No, I think we never should indeed.

Berinthia. We! why, monster, you don't pretend that I ever entertained a thought?

Loveless. Why then, sincerely and honestly, Berinthia, there is something in my wife's conduct which strikes me so forcibly, that if it were not for shame, and the fear of hurting you in her opinion, I swear I would follow her, confess my error, and trust to her generosity for forgiveness.

Berinthia. Nay, pr'ythee, don't let your respect for me

prevent you; for as my object in trifling with you was
nothing more than to pique Townly, and as I perceive he
has been actuated by a similar motive, you may depend
on't I shall make no mystery of the matter to him.

Loveless. By no means inform him: for though I may
choose to pass by his conduct without resentment, how
will he presume to look me in the face again?

Berinthia. How will you presume to look him in the face
again?

Loveless. He, who has dared to attempt the honour of
my wife!

Berinthia. You who have dared to attempt the honour of
his mistress! Come, come, be ruled by me, who affect more
levity than I have, and don't think of anger in this cause.
A readiness to resent injuries is a virtue only in those who
are slow to injure.

Loveless. Then I will be ruled by you; and when you
think proper to undeceive Townly, may your good qualities
make as sincere a convert of him as Amanda's have of me.
—When truth's extorted from us, then we own the robe
of virtue is a sacred habit.

> Could women but our secret counsel scan—
> Could they but reach the deep reserve of man—
> To keep our love they'd rate their virtue high,
> They live together, and together die.   [*Exeunt.*

SCENE II—*A Room in* Sir Tunbelly Clumsy's *House*

Enter Miss Hoyden, Nurse, *and* Tom Fashion.

Fashion. This quick despatch of the chaplain's I take
so kindly it shall give him claim to my favour as long as
I live, I assure you.

Miss Hoyden. And to mine too, I promise you.

Nurse. I most humbly thank your honours; and may
your children swarm about you like bees about a honey-
comb!

Miss Hoyden. Ecod, with all my heart—the more the
merrier, I say—ha, nurse?

Enter Lory.

Lory. One word with you, for Heaven's sake.
                    [*Taking* Tom Fashion *hastily aside.*

Fashion. What the devil's the matter?

Lory. Sir, your fortune's ruined if you are not married. Yonder's your brother arrived, with two coaches and six horses, twenty footmen, and a coat worth fourscore pounds —so judge what will become of your lady's heart.

Fashion. Is he in the house yet?

Lory. No, they are capitulating with him at the gate. Sir Tunbelly luckily takes him for an impostor; and I have told him that we have heard of this plot before.

Fashion. That's right.—[*Turning to* MISS HOYDEN.] My dear, here's a troublesome business my man tells me of, but don't be frightened; we shall be too hard for the rogue. Here's an impudent fellow at the gate (not knowing I was come hither incognito) has taken my name upon him, in hopes to run away with you.

Miss Hoyden. Oh, the brazen-faced varlet! it's well we are married, or maybe we might never have been so.

Fashion. [*Aside.*] Egad, like enough.—[*Aloud.*] Pr'ythee, nurse, run to Sir Tunbelly, and stop him from going to the gate before I speak to him.

Nurse. An't please your honour, my lady and I had better lock ourselves up till the danger be over.

Fashion. Do so, if you please.

Miss Hoyden. Not so fast; I won't be locked up any more, now I'm married.

Fashion. Yes, pray, my dear, do, till we have seized this rascal.

Miss Hoyden. Nay, if you'll pray me, I'll do anything.
[*Exit with* NURSE.

Fashion. Hark you, sirrah, things are better than you imagine. The wedding's over.

Lory. The devil it is, sir!   [*Capers about.*

Fashion. Not a word—all's safe—but Sir Tunbelly don't know it, nor must not yet. So I am resolved to brazen the brunt of the business out, and have the pleasure of turning the impostor upon his lordship, which I believe may easily be done.

Enter SIR TUNBELLY CLUMSY.

Did you ever hear, sir, of so impudent an undertaking?

Sir Tunbelly. Never, by the mass; but we'll tickle him, I'll warrant you.

Fashion. They tell me, sir, he has a great many people with him, disguised like servants.

Sir Tunbelly. Ay, ay, rogues enow, but we have mastered them. We only fired a few shot over their heads, and the regiment scoured in an instant.—Here, Tummus, bring in your prisoner.

Fashion. If you please, Sir Tunbelly, it will be best for me not to confront this fellow yet, till you have heard how far his impudence will carry him.

Sir Tunbelly. Egad, your lordship is an ingenious person. Your lordship, then, will please to step aside.

Lory. [*Aside.*] 'Fore heavens, I applaud my master's modesty!   [*Exit with* TOM FASHION.

Enter SERVANTS, *with* LORD FOPPINGTON *disarmed.*

Sir Tunbelly. Come, bring him along, bring him along.

Lord Foppington. What the plague do you mean, gentlemen? is it fair time, that you are all drunk before supper?

Sir Tunbelly. Drunk, sirrah! here's an impudent rogue for you now. Drunk or sober, bully, I'm a justice o' the peace, and know how to deal with strollers.

Lord Foppington. Strollers!

Sir Tunbelly. Ay, strollers. Come, give an account of yourself. What's your name? where do you live? do you pay scot and lot? Come, are you a freeholder or a copyholder?

Lord Foppington. And why dost thou ask me so many impertinent questions?

Sir Tunbelly. Because I'll make you answer 'em, before I have done with you, you rascal, you!

Lord Foppington. Before Gad, all the answer I can make to them is, that you are a very extraordinary old fellow, stap my vitals.

Sir Tunbelly. Nay, if thou art joking deputy-lieutenants, we know how to deal with you.—Here, draw a warrant for him immediately.

Lord Foppington. A warrant! What the devil is't thou wouldst be at, old gentleman?

Sir Tunbelly. I would be at you, sirrah, if my hands were not tied as a magistrate, and with these two double fists beat your teeth down your throat, you dog, you!
                                          [*Driving him.*

Lord Foppington. And why wouldst thou spoil my face at that rate?

Sir Tunbelly. For your design to rob me of my daughter, villain.

Lord Foppington. Rob thee of thy daughter! Now do I begin to believe I am in bed and asleep, and that all this is but a dream. Pr'ythee, old father, wilt thou give me leave to ask thee one question?

Sir Tunbelly. I can't tell whether I will or not, till I know what it is.

Lord Foppington. Why, then, it is, whether thou didst not write to my Lord Foppington, to come down and marry thy daughter?

Sir Tunbelly. Yes, marry, did I, and my Lord Foppington is come down, and shall marry my daughter before she's a day older.

Lord Foppington. Now give me thy hand, old dad; I thought we should understand one another at last.

Sir Tunbelly. The fellow's mad!—Here, bind him hand and foot.   [*They bind him.*

Lord Foppington. Nay, pr'ythee, knight, leave fooling; thy jest begins to grow dull.

Sir Tunbelly. Bind him, I say—he's mad: bread and water, a dark room, and a whip, may bring him to his senses again.

Lord Foppington. Pr'ythee, Sir Tunbelly, why should you take such an aversion to the freedom of my address as to suffer the rascals thus to skewer down my arms like a rabbit?—[*Aside.*] Egad, if I don't awake, by all that I can see, this is like to prove one of the most impertinent dreams that ever I dreamt in my life.

Re-enter MISS HOYDEN *and* NURSE.

Miss Hoyden. [*Going up to* LORD FOPPINGTON.] Is this he that would have run—Fough, how he stinks of sweets! —Pray, father, let him be dragged through the horse-pond.

Lord Foppington. This must be my wife, by her natural inclination to her husband.   [*Aside.*

Miss Hoyden. Pray, father, what do you intend to do with him—hang him?

Sir Tunbelly. That, at least, child.

Nurse. Ay, and it's e'en too good for him too.

Lord Foppington. Madame la gouvernante, I presume: hitherto this appears to me to be one of the most extraordinary families that ever man of quality matched into.

[*Aside.*

Sir Tunbelly. What's become of my lord, daughter?

Miss Hoyden. He's just coming, sir.

Lord Foppington. My lord! what does he mean by that,
now?   [*Aside.*

Re-enter TOM FASHION *and* LORY.

Stap my vitals, Tam, now the dream's out!   [*Runs.*

Fashion. Is this the fellow, sir, that designed to trick me
of your daughter?

Sir Tunbelly. This is he, my lord. How do you like him?
Is not he a pretty fellow to get a fortune?

Fashion. I find by his dress he thought your daughter
might be taken with a beau.

Miss Hoyden. Oh, gemini! is this a beau? let me see
him again. [*Surveys him.*] Ha! I find a beau is no such
ugly thing, neither.

Fashion. [*Aside.*] Egad, she'll be in love with him
presently—I'll e'en have him sent away to jail.—[*To* LORD
FOPPINGTON.] Sir, though your undertaking shows you a
person of no extraordinary modesty, I suppose you ha'n't
confidence enough to expect much favour from me?

Lord Foppington. Strike me dumb, Tam, thou art a
very impudent fellow.

Nurse. Look, if the varlet has not the effrontery to call
his lordship plain Thomas!

Lord Foppington. My Lord Foppington, shall I beg one
word with your lordship?

Nurse. Ho, ho! it's my lord with him now! See how
afflictions will humble folks.

Miss Hoyden. Pray, my lord—[*To* FASHION.]—don't let
him whisper too close, lest he bite your ear off.

Lord Foppington. I am not altogether so hungry as
your ladyship is pleased to imagine.—[*Aside to* TOM
FASHION.] Look you, Tam, I am sensible I have not been
so kind to you as I ought, but I hope you'll forgive what's
past, and accept of the five thousand pounds I offer—thou
mayst live in extreme splendour with it, stap my vitals!

Fashion. It's a much easier matter to prevent a disease
than to cure it. A quarter of that sum would have secured
your mistress, twice as much cannot redeem her.

[*Aside to* LORD FOPPINGTON.

Sir Tunbelly. Well, what says he?

Fashion. Only the rascal offered me a bribe to let him
go.

Sir Tunbelly. Ay, he shall go, with a plague to him!—
lead on, constable.

Enter SERVANT.

Servant. Sir, here is Muster Loveless, and Muster Colonel Townly, and some ladies to wait on you.

[*To* TOM FASHION.

Lory. [*Aside to* TOM FASHION.] So, sir, what will you do now?

Fashion. [*Aside to* LORY.] Be quiet; they are in the plot. —[*Aloud.*] Only a few friends, Sir Tunbelly, whom I wish to introduce to you.

Lord Foppington. Thou art the most impudent fellow, Tam, that ever nature yet brought into the world.—Sir Tunbelly, strike me speechless, but these are my friends and acquaintances, and my guests, and they will soon inform thee whether I am the true Lord Foppington or not.

Enter LOVELESS, COLONEL TOWNLY, AMANDA, *and* BERINTHIA.—LORD FOPPINGTON *accosts them as they pass, but none answer him.*

Fashion. So, gentlemen, this is friendly; I rejoice to see you.

Colonel Townly. My lord, we are fortunate to be the witnesses of your lordship's happiness.

Loveless. But your lordship will do us the honour to introduce us to Sir Tunbelly Clumsy?

Amanda. And us to your lady.

Lord Foppington. Gad take me, but they are all in a story!   [*Aside.*

Sir Tunbelly. Gentlemen, you do me much honour; my Lord Foppington's friends will ever be welcome to me and mine.

Fashion. My love, let me introduce you to these ladies.

Miss Hoyden. By goles, they look so fine and so stiff, I am almost ashamed to come nigh 'em.

Amanda. A most engaging lady indeed!

Miss Hoyden. Thank ye, ma'am.

Berinthia. And I doubt not will soon distinguish herself in the beau monde.

Miss Hoyden. Where is that?

Fashion. You'll soon learn, my dear.

Loveless. But Lord Foppington——

Lord Foppington. Sir!

Loveless. Sir! I was not addressing myself to you, sir!— Pray who is this gentleman? He seems rather in a singular predicament——

Colonel Townly. For so well-dressed a person, a little oddly circumstanced, indeed.

Sir Tunbelly. Ha! ha! ha!—So, these are your friends and your guests, ha, my adventurer?

Lord Foppington. I am struck dumb with their impudence, and cannot positively say whether I shall ever speak again or not.

Sir Tunbelly. Why, sir, this modest gentleman wanted to pass himself upon me as Lord Foppington, and carry off my daughter.

Loveless. A likely plot to succeed, truly, ha! ha!

Lord Foppington. As Gad shall judge me, Loveless, I did not expect this from thee. Come, pr'ythee confess the joke; tell Sir Tunbelly that I am the real Lord Foppington, who yesterday made love to thy wife; was honoured by her with a slap on the face, and afterwards pinked through the body by thee.

Sir Tunbelly. A likely story, truly, that a peer would behave thus.

Loveless. A pretty fellow, indeed, that would scandalize the character he wants to assume; but what will you do with him, Sir Tunbelly?

Sir Tunbelly. Commit him, certainly, unless the bride and bridegroom choose to pardon him.

Lord Foppington. Bride and bridegroom! For Gad's sake, Sir Tunbelly, 'tis tarture to me to hear you call 'em so.

Miss Hoyden. Why, you ugly thing, what would you have him call us—dog and cat?

Lord Foppington. By no means, miss; for that sounds ten times more like man and wife than t'other.

Sir Tunbelly. A precious rogue this to come a-wooing!

Re-enter SERVANT.

Servant. There are some gentlefolks below to wait upon Lord Foppington.   [*Exit.*

Colonel Townly. 'Sdeath, Tom, what will you do now?
[*Aside to* TOM FASHION.

Lord Foppington. Now, Sir Tunbelly, here are witnesses who I believe are not corrupted.

Sir Tunbelly. Peace, fellow!—Would your lordship choose to have your guests shown here, or shall they wait till we come to 'em?

Fashion. I believe, Sir Tunbelly, we had better not have these visitors here yet.—[*Aside.*] Egad, all must out.

Loveless. Confess, confess; we'll stand by you.

[*Aside to* TOM FASHION.

Lord Foppington. Nay, Sir Tunbelly, I insist on your calling evidence on both sides—and if I do not prove that fellow an impostor——

Fashion. Brother, I will save you the trouble, by now confessing that I am not what I have passed myself for.— Sir Tunbelly, I am a gentleman, and I flatter myself a man of character; but 'tis with great pride I assure you I am not Lord Foppington.

Sir Tunbelly. Ouns!—what's this?—an impostor?—a cheat?—fire and faggots, sir, if you are not Lord Foppington, who the devil are you?

Fashion. Sir, the best of my condition is, I am your son-in-law; and the worst of it is, I am brother to that noble peer.

Lord Foppington. Impudent to the last, Gad dem me!

Sir Tunbelly. My son-in-law! not yet, I hope.

Fashion. Pardon me, sir; thanks to the goodness of your chaplain, and the kind offices of this gentlewoman.

Lory. 'Tis true indeed, sir; I gave your daughter away, and Mrs. Nurse, here, was clerk.

Sir Tunbelly. Knock that rascal down!—But speak, Jezebel, how's this?

Nurse. Alas! your honour, forgive me; I have been over-reached in this business as well as you. Your worship knows, if the wedding-dinner had been ready, you would have given her away with your own hands.

Sir Tunbelly. But how durst you do this without acquainting me?

Nurse. Alas! if your worship had seen how the poor thing begged and prayed, and clung and twined about me like ivy round an old wall, you would say, I who had nursed it, and reared it, must have had a heart like stone to refuse it.

Sir Tunbelly. Ouns! I shall go mad! Unloose my lord there, you scoundrels!

Lord Foppington. Why, when these gentlemen are at leisure, I should be glad to congratulate you on your son-in-law, with a little more freedom of address.

Miss Hoyden. Egad, though, I don't see which is to be my husband after all.

Loveless. Come, come, Sir Tunbelly, a man of your understanding must perceive that an affair of this kind is not to be mended by anger and reproaches.

Colonel Townly. Take my word for it, Sir Tunbelly, you are only tricked into a son-in-law you may be proud of: my friend Tom Fashion is as honest a fellow as ever breathed.

Loveless. That he is, depend on't; and will hunt or drink with you most affectionately: be generous, old boy, and forgive them——

Sir Tunbelly. Never! the hussy!—when I had set my heart on getting her a title.

Lord Foppington. Now, Sir Tunbelly, that I am untrussed—give me leave to thank thee for the very extraordinary reception I have met with in thy damned, execrable mansion; and at the same time to assure you, that of all the bumpkins and blockheads I have had the misfortune to meet with, thou art the most obstinate and egregious, strike me ugly!

Sir Tunbelly. What's this! I believe you are both rogues alike.

Lord Foppington. No, Sir Tunbelly, thou wilt find to thy unspeakable mortification, that I am the real Lord Foppington, who was to have disgraced myself by an alliance with a clod; and that thou hast matched thy girl to a beggarly younger brother of mine, whose title deeds might be contained in thy tobacco-box.

Sir Tunbelly. Puppy! puppy!—I might prevent their being beggars, if I chose it; for I could give 'em as good a rent-roll as your lordship.

Lord Foppington. Ay, old fellow, but you will not do that—for that would be acting like a Christian, and thou art a barbarian, stap my vitals.

Sir Tunbelly. Udzookers! now six such words more, and I'll forgive them directly.

Loveless. 'Slife, Sir Tunbelly, you should do it, and bless yourself—Ladies, what say you?

Amanda. Good Sir Tunbelly, you must consent.

Berinthia. Come, you have been young yourself, Sir Tunbelly.

Sir Tunbelly. Well then, if I must, I must; but turn—turn that sneering lord out, however, and let me be revenged on somebody. But first look whether I am a barbarian or not; there, children, I join your hands; and when I'm in a better humour, I'll give you my blessing.

Loveless. Nobly done, Sir Tunbelly! and we shall see you dance at a grandson's christening yet.

Miss Hoyden. By goles, though, I don't understand this! What! an't I to be a lady after all? only plain Mrs.—— What's my husband's name, nurse?

Nurse. Squire Fashion.

Miss Hoyden. Squire, is he?—Well, that's better than nothing.

Lord Foppington. [*Aside.*] Now I will put on a philosophic air, and show these people, that it is not possible to put a man of my quality out of countenance.—[*Aloud.*] Dear Tam, since things are fallen out, pr'ythee give me leave to wish thee joy; I do it *de bon cœur*, strike me dumb! You have married into a family of great politeness and uncommon elegance of manners, and your bride appears to be a lady beautiful in person, modest in her deportment, refined in her sentiments, and of nice morality, split my windpipe!

Miss Hoyden. By goles, husband, break his bones if he calls me names!

Fashion. Your lordship may keep up your spirits with your grimace, if you please; I shall support mine, by Sir Tunbelly's favour, with this lady and three thousand pounds a year.

Lord Foppington. Well, adieu, Tam!—Ladies, I kiss your hands!—Sir Tunbelly, I shall now quit this thy den; but while I retain the use of my arms, I shall ever remember thou art a demned horrid savage; Ged demn me! [*Exit.*

Sir Tunbelly. By the mass, 'tis well he's gone—for I should ha' been provoked, by-and-by, to ha' dun un a mischief. Well, if this is a lord, I think Hoyden has luck on her side, in troth.

Colonel Townly. She has, indeed, Sir Tunbelly.—But I hear the fiddles; his lordship, I know, has provided 'em.

Loveless. Oh, a dance and a bottle, Sir Tunbelly, by all means!

Sir Tunbelly. I had forgot the company below; well— what—we must be merry, then, ha? and dance and drink, ha? Well, 'fore George, you shan't say I do these things by halves. Son-in-law there looks like a hearty rogue, so we'll have a night on't: and which of these ladies will be the old man's partner, ha?—Ecod, I don't know how I came to be in so good a humour.

Berinthia. Well, Sir Tunbelly, my friend and I both will endeavour to keep you so: you have done a generous action, and are entitled to our attention. If you should be at a loss to divert your new guests, we will assist you to relate to them the plot of your daughter's marriage, and his lordship's deserved mortification; a subject which perhaps may afford no bad evening's entertainment.

Sir Tunbelly. Ecod, with all my heart; though I am a main bungler at a long story.

Berinthia. Never fear; we will assist you, if the tale is judged worth being repeated; but of this you may be assured, that while the intention is evidently to please, British auditors will ever be indulgent to the errors of the performance.   [*Exeunt omnes.*

THE SCHOOL FOR SCANDAL

A Comedy

A PORTRAIT

By R. B. Sheridan, Esq.

TELL me, ye prim adepts in Scandal's school,
Who rail by precept, and detract by rule,
Lives there no character, so tried, so known,
So decked with grace, and so unlike your own,
That even you assist her fame to raise,
Approve by envy, and by silence praise!
Attend!—a model shall attract your view—
Daughters of calumny, I summon you!
You shall decide if this a portrait prove,
Or fond creation of the Muse and Love.
Attend, ye virgin critics, shrewd and sage,
Ye matron censors of this childish age,
Whose peering eye and wrinkled front declare
A fixed antipathy to young and fair;
By cunning, cautious; or by nature, cold,
In maiden madness, virulently bold!
Attend, ye skilled to coin the precious tale,
Creating proof, where innuendos fail!
Whose practised memories, cruelly exact,
Omit no circumstance, except the fact!—
Attend, all ye who boast,—or old or young,—
The living libel of a slanderous tongue!
So shall my theme as far contrasted be,
As saints by fiends or hymns by calumny.

[1] Sheridan's dedicatory verses to Mrs. Crewe, according to his own subsequent account, 'were sent with a MS. copy of the play finely bound' [the Crewe MS. copy, with the author's handwritten corrections]. They early circulated in manuscript, as Horace Walpole attests in a letter of October 8, 1777, but his hope that 'they will not long retain their MS.-hood' proved idle. An undated letter of Sheridan, written late in life to his second wife, was prompted by their unauthorized appearance, 'incorrectly printed,' in a 'newspaper professing to *publish* for the *first time* some verses of mine to Mrs. (now Lady) Crewe.' After Sheridan's death, they were included in the Murray (1821) edition of Sheridan's *Works* (II, 3-7) in the form thereafter habitually accepted.

Come, gentle Amoret (for 'neath that name[2]
In worthier verse is sung thy beauty's fame),
Come—for but thee who seeks the Muse? and while
Celestial blushes check thy conscious smile,
With timid grace and hesitating eye,
The perfect model which I boast supply:—
Vain Muse! couldst thou the humblest sketch create
Of her, or slightest charm couldst imitate—
Could thy blest strain in kindred colors trace
The faintest wonder of her form and face—
Poets would study the immortal line,
And Reynolds[3] own *his* art subdued by thine;
That art, which well might added lustre give
To nature's best and heaven's superlative:
On Granby's[4] cheek might bid new glories rise,
Or point a purer beam from Devon's[5] eyes!
Hard is the task to shape that beauty's praise,
Whose judgment scorns the homage flattery pays?
But praising Amoret we cannot err,
No tongue o'ervalues heaven, or flatters her!
Yet she by fate's perverseness—she alone
Would doubt our truth, nor deem such praise her own!
Adorning fashion, unadorned by dress,
Simple from taste, and not from carelessness;
Discreet in gesture, in deportment mild,
Not stiff with prudence, nor uncouthly wild:
No state has Amoret; no studied mien;
She frowns no *goddess*, and she moves no *queen*,
The softer charm that in her manner lies
Is framed to captivate, yet not surprise;
It justly suits th' expression of her face,—
'Tis less than dignity, and more than grace!
On her pure cheek the native hue is such,
That, formed by heaven to be admired so much,
The hand divine, with a less partial care,
Might well have fixed a fainter crimson there,
And bade the gentle inmate of her breast—
Inshrinèd Modesty—supply the rest.
But who the peril of her lips shall paint?

[2] Fox had extolled Mrs. Crewe as *Amoret* in verses printed at Walpole's
Strawberry Hill Press in 1775.
[3] Sir Joshua Reynolds (1723-1792) had portrayed Mrs. Sheridan as St.
Cecilia in 1775.
[4] Mary Isabella, Marchioness of Granby, later Duchess of Rutland.
[5] Georgiana, Duchess of Devonshire.

Strip them of smiles—still, still all words are faint!
But moving Love himself appears to teach
Their action, though denied to rule her speech;
And thou who seest her speak, and dost not hear,
Mourn not her distant accents 'scape thine ear;
Viewing those lips, thou still may'st make pretense
To judge of what she says, and swear 'tis sense:
Clothed with such grace, with such expression fraught,
They move in meaning, and they pause in thought!
But dost thou farther watch, with charmed surprise,
The mild irresolution of her eyes,
Curious to mark how frequent they repose,
In brief eclipse and momentary close—
Ah! seest thou not an ambushed Cupid there,
Too tim'rous of his charge, with jealous care
Veils and unveils those beams of heav'nly light,
Too full, too fatal else, for mortal sight?
Nor yet, such pleasing vengeance fond to meet,
In pard'ning dimples hope a safe retreat.
What though her peaceful breast should ne'er allow
Subduing frowns to arm her altered brow,
By Love, I swear, and by his gentle wiles,
More fatal still the mercy of her smiles!
Thus lovely, thus adorned, possessing all
Of bright or fair that can to woman fall,
The height of vanity might well be thought
Prerogative in her, and Nature's fault.
Yet gentle Amoret, in mind supreme
As well as charms, rejects the vainer theme;
And, half mistrustful of her beauty's store,
She barbs with wit those darts too keen before:—
Read in all knowledge that her sex should reach,
Though Greville,[6] or the Muse, should deign to teach,
Fond to improve, nor tim'rous to discern
How far it is a woman's grace to learn;
In Millar's[7] dialect she would not prove
Apollo's priestess, but Apollo's love,
Graced by those signs which truth delights to own,
The timid blush, and mild submitted tone:
Whate'er she says, though sense appear throughout,

[6] Mrs. Fulke Greville, mother of Mrs. Crewe. Sheridan dedicated *The Critic* 'To Mrs. Greville' (see p. 313).
[7] Lady Miller (Millar), an eighteenth-century Mrs. Leo Hunter, whose literary 'assemblies' near Bath were notorious.

Displays the tender hue of female doubt;
Decked with that charm, how lovely wit appears,
How graceful *science*, when that robe she wears!
Such too her talents, and her bent of mind,
As speak a sprightly heart by thought refined:
A taste for mirth, by contemplation schooled,
A turn for ridicule, by candor ruled,
A scorn of folly, which she tries to hide;
An awe of talent, which she owns with pride!

   Peace, idle Muse! no more thy strain prolong,
But yield a theme, thy warmest praises wrong;
Just to her merit, though thou canst not raise
Thy feeble verse, behold th' acknowledged praise
Has spread conviction through the envious train,
And cast a fatal gloom o'er Scandal's reign!
And lo! each pallid hag, with blistered tongue,
Mutters assent to all thy zeal has sung—
Owns all the colors just—the outline true:
Thee my inspirer, and my *model*—CREWE!

DRAMATIS PERSONÆ

Sir Peter Teazle	Mr. King
Sir Oliver Surface	Mr. Yates
Joseph Surface	Mr. Palmer
Charles Surface	Mr. Smith
Crabtree	Mr. Parsons
Sir Benjamin Backbite	Mr. Dodd
Rowley	Mr. Aickin
Trip	Mr. LaMash
Moses	Mr. Baddeley
Snake	Mr. Packer
Careless	Mr. Farren
Lady Teazle	Mrs. Abington
Maria	Miss P. Hopkins
Lady Sneerwell	Miss Sherry
Mrs. Candour	Miss Pope

and other Companions to Charles [Surface],
Servants, etc.

[Scene—London]

DRAMATIS PERSONÆ] The Crewe MS. is here followed both in the order
of characters and in indication of actors' names. The cast is that of the
original production in May, 1777. The part of Sir Toby Bumper appears
neither in the *Dram. Pers.* nor in the heading of the scene (III. iii) in
which he figures as one of the 'other Companions to Charles.' Originally,
his song was given to Careless (Rae text), and later (in the Crewe MS.)
provision for its transfer was made by introducing Sir Toby Bumper into
the text. The rôle was early taken by Mr. Gaudry, but, as here indicated,
the stress was on the song and not on the nominal character-part that
served the turn. Neither the Crewe MS. nor Sheridan in correcting it
specified Sir Toby in the *Dram. Pers.* (For M.'s change to Sir Harry, see
text, III. iii.)

PROLOGUE

SPOKEN BY MR. KING[1]

Written by D. Garrick, Esq.

A School for Scandal! tell me, I beseech you,
Needs there a school this modish art to teach you?
No need of lessons now, the knowing think—
We might as well be taught to eat and drink.
Caused by a dearth of scandal, should the vapors
Distress our fair ones—let 'em read the papers;
Their pow'rful mixtures such disorders hit;
Crave what they will, there's *quantum sufficit*.[2]
  'Lord!' cries my Lady Wormwood (who loves tattle,
And puts much salt and pepper in her prattle),
Just ris'n at noon, all night at cards when threshing
Strong tea and scandal—'Bless me, how refreshing!
Give me the papers, Lisp—how bold and free! [*Sips.*]
Last night Lord L—— [sips] was caught with Lady
  D——
For aching heads what charming sal volatile! [*Sips.*]
If Mrs. B—— will still continue flirting,
We hope she'll DRAW, *or we'll* UNDRAW *the curtain.*
Fine satire, poz[3]—in public all abuse it,
But, by ourselves [*sips*], our praise we can't refuse it.
Now, Lisp, read *you*—there, at that dash and star.'[4]
'Yes, ma'am.—*A certain Lord had best beware,*
Who lives not twenty miles from Grosv'nor Square;
For should he Lady W—— find willing,
WORMWOOD *is bitter*'——'Oh! that's me! the villain!
Throw it behind the fire, and never more
Let that vile paper come within my door.'—
  Thus at our friends we laugh, who feel the dart;

---

[1] Thomas King, the original Sir Peter Teazle.
[2] Plenty.
[3] Positively.
[4] A frequent method of veiled reference to the names of those involved in fashionable intrigues. See the early allusion to the *Têtes-à-Têtes* in the *Town and Country Magazine* (S. for S., I. i.).

To reach our feelings, we ourselves must smart.
Is our young bard so young, to think that he
Can stop the full spring-tide of calumny?
Knows he the world so little, and its trade?
Alas! the devil is sooner raised than laid.
So strong, so swift, the monster there's no gagging:
Cut Scandal's head off—still the tongue is wagging.
Proud of your smiles once lavishly bestow'd,
Again your young Don Quixote[5] takes the road:
To show his gratitude, he draws his pen,
And seeks this hydra, Scandal, in his den.
For your applause all perils he would through— ⎫
He'll fight—that's *write*—a cavalliero true,   ⎬
Till every drop of blood—that's *ink*—is spilt for you. ⎭

[5] Sheridan had first ridiculed the sentimental drama and novel in *The Rivals*.

THE SCHOOL FOR SCANDAL

ACT ONE

SCENE I—LADY SNEERWELL's *house*

LADY SNEERWELL *at the dressing-table*—SNAKE
drinking chocolate

LADY SNEERWELL. The paragraphs, you say, Mr. Snake, were all inserted?

Snake. They were, madam, and as I copied them myself in a feigned hand, there can be no suspicion whence they came.

Lady Sneerwell. Did you circulate the reports of Lady Brittle's intrigue with Captain Boastall?

Snake. That is in as fine a train as your ladyship could wish,—in the common course of things, I think it must reach Mrs. Clackit's ears within four-and-twenty hours; and then, you know, the business is as good as done.

Lady Sneerwell. Why, truly, Mrs. Clackit has a very pretty talent, and a great deal of industry.

Snake. True, madam, and has been tolerably successful in her day:—to my knowledge, she has been the cause of six matches being broken off, and three sons being disinherited, of four forced elopements, as many close confinements, nine separate maintenances, and two divorces;—nay, I have more than once traced her causing a *Tête-à-Tête* in the *Town and Country Magazine,* when the parties perhaps had never seen each other's faces before in the course of their lives.

Lady Sneerwell. She certainly has talents, but her manner is gross.

Snake. 'Tis very true,—she generally designs well, has a free tongue, and a bold invention; but her coloring is too dark, and her outline often extravagant. She wants that *delicacy* of *hint*, and *mellowness* of *sneer*, which distinguish your ladyship's scandal.

Lady Sneerwell. Ah! you are partial, Snake.

Snake. Not in the least; everybody allows that Lady Sneerwell can do more with a *word* or a *look* than many can with the most labored detail, even when they happen to have a little truth on their side to support it.

Lady Sneerwell. Yes, my dear Snake; and I am no hypocrite to deny the satisfaction I reap from the success of my efforts. Wounded myself, in the early part of my life, by the envenomed tongue of slander, I confess I have since known no pleasure equal to the reducing others to the level of my own injured reputation.

Snake. Nothing can be more natural. But, Lady Sneerwell, there is one affair in which you have lately employed me, wherein, I confess, I am at a loss to guess your motives.

Lady Sneerwell. I conceive you mean with respect to my neighbor, Sir Peter Teazle, and his family?

Snake. I do; here are two young men, to whom Sir Peter has acted as a kind of guardian since their father's death; the elder possessing the most amiable character, and universally well spoken of; the youngest, the most dissipated and extravagant young fellow in the kingdom, without friends or character,—the former an avowed admirer of your ladyship, and apparently your favorite; the latter attached to Maria, Sir Peter's ward, and confessedly beloved by her. Now, on the face of these circumstances, it is utterly unaccountable to me, why you, the widow of a city knight, with a good jointure, should not close with the passion of a man of such character and expectations as Mr. Surface; and more so why you should be so uncommonly earnest to destroy the mutual attachment subsisting between his brother Charles and Maria.

Lady Sneerwell. Then, at once to unravel this mystery, I must inform you that love has no share whatever in the intercourse between Mr. Surface and me.

Snake. No!

Lady Sneerwell. His real attachment is to Maria, or her fortune; but, finding in his brother a favored rival, he has been obliged to mask his pretensions, and profit by my assistance.

Snake. Yet still I am more puzzled why you should interest yourself in his success.

Lady Sneerwell. Heav'ns! how dull you are! Cannot you surmise the weakness which I hitherto, through shame, have concealed even from *you?* Must I confess that Charles—that libertine, that extravagant, that bankrupt in fortune and reputation—that he it is for whom I am thus anxious and malicious, and to gain whom I would sacrifice everything?

Snake. Now, indeed, your conduct appears consistent; but how came you and Mr. Surface so confidential?

Lady Sneerwell. For our mutual interest. I have found him out a long time since—I know him to be artful, selfish, and malicious—in short, a sentimental knave.

Snake. Yet, Sir Peter vows he has not his equal in England—and, above all, he praises him as a man of sentiment.

Lady Sneerwell. True; and with the assistance of his sentiment and hypocrisy he has brought him [Sir Peter] entirely into his interest with regard to Maria.

Enter Servant.

Servant. Mr. Surface.

Lady Sneerwell. Show him up.   [*Exit Servant.*
He generally calls about this time. I don't wonder at people's giving him to me for a lover.

Enter JOSEPH SURFACE.

Joseph Surface. My dear Lady Sneerwell, how do you do to-day? Mr. Snake, your most obedient.

Lady Sneerwell. Snake has just been arraigning me on our mutual attachment, but I have informed him of our real views; you know how useful he has been to us; and, believe me, the confidence is not ill placed.

Joseph Surface. Madam, it is impossible for me to suspect a man of Mr. Snake's sensibility and discernment.

Lady Sneerwell. Well, well, no compliments now;—but tell me when you saw your mistress, Maria—or, what is more material to me, your brother.

Joseph Surface. I have not seen either since I left you; but I can inform you that they never meet. Some of your stories have taken a good effect on Maria.

Lady Sneerwell. Ah, my dear Snake! the merit of this belongs to you. But do your brother's distresses increase?

Joseph Surface. Every hour;—I am told he has had another execution in the house yesterday; in short, his dissipation and extravagance exceed any thing I ever heard of.

Lady Sneerwell. Poor Charles!

Joseph Surface. True, madam;—notwithstanding his vices, one can't help feeling for him.—Aye, poor Charles! I'm sure I wish it was in *my* power to be of any essential service to him.—For the man who does not share in the distresses of a brother, even though merited by his own misconduct, deserves——

Lady Sneerwell. O lud! you are going to be moral, and forget that you are among friends.

Joseph Surface. Egad, that's true!—I'll keep that sentiment till I see Sir Peter. However, it is certainly a charity to rescue Maria from such a libertine, who, if he is to be reclaimed, can be so only by a person of your ladyship's superior accomplishments and understanding.

Snake. I believe, Lady Sneerwell, here's company coming,—I'll go and copy the letter I mentioned to you.—Mr. Surface, your most obedient. [*Exit* SNAKE.

Joseph Surface. Sir, your very devoted.—Lady Sneerwell, I am very sorry you have put any further confidence in that fellow.

Lady Sneerwell. Why so?

Joseph Surface. I have lately detected him in frequent conference with old Rowley, who was formerly my father's steward, and has never, you know, been a friend of mine.

Lady Sneerwell. And do you think he would betray us?

Joseph Surface. Nothing more likely: take my word for't, Lady Sneerwell, that fellow hasn't virtue enough to be faithful even to his own villainy.—Hah! Maria!

Enter MARIA.

Lady Sneerwell. Maria, my dear, how do you do?—What's the matter?

Maria. Oh! there is that disagreeable lover of mine, Sir Benjamin Backbite, has just called at my guardian's, with his odious uncle, Crabtree; so I slipped out, and run hither to avoid them.

Lady Sneerwell. Is that all?

Joseph Surface. If my brother Charles had been of the party, ma'am, perhaps you would not have been so much alarmed.

Lady Sneerwell. Nay, now you are severe; for I dare swear the truth of the matter is, Maria heard *you* were here;—but, my dear, what has Sir Benjamin done, that you should avoid him so?

Maria. Oh, he has done nothing—but 'tis for what he has said,—his conversation is a perpetual libel on all his acquaintance.

Joseph Surface. Aye, and the worst of it is, there is no advantage in not knowing him; for he'll abuse a stranger just as soon as his best friend—and his uncle's as bad.

Lady Sneerwell. Nay, but we should make allowance; Sir Benjamin is a wit and a poet.

Maria. For my part, I own, madam, wit loses its respect with me, when I see it in company with malice.—What do you think, Mr. Surface?

Joseph Surface. Certainly, madam; to smile at the jest which plants a thorn in another's breast is to become a principal in the mischief.

Lady Sneerwell. Pshaw! there's no possibility of being witty without a little ill nature: the malice of a good thing is the barb that makes it stick.—What's your opinion, Mr. Surface?

Joseph Surface. To be sure, madam, that conversation, where the spirit of raillery is suppressed, will ever appear tedious and insipid.

Maria. Well, I'll not debate how far scandal may be allowable; but in a man, I am sure, it is always contemptible.—We have pride, envy, rivalship, and a thousand motives to depreciate each other; but the male slanderer must have the cowardice of a woman before he can traduce one.

Enter Servant.

Servant. Madam, Mrs. Candour is below, and, if your ladyship's at leisure, will leave her carriage.

Lady Sneerwell. Beg her to walk in. [*Exit Servant.*] Now Maria, however here is a character to your taste; for, though Mrs. Candour is a little talkative, everybody allows her to be the best-natured and best sort of woman.

Maria. Yes, with a very gross affectation of good nature and benevolence, she does more mischief than the direct malice of old Crabtree.

Joseph Surface. I'faith 'tis very true, Lady Sneerwell; whenever I hear the current running against the characters of my friends, I never think them in such danger as when Candour undertakes their defence.

Lady Sneerwell. Hush!—here she is!

Enter MRS. CANDOUR.

Mrs. Candour. My dear Lady Sneerwell, how have you been this century?—Mr. Surface, what news do you hear? —though indeed it is no matter, for I think one hears nothing else but scandal.

Joseph Surface. Just so, indeed, madam.

Mrs. Candour. Ah, Maria! child,—what, is the whole affair off between you and Charles? His extravagance, I presume—the town talks of nothing else.

Maria. I am very sorry, ma'am, the town has so little to do.

Mrs. Candour. True, true, child: but there is no stopping people's tongues.—I own I was hurt to hear it, as indeed I was to learn, from the same quarter, that your guardian, Sir Peter, and Lady Teazle have not agreed lately so well as could be wished.

Maria. 'Tis strangely impertinent for people to busy themselves so.

Mrs. Candour. Very true, child, but what's to be done? People will talk—there's no preventing it.—Why, it was but yesterday I was told that Miss Gadabout had eloped with Sir Filigree Flirt.—But, Lord! there's no minding what one hears—though, to be sure, I had this from very good authority.

Maria. Such reports are highly scandalous.

Mrs. Candour. So they are, child—shameful, shameful! But the world is so censorious, no character escapes.— Lord, now who would have suspected your friend, Miss Prim, of an indiscretion? Yet such is the ill-nature of people, that they say her uncle stopped her last week, just as she was stepping into the York Diligence with her dancing-master.

Maria. I'll answer for't there are no grounds for the report.

Mrs. Candour. Oh, no foundation in the world, I dare swear; no more, probably, than for the story circulated last month, of Mrs. Festino's affair with Colonel Cassino; —though, to be sure, that matter was never rightly cleared up.

Joseph Surface. The license of invention some people take is monstrous indeed.

Maria. 'Tis so.—But, in my opinion, those who report such things are equally culpable.

Mrs. Candour. To be sure they are; tale-bearers are as bad as the tale-makers—'tis an old observation, and a very true one—but what's to be done, as I said before? how will you prevent people from talking?—To-day, Mrs. Clackit assured me Mr. and Mrs. Honeymoon were at last become mere man and wife, like the rest of their acquaintances.—She likewise hinted that a certain widow, in the next street, had got rid of her dropsy and recovered her shape in a most surprising manner. And at the same time Miss Tattle, who was by, affirmed that Lord Buffalo had discovered his lady at a house of no extraordinary fame— and that Sir Harry Bouquet and Tom Saunter were to measure swords on a similar provocation. But, Lord, do you think I would report these things! No, no! tale-bearers, as I said before, are just as bad as tale-makers.

Joseph Surface. Ah! Mrs. Candour, if everybody had your forbearance and good nature!

Mrs. Candour. I confess, Mr. Surface, I cannot bear to hear people attacked behind their backs, and when ugly circumstances come out against one's acquaintance I own I always love to think the best.—By the bye, I hope it is not true that your brother is absolutely ruined?

Joseph Surface. I am afraid his circumstances are very bad indeed, ma'am.

Mrs. Candour. Ah!—I heard so—but you must tell him to keep up his spirits—everybody almost is in the same way! Lord Spindle, Sir Thomas Splint, Captain Quinze, and Mr. Nickit—all up, I hear, within this week; so, if Charles is undone, he'll find half his acquaintances ruined too—and that, you know, is a consolation.

Joseph Surface. Doubtless, ma'am—a very great one.

Enter Servant.

Servant. Mr. Crabtree and Sir Benjamin Backbite.

[*Exit Servant.*

Lady Sneerwell. So, Maria, you see your lover pursues you; positively you shan't escape.

Enter CRABTREE and SIR BENJAMIN BACKBITE.

Crabtree. Lady Sneerwell, I kiss your hands. Mrs. Candour, I don't believe you are acquainted with my

nephew, Sir Benjamin Backbite? Egad, ma'am, he has a
pretty wit, and is a pretty poet too; isn't he, Lady Sneerwell?

Sir Benjamin. O fie, uncle!

Crabtree. Nay, egad it's true—I'll back him at a rebus
or a charade against the best rhymer in the kingdom. Has
your ladyship heard the epigram he wrote last week on
Lady Frizzle's feather catching fire?—Do, Benjamin, repeat it—or the charade you made last night extempore at
Mrs. Drowzie's conversazione.—Come now; your *first* is
the name of a fish, your *second* a great naval commander,
and——

Sir Benjamin. Uncle, now—prithee——

Crabtree. I'faith, ma'am, 'twould surprise you to hear
how ready he is at these things.

Lady Sneerwell. I wonder, Sir Benjamin, you never publish anything.

Sir Benjamin. To say truth, ma'am, 'tis very vulgar to
print; and, as my little productions are mostly satires and
lampoons on particular people, I find they circulate more
by giving copies in confidence to the friends of the parties
—however, I have some love elegies, which, when favored
with this lady's smiles, I mean to give to the public.

Crabtree. 'Fore heav'n, ma'am, they'll immortalize you!
—you'll be handed down to posterity like Petrarch's Laura,
or Waller's Sacharissa.[1]

Sir Benjamin. Yes, madam, I think you will like them,
when you shall see them on a beautiful quarto page,
where a neat rivulet of text shall murmur through a
meadow of margin. 'Fore gad, they will be the most elegant things of their kind!

Crabtree. But, ladies, that's true—have you heard the
news?

Mrs. Candour. What, sir, do you mean the report of—

Crabtree. No, ma'am, that's not it.—Miss Nicely is going to be married to her own footman.

Mrs. Candour. Impossible!

Crabtree. Ask Sir Benjamin.

Sir Benjamin. 'Tis very true, ma'am—everything is fixed,
and the wedding liveries bespoke.

Crabtree. Yes—and they *do* say there were pressing
reasons for it.

---

[1] Edmund Waller's poetical name for Lady Dorothy Sidney.

Lady Sneerwell. Why, I *have* heard something of this before.

Mrs. Candour. It can't be—and I wonder anyone should believe such a story of so prudent a lady as Miss Nicely.

Sir Benjamin. O lud! ma'am, that's the very reason 'twas believed at once. She has always been so *cautious* and so *reserved*, that everybody was sure there was some reason for it at bottom.

Mrs. Candour. Why, to be sure, a tale of scandal is as fatal to the credit of a prudent lady of her stamp as a fever is generally to those of the strongest constitutions; but there is a sort of puny, sickly reputation that is always ailing, yet will outlive the robuster characters of a hundred prudes.

Sir Benjamin. True, madam, there are valetudinarians in reputation as well as constitution, who, being conscious of their weak part, avoid the least breath of air, and supply their want of stamina by care and circumspection.

Mrs. Candour. Well, but this may be all a mistake. You know, Sir Benjamin, very trifling circumstances often give rise to the most injurious tales.

Crabtree. That they do, I'll be sworn, ma'am. Did you ever hear how Miss Piper came to lose her lover and her character last summer at Tunbridge?—Sir Benjamin, you remember it?

Sir Benjamin. Oh, to be sure!—the most whimsical circumstance—

Lady Sneerwell. How was it, pray?

Crabtree. Why, one evening, at Mrs. Ponto's assembly, the conversation happened to turn on the difficulty of breeding Nova Scotia sheep in this country. Says a young lady in company, 'I have known instances of it; for Miss Letitia Piper, a first cousin of mine, had a Nova Scotia sheep that produced her twins.' 'What!' cries the old Dowager Lady Dundizzy (who you know is as deaf as a post), 'has Miss Piper had twins?' This mistake, as you may imagine, threw the whole company into a fit of laughing. However, 'twas the next morning everywhere reported, and in a few days believed by the whole town, that Miss Letitia Piper had actually been brought to bed of a fine boy and a girl—and in less than a week there were people who could name the father, and the farmhouse where the babies were put out to nurse!

Lady Sneerwell. Strange, indeed!

Crabtree. Matter of fact, I assure you.—O lud! Mr. Surface, pray is it true that your uncle, Sir Oliver, is coming home?

Joseph Surface. Not that I know of, indeed, sir.

Crabtree. He has been in the East Indias a long time. You can scarcely remember him, I believe.—Sad comfort, whenever he returns, to hear how your brother has gone on!

Joseph Surface. Charles has been imprudent, sir, to be sure; but I hope no busy people have already prejudiced Sir Oliver against him,—he may reform.

Sir Benjamin. To be sure he may—for my part I never believed him to be so utterly void of principle as people say—and though he has lost all his friends, I am told nobody is better spoken of by the Jews.

Crabtree. That's true, egad, nephew. If the old Jewry were a ward, I believe Charles would be an alderman; no man more popular there, 'fore gad! I hear he pays as many annuities as the Irish tontine;[2] and that, whenever he's sick, they have prayers for the recovery of his health in the Synagogue.

Sir Benjamin. Yet no man lives in greater splendor.— They tell me, when he entertains his friends, he can sit down to dinner with a dozen of his own securities; have a score [of] tradesmen waiting in the antechamber, and an officer behind every guest's chair.

Joseph Surface. This may be entertainment to you, gentlemen, but you pay very little regard to the feelings of a brother.

Maria. Their malice is intolerable!—Lady Sneerwell, I must wish you a good morning—I'm not very well.

[*Exit* MARIA.

Mrs. Candour. O dear! she changes color very much!

Lady Sneerwell. Do, Mrs. Candour, follow her—she may want assistance.

Mrs. Candour. That I will, with all my soul, ma'am.— Poor dear girl! who knows what her situation may be!

[*Exit* MRS. CANDOUR.

Lady Sneerwell. 'Twas nothing but that she could not bear to hear Charles reflected on, notwithstanding their difference.

---

[2] In 1773 and thereafter, the Irish parliament raised considerable revenues by selling life annuities to subscribers. The 'tontine' plan took its name from the inventor, Tonti, an Italian banker.

Sir Benjamin. The young lady's *penchant* is obvious.

Crabtree. But, Benjamin, you mustn't give up the pursuit for that; follow her, and put her into good humor. Repeat her some of your own verses.—Come, I'll assist you.

Sir Benjamin. Mr. Surface, I did not mean to hurt you; but depend upon't your brother is utterly undone. [*Going.*

Crabtree. O lud, aye! undone as ever man was—can't raise a guinea. [*Going.*

Sir Benjamin. And everything sold, I'm told, that was movable. [*Going.*

Crabtree. I have seen one that was at his house—not a thing left but some empty bottles that were overlooked, and the family pictures, which I believe are framed in the wainscot. [*Going.*

Sir Benjamin. And I am very sorry to hear also some bad stories against him. [*Going.*

Crabtree. Oh, he has done many mean things, that's certain. [*Going.*

Sir Benjamin. But, however, as he's your brother—— [*Going.*

Crabtree. We'll tell you all, another opportunity.

[*Exeunt* CRABTREE *and* SIR BENJAMIN.

Lady Sneerwell. Ha, ha! ha! 'tis very hard for them to leave a subject they have not quite run down.

Joseph Surface. And I believe the abuse was no more acceptable to your ladyship than to Maria.

Lady Sneerwell. I doubt [3] her affections are farther engaged than we imagined; but the family are to be here this evening, so you may as well dine where you are, and we shall have an opportunity of observing farther;—in the meantime, I'll go and plot mischief, and you shall study sentiments. [*Exeunt.*

SCENE II—SIR PETER TEAZLE's *house*

Enter SIR PETER.

Sir Peter. When an old bachelor takes a young wife, what is he to expect?—'Tis now six months since Lady Teazle made me the happiest of men—and I have been the miserablest dog ever since that ever committed wedlock! We tift a little going to church, and came **to a**

[3] Suspect.

quarrel before the bells were done ringing. I was more
than once nearly choked with gall during the honeymoon,
and had lost all comfort in life before my friends had done
wishing me joy! Yet I chose with caution—a girl bred
wholly in the country, who never knew luxury beyond
one silk gown, nor dissipation above the annual gala of a
race ball. Yet now she plays her part in all the extravagant
fopperies of the fashion and the town, with as ready a
grace as if she had never seen a bush nor a grass-plat out
of Grosvenor Square! I am sneered at by my old acquaintance—paragraphed in the newspapers. She dissipates my
fortune, and contradicts all my humors; yet the worst of it
is, I doubt I love her, or I should never bear all this.
However, I'll never be weak enough to own it.

Enter ROWLEY.

Rowley. Oh! Sir Peter, your servant,—how is it with
you, sir?

Sir Peter. Very bad, Master Rowley, very bad;—I meet
with nothing but crosses and vexations.

Rowley. What can have happened to trouble you since
yesterday?

Sir Peter. A good question to a married man!

Rowley. Nay, I'm sure your lady, Sir Peter, can't be the
cause of your uneasiness.

Sir Peter. Why, has anyone told you she was dead?

Rowley. Come, come, Sir Peter, you love her, notwithstanding your tempers don't exactly agree.

Sir Peter. But the fault is entirely hers, Master Rowley.
I am, myself, the sweetest-tempered man alive, and hate a
teasing temper—and so I tell her a hundred times a day.

Rowley. Indeed!

Sir Peter. Aye; and what is very extraordinary, in all our
disputes she is always in the wrong! But Lady Sneerwell,
and the set she meets at her house, encourage the perverseness of her disposition. Then, to complete my vexations,
Maria, my ward, whom I ought to have the power of a
father over, is determined to turn rebel too, and absolutely
refuses the man whom I have long resolved on for her
husband;—meaning, I suppose, to bestow herself on his
profligate brother.

Rowley. You know, Sir Peter, I have always taken the
liberty to differ with you on the subject of these two young

gentlemen. I only wish you may not be deceived in your opinion of the elder. For Charles, my life on't! he will retrieve his errors yet. Their worthy father, once my honored master, was, at his years, nearly as wild a spark; yet, when he died, he did not leave a more benevolent heart to lament his loss.

Sir Peter. You are wrong, Master Rowley. On their father's death, you know, I acted as a kind of guardian to them both, till their uncle Sir Oliver's Eastern liberality gave them an early independence; of course, no person could have more opportunities of judging of their hearts, and I was never mistaken in my life. Joseph is indeed a model for the young men of the age. He is a man of sentiment, and acts up to the sentiments he professes; but, for the other, take my word for't, if he had any grains of virtue by descent, he has dissipated them with the rest of his inheritance. Ah! my old friend, Sir Oliver, will be deeply mortified when he finds how part of his bounty has been misapplied.

Rowley. I am sorry to find you so violent against the young man, because this may be the most critical period of his fortune. I came hither with news that will surprise you.

Sir Peter. What! let me hear.

Rowley. Sir Oliver *is* arrived, and at this moment in town.

Sir Peter. How! you astonish me! I thought you did not expect him this month.

Rowley. I did not; but his passage has been remarkably quick.

Sir Peter. Egad, I shall rejoice to see my old friend,— 'tis sixteen years since we met—we have had many a day together; but does he still enjoin us not to inform his nephews of his arrival?

Rowley. Most strictly. He means, before it is known, to make some trial of their dispositions.

Sir Peter. Ah! There needs no art to discover their merits—however, he shall have his way; but, pray, does he know I am married?

Rowley. Yes, and will soon wish you joy.

Sir Peter. What, as we drink health to a friend in a consumption! Ah, Oliver will laugh at me—we used to rail at matrimony together—but he has been steady to his text.

Well, he must be at my house, though—I'll instantly give orders for his reception. But, Master Rowley, don't drop a word that Lady Teazle and I ever disagree.

Rowley. By no means.

Sir Peter. For I should never be able to stand Noll's jokes; so I'd have him think, Lord forgive me! that we are a very happy couple.

Rowley. I understand you—but then you must be very careful not to differ while he's in the house with you.

Sir Peter. Egad, and so we must—and that's impossible. Ah! Master Rowley, when an old bachelor marries a young wife, he deserves—no—the crime carries the punishment along with it. [*Exeunt.*

ACT TWO

SCENE I—SIR PETER TEAZLE'S *house*

Enter SIR PETER *and* LADY TEAZLE.

Sir Peter. Lady Teazle, Lady Teazle, I'll not bear it!

Lady Teazle. Sir Peter, Sir Peter, you may bear it or not, as you please; but I ought to have my own way in everything, and what's more, I *will* too.—What! though I was educated in the country, I know very well that women of fashion in London are accountable to nobody after they are married.

Sir Peter. Very well, ma'am, very well,—so a husband is to have no influence, no authority?

Lady Teazle. Authority! No, to be sure—if you wanted authority over me, you should have adopted me, and not married me; I am sure you were old enough.

Sir Peter. Old enough!—aye, there it is!—Well, well, Lady Teazle, though my life may be made unhappy by your temper, I'll not be ruined by your extravagance.

Lady Teazle. My extravagance! I'm sure I'm not more extravagant than a woman of fashion ought to be.

Sir Peter. No, no, madam, you shall throw away no more sums on such unmeaning luxury. 'Slife! to spend as much to furnish your dressing-room with flowers in winter as would suffice to turn the Pantheon[4] into a greenhouse, and give a *fête champêtre*[5] at Christmas!

[4] A fashionable concert-hall in Oxford Street.
[5] An open-air festival.

Lady Teazle. Lord, Sir Peter, am I to blame because flowers are dear in cold weather? You should find fault with the climate, and not with me. For my part, I am sure I wish it was spring all the year round, and that roses grew under one's feet!

Sir Peter. Oons! madam—if you had been born to this, I shouldn't wonder at your talking thus.—But you forget what your situation was when I married you.

Lady Teazle. No, no, I don't; 'twas a very disagreeable one, or I should never have married *you.*

Sir Peter. Yes, yes, madam, you were then in somewhat an humbler style—the daughter of a plain country squire. Recollect, Lady Teazle, when I saw you first, sitting at your tambour,⁶ in a pretty figured linen gown, with a bunch of keys by your side, your hair combed smooth over a roll, and your apartment hung round with fruits in worsted, of your own working.

Lady Teazle. O, yes! I remember it very well, and a curious life I led—my daily occupation to inspect the dairy, superintend the poultry, make extracts from the family receipt-book, and comb my aunt Deborah's lap-dog.

Sir Peter. Yes, yes, ma'am, 'twas so indeed.

Lady Teazle. And then, you know, my evening amusements! To draw patterns for ruffles, which I had not the materials to make; to play Pope Joan⁷ with the curate; to read a novel to my aunt; or to be stuck down to an old spinet to strum my father to sleep after a fox-chase.

Sir Peter. I am glad you have so good a memory. Yes, madam, these were the recreations I took you from; but now you must have your coach—*vis-à-vis*—and three powdered footmen before your chair and, in summer, a pair of white cats⁸ to draw you to Kensington Gardens.— No recollection, I suppose, when you were content to ride double, behind the butler, on a docked coach-horse?

Lady Teazle. No—I swear I never did that—I deny the butler and the coach-horse.

Sir Peter. This, madam, was your situation—and what have I not done for you? I have made you a woman of fashion, of fortune, of rank—in short, I have made you my wife.

Lady Teazle. Well, then, and there is but one thing

---

⁶ Embroidery-frame.

⁷ An old-fashioned game of cards.

⁸ Ponies (Rae text reads *cobs*).

more you can make me to add to the obligation—and that
is——

Sir Peter. My widow, I suppose?

Lady Teazle. Hem! hem!

Sir Peter. Thank you, madam—but don't flatter yourself; for though your ill-conduct may disturb my peace, it
shall never break my heart, I promise you: however, I am
equally obliged to you for the hint.

Lady Teazle. Then why will you endeavor to make yourself so disagreeable to me, and thwart me in every little
elegant expense?

Sir Peter. 'Slife, madam, I say, had you any of these
elegant expenses when you married me?

Lady Teazle. Lud, Sir Peter! would you have me be out
of the fashion?

Sir Peter. The fashion, indeed! what had you to do with
the fashion before you married me?

Lady Teazle. For my part, I should think you would
like to have your wife thought a woman of taste.

Sir Peter. Aye—there again—taste! Zounds! madam,
you had no taste when you married *me!*

Lady Teazle. That's very true, indeed, Sir Peter! and,
after having married you, I am sure I should never pretend to taste again! But now, Sir Peter, if we have finished
our daily jangle, I presume I may go to my engagement of
[at] Lady Sneerwell's?

Sir Peter. Aye—there's another precious circumstance!
—a charming set of acquaintances you have made there!

Lady Teazle. Nay, Sir Peter, they are people of rank and
fortune, and remarkably tenacious of reputation.

Sir Peter. Yes, egad, they are tenacious of reputation
with a vengeance; for they don't choose anybody should
have a character but themselves! Such a crew! Ah! many
a wretch has rid on a hurdle[9] who has done less mischief
than those utterers of forged tales, coiners of scandal,—
and clippers of reputation.

Lady Teazle. What! would you restrain the freedom of
speech?

Sir Peter. Oh! they have made you just as bad as any
one of the society.

[9] Rough cart on which criminals were taken to the place of execution.
'Hurdles, with four, five, six wretches convicted of counterfeiting or muti-
lating the money of the realm, were dragged month after month up Hol-
born Hill.'

Lady Teazle. Why, I believe I do bear a part with a tolerable grace. But I vow I have no malice against the people I abuse; when I say an ill-natured thing, 'tis out of pure good humor—and I take it for granted they deal exactly in the same manner with me. But, Sir Peter, you know you promised to come to Lady Sneerwell's too.

Sir Peter. Well, well, I'll call in just to look after my own character.

Lady Teazle. Then, indeed, you must make haste after me or you'll be too late.—So good-bye to ye.

[*Exit* LADY TEAZLE.

Sir Peter. So—I have gained much by my intended expostulations! Yet with what a charming air she contradicts everything I say, and how pleasingly she shows her contempt of my authority! Well, though I can't make her love me, there is a great satisfaction in quarrelling with her; and I think she never appears to such advantage as when she's doing everything in her power to plague me.   [*Exit.*

SCENE II—LADY SNEERWELL'S

LADY SNEERWELL, MRS. CANDOUR, CRABTREE, SIR BENJAMIN BACKBITE, *and* JOSEPH SURFACE.

Lady Sneerwell. Nay, positively, we will hear it.

Joseph Surface. Yes, yes, the epigram, by all means.

Sir Benjamin. Plague on't, uncle! 'tis mere nonsense.

Crabtree. No, no; 'fore gad, very clever for an extempore!

Sir Benjamin. But, ladies, you should be acquainted with the circumstance,—you must know, that one day last week, as Lady Betty Curricle was taking the dust in Hyde Park, in a sort of duodecimo[10] phaëton, she desired me to write some verses on her ponies; upon which, I took out my pocket-book, and in one moment produced the following:

'Sure never were seen two such beautiful ponies!
Other horses are clowns, and these macaronies!
Nay, to give 'em this title I'm sure isn't wrong—
Their legs are so slim, and their tails are so long.'

Crabtree. There, ladies—done in the smack of a whip, and on horseback too!

[10] Diminutive.

Joseph Surface. A very Phœbus, mounted—indeed, Sir Benjamin.

Sir Benjamin. O dear sir—trifles—trifles.

Enter LADY TEAZLE *and* MARIA.

Mrs. Candour. I must have a copy.

Lady Sneerwell. Lady Teazle, I hope we shall see Sir Peter.

Lady Teazle. I believe he'll wait on your ladyship presently.

Lady Sneerwell. Maria, my love, you look grave. Come, you shall sit down to cards with Mr. Surface.

Maria. I take very little pleasure in cards—however, I'll do as your ladyship pleases.

Lady Teazle. [*Aside.*] I am surprised Mr. Surface should sit down with *her.*—I thought he would have embraced this opportunity of speaking to me before Sir Peter came.

Mrs. Candour. Now, I'll die but you are so scandalous, I'll forswear your society.

Lady Teazle. What's the matter, Mrs. Candour?

Mrs. Candour. They'll not allow our friend Miss Vermilion to be handsome.

Lady Sneerwell. Oh, surely, she's a pretty woman.

Crabtree. I am very glad you think so, ma'am.

Mrs. Candour. She has a charming fresh color.

Lady Teazle. Yes, when it is fresh put on.

Mrs. Candour. O fie! I'll swear her color is natural—I have seen it come and go.

Lady Teazle. I dare swear you have, ma'am—it goes of a night, and comes again in the morning.

Mrs. Candour. Ha! ha! ha! how I hate to hear you talk so! But surely, now, her sister *is,* or *was,* very handsome.

Crabtree. Who? Mrs. Evergreen?—O Lord! she's six-and-fifty if she's an hour!

Mrs. Candour. Now positively you wrong her; fifty-two or fifty-three is the utmost—and I don't think she looks more.

Sir Benjamin. Ah! there is no judging by her looks, unless one could see her face.

Lady Sneerwell. Well, well, if Mrs. Evergreen *does* take some pains to repair the ravages of time, you must allow she effects it with great ingenuity; and surely that's

better than the careless manner in which the widow
Ochre caulks her wrinkles.

Sir Benjamin. Nay, now, Lady Sneerwell, you are severe
upon the widow. Come, come, it is not that she paints so
ill—but, when she has finished her face, she joins it on
so badly to her neck, that she looks like a mended statue,
in which the connoisseur may see at once that the head's
modern, though the trunk's antique!

Crabtree. Ha! ha! ha! Well said, nephew!

Mrs. Candour. Ha! ha! ha! Well, you make me laugh,
but I vow I hate you for't.—What do you think of Miss
Simper?

Sir Benjamin. Why, she has very pretty teeth.

Lady Teazle. Yes; and on that account, when she is
neither speaking nor laughing (which very seldom happens), she never absolutely shuts her mouth, but leaves it
always on a jar, as it were.

Mrs. Candour. How can you be so ill-natured?

Lady Teazle. Nay, I allow even that's better than the
pains Mrs. Prim takes to conceal her losses in front. She
draws her mouth till it positively resembles the aperture
of a poor's-box,[11] and all her words appear to slide out
edgeways.

Lady Sneerwell. Very well, Lady Teazle; I see you can
be a little severe.

Lady Teazle. In defence of a friend it is but justice;—
but here comes Sir Peter to spoil our pleasantry.

Enter SIR PETER TEAZLE.

Sir Peter. Ladies, your most obedient—Mercy on me,
here is the whole set! a character dead at every word, I
suppose.   [*Aside.*

Mrs. Candour. I am rejoiced you are come, Sir Peter.
They have been *so* censorious. They will allow good quali-
ties to nobody—not even good nature to our friend Mrs.
Pursy.

Lady Teazle. What, the fat dowager who was at Mrs.
Codille's last night?

Mrs. Candour. Nay, her bulk is her misfortune; and,
when she takes such pains to get rid of it, you ought not
to reflect on her.

Lady Sneerwell. That's very true, indeed.

---

11 Referring to the narrow slit in the top of the church contribution-box
for the poor of the parish.

Lady Teazle. Yes, I know she almost lives on acids and small whey; laces herself by pulleys; and often, in the hottest noon of summer, you may see her on a little squat pony, with her hair platted up behind like a drummer's, and puffing round the Ring[12] on a full trot.

Mrs. Candour. I thank you, Lady Teazle, for defending her.

Sir Peter. Yes, a good defence, truly.

Mrs. Candour. But Sir Benjamin is as censorious as Miss Sallow.

Crabtree. Yes, and she is a curious being to pretend to be censorious!—an awkward gawky, without any one good point under heaven.

Mrs. Candour. Positively you shall not be so very severe. Miss Sallow is a relation of mine by marriage, and, as for her person, great allowance is to be made; for, let me tell you, a woman labors under many disadvantages who tries to pass for a girl at six-and-thirty.

Lady Sneerwell. Though, surely, she is handsome still —and for the weakness in her eyes, considering how much she reads by candle-light, it is not to be wondered at.

Mrs. Candour. True; and then as to her manner, upon my word I think it is particularly graceful, considering she never had the least education; for you know her mother was a Welch milliner, and her father a sugar-baker at Bristol.

Sir Benjamin. Ah! you are both of you too good-natured!

Sir Peter. Yes, damned good-natured! This their own relation! mercy on me!   [*Aside.*

Sir Benjamin. And Mrs. Candour is of so moral a turn she can sit for an hour to hear Lady Stucco talk sentiment.

Lady Teazle. Nay, I vow Lady Stucco is very well with the dessert after dinner; for she's just like the French fruit one cracks for mottoes—made up of paint and proverb.

Mrs. Candour. Well, I never will join in ridiculing a friend; and so I constantly tell my cousin Ogle, and you all know what pretensions she has to be critical in beauty.

Crabtree. Oh, to be sure! she has herself the oddest countenance that ever was seen; 'tis a collection of features from all the different countries of the globe.

Sir Benjamin. So she has, indeed—an Irish front!

Crabtree. Caledonian locks!

[12] The fashionable drive originally laid out in Hyde Park by Charles II.

Sir Benjamin. Dutch nose!

Crabtree. Austrian lip!

Sir Benjamin. Complexion of a Spaniard!

Crabtree. And teeth *à la Chinoise!*

Sir Benjamin. In short, her face resembles a *table d'hôte* at Spa—where no two guests are of a nation——

Crabtree. Or a congress at the close of a general war—wherein all the members, even to her eyes, appear to have a different interest, and her nose and chin are the only parties likely to join issue.

Mrs. Candour. Ha! ha! ha!

Sir Peter. Mercy on my life!—a person they dine with twice a week!   [*Aside.*

Lady Sneerwell. Go—go—you are a couple of provoking toads.

Mrs. Candour. Nay, but I vow you shall not carry the laugh off so—for give me leave to say, that Mrs. Ogle——

Sir Peter. Madam, madam, I beg your pardon—there's no stopping these good gentlemen's tongues. But when I tell *you*, Mrs. Candour, that the lady they are abusing is a particular friend of mine—I hope you'll not take her part.

Lady Sneerwell. Well said, Sir Peter! but you are a cruel creature—too phlegmatic yourself for a jest, and too peevish to allow wit on others.

Sir Peter. Ah, madam, true wit is more nearly allied to good nature than your ladyship is aware of.

Lady Teazle. True, Sir Peter; I believe they are so near akin that they can never be united.

Sir Benjamin. Or rather, madam, suppose them man and wife, because one so seldom sees them together.

Lady Teazle. But Sir Peter is such an enemy to scandal, I believe he would have it put down by parliament.

Sir Peter. 'Fore heaven, madam, if they were to consider the sporting with reputation of as much importance as poaching on manors, and pass *An Act for the Preservation of Fame,* I believe many would thank them for the bill.

Lady Sneerwell. O lud! Sir Peter; would you deprive us of our privileges?

Sir Peter. Aye, madam; and then no person should be permitted to kill characters or run down reputations, but qualified old maids and disappointed widows.

Lady Sneerwell. Go, you monster!

Mrs. Candour. But sure you would not be quite so severe on those who only report what they hear.

Sir Peter. Yes, madam, I would have law merchant[13] for them too; and in all cases of slander currency, whenever the drawer of the lie was not to be found, the injured parties should have a right to come on any of the indorsers.

Crabtree. Well, for my part, I believe there never was a scandalous tale without some foundation.

Lady Sneerwell. Come, ladies, shall we sit down to cards in the next room?

Enter Servant and whispers Sir Peter.

Sir Peter. I'll be with them directly.—[*Exit Servant.*] I'll get away unperceived. [*Aside.*]

Lady Sneerwell. Sir Peter, you are not leaving us?

Sir Peter. Your ladyship must excuse me; I'm called away by particular business—but I leave my character behind me.   [*Exit* Sir Peter.

Sir Benjamin. Well certainly, Lady Teazle, that lord of yours is a strange being; I could tell you some stories of him would make you laugh heartily, if he wasn't your husband.

Lady Teazle. O pray don't mind that—come, do let's hear them.

[*They join the rest of the company, all talking as they are going into the next room.*

Joseph Surface. [*Rising with* Maria.] Maria, I see you have no satisfaction in this society.

Maria. How is it possible I should? If to raise malicious smiles at the infirmities and misfortunes of those who have never injured us be the province of wit or humor, heaven grant me a double portion of dulness!

Joseph Surface. Yet they appear more ill-natured than they are; they have no malice at heart.

Maria. Then is their conduct still more contemptible; for, in my opinion, nothing could excuse the intemperance of their tongues but a natural and ungovernable bitterness of mind.

Joseph Surface. But can you, Maria, feel thus for others, and be unkind to me alone? Is hope to be denied the tenderest passion?

[13] Mercantile law.

Maria. Why will you distress me by renewing this subject?

Joseph Surface. Ah, Maria! you would not treat me thus, and oppose your guardian, Sir Peter's will, but that I see that profligate Charles is still a favored rival.

Maria. Ungenerously urged! But, whatever my sentiments of that unfortunate young man are, be assured I shall not feel more bound to give him up, because his distresses have lost him the regard even of a brother.

LADY TEAZLE *returns.*

Joseph Surface. Nay, but, Maria, do not leave me with a frown—by all that's honest, I swear——Gad's life, here's Lady Teazle. [*Aside.*]—You must not—no, you shall not —for, though I have the greatest regard for Lady Teazle——

Maria. Lady Teazle!

Joseph Surface. Yet were Sir Peter to suspect——

Lady Teazle. [*Coming forward.*] What's this, pray? Do you take her for me?—Child, you are wanted in the next room.——   [*Exit* MARIA.
What is all this, pray?

Joseph Surface. Oh, the most unlucky circumstance in nature! Maria has somehow suspected the tender concern I have for your happiness, and threatened to acquaint Sir Peter with her suspicions, and I was just endeavoring to reason with her when you came.

Lady Teazle. Indeed! but you seemed to adopt a very tender mode of reasoning—do you *usually* argue on your knees?

Joseph Surface. Oh, she's a child—and I thought a little bombast——but, Lady Teazle, when are you to give me your judgment on my library, as you promised?

Lady Teazle. No, no,—I begin to think it would be imprudent, and you know I admit you as a lover no further than *fashion* requires.

Joseph Surface. True—a mere Platonic cicisbeo,[14] what every London wife is *entitled* to.

Lady Teazle. Certainly, one must not be out of the fashion; however, I have so many of my country prejudices left, that, though Sir Peter's ill humor may vex me ever so, it never shall provoke me to——

---

[14] Gallant to a married woman.

Joseph Surface. The only revenge in your power. Well, I applaud your moderation.

Lady Teazle. Go——you are an insinuating wretch! But we shall be missed——let us join the company.

Joseph Surface. But we had best not return together.

Lady Teazle. Well, don't stay——for Maria shan't come to hear any more of your *reasoning,* I promise you.

[*Exit* Lady Teazle.

Joseph Surface. A curious dilemma, truly, my politics have run me into! I wanted, at first, only to ingratiate myself with Lady Teazle, that she might not be my enemy with Maria; and I have, I don't know how, become her serious lover. Sincerely I begin to wish I had never made such a point of gaining so *very good* a character, for it has led me into so many cursed rogueries that I doubt I shall be exposed at last.   [*Exit.*

SCENE III—Sir Peter's

Enter Sir Oliver Surface *and* Rowley.

Sir Oliver. Ha! ha! ha! and so my old friend is married, hey?—a young wife out of the country.—Ha! ha! ha!—that he should have stood bluff [15] to old bachelor so long, and sink into a husband at last!

Rowley. But you must not rally him on the subject, Sir Oliver; 'tis a tender point, I assure you, though he has been married only seven months.

Sir Oliver. Then he has been just half a year on the stool of repentance!—Poor Peter! But you say he has entirely given up Charles—never sees him, hey?

Rowley. His prejudice against him is astonishing, and I am sure greatly increased by a jealousy of him with Lady Teazle, which he has been industriously led into by a scandalous society in the neighborhood, who have contributed not a little to Charles's ill name; whereas the truth is, I believe, if the lady is partial to either of them, his brother is the favorite.

Sir Oliver. Aye,—I know there are a set of malicious, prating, prudent gossips, both male and female, who murder characters to kill time, and will rob a young fellow of his good name before he has years to know the value of

[15] Steadfast.

it,—but I am not to be prejudiced against my nephew by such, I promise you! No, no;—if Charles has done nothing false or mean, I shall compound for his extravagance.

Rowley. Then, my life on't, you will reclaim him.—Ah, sir, it gives me new life to find that *your* heart is not turned against him, and that the son of my good old master has one friend, however, left.

Sir Oliver. What! shall I forget, Master Rowley, when I was at his years myself? Egad, my brother and I were neither of us very *prudent* youths—and yet, I believe, you have not seen many better men than your old master was?

Rowley. Sir, 'tis this reflection gives me assurance that Charles may yet be a credit to his family.—But here comes Sir Peter.

Sir Oliver. Egad, so he does!—Mercy on me, he's greatly altered, and seems to have a settled married look! One may read husband in his face at this distance!

Enter SIR PETER TEAZLE.

Sir Peter. Hah! Sir Oliver—my old friend! Welcome to England a thousand times!

Sir Oliver. Thank you, thank you, Sir Peter! and i'faith I am glad to find you well, believe me!

Sir Peter. Ah! 'tis a long time since we met—sixteen years, I doubt, Sir Oliver, and many a cross accident in the time.

Sir Oliver. Aye, I have had my share—but, what! I find you are married, hey, my old boy?—Well, well, it can't be helped—and so I wish you joy with all my heart!

Sir Peter. Thank you, thank you, Sir Oliver.—Yes, I have entered into the happy state—but we'll not talk of that now.

Sir Oliver. True, true, Sir Peter; old friends should not begin on grievances at first meeting. No, no, no.

Rowley. [*To* SIR OLIVER.] Take care, pray, sir.

Sir Oliver. Well, so one of my nephews is a wild rogue, hey?

Sir Peter. Wild! Ah! my old friend, I grieve for your disappointment there—he's a lost young man, indeed; however, his brother will make you amends; Joseph is, indeed, what a youth should be—everybody in the world speaks well of him.

Sir Oliver. I am sorry to hear it—he has too good a character to be an honest fellow.—Everybody speaks well of him! Psha! then he has bowed as low to knaves and fools as to the honest dignity of genius or virtue.

Sir Peter. What, Sir Oliver! do you blame him for not making enemies?

Sir Oliver. Yes, if he has merit enough to deserve them.

Sir Peter. Well, well—you'll be convinced when you know him. 'Tis edification to hear him converse—he professes the noblest sentiments.

Sir Oliver. Ah, plague of his sentiments! If he salutes me with a scrap of morality in his mouth, I shall be sick directly. But, however, don't mistake me, Sir Peter; I don't mean to defend Charles's errors—but, before I form my judgment of either of them, I intend to make a trial of their hearts—and my friend Rowley and I have planned something for the purpose.

Rowley. And Sir Peter shall own for once he has been mistaken.

Sir Peter. Oh, my life on Joseph's honor!

Sir Oliver. Well, come, give us a bottle of good wine, and we'll drink the lad's health, and tell you our scheme.

Sir Peter. Allons, then!

Sir Oliver. And don't, Sir Peter, be so severe against your old friend's son. Odds my life! I am not sorry that he has run out of the course a little; for my part, I hate to see prudence clinging to the green succors of youth; 'tis like ivy round a sapling, and spoils the growth of the tree.

[*Exeunt.*

ACT THREE

SCENE I—Sir Peter's

Sir Peter Teazle, Sir Oliver Surface, *and* Rowley.

Sir Peter. Well, then—we will see this fellow first, and have our wine afterwards. But how is this, Master Rowley? I don't see the jet[16] of your scheme.

Rowley. Why, sir, this Mr. Stanley, whom I was speaking of, is nearly related to them, by their mother; he was once a merchant in Dublin, but has been ruined by a series of undeserved misfortunes. He has applied, by letter, since his confinement, both to Mr. Surface and Charles—from

---
16 Point, gist.

the former he has received nothing but evasive promises of future service, while Charles has done all that his extravagance has left him power to do; and he is, at this time, endeavoring to raise a sum of money, part of which, in the midst of his own distresses, I know he intends for the service of poor Stanley.

Sir Oliver. Ah! he is my brother's son.

Sir Peter. Well, but how is Sir Oliver personally to——

Rowley. Why, sir, I will inform Charles and his brother that Stanley has obtained permission to apply in person to his friends, and, as they have neither of them ever seen him, let Sir Oliver assume his character, and he will have a fair opportunity of judging at least of the benevolence of their dispositions; and believe me, sir, you will find in the youngest brother one who, in the midst of folly and dissipation, has still, as our immortal bard expresses it,—

> 'a tear for pity, and a hand
> Open as day, for melting charity.' [17]

Sir Peter. Psha! What signifies his having an open hand or purse either, when he has nothing left to give? Well, well, make the trial, if you please; but where is the fellow whom you brought for Sir Oliver to examine, relative to Charles's affairs?

Rowley. Below, waiting his commands, and no one can give him better intelligence.—This, Sir Oliver, is a friendly Jew, who, to do him justice, has done everything in his power to bring your nephew to a proper sense of his extravagance.

Sir Peter. Pray let us have him in.

Rowley. Desire Mr. Moses to walk upstairs.

Sir Peter. But why should you suppose he will speak the truth?

Rowley. Oh, I have convinced him that he has no chance of recovering certain sums advanced to Charles but through the bounty of Sir Oliver, who he knows is arrived; so that you may depend on his fidelity to his [own] interest. I have also another evidence in my power, one Snake, whom I have detected in a matter little short of forgery, and shall shortly produce to remove some of *your* prejudices, Sir Peter, relative to Charles and Lady Teazle.

[17] From *Henry IV, Part II*, IV. iv. 31-32. (Quoted correctly, but not transcribed as verse.)

Sir Peter. I have heard too much on that subject.

Rowley. Here comes the honest Israelite.

Enter MOSES.

—This is Sir Oliver.

Sir Oliver. Sir, I understand you have lately had great dealings with my nephew Charles.

Moses. Yes, Sir Oliver—I have done all I could for him, but he was ruined before he came to me for assistance.

Sir Oliver. That was unlucky, truly—for you have had no opportunity of showing your talents.

Moses. None at all—I hadn't the pleasure of knowing his distresses—till he was some thousands worse than nothing.

Sir Oliver. Unfortunate, indeed! But I suppose you have done all in your power for him, honest Moses?

Moses. Yes, he knows that. This very evening I was to have brought him a gentleman from the city, who doesn't know him, and will, I believe, advance him some money.

Sir Peter. What, one Charles has never had money from before?

Moses. Yes; Mr. Premium, of Crutched Friars[18]—formerly a broker.

Sir Peter. Egad, Sir Oliver, a thought strikes me!—Charles, you say, doesn't know Mr. Premium?

Moses. Not at all.

Sir Peter. Now then, Sir Oliver, you may have a better opportunity of satisfying yourself than by an old romancing tale of a poor relation;—go with my friend Moses, and represent Mr. Premium, and then, I'll answer for't, you will see your nephew in all his glory.

Sir Oliver. Egad, I like this idea better than the other, and I may visit Joseph afterwards, as old Stanley.

Sir Peter. True—so you may.

Rowley. Well, this is taking Charles rather at a disadvantage, to be sure. However, Moses—you understand Sir Peter, and will be faithful?

Moses. You may depend upon me,—this is near the time I was to have gone.

Sir Oliver. I'll accompany you as soon as you please, Moses; but hold! I have forgot one thing—how the plague shall I be able to pass for a Jew?

---

[18] A street, not far from the Tower of London, named from an old Convent of Crossed or Crouched Friars.

Moses. There's no need—the principal is Christian.

Sir Oliver. Is he?—I'm sorry to hear it—but, then again, an't I rather too smartly dressed to look like a money-lender?

Sir Peter. Not at all; 'twould not be out of character, if you went in your own carriage—would it, Moses?

Moses. Not in the least.

Sir Oliver. Well, but how must I talk? there's certainly some cant of usury, and mode of treating, that I ought to know.

Sir Peter. Oh, there's not much to learn—the great point, as I take it, is to be exorbitant enough in your demands—hey, Moses?

Moses. Yes, that's a very great point.

Sir Oliver. I'll answer for't I'll not be wanting in that. I'll ask him eight or ten per cent on the loan, at least.

Moses. If you ask him no more than that, you'll be discovered immediately.

Sir Oliver. Hey! what the plague! how much then?

Moses. That depends upon the circumstances. If he appears not very anxious for the supply, you should require only forty or fifty per cent; but if you find him in great distress, and want the moneys very bad—you may ask double.

Sir Peter. A good honest trade you're learning, Sir Oliver!

Sir Oliver. Truly I think so—and not unprofitable.

Moses. Then, you know, you haven't the moneys yourself, but are forced to borrow them for him of a friend.

Sir Oliver. Oh! I borrow it of a friend, do I?

Moses. Yes, and your friend is an unconscionable dog, but you can't help it.

Sir Oliver. My friend is an unconscionable dog, is he?

Moses. Yes, and he himself has not the moneys by him —but is forced to sell stock at a great loss.

Sir Oliver. He is forced to sell stock, is he, at a great loss, is he? Well, that's very kind of him.

Sir Peter. I'faith, Sir Oliver—Mr. Premium, I mean— you'll soon be master of the trade. But, Moses! wouldn't you have him run out a little against the Annuity Bill? [19] That would be in character, I should think.

---

[19] The Annuity Bill, presented in the House of Commons April 29, 1777, and passed in May (after the first performance of *The S. for S.*) was aimed to safeguard minors against grantors of life annuities.

Moses. Very much.

Rowley. And lament that a young man now must be at years of discretion before he is suffered to ruin himself?

Moses. Aye, great pity!

Sir Peter. And abuse the public for allowing merit to an act whose only object is to snatch misfortune and imprudence from the rapacious relief of usury, and give the minor a chance of inheriting his estate without being undone by coming into possession.

Sir Oliver. So, so—Moses shall give me further instructions as we go together.

Sir Peter. You will not have much time, for your nephew lives hard by.

Sir Oliver. Oh, never fear! my tutor appears so able, that though Charles lived in the next street, it must be my own fault if I am not a complete rogue before I turn the corner.   [*Exeunt* SIR OLIVER *and* MOSES.

Sir Peter. So now I think Sir Oliver will be convinced; —you are partial, Rowley, and would have prepared Charles for the other plot.

Rowley. No, upon my word, Sir Peter.

Sir Peter. Well, go bring me this Snake, and I'll hear what he has to say presently.—I see Maria, and want to speak with her.—[*Exit* ROWLEY.] I should be glad to be convinced my suspicions of Lady Teazle and Charles were unjust. I have never yet opened my mind on this subject to my friend Joseph—I'm determined I will do it—*he* will give me his opinion sincerely.

Enter MARIA.

So, child, has Mr. Surface returned with you?

Maria. No, sir—he was engaged.

Sir Peter. Well, Maria, do you not reflect, the more you converse with that amiable young man, what return his partiality for you deserves?

Maria. Indeed, Sir Peter, your frequent importunity on this subject distresses me extremely—you compel me to declare, that I know no man who has ever paid me a particular attention whom I would not prefer to Mr. Surface.

Sir Peter. So—here's perverseness! No, no, Maria, 'tis Charles only whom you would prefer—'tis evident his vices and follies have won your heart.

Maria. This is unkind, sir—you know I have obeyed you in neither seeing nor corresponding with him; I have heard enough to convince me that he is unworthy my regard. Yet I cannot think it culpable, if, while my understanding severely condemns his vices, my heart suggests some pity for his distresses.

Sir Peter. Well, well, pity him as much as you please, but give your heart and hand to a worthier object.

Maria. Never to his brother!

Sir Peter. Go, perverse and obstinate! But take care, madam; you have never yet known what the authority of a guardian is—don't compel me to inform you of it.

Maria. I can only say, you shall not have *just* reason. 'Tis true, by my father's will, I am for a short period bound to regard you as his substitute, but must cease to think you so, when you would compel me to be miserable.

[*Exit* MARIA.

Sir Peter. Was ever man so crossed as I am! everything conspiring to fret me!—I had not been involved in matrimony a fortnight, before her father, a hale and hearty man, died—on purpose, I believe, for the pleasure of plaguing me with the care of his daughter. But here comes my helpmate! She appears in great good humor. How happy I should be if I could tease her into loving me, though but a little!

Enter LADY TEAZLE.

Lady Teazle. Lud! Sir Peter, I hope you haven't been quarrelling with Maria—it isn't using me well to be ill humored when I am not by.

Sir Peter. Ah, Lady Teazle, you might have the power to make me good humored at all times.

Lady Teazle. I am sure I wish I had—for I want you to be in charming sweet temper at this moment. Do be good humored now, and let me have two hundred pounds, will you?

Sir Peter. Two hundred pounds! what, an't I to be in a good humor without paying for it! But speak to me thus, and i'faith there's nothing I could refuse you. You shall have it; but seal me a bond for the repayment.

Lady Teazle. O, no—there—my note of hand will do as well.

Sir Peter. [*Kissing her hand.*] And you shall no longer reproach me with not giving you an independent settlement,—I mean shortly to surprise you; but shall we always live thus, hey?

Lady Teazle. If you please. I'm sure I don't care how soon we leave off quarrelling, provided you'll own *you* were tired first.

Sir Peter. Well—then let our future contest be, who shall be most obliging.

Lady Teazle. I assure you, Sir Peter, good nature becomes you. You look now as you did before we were married!—when you used to walk with me under the elms, and tell me stories of what a gallant you were in your youth, and chuck me under the chin, you would, and ask me if I thought I could love an old fellow, who would deny me nothing—didn't you?

Sir Peter. Yes, yes, and you were as kind and attentive.

Lady Teazle. Aye, so I was, and would always take your part, when my acquaintance used to abuse you, and turn you into ridicule.

Sir Peter. Indeed!

Lady Teazle. Aye, and when my cousin Sophy has called you a stiff, peevish old bachelor, and laughed at me for thinking of marrying one who might be my father, I have always defended you—and said, I didn't think you so ugly by any means, and that I dared say you'd make a very good sort of a husband.

Sir Peter. And you prophesied right—and we shall certainly now be the happiest couple——

Lady Teazle. And never differ again!

Sir Peter. No, never!—though at the same time, indeed, my dear Lady Teazle, you must watch your temper very narrowly; for in all our little quarrels, my dear, if you recollect, my love, you always began first.

Lady Teazle. I beg your pardon, my dear Sir Peter: indeed, you always gave the provocation.

Sir Peter. Now, see, my angel! take care—*contradicting* isn't the way to keep friends.

Lady Teazle. Then, don't *you* begin it, my love!

Sir Peter. There, now! you—you are going on—you don't perceive, my life, that you are just doing the very thing which you know always makes me angry.

Lady Teazle. Nay, you know if you will be angry without any reason——

Sir Peter. There now! you want to quarrel again.

Lady Teazle. No, I am sure I don't—but, if you will be so peevish——

Sir Peter. There now! who begins first?

Lady Teazle. Why, you, to be sure. I said nothing—but there's no bearing your temper.

Sir Peter. No, no, madam, the fault's in your own temper.

Lady Teazle. Aye, you are just what my cousin Sophy said you would be.

Sir Peter. Your cousin Sophy is a forward, impertinent gipsy.

Lady Teazle. You are a great bear, I'm sure, to abuse my relations.

Sir Peter. Now may all the plagues of marriage be doubled on me, if ever I try to be friends with you any more!

Lady Teazle. So much the better.

Sir Peter. No, no, madam; 'tis evident you never cared a pin for me, and I was a madman to marry you—a pert, rural coquette, that had refused half the honest squires in the neighborhood!

Lady Teazle. And I am sure I was a fool to marry you—an old dangling bachelor, who was single at fifty, only because he never could meet with any one who would have him.

Sir Peter. Aye, aye, madam; but you were pleased enough to listen to me—*you* never had such an offer before.

Lady Teazle. No! didn't I refuse Sir Twivy Tarrier, who everybody said would have been a better match—for his estate is just as good as yours—and he has broke his neck since we have been married.

Sir Peter. I have done with you, madam! You are an unfeeling, ungrateful—but there's an end of everything. I believe you capable of anything that's bad. Yes, madam, I now believe the reports relative to you and Charles, madam—yes, madam, you and Charles—are not without grounds——

Lady Teazle. Take care, Sir Peter! you had better not insinuate any such thing! I'll not be suspected with*out cause,* I promise you.

Sir Peter. Very well, madam! very well! a separate maintenance as soon as you please. Yes, madam, or a divorce! I'll make an example of myself for the benefit of all old bachelors. Let us separate, madam.

Lady Teazle. Agreed! agreed! And now, my dear Sir Peter, we are of a mind once more, we may be the *hap-*

piest couple, and *never differ again,* you know: ha! ha!
Well, you are going to be in a passion, I see, and I shall
only interrupt you—so, bye! bye!   [*Exit.*

Sir Peter. Plagues and tortures! can't I make her angry
neither? Oh, I am the miserablest fellow! But I'll not bear
her presuming to keep her temper—no! she may break my
heart, but she shan't keep her temper.   [*Exit.*

SCENE II—CHARLES'S *house*

Enter TRIP, MOSES, *and* SIR OLIVER SURFACE.

Trip. Here, Master Moses! if you'll stay a moment, I'll
try whether—what's the gentleman's name?

Sir Oliver. Mr. Moses, what *is* my name?   [*Aside.*

Moses. Mr. Premium.

Trip. Premium—very well.   [*Exit* TRIP, *taking snuff.*

Sir Oliver. To judge by the servants, one wouldn't believe the master was ruined. But what!—sure, this was my
brother's house?

Moses. Yes, sir; Mr. Charles bought it of Mr. Joseph,
with the furniture, pictures, &c., just as the old gentleman left it—Sir Peter thought it a great piece of extravagance in him.

Sir Oliver. In my mind, the other's economy in *selling*
it to him was more reprehensible by half.

Re-enter TRIP.

Trip. My master says you must wait, gentlemen; he
has company, and can't speak with you yet.

Sir Oliver. If he knew *who* it was wanted to see him,
perhaps he wouldn't have sent such a message?

Trip. Yes, yes, sir; he knows *you* are here—I didn't
forget little Premium—no, no, no.

Sir Oliver. Very well—and I pray, sir, what may be your
name?

Trip. Trip, sir—my name is Trip, at your service.

Sir Oliver. Well, then, Mr. Trip, you have a pleasant
sort of a place here, I guess.

Trip. Why, yes—here are three or four of us pass our
time agreeably enough; but then our wages are sometimes a little in arrear—and not very great either—but
fifty pounds a year, and find our own bags and bouquets.[20]

[20] Footman's trappings. The back-hair of the bag-wig was enclosed in
an ornamental bag.

Sir Oliver. [*Aside.*] Bags and bouquets! halters and bastinadoes!

Trip. But *à propos*, Moses, have you been able to get me that little bill discounted?

Sir Oliver. [*Aside.*] Wants to raise money, too!—mercy on me! Has his distresses, I warrant, like a lord,—and affects creditors and duns.

Moses. 'Twas not to be done, indeed, Mr. Trip.
                                    [*Gives the note.*

Trip. Good lack, you surprise me! My friend *Brush* has indorsed it, and I thought when he put his mark on the back of a bill 'twas as good as cash.

Moses. No, 'twouldn't do.

Trip. A small sum—but twenty pounds. Hark'ee, Moses, do you think you couldn't get it me by way of annuity?

Sir Oliver. [*Aside.*] An annuity! ha! ha! ha! a footman raise money by way of annuity! Well done, luxury, egad!

Moses. But you must insure your place.

Trip. Oh, with all my heart! I'll insure my place, and my life too, if you please.

Sir Oliver. [*Aside.*] It's more than I would your neck.

Trip. But then, Moses, it must be done before this d—d register[21] takes place—one wouldn't like to have one's name made public, you know.

Moses. No, certainly. But is there nothing you could deposit?

Trip. Why, nothing capital of my master's wardrobe has dropped lately; but I could give you a mortgage on some of his winter clothes, with equity of redemption before November—or you shall have the reversion of the French velvet, or a post-obit[22] on the blue and silver;—these, I should think, Moses, with a few pair of point ruffles, as a collateral security—hey, my little fellow?

Moses. Well, well.   [*Bell rings.*

Trip. Gad, I heard the bell! I believe, gentlemen, I can now introduce you. Don't forget the annuity, little Moses! This way, gentlemen, insure my place, you know.

Sir Oliver. [*Aside.*] If the man be a shadow of his master, this is the temple of dissipation indeed!   [*Exeunt.*

[21] Another reference to the Annuity Bill of 1777, proposed on April 29, and passed in May. It provided 'for registering the Grants of Life Annuities.'
[22] Future claim.

SCENE III—CHARLES SURFACE, CARELESS, &C., &C.,
at a table with wine, &c.

Charles Surface. 'Fore heaven, 'tis true!—there's the great degeneracy of the age. Many of our acquaintance have taste, spirit, and politeness; but, plague on't, they won't drink.

Careless. It is so, indeed, Charles! they give in to all the substantial luxuries of the table, and abstain from nothing but wine and wit.

Charles Surface. Oh, certainly society suffers by it intolerably! for now, instead of the social spirit of raillery that used to mantle over a glass of bright Burgundy, their conversation is become just like the Spa-water they drink, which has all the pertness and flatulence of champagne, without its spirit or flavor.

1 Gentleman. But what are *they* to do who love play better than wine?

Careless. True! there's Harry diets himself for gaming, and is now under a hazard regimen.[23]

Charles Surface. Then he'll have the worst of it. What! you wouldn't train a horse for the course by keeping him from corn! For my part, egad, I am now never so successful as when I am a little merry—let me throw on a bottle of champagne, and I never lose—at least I never feel my losses, which is exactly the same thing.

2 Gentleman. Aye, that I believe.

Charles Surface. And, then, what man can pretend to be a believer in love, who is an abjurer of wine? 'Tis the test by which the lover knows his own heart. Fill a dozen bumpers to a dozen beauties, and she that floats at top is the maid that has bewitched you.

Careless. Now then, Charles, be honest, and give us your real favorite.

Charles Surface. Why, I have withheld her only in compassion to you. If I toast her, you must give a round of her peers—which is impossible—on earth.

Careless. Oh, then we'll find some canonised vestals or heathen goddesses that will do, I warrant!

Charles Surface. Here then, bumpers, you rogues! bumpers! Maria! Maria—   [*Drink.*

[23] 'Keeps in strict training for gambling.'

1 Gentleman. Maria who?

Charles Surface. O, damn the surname!—'tis too formal to be registered in Love's calendar—but now, Sir Toby Bumper, beware—we must have beauty superlative.

Careless. Nay, never study, Sir Toby: we'll stand to the toast, though your mistress should want an eye—and you know you have a song will excuse you.

Sir Toby. Egad, so I have! and I'll give him the song instead of the lady.　　　　　　　　　　　　　[*Sings.*

SONG AND CHORUS.

> Here's to the maiden of bashful fifteen;
> 　　Here's to the widow of fifty;
> Here's to the flaunting extravagant quean,
> 　　And here's to the housewife that's thrifty.
> *Chorus.*　Let the toast pass—
> 　　　　Drink to the lass—
> I'll warrant she'll prove an excuse for the glass.
>
> Here's to the charmer whose dimples we prize;
> 　　Now to the maid who has none, sir;
> Here's to the girl with a pair of blue eyes,
> 　　And here's to the nymph with but one, sir.
> *Chorus.*　Let the toast pass, &c.
>
> Here's to the maid with a bosom of snow:
> 　　Now to *her* that's as brown as a berry:
> Here's to the wife with a face full of woe,
> 　　And now for the damsel that's merry.
> *Chorus.*　Let the toast pass, &c.
>
> For let 'em be clumsy, or let 'em be slim,
> 　　Young or ancient, I care not a feather:
> So fill a pint bumper quite up to the brim,
> 　　—And let us e'en toast 'em together.
> *Chorus.*　Let the toast pass, &c.

All. Bravo! Bravo!

Enter TRIP, *and whispers* CHARLES SURFACE.

Charles Surface. Gentlemen, you must excuse me a little.—Careless, take the chair, will you?

Careless. Nay, prithee, Charles, what now? This is one of your peerless beauties, I suppose, has dropped in by chance?

Charles Surface. No, faith! To tell you the truth, 'tis a
Jew and a broker, who are come by appointment.

Careless. Oh, damn it! let's have the Jew in—

1 Gentleman. Aye, and the broker too, by all means.

2 Gentleman. Yes, yes, the Jew and the broker.

Charles Surface. Egad, with all my heart!—Trip, bid
the gentlemen walk in.—   [*Exit* TRIP.
Though there's one of them a stranger, I can tell you.

Careless. Charles, let us give them some generous
Burgundy, and perhaps they'll grow conscientious.

Charles Surface. Oh, hang 'em, no! wine does but draw
forth a man's *natural* qualities; and to make *them* drink
would only be to whet their knavery.

Enter TRIP, SIR OLIVER SURFACE, *and* MOSES.

Charles Surface. So, honest Moses; walk in, pray, Mr.
Premium—that's the gentleman's name, isn't it, Moses?

Moses. Yes, sir.

Charles Surface. Set chairs, Trip.—Sit down, Mr.
Premium.—Glasses, Trip.—Sit down, Moses.—Come, Mr.
Premium, I'll give you a sentiment; here's 'Success to
usury!'—Moses, fill the gentleman a bumper.

Moses. Success to usury!

Careless. Right, Moses—usury is prudence and industry,
and deserves to succeed.

Sir Oliver. Then here's—All the success it deserves!

Careless. No, no, that won't do! Mr. Premium, you have
demurred to the toast, and must drink it in a pint bumper.

1 Gentleman. A pint bumper, at least.

Moses. Oh, pray, sir, consider—Mr. Premium's a gentleman.

Careless. And therefore loves good wine.

2 Gentleman. Give Moses a quart glass—this is mutiny,
and a high contempt of the chair.

Careless. Here, now for't! I'll see justice done, to the
last drop of my bottle.

Sir Oliver. Nay, pray, gentlemen—I did not expect this
usage.

Charles Surface. No, hang it, Careless, you shan't; Mr.
Premium's a stranger.

Sir Oliver. [*Aside.*] Odd! I wish I was well out of this
company.

Careless. Plague on 'em then! if they won't drink, we'll
not sit down with 'em. Come, Harry, the dice are in the

next room.—Charles, you'll join us—when you have finished your business with these gentlemen?

Charles Surface. I will! I will!—[*Exeunt Gentlemen.*]
Careless!

Careless. [*Returning.*] Well!

Charles Surface. Perhaps I may want *you.*

Careless. Oh, you know I am always ready—word, note,
or bond, 'tis all the same to me.   [*Exit.*

Moses. Sir, this is Mr. Premium, a gentleman of the
strictest honor and secrecy; and always performs what he
undertakes. Mr. Premium, this is——

Charles Surface. Pshaw! have done! Sir, my friend
Moses is a very honest fellow, but a little slow at expression; he'll be an hour giving us our titles. Mr. Premium,
the plain state of the matter is this—I am an extravagant
young fellow who wants money to borrow; you I take
to be a prudent old fellow, who has got money to lend.
I am blockhead enough to give fifty per cent sooner than
not have it; and you, I presume, are rogue enough to take
a hundred if you could get it. Now, sir, you see we are
acquainted at once, and may proceed to business without
farther ceremony.

Sir Oliver. Exceeding frank, upon my word. I see, sir,
you are not a man of many compliments.

Charles Surface. Oh, no, sir! plain dealing in business I
always think best.

Sir Oliver. Sir, I like you the better for't. However, you
are mistaken in one thing—I have no money to lend, but
I believe I could procure some of a friend; but then he's
an unconscionable dog—isn't he, Moses? And must sell
stock to accommodate you—mustn't he, Moses?

Moses. Yes, indeed! You know I always speak the truth,
and scorn to tell a lie!

Charles Surface. Right! People that expect truth generally do. But these are trifles, Mr. Premium. What! I
know money isn't to be bought without paying for't!

Sir Oliver. Well, but what security could you give? You
have no land, I suppose?

Charles Surface. Not a mole-hill, nor a twig, but what's
in beau-pots[24] out at the window!

Sir Oliver. Nor any stock, I presume?

Charles Surface. Nothing but live stock—and that's only

---

[24] Large ornamental flower-pots.

a few pointers and ponies. But pray, Mr. Premium, are you acquainted at all with any of my connections?

Sir Oliver. Why, to say truth, I am.

Charles Surface. Then you must know that I have a devilish rich uncle in the East Indies, Sir *Oliver Surface,* from whom I have the greatest expectations.

Sir Oliver. That you have a wealthy uncle, I have heard —but how your expectations will turn out is more, I believe, than you can tell.

Charles Surface. Oh, no!—there can be no doubt—they tell me I'm a prodigious favorite—and that he talks of leaving me everything.

Sir Oliver. Indeed! this is the first I've heard on't.

Charles Surface. Yes, yes, 'tis just so.—Moses knows 'tis true; don't you, Moses?

Moses. Oh, yes! I'll swear to't.

Sir Oliver. [*Aside.*] Egad, they'll persuade me presently I'm at Bengal.

Charles Surface. Now I propose, Mr. Premium, if it's agreeable to you, a post-obit on Sir Oliver's life; though at the same time the old fellow has been so liberal to me that I give you my word I should be very sorry to hear anything had happened to him.

Sir Oliver. Not more than *I* should, I assure you. But the bond you mention happens to be just the worst security you could offer me—for I might live to a hundred and never recover the principal.

Charles Surface. Oh, yes, you would!—the moment Sir Oliver dies, you know, you'd come on me for the money.

Sir Oliver. Then I believe I should be the most unwelcome dun you ever had in your life.

Charles Surface. What! I suppose you are afraid now that Sir Oliver is too good a life?

Sir Oliver. No, indeed I am not—though I have heard he is as hale and healthy as any man of his years in Christendom.

Charles Surface. There again you are misinformed. No, no, the climate has hurt him considerably, poor uncle Oliver. Yes, he breaks apace, I'm told—and so much altered lately that his nearest relations don't know him.

Sir Oliver. No! Ha! ha! ha! so much altered lately that his relations don't know him! Ha! ha! ha! that's droll, egad —ha! ha! ha!

Charles Surface. Ha! ha!—you're glad to hear that, little Premium.

Sir Oliver. No, no, I'm not.

Charles Surface. Yes, yes, you are—ha! ha! ha!—you know that mends your chance.

Sir Oliver. But I'm told Sir Oliver is coming over—nay, some say he is actually arrived.

Charles Surface. Pshaw! sure I must know better than you whether he's come or not. No, no, rely on't, he is at this moment at Calcutta, isn't he, Moses?

Moses. Oh, yes, certainly.

Sir Oliver. Very true, as you say, you must know better than I, though I have it from pretty good authority—haven't I, Moses?

Moses. Yes, most undoubted!

Sir Oliver. But, sir, as I understand you want a few hundreds immediately, is there nothing you would dispose of?

Charles Surface. How do you mean?

Sir Oliver. For instance, now—I have heard—that your father left behind him a great quantity of massy old plate.

Charles Surface. O lud! that's gone long ago—Moses can tell you how better than I can.

Sir Oliver. Good lack! all the family race-cups and corporation-bowls! [*Aside.*]—Then it was also supposed that his library was one of the most valuable and complete.

Charles Surface. Yes, yes, so it was—vastly too much so for a private gentleman—for my part, I was always of a communicative disposition, so I thought it a shame to keep so much knowledge to myself.

Sir Oliver. [*Aside.*] Mercy on me! learning that had run in the family like an heirloom!—[*Aloud.*] Pray, what are become of the books?

Charles Surface. You must inquire of the auctioneer, Master Premium, for I don't believe even Moses can direct you there.

Moses. I never meddle with books.

Sir Oliver. So, so, nothing of the family property left, I suppose?

Charles Surface. Not much, indeed; unless you have a mind to the family pictures. I have got a room full of ancestors above—and if you have a taste for old paintings, egad, you shall have 'em a bargain!

Sir Oliver. Hey! and the devil! sure, you wouldn't sell your forefathers, would you?

Charles Surface. Every man of 'em, to the best bidder.

Sir Oliver. What! your great-uncles and aunts?

Charles Surface. Aye, and my great-grandfathers and grandmothers too.

Sir Oliver. Now I give him up!—[*Aside.*]—What the plague, have you no bowels for your own kindred? Odd's life! do you take me for Shylock in the play, that you would raise money of me on your own flesh and blood?

Charles Surface. Nay, my little broker, don't be angry: what need *you* care, if you have your money's worth?

Sir Oliver. Well, I'll be the purchaser—I think I can dispose of the family.—[*Aside.*] Oh, I'll never forgive him this! never!

Enter CARELESS.

Careless. Come, Charles, what keeps you?

Charles Surface. I can't come yet. I'faith! we are going to have a sale above—here's little Premium will buy all my ancestors!

Careless. Oh, burn your ancestors!

Charles Surface. No, he may do that afterwards, if he pleases. Stay, Careless, we want you; egad, you shall be auctioneer—so come along with us.

Careless. Oh, have with you, if that's the case.—I can handle a hammer as well as a dice box!

Sir Oliver. Oh, the profligates!   [*Aside.*

Charles Surface. Come, Moses, you shall be appraiser, if we want one.—Gad's life, little Premium, you don't seem to like the business.

Sir Oliver. Oh, yes, I do, vastly! Ha! ha! yes, yes, I think it a rare joke to sell one's family by auction—ha! ha! —[*Aside.*] Oh, the prodigal!

Charles Surface. To be sure! when a man wants money, where the plague should he get assistance, if he can't make free with his own relations?   [*Exeunt.*

ACT FOUR

SCENE I—*Picture-room at* CHARLES'S

Enter CHARLES SURFACE, SIR OLIVER SURFACE,
MOSES, *and* CARELESS.

CHARLES SURFACE. Walk in, gentlemen, pray walk in!—
here they are, the family of the Surfaces, up to the Conquest.

Sir Oliver. And, in my opinion, a goodly collection.

Charles Surface. Aye, aye, these are done in true spirit
of portrait-painting—no volunteer grace or expression—
not like the works of your modern Raphael, who gives you
the strongest resemblance, yet contrives to make your own
portrait independent of you; so that you may sink the
original and not hurt the picture. No, no; the merit of
these is the inveterate likeness—all stiff and awkward as
the originals, and like nothing in human nature beside!

Sir Oliver. Ah! we shall never see such figures of men
again.

Charles Surface. I hope not. Well, you see, Master
Premium, what a domestic character I am—here I sit of
an evening surrounded by my family. But come, get to
your pulpit, Mr. Auctioneer—here's an old gouty chair of
my grandfather's will answer the purpose.

Careless. Aye, aye, this will do. But, Charles, I have
ne'er a hammer; and what's an auctioneer without his
hammer?

Charles Surface. Egad, that's true. What parchment
have we here? [*Takes down a roll.*] *Richard, heir to
Thomas*—our genealogy in full. Here, Careless, you shall
have no common bit of mahogany—here's the family tree
for you, you rogue—this shall be your hammer, and now
you may knock down my ancestors with their own
pedigree.

Sir Oliver. [*Aside.*] What an unnatural rogue!—an *ex
post facto* parricide!

Careless. Yes, yes, here's a list of your generation indeed;—faith, Charles, this is the most convenient thing
you could have found for the business, for 'twill serve not
only as a hammer, but a catalogue into the bargain.—But
come, begin—A-going, a-going, a-going!

Charles Surface. Bravo, Careless! Well, here's my great uncle, Sir Richard Raviline, a marvellous good general in his day, I assure you. He served in all the Duke of Marlborough's wars, and got that cut over his eye at the battle of Malplaquet.[25] What say you, Mr. Premium? look at him—there's a hero for you! not cut out of his feathers, as your modern clipped captains are, but enveloped in wig and regimentals, as a general should be. What do you bid?

Moses. Mr. Premium would have you speak.

Charles Surface. Why, then, he shall have him for ten pounds, and I am sure that's not dear for a staff-officer.

Sir Oliver. Heaven deliver me! his famous uncle Richard for ten pounds! [*Aside.*]—Very well, sir, I take him at that.

Charles Surface. Careless, knock down my uncle Richard.—Here, now, is a maiden sister of his, my great-aunt Deborah, done by Kneller,[26] thought to be in his best manner, and a very formidable likeness. There she is, you see, a shepherdess feeding her flock. You shall have her for five pounds ten—the sheep are worth the money.

Sir Oliver. Ah! poor Deborah! a woman who set such a value on herself! [*Aside.*]—Five pound ten—she's mine.

Charles Surface. Knock down my aunt Deborah! Here, now, are two that were a sort of cousins of theirs.—You see, Moses, these pictures were done some time ago, when beaux wore wigs, and the ladies wore their own hair.

Sir Oliver. Yes, truly, head-dresses appear to have been a little lower in those days.

Charles Surface. Well, take that couple for the same.

Moses. 'Tis a good bargain.

Charles Surface. Careless!—This, now, is a grandfather of my mother's, a learned judge, well known on the western circuit.—What do you rate him at, Moses?

Moses. Four guineas.

Charles Surface. Four guineas! Gad's life, you don't bid me the price of his wig.—Mr. Premium, *you* have more respect for the woolsack;[27] do let us knock his lordship down at fifteen.

Sir Oliver. By all means.

Careless. Gone!

25 On September 11, 1709.
26 Sir Godfrey Kneller (1648-1723), who painted many portraits of English sovereigns and nobles.
27 'For lawyers.' The reference to the Lord Chancellor's seat on the Woolsack in the House of Lords is here meant as the symbol of the profession of law.

Charles Surface. And there are two brothers of his, William and Walter Blunt, Esquires, both members of Parliament, and noted speakers; and, what's very extraordinary, I believe that is the first time they were ever bought and sold.

Sir Oliver. That's very extraordinary, indeed! I'll take them at your own price, for the honor of Parliament.

Careless. Well said, little Premium! I'll knock 'em down at forty.

Charles Surface. Here's a jolly fellow—I don't know what relation, but he was mayor of Manchester; take him at eight pounds.

Sir Oliver. No, no—six will do for the mayor.

Charles Surface. Come, make it guineas, and I'll throw you the two aldermen there into the bargain.

Sir Oliver. They're mine.

Charles Surface. Careless, knock down the mayor and aldermen. But, plague on't! we shall be all day retailing in this manner; do let us deal wholesale—what say you, little Premium? Give me three hundred pounds for the rest of the family in the lump.

Careless. Aye, aye, that will be the best way.

Sir Oliver. Well, well, anything to accommodate you; they are mine. But there is one portrait which you have always passed over.

Careless. What, that ill-looking little fellow over the settee?

Sir Oliver. Yes, sir, I mean that; though I don't think him so ill-looking a little fellow, by any means.

Charles Surface. What, that? Oh, that's my uncle Oliver! 'Twas done before he went to India.

Careless. Your uncle Oliver! Gad, then you'll never be friends, Charles. That, now, to me, is as stern a looking rogue as ever I saw—an unforgiving eye, and a damned disinheriting countenance! an inveterate knave, depend on't. Don't you think so, little Premium?

Sir Oliver. Upon my soul, sir, I do not; I think it is as honest a looking face as any in the room, dead or alive. But I suppose your uncle Oliver goes with the rest of the lumber?

Charles Surface. No, hang it! I'll not part with poor Noll. The old fellow has been very good to me, and egad, I'll keep his picture while I've a room to put it in.

Sir Oliver. The rogue's my nephew after all! [*Aside.*]

—But, sir, I have somehow taken a fancy to that picture.

Charles Surface. I'm sorry for't, for you certainly will not have it. Oons! haven't you got enough of 'em?

Sir Oliver. I forgive him everything! [*Aside.*]—But, sir, when I take a whim in my head, I don't value money. I'll give you as much for that as for all the rest.

Charles Surface. Don't tease me, master broker; I tell you I'll not part with it, and there's an end on't.

Sir Oliver. How like his father the dog is!—[*Aloud.*] Well, well, I have done.—I did not perceive it before, but I think I never saw such a resemblance.—Well, sir—here is a draught for your sum.

Charles Surface. Why, 'tis for eight hundred pounds!

Sir Oliver. You will not let Sir Oliver go?

Charles Surface. Zounds! no! I tell you, once more.

Sir Oliver. Then never mind the difference; we'll balance another time. But give me your hand on the bargain; you are an honest fellow, Charles—I beg pardon, sir, for being so free.—Come, Moses.

Charles Surface. Egad, this is a whimsical old fellow!— but hark'ee, Premium, you'll prepare lodgings for these gentlemen.

Sir Oliver. Yes, yes, I'll send for them in a day or two.

Charles Surface. But hold—do now—send a genteel conveyance for them, for, I assure you, they were most of them used to ride in their own carriages.

Sir Oliver. I will, I will, for all but—Oliver.

Charles Surface. Aye, all but the little honest nabob.

Sir Oliver. You're fixed on that?

Charles Surface. Peremptorily.

Sir Oliver. A dear extravagant rogue! [*Aside.*]—Good day!—Come, Moses.—Let me hear now who dares call him profligate!   [*Exeunt* SIR OLIVER *and* MOSES.

Careless. Why, this is the oddest genius of the sort I ever saw!

Charles Surface. Egad, he's the prince of brokers, I think. I wonder how the devil Moses got acquainted with so honest a fellow.—Ha! here's Rowley.—Do, Careless, say I'll join the company in a moment.

Careless. I will—but don't let that old blockhead persuade you to squander any of that money on old musty debts, or any such nonsense; for tradesmen, Charles, are the most exorbitant fellows!

Charles Surface. Very true, and paying them is only encouraging them.

Careless. Nothing else.

Charles Surface. Aye, aye, never fear.—[*Exit* CARELESS.] So! this was an odd old fellow, indeed! Let me see, two-thirds of this is mine by right—five hundred and thirty pounds. 'Fore heaven! I find one's ancestors are more valuable relations than I took 'em for!—Ladies and gentlemen, your most obedient and very grateful humble servant.

Enter ROWLEY.

Ha! old Rowley! egad, you are just come in time to take leave of your old acquaintance.

Rowley. Yes, I heard they were going. But I wonder you can have such spirits under so many distresses.

Charles Surface. Why, there's the point—my distresses are so many, that I can't afford to part with my spirits; but I shall be rich and splenetic, all in good time. However, I suppose you are surprised that I am not more sorrowful at parting with so many near relations; to be sure, 'tis very affecting; but, rot 'em, you see they never move a muscle, so why should I?

Rowley. There's no making you serious a moment.

Charles Surface. Yes, faith: I am so now. Here, my honest Rowley, here, get me this changed, and take a hundred pounds of it immediately to old Stanley.

Rowley. A hundred pounds! Consider only——

Charles Surface. Gad's life, don't talk about it! poor Stanley's wants are pressing, and, if you don't make haste, we shall have some one call that has a better right to the money.

Rowley. Ah! there's the point! I never will cease dunning you with the old proverb——

Charles Surface. 'Be *just* before you're *generous*,' hey!— Why, so I would if I could; but Justice is an old lame hobbling beldame, and I can't get her to keep pace with Generosity, for the soul of me.

Rowley. Yet, Charles, believe me, one hour's reflection——

Charles Surface. Aye, aye, it's all very true; but, hark'ee, Rowley, while I have, by heaven I'll give—so, damn your economy! and now for hazard.   [*Exit.*

SCENE II—*The parlor*

Enter SIR OLIVER SURFACE *and* MOSES.

Moses. Well, sir, I think, as Sir Peter said, you have seen Mr. Charles in high glory; 'tis great pity he's so extravagant.

Sir Oliver. True, but he wouldn't sell my picture.

Moses. And loves wine and women so much.

Sir Oliver. But he wouldn't sell my picture!

Moses. And games so deep.

Sir Oliver. But he wouldn't sell my picture. Oh, here's Rowley.

Enter ROWLEY.

Rowley. So, Sir Oliver, I find you have made a purchase——

Sir Oliver. Yes, yes, our young rake has parted with his ancestors like old tapestry.

Rowley. And here has he commissioned me to redeliver you part of the purchase-money—I mean, though, in your necessitous character of old Stanley.

Moses. Ah! there is the pity of all: he is so damned charitable.

Rowley. And I left a hosier and two tailors in the hall, who, I'm sure, won't be paid, and this hundred would satisfy 'em.

Sir Oliver. Well, well, I'll pay his debts—and his benevolence too; but now I am no more a broker, and you shall introduce me to the elder brother as old Stanley.

Rowley. Not yet awhile; Sir Peter, I know, means to call there about this time.

Enter TRIP.

Trip. O gentlemen, I beg pardon for not showing you out; this way—Moses, a word.   [*Exeunt* TRIP *and* MOSES.

Sir Oliver. There's a fellow for you! Would you believe it, that puppy intercepted the Jew on our coming, and wanted to raise money before he got to his master!

Rowley. Indeed!

Sir Oliver. Yes, they are now planning an annuity business. Ah, Master Rowley, in my days, servants were content with the follies of their masters, when they were worn a little threadbare—but now they have their vices, like their birthday clothes,[28] with the gloss on.

SCENE III—*A library in* JOSEPH SURFACE'S *house*

JOSEPH SURFACE *and* Servant.

Joseph Surface. No letter from Lady Teazle?

Servant. No, sir.

Joseph Surface. [*Aside.*] I am surprised she hasn't sent, if she is prevented from coming. Sir Peter certainly does not suspect me. Yet I wish I may not lose the heiress, through the scrape I have drawn myself in with the wife; however, Charles's imprudence and bad character are great points in my favor.   [*Knocking.*

Servant. Sir, I believe that must be Lady Teazle.

Joseph Surface. Hold! See whether it is or not, before you go to the door—I have a particular message for you, if it should be my brother.

Servant. 'Tis her ladyship, sir; she always leaves her chair at the milliner's in the next street.

Joseph Surface. Stay, stay—draw that screen before the window—that will do;—my opposite neighbor is a maiden lady of so curious a temper.—[*Servant draws the screen, and exit.*] I have a difficult hand to play in this affair. Lady Teazle has lately suspected my views on Maria; but she must by no means be let into that secret,—at least, not till I have her more in my power.

Enter LADY TEAZLE.

Lady Teazle. What, sentiment in soliloquy! Have you been very impatient now? O lud! don't pretend to look grave. I vow I couldn't come before.

Joseph Surface. O madam, punctuality is a species of constancy, a very unfashionable quality in a lady.

Lady Teazle. Upon my word, you ought to pity me. Do you know that Sir Peter is grown so ill-tempered to me of late, and so jealous of Charles too—that's the best of the story, isn't it?

Joseph Surface. [*Aside.*] I am glad my scandalous friends keep that up.

Lady Teazle. I am sure I wish he would let Maria

---

[28] Ceremonial dress for the King's Birthday celebrations.

marry him, and then perhaps he would be convinced; don't you, Mr. Surface?

Joseph Surface. [*Aside.*] Indeed I do not.—Oh, certainly I do! for then my dear Lady Teazle would also be convinced how wrong her suspicions were of my having any design on the silly girl.

Lady Teazle. Well, well, I'm inclined to believe you. But isn't it provoking, to have the most ill-natured things said to one? And there's my friend Lady Sneerwell has circulated I don't know how many scandalous tales of me! and all without any foundation, too—that's what vexes me.

Joseph Surface. Aye, madam, to be sure, that *is* the provoking circumstance—without foundation! yes, yes, there's the mortification, indeed; for, when a scandalous story is believed against one, there certainly is no comfort like the consciousness of having deserved it.

Lady Teazle. No, to be sure—then I'd forgive their malice; but to attack me, who am really so innocent, and who never say an ill-natured thing of anybody—that is, of **any** friend—and then Sir Peter, too, to have him so peevish, and so suspicious, when I know the integrity of my own heart—indeed 'tis monstrous!

Joseph Surface. But, my dear Lady Teazle, 'tis your own fault if you suffer it. When a husband entertains a groundless suspicion of his wife, and withdraws his confidence from her, the original compact is broke, and she owes it to the honor of her sex to endeavor to outwit him.

Lady Teazle. Indeed! So that, if he suspects me without cause, it follows that the best way of curing his jealousy is to give him reason for't?

Joseph Surface. Undoubtedly—for your husband should never be deceived in you: and in that case it becomes *you* to be frail in compliment to *his* discernment.

Lady Teazle. To be sure, what you say is very reasonable, and when the consciousness of my own innocence——

Joseph Surface. Ah, my dear madam, there is the great mistake; 'tis this very conscious innocence that is of the greatest prejudice to you. What is it makes you negligent of forms, and careless of the world's opinion? why, the *consciousness* of your innocence. What makes you thoughtless in your conduct, and apt to run into a thousand little imprudences? why, the *consciousness* of your innocence. What makes you impatient of Sir Peter's temper and outrageous at his suspicions? why, the *consciousness* of your own innocence!

Lady Teazle. 'Tis very true!

Joseph Surface. Now, my dear Lady Teazle, if you would but once make a trifling *faux pas,* you can't conceive how cautious you would grow—and how ready to humor and agree with your husband.

Lady Teazle. Do you think so?

Joseph Surface. Oh, I'm sure on't; and then you would find all scandal would cease at once, for—in short, your character at present is like a person in a plethora, absolutely dying of too much health.

Lady Teazle. So, so; then I perceive your prescription is, that I must sin in my own defence, and part with my virtue to preserve my reputation?

Joseph Surface. Exactly so, upon my credit, ma'am.

Lady Teazle. Well, certainly this is the oddest doctrine, and the newest receipt for avoiding calumny?

Joseph Surface. An infallible one, believe me. *Prudence,* like *experience,* must be paid for.

Lady Teazle. Why, if my understanding were once convinced——

Joseph Surface. Oh, certainly, madam, your understanding *should* be convinced. Yes, yes—heaven forbid I should persuade you to do anything you *thought* wrong. No, no, I have too much honor to desire it.

Lady Teazle. Don't you think we may as well leave honor out of the argument?

Joseph Surface. Ah, the ill effects of your country education, I see, still remain with you.

Lady Teazle. I doubt they do, indeed; and I will fairly own to you, that if I could be persuaded to do wrong, it would be by Sir Peter's ill-usage sooner than your honorable logic, after all.

Joseph Surface. Then, by this hand, which he is unworthy of——   *[Taking her hand.*

Re-enter Servant.

'Sdeath, you blockhead—what do you want?

Servant. I beg pardon, sir, but I thought you wouldn't choose Sir Peter to come up without announcing him.

Joseph Surface. Sir Peter!—Oons—the devil!

Lady Teazle. Sir Peter! O lud! I'm ruined! I'm ruined!

Servant. Sir, 'twasn't I let him in.

Lady Teazle. Oh! I'm undone! What will become of me, now, Mr. Logic?—Oh! mercy, he's on the stairs—I'll get behind here—and if ever I'm so imprudent again——

[*Goes behind the screen.*

Joseph Surface. Give me that book.

[*Sits down. Servant pretends to adjust his hair.*

Enter SIR PETER TEAZLE.

Sir Peter. Aye, ever improving himself!—Mr. Surface, Mr. Surface——

Joseph Surface. Oh, my dear Sir Peter, I beg your pardon. [*Gaping, and throws away the book.*] I have been dozing over a stupid book. Well, I am much obliged to you for this call. You haven't been here, I believe, since I fitted up this room. Books, you know, are the only things I am a coxcomb in.

Sir Peter. 'Tis very neat indeed. Well, well, that's proper; and you make even your screen a source of knowledge—hung, I perceive, with maps.

Joseph Surface. Oh, yes, I find great use in that screen.

Sir Peter. I dare say you must—certainly—when you want to find anything in a hurry.

Joseph Surface. [*Aside.*] Aye, or to hide anything in a hurry either.

Sir Peter. Well, I have a little private business——

Joseph Surface. You needn't stay.   [*To Servant.*

Servant. No, sir.   [*Exit.*

Joseph Surface. Here's a chair, Sir Peter—I beg——

Sir Peter. Well, now we are alone, there is a subject, my dear friend, on which I wish to unburden my mind to you—a point of the greatest moment to my peace: in short, my good friend, Lady Teazle's conduct of late has made me extremely unhappy.

Joseph Surface. Indeed! I am very sorry to hear it.

Sir Peter. Yes, 'tis but too plain she has not the least regard for me; but, what's worse, I have pretty good authority to suspect she must have formed an attachment to another.

Joseph Surface. You astonish me!

Sir Peter. Yes! and, between ourselves, I think I have discovered the person.

Joseph Surface. How! you alarm me exceedingly.

Sir Peter. Aye, my dear friend, I knew you would sympathize with me!

Joseph Surface. Yes, believe me, Sir Peter, such a discovery would hurt me just as much as it would you.

Sir Peter. I am convinced of it.—Ah! it is a happiness to have a friend whom one can trust even with one's family secrets. But have you no guess who I mean?

Joseph Surface. I haven't the most distant idea. It can't be Sir Benjamin Backbite!

Sir Peter. O, no! What say you to Charles?

Joseph Surface. My brother! impossible!

Sir Peter. Ah, my dear friend, the goodness of your own heart misleads you—you judge of others by yourself.

Joseph Surface. Certainly, Sir Peter, the heart that is conscious of its own integrity is ever slow to credit another's treachery.

Sir Peter. True; but your brother has no sentiment—you never hear him talk so.

Joseph Surface. Yet I can't but think Lady Teazle herself has too much principle——

Sir Peter. Aye; but what's her principle against the flattery of a handsome, lively young fellow?

Joseph Surface. That's very true.

Sir Peter. And then, you know, the difference of our ages makes it very improbable that she should have any great affection for me; and if she were to be frail, and I were to make it public, why the town would only laugh at me, the foolish old bachelor who had married a girl.

Joseph Surface. That's true, to be sure—they *would* laugh.

Sir Peter. Laugh! aye, and make ballads, and paragraphs, and the devil knows what of me.

Joseph Surface. No, you must never make it public.

Sir Peter. But then again—that the nephew of my old friend, Sir Oliver, should be the person to attempt such a wrong, hurts me more nearly.

Joseph Surface. Aye, there's the point. When ingratitude barbs the dart of injury, the wound has double danger in it.

Sir Peter. Aye—I, that was, in a manner, left his guardian—in whose house he had been so often entertained—who never in my life denied him—my advice!

Joseph Surface. Oh, 'tis not to be credited! There *may* be a man capable of such baseness, to be sure; but, for my part, till you can give me positive proofs, I cannot but doubt it. However, if it should be proved on him, he is no longer a brother of mine! I disclaim kindred with him—for the man who can break through the laws of hospitality, and attempt the wife of his friend, deserves to be branded as the pest of society.

Sir Peter. What a difference there is between you! What noble sentiments!

Joseph Surface. Yet I cannot suspect Lady Teazle's honor.

Sir Peter. I am sure I wish to think well of her, and to remove all ground of quarrel between us. She has lately reproached me more than once with having made no settlement on her; and, in our last quarrel, she almost hinted that she should not break her heart if I was dead. Now, as we seem to differ in our ideas of expense, I have resolved she shall be her own mistress in that respect for the future; and, if I *were* to die, she shall find that I have not been inattentive to her interest while living. Here, my friend, are the drafts of two deeds, which I wish to have your opinion on. By one, she will enjoy eight hundred a year independent while I live; and, by the other, the bulk of my fortune after my death.

Joseph Surface. This conduct, Sir Peter, is indeed truly generous.—[*Aside.*] I wish it may not corrupt my pupil.

Sir Peter. Yes, I am determined she shall have no cause to complain, though I would not have her acquainted with the latter instance of my affection yet awhile.

Joseph Surface. Nor I, if I could help it.   [*Aside.*

Sir Peter. And now, my dear friend, if you please, we will talk over the situation of your hopes with Maria.

Joseph Surface. [*Softly.*] No, no, Sir Peter; another time, if you please.

Sir Peter. I am sensibly chagrined at the little progress you seem to make in her affection.

Joseph Surface. I beg you will not mention it. What are my disappointments when your happiness is in debate! [*Softly.*]—'Sdeath, I shall be ruined every way!   [*Aside.*

Sir Peter. And though you are so averse to my acquainting Lady Teazle with your passion, I am sure she's not your enemy in the affair.

Joseph Surface. Pray, Sir Peter, now oblige me. I am really too much affected by the subject we have been speaking on to bestow a thought on my own concerns. The man who is entrusted with his friend's distresses can never——

Enter Servant.

Well, sir?

Servant. Your brother, sir, is speaking to a gentleman in the street, and says he knows you are within.

Joseph Surface. 'Sdeath, blockhead—I'm not within —I'm out for the day.

Sir Peter. Stay—hold—a thought has struck me—you shall be at home.

Joseph Surface. Well, well, let him up.—[*Exit Servant.*] He'll interrupt Sir Peter—however—

Sir Peter. Now, my good friend, oblige me, I entreat you. Before Charles comes, let me conceal myself somewhere; then do you tax him on the point we have been talking on, and his answers may satisfy me at once.

Joseph Surface. O, fie, Sir Peter! would you have me join in so mean a trick?—to trepan my brother to?

Sir Peter. Nay, you tell me you are *sure* he is innocent; if so, you do him the greatest service by giving him an opportunity to clear himself, and you will set my heart at rest. Come, you shall not refuse me; here, behind the screen will be [*Goes to the screen.*]—Hey! what the devil! there seems to be *one* listener here already—I'll swear I saw a petticoat!

Joseph Surface. Ha! ha! ha! Well, this is ridiculous enough. I'll tell you, Sir Peter, though I hold a man of intrigue to be a most despicable character, yet you know, it doesn't follow that one is to be an absolute Joseph either! Hark'ee! 'tis a little French milliner, a silly rogue that plagues me—and having some character—on your coming, she ran behind the screen.

Sir Peter. Ah, you rogue!—But, egad, she has overhead all I have been saying of my wife.

Joseph Surface. Oh, 'twill never go any further, you may depend on't!

Sir Peter. No! then, i'faith, let her hear it out.—Here's a closet will do as well.

Joseph Surface. Well, go in then.

Sir Peter. Sly rogue! sly rogue!   [*Goes into the closet.*

Joseph Surface. A very narrow escape, indeed! and a curious situation I'm in, to part man and wife in this manner.

Lady Teazle. [*Peeping from the screen.*] Couldn't I steal off?

Joseph Surface. Keep close, my angel!

Sir Peter. [*Peeping out.*] Joseph, tax him home.

Joseph Surface. Back, my dear friend!

Lady Teazle. [*Peeping.*] Couldn't you lock Sir Peter in?

Joseph Surface. Be still, my life!

Sir Peter. [*Peeping.*] You're sure the little milliner won't blab?

Joseph Surface. In, in, my dear Sir Peter!—'Fore gad, I wish I had a key to the door.

Enter CHARLES SURFACE.

Charles Surface. Hollo! brother, what has been the matter? Your fellow would not let me up at first. What! have you had a Jew or a wench with you?

Joseph Surface. Neither, brother, I assure you.

Charles Surface. But what has made Sir Peter steal off? I thought he had been with you.

Joseph Surface. He was, brother; but, hearing *you* were coming, he did not choose to stay.

Charles Surface. What! was the old gentleman afraid I wanted to borrow money of him!

Joseph Surface. No, sir: but I am sorry to find, Charles, that you have lately given that worthy man grounds for great uneasiness.

Charles Surface. Yes, they tell me I do that to a great many worthy men. But how so, pray?

Joseph Surface. To be plain with you, brother, he thinks you are endeavoring to gain Lady Teazle's affections from him.

Charles Surface. Who, I? O lud! not I, upon my word. —Ha! ha! ha! so the old fellow has found out that he has got a young wife, has he?—or, what's worse, has her ladyship discovered that she has an old husband?

Joseph Surface. This is no subject to jest on, brother.— He who can laugh——

Charles Surface. True, true, as you were going to say— then, seriously, I never had the least idea of what you charge me with, upon my honor.

Joseph Surface. Well, it will give Sir Peter great satisfaction to hear this.   [*Aloud.*

Charles Surface. To be sure, I once thought the lady seemed to have taken a fancy to me; but, upon my soul, I never gave her the least encouragement. Besides, you know my attachment to Maria.

Joseph Surface. But sure, brother, even if Lady Teazle had betrayed the fondest partiality for you——

Charles Surface. Why, look'ee, Joseph, I hope I shall never deliberately do a dishonorable action—but if a pretty woman were purposely to throw herself in my way —and that pretty woman married to a man old enough to be her father——

Joseph Surface. Well!

Charles Surface. Why, I believe I should be obliged to borrow a little of your morality, that's all.—But, brother, do you know now that you surprise me exceedingly, by naming *me* with Lady Teazle; for, faith, I always understood *you* were her favorite.

Joseph Surface. Oh, for shame, Charles! This retort is foolish.

Charles Surface. Nay, I swear I have seen you exchange such significant glances——

Joseph Surface. Nay, nay, sir, this is no jest——

Charles Surface. Egad, I'm serious! Don't you remember —one day, when I called here——

Joseph Surface. Nay, prithee, Charles——

Charles Surface. And found you together——

Joseph Surface. Zounds, sir, I insist——

Charles Surface. And another time, when your servant——

Joseph Surface. Brother, brother, a word with you!— [*Aside.*] Gad, I must stop him.

Charles Surface. Informed me, I say, that——

Joseph Surface. Hush! I beg your pardon, but Sir Peter has overheard all we have been saying—I knew you would clear yourself, or I should not have consented.

Charles Surface. How, Sir Peter! Where is he?

Joseph Surface. Softly, there!   [*Points to the closet.*

Charles Surface. Oh, 'fore heaven, I'll have him out.— Sir Peter, come forth!

Joseph Surface. No, no——

Charles Surface. I say, Sir Peter, come into court.— [*Pulls in* Sir Peter.] What! my old guardian!—What— turn inquisitor, and take evidence, incog.?

Sir Peter. Give me your hand, Charles—I believe I have suspected you wrongfully—but you mustn't be angry with Joseph—'twas my plan!

Charles Surface. Indeed!

Sir Peter. But I acquit you. I promise you I don't think

near so ill of you as I did. What I have heard has given me great satisfaction.

Charles Surface. Egad, then, 'twas lucky you didn't hear any more. Wasn't it, Joseph?   [*Half aside.*

Sir Peter. Ah! you would have retorted on him.

Charles Surface. Aye, aye, that was a joke.

Sir Peter. Yes, yes, I know his honor too well.

Charles Surface. But you might as well have suspected him as me in this matter, for all that. Mightn't he, Joseph?
                                                        [*Half aside.*

Sir Peter. Well, well, I believe you.

Joseph Surface. Would they were both out of the room!
                                                        [*Aside.*

Sir Peter. And in future, perhaps, we may not be such strangers.

Enter Servant who whispers JOSEPH SURFACE.

Joseph Surface. Lady Sneerwell!—stop her by all means —[*Exit Servant.*] Gentlemen—I beg pardon—I must wait on you downstairs—here's a person come on particular business.

Charles Surface. Well, you can see him in another room. Sir Peter and I haven't met a long time, and I have something to say to him.

Joseph Surface. They must not be left together.—I'll send Lady Sneerwell away, and return directly.—[*Aside.*] Sir Peter, not a word of the French milliner.

                                        [*Exit* JOSEPH SURFACE.

Sir Peter. Oh! not for the world!—Ah, Charles, if you associated more with your brother, one might indeed hope for your reformation. He is a man of sentiment.—Well, there is nothing in the world so noble as a man of sentiment!

Charles Surface. Pshaw! he is too moral by half, and so apprehensive of his good name, as he calls it, that I suppose he would as soon let a priest into his house as a girl.

Sir Peter. No, no,—come, come,—you wrong him. No, no, Joseph is no rake, but he is not such a saint in that respect either,—I have a great mind to tell him—we should have a laugh!   [*Aside.*

Charles Surface. Oh, hang him! he's a very anchorite, a young hermit!

Sir Peter. Hark'ee—you must not abuse him; he may chance to hear of it again, I promise you.

Charles Surface. Why, you won't tell him?

Sir Peter. No—but—this way.—[*Aside.*] Egad, I'll tell him.—Hark'ee, have you a mind to have a good laugh at Joseph?

Charles Surface. I should like it of all things.

Sir Peter. Then, i'faith, we will!—I'll be quit with him for discovering me. [*Aside.*]—He had a girl with him when I called.

Charles Surface. What! Joseph? you jest.

Sir Peter. Hush!—a little—French milliner—and the best of the jest is—she's in the room now.

Charles Surface. The devil she is!

Sir Peter. Hush! I tell you.   [*Points to the screen.*

Charles Surface. Behind the screen! 'Slife, let's unveil her!

Sir Peter. No, no, he's coming:—you shan't, indeed!

Charles Surface. Oh, egad, we'll have a peep at the little milliner!

Sir Peter. Not for the world!—Joseph will never forgive me.

Charles Surface. I'll stand by you——

Sir Peter. [*Struggling with Charles.*] Odds, here he is!

JOSEPH SURFACE *enters just as* CHARLES *throws down the screen.*

Charles Surface. Lady Teazle, by all that's wonderful!

Sir Peter. Lady Teazle, by all that's horrible!

Charles Surface. Sir Peter, this is one of the smartest French milliners I ever saw. Egad, you seem all to have been diverting yourselves here at hide and seek—and I don't see who is out of the secret. Shall I beg your lady-ship to inform me?—Not a word!—Brother, will you please to explain this matter? What! Morality dumb too!—Sir Peter, though I *found* you in the dark, perhaps you are not so now! all mute! Well—though *I* can make nothing of the affair, I suppose you perfectly understand one an-other; so I'll leave you to yourselves.—[*Going.*] Brother, I'm sorry to find you *have given that worthy man so much uneasiness.*—Sir Peter! there's nothing *in the world* so *noble as a man of sentiment!*   [*Exit* CHARLES.

[*They stand for some time looking at each other.*

Joseph Surface. Sir Peter—notwithstanding I confess that appearances are against me—if you will afford me your patience—I make no doubt but I shall explain every-thing to your satisfaction.

Sir Peter. If you please—

Joseph Surface. The fact is, sir, that Lady Teazle, knowing my pretensions to your ward Maria—I say, sir, Lady Teazle, being apprehensive of the jealousy of your temper —and knowing my friendship to the family—she, sir, I say—called here—in order that—I might explain those pretensions—but on your coming—being apprehensive— as I said—of your jealousy—she withdrew—and this, you may depend on't is the whole truth of the matter.

Sir Peter. A very clear account, upon my word; and I dare swear the lady will vouch for every article of it.

Lady Teazle. [*Coming forward.*] For not one word of it, Sir Peter!

Sir Peter. How! don't you think it worth while to agree in the lie?

Lady Teazle. There is not one syllable of truth in what that gentleman has told you.

Sir Peter. I believe you, upon my soul, ma'am!

Joseph Surface. [*Aside.*] 'Sdeath, madam, will you betray me?

Lady Teazle. Good Mr. Hypocrite, by your leave, I will speak for myself.

Sir Peter. Aye, let her alone, sir; you'll find she'll make out a better story than *you*, without prompting.

Lady Teazle. Hear me, Sir Peter!—I came here on no matter relating to your ward, and even ignorant of this gentleman's pretensions to her—but I came, seduced by his insidious arguments, at least to listen to his pretended passion, if not to sacrifice *your* honor to his baseness.

Sir Peter. Now, I believe, the truth *is* coming, indeed!

Joseph Surface. The woman's mad!

Lady Teazle. No, sir; she has recovered her senses, and your own arts have furnished her with the means.—Sir Peter, I do not expect you to credit me—but the tenderness you expressed for me, when I am sure you could not think I was a witness to it, has penetrated to my heart, and had I left the place without the shame of this discovery, my future life should have spoken the sincerity of my gratitude. As for that smooth-tongue hypocrite, who would have seduced the wife of his too credulous friend, while he affected honorable addresses to his ward —I behold him now in a light so truly despicable, that I shall never again respect myself for having listened to him.   [*Exit.*

Joseph Surface. Nothwithstanding all this, Sir Peter, heaven knows——

Sir Peter. That you are a villain!—and so I leave you to your conscience.

Joseph Surface. You are too rash, Sir Peter; you shall hear me. The man who shuts out conviction by refusing to——

Sir Peter. Oh!—

[*Exeunt,* JOSEPH SURFACE *following and speaking.*

ACT FIVE

SCENE I—*The library in* JOSEPH SURFACE'S *house*

Enter JOSEPH SURFACE *and Servant.*

JOSEPH SURFACE. Mr. Stanley! why should you think I would see him? you *must* know he comes to ask something.

Servant. Sir, I should not have let him in, but that Mr. Rowley came to the door with him.

Joseph Surface. Pshaw! blockhead! to suppose that I should *now* be in a temper to receive visits from poor relations!—Well, why don't you show the fellow up?

Servant. I will, sir.—Why, sir, it was not my fault that Sir Peter discovered my lady——

Joseph Surface. Go, fool!   [*Exit Servant.*

Sure, Fortune never played a man of my policy such a trick before! My character with Sir Peter, my hopes with Maria, destroyed in a moment! I'm in a rare humor to listen to other people's distresses! I shan't be able to bestow even a benevolent sentiment on Stanley.—So! here he comes, and Rowley with him. I must try to recover myself—and put a little charity into my face, however.

[*Exit.*

Enter SIR OLIVER SURFACE *and* ROWLEY.

Sir Oliver. What! does he avoid us? That was he, was it not?

Rowley. It was, sir—but I doubt you are come a little too abruptly—his nerves are so weak, that the sight of a poor relation may be too much for him.—I should have gone first to break you to him.

Sir Oliver. A plague of his nerves!—Yet this is he whom

Sir Peter extols as a man of the most benevolent way of thinking!

Rowley. As to his way of thinking, I cannot pretend to decide; for, to do him justice, he appears to have as much speculative benevolence as any private gentleman in the kingdom, though he is seldom so sensual as to indulge himself in the exercise of it.

Sir Oliver. Yet has a string of charitable sentiments, I suppose, at his fingers' ends!

Rowley. Or, rather, at his tongue's end, Sir Oliver; for I believe there is no sentiment he has more faith in than that 'Charity begins at home.'

Sir Oliver. And his, I presume, is of that domestic sort which never stirs abroad at all.

Rowley. I doubt you'll find it so;—but he's coming—I mustn't seem to interrupt you; and you know, immediately as you leave him, I come in to announce your arrival in your real character.

Sir Oliver. True; and afterwards you'll meet me at Sir Peter's.

Rowley. Without losing a moment.   [*Exit* ROWLEY.

Sir Oliver. So! I don't like the complaisance of his features.

Re-enter JOSEPH SURFACE.

Joseph Surface. Sir, I beg you ten thousand pardons for keeping you a moment waiting—Mr. Stanley, I presume.

Sir Oliver. At your service.

Joseph Surface. Sir, I beg you will do me the honor to sit down—I entreat you, sir.

Sir Oliver. Dear sir—there's no occasion.—Too civil by half!   [*Aside.*

Joseph Surface. I have not the pleasure of knowing you, Mr. Stanley; but I am extremely happy to see you look so well. You were nearly related to my mother, I think, Mr. Stanley?

Sir Oliver. I was, sir—so nearly that my present poverty, I fear, may do discredit to her wealthy children—else I should not have presumed to trouble you.

Joseph Surface. Dear sir, there needs no apology: he that is in distress, though a stranger, has a right to claim kindred with the wealthy;—I am sure I wish *I* was one of that class, and had it in my power to offer you even a small relief.

Sir Oliver. If your uncle, Sir Oliver, were here, I should have a friend.

Joseph Surface. I wish he were, sir, with all my heart: you should not want an advocate with him, believe me, sir.

Sir Oliver. I should not *need* one—my distresses would recommend me; but I imagined his bounty had enabled *you* to become the agent of his charity.

Joseph Surface. My dear sir, you were strangely misinformed. Sir Oliver is a worthy man, a very worthy sort of man; but—avarice, Mr. Stanley, is the vice of age. I will tell you, my good sir, in confidence, what he has done for me has been a mere nothing; though people, I know, have thought otherwise, and, for my part, I never chose to contradict the report.

Sir Oliver. What! has he never transmitted you bullion! rupees! [29] pagodas! [30]

Joseph Surface. O dear sir, nothing of the kind! No, no; a few presents now and then—china—shawls—Congo tea —avadavats,[31] and Indian crackers[32]—little more, believe me.

Sir Oliver. [*Aside.*] Here's gratitude for twelve thousand pounds!—Avadavats and Indian crackers!

Joseph Surface. Then, my dear sir, you have heard, I doubt not, of the extravagance of my brother; there are very few would credit what I have done for that unfortunate young man.

Sir Oliver. Not I, for one!   [*Aside.*

Joseph Surface. The sums I have lent him! Indeed I have been exceedingly to blame—it was an amiable weakness; however, I don't pretend to defend it—and now I feel it doubly culpable, since it has deprived me of the pleasure of serving *you,* Mr. Stanley, as my heart dictates.

Sir Oliver. [*Aside.*] Dissembler!—Then, sir, you cannot assist me?

Joseph Surface. At present, it grieves me to say, I cannot; but, whenever I have the ability, you may depend upon hearing from me.

Sir Oliver. I am extremely sorry——

Joseph Surface. Not more than I am, believe me; to pity,

---

[29] Silver coins of India, then valued at two shillings.
[30] Gold coins of India, then valued at eight shillings.
[31] Small singing-birds of India, having red and black plumage.
[32] Fire-crackers with colored wrappers.

without the power to relieve, is still more painful than to ask and be denied.

Sir Oliver. Kind sir, your most obedient humble servant.

Joseph Surface. You leave me deeply affected, Mr. Stanley.—William, be ready to open the door.

Sir Oliver. O dear sir, no ceremony.

Joseph Surface. Your very obedient.

Sir Oliver. Sir, your most obsequious.

Joseph Surface. You may depend upon hearing from me, whenever I can be of service.

Sir Oliver. Sweet sir, you are too good.

Joseph Surface. In the meantime I wish you health and spirits.

Sir Oliver. Your ever grateful and perpetual humble servant.

Joseph Surface. Sir, yours as sincerely.

Sir Oliver. Now I am satisfied!   [*Exit.*

Joseph Surface. [*Solus.*] This is one bad effect of a good character; it invites applications from the unfortunate, and there needs no small degree of address to gain the reputation of benevolence without incurring the expense. The silver ore of pure charity is an expensive article in the catalogue of a man's good qualities; whereas the sentimental French plate I use instead of it makes just as good a show, and pays no tax.

Enter ROWLEY.

Rowley. Mr. Surface, your servant—I was apprehensive of interrupting you—though my business demands immediate attention—as this note will inform you.

Joseph Surface. Always happy to see Mr. Rowley.— [*Reads.*] How! *Oliver—Surface!*—My uncle arrived!

Rowley. He is, indeed—we have just parted—quite well, after a speedy voyage, and impatient to embrace his worthy nephew.

Joseph Surface. I am astonished!—William! stop Mr. Stanley, if he's not gone.

Rowley. Oh! he's out of reach, I believe.

Joseph Surface. Why didn't you let me know this when you came in together?

Rowley. I thought you had particular business. But I must be gone to inform your brother, and appoint him here to meet his uncle. He will be with you in a quarter of an hour.

Joseph Surface. So he says. Well, I am strangely over-joyed at his coming.—[*Aside.*] Never, to be sure, was anything so damned unlucky!

Rowley. You will be delighted to see how well he looks.

Joseph Surface. Oh! I'm rejoiced to hear it.—[*Aside.*] Just at this time!

Rowley. I'll tell him how impatiently you expect him.

Joseph Surface. Do, do; pray give my best duty and affection. Indeed, I cannot express the sensations I feel at the thought of seeing him.—[*Exit* ROWLEY.] Certainly his coming just at this time is the cruellest piece of ill fortune.   [*Exit.*

SCENE II—*At* SIR PETER'S

Enter MRS. CANDOUR *and Maid.*

Maid. Indeed, ma'am, my lady will see nobody at present.

Mrs. Candour. Did you tell her it was her friend Mrs. Candour?

Maid. Yes, madam; but she begs you will excuse her.

Mrs. Candour. Do go again; I shall be glad to see her, if it be only for a moment, for I am sure she must be in great distress.—[*Exit Maid.*] Dear heart, how provoking! I'm not mistress of half the circumstances! We shall have the whole affair in the newspapers, with the names of the parties at length, before I have dropped the story at a dozen houses.

Enter SIR BENJAMIN BACKBITE.

O dear Sir Benjamin! you have heard, I suppose——

Sir Benjamin. Of Lady Teazle and Mr. Surface——

Mrs. Candour. And Sir Peter's discovery——

Sir Benjamin. Oh, the strangest piece of business, to be sure!

Mrs. Candour. Well, I never was so surprised in my life. I am so sorry for all parties, indeed I am.

Sir Benjamin. Now, I don't pity Sir Peter at all—he was so extravagantly partial to Mr. Surface.

Mrs. Candour. Mr. Surface! Why, 'twas with Charles Lady Teazle was detected.

Sir Benjamin. No such thing—Mr. Surface is the gallant.

Mrs. Candour. No, no—Charles is the man. 'Twas Mr. Surface brought Sir Peter on purpose to discover them.

Sir Benjamin. I tell you I have it from one——

Mrs. Candour. And I have it from one——

Sir Benjamin. Who had it from one, who had it——

Mrs. Candour. From one immediately——But here's Lady Sneerwell; perhaps she knows the whole affair.

Enter LADY SNEERWELL.

Lady Sneerwell. So, my dear Mrs. Candour, here's a sad affair of our friend Lady Teazle!

Mrs. Candour. Aye, my dear friend, who could have thought it——

Lady Sneerwell. Well, there's no trusting appearances; though, indeed, she was always too lively for me.

Mrs. Candour. To be sure, her manners were a little too free—but she was very young!

Lady Sneerwell. And had, indeed, some good qualities.

Mrs. Candour. So she had, indeed. But have you heard the particulars?

Lady Sneerwell. No; but everybody says that Mr. Surface——

Sir Benjamin. Aye, there, I told you—Mr. Surface was the man.

Mrs. Candour. No, no, indeed—the assignation was with Charles.

Lady Sneerwell. With Charles! You alarm me, Mrs. Candour.

Mrs. Candour. Yes, yes, he was the lover. Mr. Surface—do him justice—was only the informer.

Sir Benjamin. Well, I'll not dispute with you, Mrs. Candour; but, be it which it may, I hope that Sir Peter's wound will not——

Mrs. Candour. Sir Peter's wound! Oh, mercy! I didn't hear a word of their fighting.

Lady Sneerwell. Nor I, a syllable.

Sir Benjamin. No! what, no mention of the duel?

Mrs. Candour. Not a word.

Sir Benjamin. O Lord—yes, yes—they fought before they left the room.

Lady Sneerwell. Pray let us hear.

Mrs. Candour. Aye, do oblige us with the duel.

Sir Benjamin. 'Sir,' says Sir Peter—immediately after the discovery—'you are a most ungrateful fellow.'

Mrs. Candour. Aye, to Charles——

Sir Benjamin. No, no—to Mr. Surface—'a most ungrateful fellow; and old as I am, sir,' says he, 'I insist on immediate satisfaction.'

Mrs. Candour. Aye, that must have been to Charles; for 'tis very unlikely Mr. Surface should go to fight in his house.

Sir Benjamin. 'Gad's life, ma'am, not at all—'giving me immediate satisfaction.'—On this, madam, Lady Teazle, seeing Sir Peter in such danger, ran out of the room in strong hysterics, and Charles after her, calling out for hartshorn and water! Then, madam, they began to fight with swords——

Enter CRABTREE.

Crabtree. With pistols, nephew—I have it from undoubted authority.

Mrs. Candour. O Mr. Crabtree, then it is all true!

Crabtree. Too true, indeed, ma'am, and Sir Peter's dangerously wounded——

Sir Benjamin. By a thrust of in *seconde*[33] quite through his left side——

Crabtree. By a bullet lodged in the thorax.

Mrs. Candour. Mercy on me! Poor Sir Peter!

Crabtree. Yes, ma'am—though Charles would have avoided the matter, if he could.

Mrs. Candour. I knew Charles was the person.

Sir Benjamin. Oh, my uncle, I see, knows nothing of the matter.

Crabtree. But Sir Peter taxed him with the basest ingratitude——

Sir Benjamin. That I told you, you know.

Crabtree. Do, nephew, let me speak!—and insisted on an immediate——

Sir Benjamin. Just as I said.

Crabtree. Odds life, nephew, allow others to know something too! A pair of pistols lay on the bureau (for Mr. Surface, it seems, had come the night before late from Salt-Hill, where he had been to see the Montem[34] with a friend, who has a son at Eton), so, unluckily, the pistols were left charged.

[33] A term in fencing.
[34] It was formerly the custom of Eton school boys to go to Salt-Hill (*processus ad montem*) every third year on Whit-Tuesday, and levy *salt-money* from the onlookers at the ceremony.

Sir Benjamin. I heard nothing of this.

Crabtree. Sir Peter forced Charles to take one, and they fired, it seems, pretty nearly together. Charles's shot took place, as I told you, and Sir Peter's missed; but, what is very extraordinary, the ball struck against a little bronze Pliny that stood over the chimney-piece, grazed out of the window at a right angle, and wounded the postman, who was just coming to the door with a double letter from Northamptonshire.

Sir Benjamin. My uncle's account is more circumstantial, I must confess; but I believe mine is the true one, for all that.

Lady Sneerwell. [*Aside.*] I am more interested in this affair than they imagine, and must have better information.   [*Exit* LADY SNEERWELL.

Sir Benjamin. [*After a pause looking at each other.*] Ah! Lady Sneerwell's alarm is very easily accounted for.

Crabtree. Yes, yes, they certainly *do* say—but that's neither here nor there.

Mrs. Candour. But, pray, where is Sir Peter at present?

Crabtree. Oh! they brought him home, and he is now in the house, though the servants are ordered to deny it.

Mrs. Candour. I believe so, and Lady Teazle, I suppose, attending him.

Crabtree. Yes, yes; I saw one of the faculty enter just before me.

Sir Benjamin. Hey! who comes here?

Crabtree. Oh, this is he—the physician, depend on't.

Mrs. Candour. Oh, certainly! it must be the physician; and now we shall know.

Enter SIR OLIVER SURFACE.

Crabtree. Well, doctor, what hopes?

Mrs. Candour. Aye, doctor, how's your patient?

Sir Benjamin. Now, doctor, isn't it a wound with a small-sword?

Crabtree. A bullet lodged in the thorax, for a hundred!

Sir Oliver. Doctor! a wound with a small-sword! and a bullet in the thorax?—Oons! are you mad, good people?

Sir Benjamin. Perhaps, sir, you are not a doctor?

Sir Oliver. Truly, I am to thank you for my degree, if I am.

Crabtree. Only a friend of Sir Peter's, then, I presume. But, sir, you must have heard of this accident?

Sir Oliver. Not a word!

Crabtree. Not of his being dangerously wounded?

Sir Oliver. The devil he is!

Sir Benjamin. Run through the body——

Crabtree. Shot in the breast——

Sir Benjamin. By one Mr. Surface——

Crabtree. Aye, the younger.

Sir Oliver. Hey! what the plague! you seem to differ strangely in your accounts—however, you agree that Sir Peter is dangerously wounded.

Sir Benjamin. Oh, yes, we agree there.

Crabtree. Yes, yes, I believe there can be no doubt of that.

Sir Oliver. Then, upon my word, for a person in that situation, he is the most imprudent man alive—for here he comes, walking as if nothing at all were the matter.

Enter SIR PETER TEAZLE.

Odds heart, Sir Peter! you are come in good time, I promise you; for we had just *given you over.*

Sir Benjamin. Egad, uncle, this is the most sudden recovery!

Sir Oliver. Why, man! what do you do out of bed with a small-sword through your body, and a bullet lodged in your thorax?

Sir Peter. A small-sword and a bullet?

Sir Oliver. Aye; these gentlemen would have killed you without law or physic, and wanted to dub me a doctor— to make me an accomplice.

Sir Peter. Why, what is all this?

Sir Benjamin. We rejoice, Sir Peter, that the story of the duel is not true, and are sincerely sorry for your other misfortunes.

Sir Peter. So; so; all over the town already.   [*Aside.*

Crabtree. Though, Sir Peter, you were certainly vastly to blame to marry at all, at your years.

Sir Peter. Sir, what business is that of yours?

Mrs. Candour. Though, indeed, as Sir Peter made so good a husband, he's very much to be pitied.

Sir Peter. Plague on your pity, ma'am! I desire none of it.

Sir Benjamin. However, Sir Peter, you must not mind the laughing and jests you will meet with on this occasion.

Sir Peter. Sir, I desire to be master in my own house.

Crabtree. 'Tis no uncommon case, that's one comfort.

Sir Peter. I insist on being left to myself: without ceremony, I insist on your leaving my house directly!

Mrs. Candour. Well, well, we are going; and depend on't, we'll make the best report of you we can.

Sir Peter. Leave my house!

Crabtree. And tell how hardly you have been treated.

Sir Peter. Leave my house!

Sir Benjamin. And how patiently you bear it.

Sir Peter. Fiends! vipers! furies! Oh! that their own venom would choke them!

[*Exeunt* MRS. CANDOUR, SIR BENJAMIN BACK-
BITE, CRABTREE, &c.

Sir Oliver. They are very provoking indeed, Sir Peter.

Enter ROWLEY.

Rowley. I heard high words—what has ruffled you, Sir Peter?

Sir Peter. Pshaw! what signifies asking? Do I ever pass a day without my vexations?

Sir Oliver. Well, I'm not inquisitive—I come only to tell you that I have seen both my nephews in the manner we proposed.

Sir Peter. A precious couple they are!

Rowley. Yes, and Sir Oliver is convinced that your judgment was right, Sir Peter.

Sir Oliver. Yes, I find Joseph is indeed the man, after all.

Rowley. Yes, as Sir Peter says, he's a man of sentiment.

Sir Oliver. And acts up to the sentiments he professes.

Rowley. It certainly is edification to hear him talk.

Sir Oliver. Oh, he's a model for the young men of the age! But how's this, Sir Peter? you don't join in your friend Joseph's praise, as I expected.

Sir Peter. Sir Oliver, we live in a damned wicked world, and the fewer we praise the better.

Rowley. What! do *you* say so, Sir Peter, who were never mistaken in your life?

Sir Peter. Pshaw! plague on you both! I see by your

sneering you have heard the whole affair. I shall go mad among you!

Rowley. Then, to fret you no longer, Sir Peter, we are indeed acquainted with it all. I met Lady Teazle coming from Mr. Surface's, so humbled that she deigned to request me to be her advocate with you.

Sir Peter. And does Sir Oliver know all too?

Sir Oliver. Every circumstance.

Sir Peter. What, of the closet—and the screen, hey?

Sir Oliver. Yes, yes, and the little French milliner. Oh, I have been vastly diverted with the story! ha! ha!

Sir Peter. 'Twas very pleasant.

Sir Oliver. I never laughed more in my life, I assure you: ha! ha!

Sir Peter. O, vastly diverting! ha! ha!

Rowley. To be sure, Joseph with his sentiments! ha! ha!

Sir Peter. Yes, yes, his sentiments! ha! ha! A hypocritical villain!

Sir Oliver. Aye, and that rogue Charles to pull Sir Peter out of the closet: ha! ha!

Sir Peter. Ha! ha! 'twas devilish entertaining, to be sure!

Sir Oliver. Ha! ha! Egad, Sir Peter, I should like to have seen your face when the screen was thrown down: ha! ha!

Sir Peter. Yes, yes, my face when the screen was thrown down: ha! ha! Oh, I must never show my head again!

Sir Oliver. But come, come, it isn't fair to laugh at you neither, my old friend—though, upon my soul, I can't help it.

Sir Peter. Oh, pray don't restrain your mirth on my account—it does not hurt me at all! I laugh at the whole affair myself. Yes, yes, I think being a standing jest for all one's acquaintances a very happy situation. O yes, and then of a morning to read the paragraphs about Mr. S——, Lady T——, and Sir P——, will be so entertaining!

Rowley. Without affectation, Sir Peter, you may despise the ridicule of fools. But I see Lady Teazle going towards the next room; I am sure you must desire a reconciliation as earnestly as she does.

Sir Oliver. Perhaps my being here prevents her coming to you. Well, I'll leave honest Rowley to mediate between you; but he must bring you all presently to Mr. Surface's, where I am now returning, if not to reclaim a libertine, at least to expose hypocrisy.

Sir Peter. Ah! I'll be present at your discovering yourself there with all my heart—though 'tis a vile unlucky place for discoveries!

Rowley. We'll follow.   [*Exit* SIR OLIVER SURFACE.

Sir Peter. She is not coming here, you see, Rowley.

Rowley. No, but she has left the door of that room open, you perceive. See, she is in tears!

Sir Peter. Certainly a little mortification appears very becoming in a wife! Don't you think it will do her good to let her pine a little?

Rowley. Oh, this is ungenerous in you!

Sir Peter. Well, I know not what to think. You remember, Rowley, the letter I found of hers, evidently intended for Charles!

Rowley. A mere forgery, Sir Peter! laid in your way on purpose. This is one of the points which I intend Snake shall give you conviction on.

Sir Peter. I wish I were once satisfied of that. She looks this way. What a remarkably elegant turn of the head she has! Rowley, I'll go to her.

Rowley. Certainly.

Sir Peter. Though, when it is known that we are reconciled, people will laugh at me ten times more!

Rowley. Let them laugh, and retort their malice only by showing them you are happy in spite of it.

Sir Peter. I'faith, so I will! and, if I'm not mistaken, we may yet be the happiest couple in the country.

Rowley. Nay, Sir Peter—he who once lays aside suspicion——

Sir Peter. Hold, my dear Rowley! if you have any regard for me, never let me hear you utter anything like a sentiment—I have had enough of them to serve me the rest of my life.   [*Exeunt.*

SCENE III—*The library in* JOSEPH SURFACE'S *house.*

JOSEPH SURFACE *and* LADY SNEERWELL.

Lady Sneerwell. Impossible! Will not Sir Peter immediately be reconciled to Charles, and of consequence no longer oppose his union with Maria? The thought is distraction to me!

Joseph Surface. Can passion furnish a remedy?

Lady Sneerwell. No, nor cunning either. Oh, I was a fool, an idiot, to league with such a blunderer!

Joseph Surface. Sure, Lady Sneerwell, *I* am the greatest sufferer; yet you see I bear the accident with calmness.

Lady Sneerwell. Because the disappointment doesn't reach your *heart;* your *interest* only attached you to Maria. Had you felt for *her* what *I* have for that ungrateful libertine, neither your temper nor hypocrisy could prevent your showing the sharpness of your vexation.

Joseph Surface. But why should your reproaches fall on *me* for this disappointment?

Lady Sneerwell. Are you not the cause of it? What had you to do to bate in your pursuit of Maria to pervert Lady Teazle by the way? Had you not a sufficient field for your roguery in blinding Sir Peter, and supplanting your brother? I hate such an avarice of crimes; 'tis an unfair monopoly, and never prospers.

Joseph Surface. Well, I admit I have been to blame. I confess I deviated from the direct road of wrong, but I don't think we're so totally defeated neither.

Lady Sneerwell. No!

Joseph Surface. You tell me you have made a trial of Snake since we met, and that you still believe him faithful to us—

Lady Sneerwell. I do believe so.

Joseph Surface. And that he has undertaken, should it be necessary, to swear and prove that Charles is at this time contracted by vows and honor to your ladyship— which some of his former letters to you will serve to support?

Lady Sneerwell. This, indeed, might have assisted.

Joseph Surface. Come, come; it is not too late yet— [*Knocking at the door.*] But hark! this is probably my uncle, Sir Oliver: retire to that room; we'll consult farther when he's gone.

Lady Sneerwell. Well! but if *he* should find you out too—

Joseph Surface. Oh, I have no fear of that. Sir Peter will hold his tongue for his own credit's sake—and you may depend on't I shall soon discover Sir Oliver's weak side!

Lady Sneerwell. I have no diffidence of your abilities— only be constant to one roguery at a time.   [*Exit.*

Joseph Surface. I will, I will! So! 'tis confounded hard,

after such bad fortune, to be baited by one's confederate in evil. Well, at all events, my character is so much better than Charles's, that I certainly—hey!—what!—this is not *Sir Oliver*, but old *Stanley* again! Plague on't! that he should return to tease me just now! We shall have Sir Oliver come and find him here—and——

Enter SIR OLIVER SURFACE.

Gad's life, Mr. Stanley, why have you come back to plagued me just at this time? You must not stay now, upon my word.

Sir Oliver. Sir, I hear your uncle Oliver is expected here, and though he has been so penurious to *you*, I'll try what he'll do for *me*.

Joseph Surface. Sir, 'tis impossible for you to stay now, so I must beg——Come any other time, and I promise you, you shall be assisted.

Sir Oliver. No: Sir Oliver and I must be acquainted.

Joseph Surface. Zounds, sir! then I insist on your quitting the room directly.

Sir Oliver. Nay, sir!

Joseph Surface. Sir, I insist on't!—Here, William! show this gentleman out. Since you compel me, sir—not one moment—this is such insolence!   [*Going to push him out.*

Enter CHARLES SURFACE.

Charles Surface. Heyday! what's the matter now? What the devil, have you got hold of my little broker here? Zounds, brother, don't hurt little Premium. What's the matter, my little fellow?

Joseph Surface. So! he has been with you, too, has he?

Charles Surface. To be sure he has! Why, 'tis as honest a little——But sure, Joseph, you have not been borrowing money too, have you?

Joseph Surface. Borrowing! no! But, brother, you know here we expect Sir Oliver every——

Charles Surface. O gad, that's true! Noll mustn't find the little broker here, to be sure.

Joseph Surface. Yet, Mr. *Stanley* insists——

Charles Surface. Stanley! why his name is *Premium*.

Joseph Surface. No, no, *Stanley*.

Charles Surface. No, no, *Premium*.

Joseph Surface. Well, no matter which—but——

Charles Surface. Aye, aye, Stanley or Premium, 'tis the

same thing, as you say; for I suppose he goes by half a hundred names, besides A.B.'s[35] at the coffee-houses.

Joseph Surface. Death! here's Sir Oliver at the door. [*Knocking again.*] Now I beg, Mr. Stanley——

Charles Surface. Aye, and I beg, Mr. Premium——

Sir Oliver. Gentlemen——

Joseph Surface. Sir, by heaven you shall go!

Charles Surface. Aye, out with him, certainly.

Sir Oliver. This violence——

Joseph Surface. 'Tis your own fault.

Charles Surface. Out with him, to be sure.

[*Both forcing* SIR OLIVER *out.*

Enter SIR PETER *and* LADY TEAZLE, MARIA, *and* ROWLEY.

Sir Peter. My old friend, Sir Oliver—hey! What in the name of wonder!—Here are dutiful nephews!—assault their uncle at the first visit!

Lady Teazle. Indeed, Sir Oliver, 'twas well we came in to rescue you.

Rowley. Truly it was; for I perceive, Sir Oliver, the character of old Stanley was no protection to you.

Sir Oliver. Nor of Premium either: the necessities of the *former* could not extort a shilling from *that* benevolent gentleman; and now, egad, I stood a chance of faring worse than my ancestors, and being knocked down without being bid for.

[*After a pause,* JOSEPH *and* CHARLES *turning to each other.*

Joseph Surface. Charles!

Charles Surface. Joseph!

Joseph Surface. 'Tis now complete!

Charles Surface. Very!

Sir Oliver. Sir Peter, my friend, and Rowley too—look on that elder nephew of mine. You know what he has already received from my bounty; and you know also how gladly I would have regarded half my fortune as held in trust for him—judge, then, my disappointment in discovering him to be destitute of truth—charity—and gratitude!

Sir Peter. Sir Oliver, I should be more surprised at this declaration, if I had not myself found him selfish, treacherous, and hypocritical!

[35] A reference to appointments at the coffee-houses made under concealed names.

Lady Teazle. And if the gentleman pleads not guilty to these, pray let him call *me* to his character.

Sir Peter. Then, I believe, we need add no more.—If he knows himself, he will consider it as the most perfect punishment that he is known to the world.

Charles Surface. [*Aside.*] If they talk this way to *Honesty,* what will they say to *me,* by and be?

[SIR PETER, LADY TEAZLE, *and* MARIA *retire.*

Sir Oliver. As for that prodigal, his brother, there——

Charles Surface. [*Aside.*] Aye, now comes my turn: the damned family pictures will ruin me!

Joseph Surface. Sir Oliver!—uncle!—will you honor me with a hearing?

Charles Surface. [*Aside.*] Now if Joseph would make one of his long speeches, I might recollect myself a little.

Sir Oliver. [*To* JOSEPH SURFACE.] I suppose you would undertake to justify yourself entirely?

Joseph Surface. I trust I could.

Sir Oliver. Pshaw!—Well, sir! and *you* [*To* CHARLES.] could justify yourself too, I suppose?

Charles Surface. Not that I know of, Sir Oliver.

Sir Oliver. What!—Little Premium has been let too much into the secret, I presume?

Charles Surface. True, sir; but they were family secrets, and should never be mentioned again, you know.

Rowley. Come, Sir Oliver, I know you cannot speak of Charles's follies with anger.

Sir Oliver. Odd's heart, no more I can—nor with gravity either. Sir Peter, do you know the rogue bargained with me for all his ancestors—sold me judges and generals by the foot—and maiden aunts as cheap as broken china.

Charles Surface. To be sure, Sir Oliver, I did make a little free with the family canvas, that's the truth on't. My ancestors may certainly rise in evidence against me, there's no denying it; but believe me sincere when I tell you—and upon my soul I would not say it if I was not—that if I do not appear mortified at the exposure of my follies, it is because I feel at this moment the warmest satisfaction in seeing you, my liberal benefactor.

Sir Oliver. Charles, I believe you. Give me your hand again; the ill-looking little fellow over the settee has made your peace.

Charles Surface. Then, sir, my gratitude to the original is still increased.

Lady Teazle. [*Pointing to* MARIA.] Yet, I believe, Sir Oliver, here is one whom Charles is still more anxious to be reconciled to.

Sir Oliver. Oh, I have heard of his attachment there; and, with the young lady's pardon, if I construe right—that blush——

Sir Peter. Well, child, speak your sentiments.

Maria. Sir, I have little to say, but that I shall rejoice to hear that he is happy; for me, whatever claim I had to his affection, I willingly resign it to one who has a better title.

Charles Surface. How, Maria!

Sir Peter. Heyday! what's the mystery now? While he appeared an incorrigible rake, you would give your hand to no one else; and now that he is likely to reform, I warrant you won't have him.

MARIA. His own heart—and Lady Sneerwell know the cause.

Charles Surface. Lady Sneerwell!

Joseph Surface. Brother, it is with great concern I am obliged to speak on this point, but my regard to justice compels me, and Lady Sneerwell's injuries can no longer be concealed. [*Goes to the door.*

Enter LADY SNEERWELL.

Sir Peter. So! another French milliner!—Egad, he has one in every room in the house, I suppose!

Lady Sneerwell. Ungrateful Charles! Well may you be surprised, and feel for the indelicate situation which your perfidy has forced me into.

Charles Surface. Pray, uncle, is this another plot of yours? For, as I have life, I don't understand it.

Joseph Surface. I believe, sir, there is but the evidence of one person more necessary to make it extremely clear.

Sir Peter. And that person, I imagine, is Mr. Snake.—Rowley, you were perfectly right to bring him with us, and pray let him appear.

Rowley. Walk in, Mr. Snake.

Enter SNAKE.

I thought his testimony might be wanted; however, it happens unluckily, that he comes to confront Lady Sneerwell, and not to support her.

Lady Sneerwell. Villain! Treacherous to me at last! [*Aside.*]—Speak, fellow, have *you* too conspired against me?

Snake. I beg your ladyship ten thousand pardons: you paid me extremely liberally for the lie in question; but I have unfortunately been offered double to speak the truth.

Sir Peter. Plot and counterplot, egad—I wish your ladyship joy of the success of your negotiation.

Lady Sneerwell. The torments of shame and disappointment on you all!

Lady Teazle. Hold, Lady Sneerwell—before you go, let me thank you for the trouble you and that gentleman have taken, in writing letters to me from Charles, and answering them yourself; and let me also request you to make my respects to the Scandalous College, of which you are president, and inform them, that Lady Teazle, licentiate, begs leave to return the diploma they granted her, as she leaves off practice, and kills characters no longer.

Lady Sneerwell. You too, madam!—provoking—insolent! May your husband live these fifty years!   [*Exit.*

Sir Peter. Oons! what a fury!

Lady Teazle. A malicious creature, indeed!

Sir Peter. Hey! not for her last wish?

Lady Teazle. Oh, no!

Sir Oliver. Well, sir, and what have you to say now?

Joseph Surface. Sir, I am so confounded, to find that Lady Sneerwell could be guilty of suborning Mr. Snake in this manner, to impose on us all, that I know not what to say; however, lest her revengeful spirit should prompt her to injure my brother, I had certainly better follow her directly.   [*Exit.*

Sir Peter. Moral to the last drop!

Sir Oliver. Aye, and marry her, Joseph, if you can.— Oil and vinegar, egad! you'll do very well together.

Rowley. I believe we have no more occasion for Mr. Snake at present.

Snake. Before I go, I beg pardon once for all, for whatever uneasiness I have been the humble instrument of causing to the parties present.

Sir Peter. Well, well, you have made atonement by a good deed at last.

Snake. But I must request of the company, that it shall never be known.

Sir Peter. Hey! what the plague! are you ashamed of having done a right thing once in your life?

Snake. Ah, sir,—consider I live by the badness of my character—I have nothing but my infamy to depend on! and, if it were once known that I had been betrayed into an honest action, I should lose every friend I have in the world.

Sir Oliver. Well, well—we'll not traduce you by saying anything in your praise, never fear.   [*Exit* SNAKE.

Sir Peter. There's a precious rogue! yet that fellow is a writer and a critic!

Lady Teazle. See, Sir Oliver, there needs no persuasion now to reconcile your nephew and Maria.

                    [CHARLES *and* MARIA *apart.*

Sir Oliver. Aye, aye, that's as it should be, and, egad, we'll have the wedding to-morrow morning.

Charles Surface. Thank you, my dear uncle.

Sir Peter. What, you rogue! don't you ask the girl's consent first?

Charles Surface. Oh, I have done that a long time— above a minute ago—and she has looked yes.

Maria. For shame, Charles!—I protest, Sir Peter, there has not been a word——

Sir Oliver. Well, then, the fewer the better—may your love for each other never know abatement.

Sir Peter. And may you live as happily together as Lady Teazle and I—intend to do!

Charles Surface. Rowley, my old friend, I am sure you congratulate me; and I suspect that I owe you much.

Sir Oliver. You do, indeed, Charles.

Rowley. If my efforts to serve you had not succeeded you would have been in my debt for the attempt—but deserve to be happy—and you overpay me.

Sir Peter. Aye, honest Rowley always said you would reform.

Charles Surface. Why as to reforming, Sir Peter, I'll make no promises, and that I take to be a proof that I intend to set about it.—But here shall be my monitor—my gentle guide.—Ah! can I leave the virtuous path those eyes illumine?

Though thou, dear maid, shouldst waive thy
            beauty's sway,

Thou still must rule, because I *will* obey:

An humbled fugitive from Folly view,
No sanctuary near but *Love* and—*You*;

[*To the audience.*

You can, indeed, each anxious fear remove,
For even *Scandal* dies, if *you* approve.

EPILOGUE

Written by G. Colman,[1] *Esq.*

SPOKEN BY MRS. ABINGTON[2]

I, WHO was late so volatile and gay,
Like a trade-wind must now blow all one way,
Bend all my cares, my studies, and my vows,
To one old rusty weathercock—my spouse!
So wills our virtuous bard—the motley Bayes[3]
Of crying epilogues and laughing plays!
    Old bachelors, who marry smart young wives,
Learn from our play to regulate your lives:
Each bring his dear to town, all faults upon her—
London will prove the very source of honor.
Plunged fairly in, like a cold bath it serves,
When principles relax, to brace the nerves.
    Such is my case;—and yet I might deplore
That the gay dream of dissipation's o'er;
And say, ye fair, was ever lively wife,
Born with a genius for the highest life,
Like me untimely blasted in her bloom,
Like me condemned to such a dismal doom?
Save money—when I just knew how to waste it!
Leave London—just as I began to taste it!
Must I then watch the early crowing cock,
The melancholy ticking of a clock;
In the lone rustic hall for ever pounded,
With dogs, cats, rats, and squalling brats surrounded?
With humble curates can I now retire,

[1] George Colman, author of *The Jealous Wife.*
[2] The original Lady Teazle.
[3] Poet, dramatist (from Bayes in *The Rehearsal*).

(While good Sir Peter boozes with the squire,)
And at backgammon mortify my soul,
That pants for loo,[4] or flutters at a vole?[5]
Seven's the main![6] Dear sound!—that must expire,
Lost at hot cockles,[7] round a Christmas fire!
The transient hour of fashion too soon spent,
Farewell the tranquil mind, farewell content![8]
Farewell the plumèd head, the cushioned tête,
That takes the cushion from its proper seat!
That spirit-stirring drum![9]—card drums I mean,
Spadille[10]—odd trick—pam[11]—basto[12]—king and queen!
And you, ye knockers, that, with brazen throat,
The welcome visitors' approach denote;
Farewell! all quality of high renown,
Pride, pomp, and circumstance of glorious town!
Farewell! your revels I partake no more,
And Lady Teazle's occupation's o'er!
All this I told our bard—he smiled, and said 'twas clear,
I ought to play deep tragedy next year.
Meanwhile he drew wise morals from his play,
And in these solemn periods stalked away:—
'Blest were the fair like you; her faults who stopped,
And closed her follies when the curtain dropped!
No more in vice or error to engage,
Or play the fool at large on life's great stage.'

[4] A favorite eighteenth-century game of cards.
[5] Winning all the tricks.
[6] In hazard, the caster of the dice 'called his *main*' by naming a number from five to nine.
[7] 'A play in which one kneels, and covering his eyes lays his head in another's lap and guesses who struck him.' (Strutt, *Sports and Pastimes.*)
[8] Lines 32-42 parody Othello's soliloquy, III. iii. 347-357.
[9] Fashionable card-party.
[10] The ace of spades. (See Pope, *The Rape of the Lock*, Canto iii.)
[11] The knave of clubs.
[12] The ace of clubs.

THE CRITIC

or, a Tragedy Rehearsed

DRAMATIS PERSONÆ

AS ORIGINALLY ACTED AT DRURY LANE THEATRE IN 1779

SIR FRETFUL PLAGIARY	Mr. Parsons
PUFF	Mr. King
DANGLE	Mr. Dodd
SNEER	Mr. Palmer
SIGNOR PASTICCIO RITORNELLO	Mr. Delpini
INTERPRETER	Mr. Baddeley
UNDER PROMPTER	Mr. Phillimore
MR. HOPKINS	Mr Hopkins
MRS. DANGLE	Mrs. Hopkins
SIGNORE PASTICCIO RITORNELLO	{ Miss Field and the Miss Abrams

Scenemen, Musicians, *and* Servants.

CHARACTERS OF THE TRAGEDY

LORD BURLEIGH	Mr. Moody
GOVERNOR OF TILBURY FORT	Mr. Wrighten
EARL OF LEICESTER	Mr. Farren
SIR WALTER RALEIGH	Mr. Burton
SIR CHRISTOPHER HATTON	Mr. Waldron
MASTER OF THE HORSE	Mr. Kenny
DON FEROLO WHISKERANDOS	Mr. Bannister, jun.
BEEFEATER	Mr. Wright
JUSTICE	Mr. Packer
SON	Mr. Lamash
CONSTABLE	Mr. Fawcett
THAMES	Mr. Gawdry
TILBURINA	Miss Pope
CONFIDANT	Mrs. Bradshaw
JUSTICE'S LADY	Mrs. Johnston
FIRST NIECE	Miss Collett
SECOND NIECE	Miss Kirby

Knights, Guards, Constables, Sentinels, Servants, Chorus, Rivers, Attendants, &c., &c.

SCENE—LONDON: *in* DANGLE'S *House during the First Act, and throughout the rest of the Play in* DRURY LANE THEATRE

TO MRS. GREVILLE

MADAM,—In requesting your permission to address the following pages to you, which, as they aim themselves to be critical, require every protection and allowance that approving taste or friendly prejudice can give them, I yet ventured to mention no other motive than the gratification of private friendship and esteem. Had I suggested a hope that your implied approbation would give a sanction to their defects, your particular reserve, and dislike to the reputation of critical taste, as well as of poetical talent, would have made you refuse the protection of your name to such a purpose. However, I am not so ungrateful as now to attempt to combat this disposition in you. I shall not here presume to argue that the present state of poetry claims and expects every assistance that taste and example can afford it; nor endeavour to prove that a fastidious concealment of the most elegant productions of judgment and fancy is an ill return for the possession of those endowments. Continue to deceive yourself in the idea that you are known only to be eminently admired and regarded for the valuable qualities that attach private friendships, and the graceful talents that adorn conversation. Enough of what you have written has stolen into full public notice to answer my purpose; and you will, perhaps, be the only person, conversant in elegant literature, who shall read this address and not perceive that by publishing your particular approbation of the following drama, I have a more interested object than to boast the true respect and regard with which I have the honour to be, Madam, your very sincere and obedient humble servant,

R. B. SHERIDAN

PROLOGUE

By the Honourable Richard Fitzpatrick

The sister Muses, whom these realms obey,
Who o'er the drama hold divided sway,
Sometimes by evil counsellors, 'tis said,
Like earth-born potentates have been misled.
In those gay days of wickedness and wit,
When Villiers criticised what Dryden writ,
The tragic queen, to please a tasteless crowd,
Had learn'd to bellow, rant, and roar so loud,
That frighten'd Nature, her best friend before,
The blustering beldam's company foreswore;
Her comic sister, who had wit 'tis true,
With all her merits, had her failings too:
And would sometimes in mirthful moments use
A style too flippant for a well-bred muse;
Then female modesty abash'd began
To seek the friendly refuge of the fan,
Awhile behind that slight intrenchment stood,
Till driven from thence, she left the stage for good.
In our more pious, and far chaster times,
These sure no longer are the Muse's crimes!
But some complain that, former faults to shun,
The reformation to extremes has run.
The frantic hero's wild delirium past,
Now insipidity succeeds bombast:
So slow Melpomene's cold numbers creep,
Here dulness seems her drowsy court to keep,
And we are scarce awake, whilst you are fast asleep.
Thalia, once so ill-behaved and rude,
Reform'd, is now become an arrant prude;
Retailing nightly to the yawning pit
The purest morals, undefiled by wit!
Our author offers, in these motley scenes,
A slight remonstrance to the drama's queens:
Nor let the goddesses be over nice;
Free-spoken subjects give the best advice.
Although not quite a novice in his trade,

His cause to-night requires no common aid.
To this, a friendly, just, and powerful court,
I come ambassador to beg support.
Can he undaunted brave the critic's rage?
In civil broils with brother bards engage?
Hold forth their errors to the public eye,
Nay more, e'en newspapers themselves defy?
Say, must his single arm encounter all?
By number vanquish'd, e'en the brave may fall;
And though no leader should success distrust,
Whose troops are willing, and whose cause is just;
To bid such hosts of angry foes defiance,
His chief dependence must be, your alliance.

THE CRITIC

ACT ONE

SCENE I—*A Room in* Dangle's *House*

Mr. *and* Mrs. Dangle *discovered at breakfast, and reading newspapers.*

Dangle. [*Reading.*] *Brutus to Lord North.—Letter the second on the State of the Army*—Psha! *To the first L dash D of the A dash Y.—Genuine extract of a Letter from St. Kitt's.—Coxheath Intelligence.—It is now confidently asserted that Sir Charles Hardy*—Psha! nothing but about the fleet and the nation!—and I hate all politics but theatrical politics.—Where's the Morning Chronicle?

Mrs. Dangle. Yes, that's your Gazette.

Dangle. So, here we have it.—[*Reads.*] *Theatrical intelligence extraordinary.—We hear there is a new tragedy in rehearsal at Drury Lane Theatre, called the Spanish Armada, said to be written by Mr. Puff, a gentleman well-known in the theatrical world. If we may allow ourselves to give credit to the report of the performers, who, truth to say, are in general but indifferent judges, this piece abounds with the most striking and received beauties of modern composition.*—So! I am very glad my friend Puff's tragedy is in such forwardness.—Mrs. Dangle, my dear, you will be very glad to hear that Puff's tragedy——

Mrs. Dangle. Lord, Mr. Dangle, why will you plague me about such nonsense?—Now the plays are begun I shall have no peace.—Isn't it sufficient to make yourself ridiculous by your passion for the theatre, without continually teasing me to join you? Why can't you ride your hobby-horse without desiring to place me on a pillion behind you, Mr. Dangle?

Dangle. Nay, my dear, I was only going to read——

Mrs. Dangle. No, no; you will never read anything that's worth listening to. You hate to hear about your country;

there are letters every day with Roman signatures, demonstrating the certainty of an invasion, and proving that the nation is utterly undone. But you never will read anything to entertain one.

Dangle. What has a woman to do with politics, Mrs. Dangle?

Mrs. Dangle. And what have you to do with the theatre, Mr. Dangle? Why should you affect the character of a critic? I have no patience with you!—haven't you made yourself the jest of all your acquaintance by your interference in matters where you have no business? Are you not called a theatrical Quidnunc, and a mock Mæcenas to second-hand authors?

Dangle. True; my power with the managers is pretty notorious. But is it no credit to have applications from all quarters for my interest—from lords to recommend fiddlers, from ladies to get boxes, from authors to get answers, and from actors to get engagements?

Mrs. Dangle. Yes, truly; you have contrived to get a share in all the plague and trouble of theatrical property, without the profit, or even the credit of the abuse that attends it.

Dangle. I am sure, Mrs. Dangle, you are no loser by it, however; you have all the advantages of it. Mightn't you, last winter, have had the reading of the new pantomime a fortnight previous to its performance? And doesn't Mr. Fosbrook let you take places for a play before it is advertised, and set you down for a box for every new piece through the season? And didn't my friend, Mr. Smatter, dedicate his last farce to you at my particular request, Mrs. Dangle?

Mrs. Dangle. Yes; but wasn't the farce damned, Mr. Dangle? And to be sure it is extremely pleasant to have one's house made the motley rendezvous of all the lackeys of literature; the very high 'Change of trading authors and jobbing critics!—Yes, my drawing-room is an absolute register-office for candidate actors, and poets without character.—Then to be continually alarmed with misses and ma'ams piping hysteric changes on Juliets and Dorindas, Pollys and Ophelias; and the very furniture trembling at the probationary starts and unprovoked rants of would-be Richards and Hamlets!—And what is worse than all, now that the manager has monopolized the Opera House, haven't we the signors and signoras calling here, sliding their smooth semibraves, and gargling glib divisions in their outlandish throats—with foreign emissaries and French spies, for aught I know, disguised like fiddlers and figure dancers?

Dangle. Mercy! Mrs. Dangle!

Mrs. Dangle. And to employ yourself so idly at such an alarming crisis as this too—when, if you had the least spirit, you would have been at the head of one of the Westminster associations—or trailing a volunteer pike in the Artillery Ground! But you—o' my conscience, I believe, if the French were landed to-morrow, your first inquiry would be, whether they had brought a theatrical troop with them.

Dangle. Mrs. Dangle, it does not signify—I say the stage is *the mirror of Nature,* and the actors are *the Abstract and brief Chronicles of the Time:* and pray what can a man of sense study better?—Besides, you will not easily persuade me that there is no credit or importance in being at the head of a band of critics, who take upon them to decide for the whole town, whose opinion and patronage all writers solicit, and whose recommendation no manager dares refuse.

Mrs. Dangle. Ridiculous!—Both managers and authors of the least merit laugh at your pretensions.—The public is their critic—without whose fair approbation they know no play can rest on the stage, and with whose applause they welcome such attacks as yours, and laugh at the malice of them, where they can't at the wit.

Dangle. Very well, madam—very well!

Enter SERVANT.

Servant. Mr. Sneer, sir, to wait on you.

Dangle. Oh, show Mr. Sneer up.—[*Exit* SERVANT.]— Plague on't, now we must appear loving and affectionate, or Sneer will hitch us into a story.

Mrs. Dangle. With all my heart; you can't be more ridiculous than you are.

Dangle. You are enough to provoke——

Enter SNEER.

Ha! my dear Sneer, I am vastly glad to see you.—My dear, here's Mr. Sneer.

Mrs. Dangle. Good-morning to you, sir.

Dangle. Mrs. Dangle and I have been diverting ourselves with the papers. Pray, Sneer, won't you go to Drury Lane Theatre the first night of Puff's tragedy?

Sneer. Yes; but I suppose one shan't be able to get in, for on the first night of a new piece they always fill the house with orders to support it. But here, Dangle, I have brought you two pieces, one of which you must exert yourself to make the managers accept, I can tell you that; for 'tis written by a person of consequence.

Dangle. So! now my plagues are beginning.

Sneer. Ay, I am glad of it, for now you'll be happy. Why, my dear Dangle, it is a pleasure to see how you enjoy your volunteer fatigue, and your solicited solicitations.

Dangle. It's a great trouble—yet, egad, it's pleasant too. —Why, sometimes of a morning I have a dozen people call on me at breakfast-time, whose faces I never saw before, nor ever desire to see again.

Sneer. That must be very pleasant indeed!

Dangle. And not a week but I receive fifty letters, and not a line in them about any business of my own.

Sneer. An amusing correspondence!

Dangle. [*Reading.*] *Bursts into tears and exit.*—What, is this a tragedy?

Sneer. No, that's a genteel comedy, not a translation— only taken from the French: it is written in a style which they have lately tried to run down; the true sentimental, and nothing ridiculous in it from the beginning to the end.

Mrs. Dangle. Well, if they had kept to that, I should not have been such an enemy to the stage; there was some edification to be got from those pieces, Mr. Sneer!

Sneer. I am quite of your opinion, Mrs. Dangle: the theatre, in proper hands, might certainly be made the school of morality; but now, I am sorry to say it, people seem to go there principally for their entertainment!

Mrs. Dangle. It would have been more to the credit of the managers to have kept it in the other line.

Sneer. Undoubtedly, madam; and hereafter perhaps to have had it recorded, that in the midst of a luxurious and dissipated age, they preserved two houses in the capital, where the conversation was always moral at least, if not entertaining!

Dangle. Now, egad, I think the worst alteration is in the nicety of the audience!—No *double-entendre*, no smart innuedo admitted; even Vanbrugh and Congreve obliged to undergo a bungling reformation!

Sneer. Yes, and our prudery in this respect is just on a
par with the artificial bashfulness of a courtesan, who in-
creases the blush upon her cheek in an exact proportion
to the diminution of her modesty.

Dangle. Sneer can't even give the public a good word!
But what have we here?—This seems a very odd——

Sneer. Oh, that's a comedy on a very new plan; replete
with wit and mirth, yet of a most serious moral! You see
it is called *The Reformed House-breaker;* where, by the
mere force of humour, house-breaking is put in so ridiculous a light, that if the piece has its proper run, I have
no doubt but that bolts and bars will be entirely useless
by the end of the season.

Dangle. Egad, this is new indeed!

Sneer. Yes; it is written by a particular friend of mine,
who has discovered that the follies and foibles of society
are subjects unworthy the notice of the comic muse, who
should be taught to stoop only to the greater vices and
blacker crimes of humanity—gibbeting capital offences in
five acts, and pillorying petty larcenies in two.—In short,
his idea is to dramatize the penal laws, and make the stage
a court of ease to the Old Bailey.

Dangle. It is truly moral.

Re-enter SERVANT.

Servant. Sir Fretful Plagiary, sir.

Dangle. Beg him to walk up.—[*Exit* SERVANT.] Now,
Mrs. Dangle, Sir Fretful Plagiary is an author to your own
taste.

Mrs. Dangle. I confess he is a favourite of mine, because
everybody else abuses him.

Sneer. Very much to the credit of your charity, madam,
if not of your judgment.

Dangle. But, egad, he allows no merit to any author but
himself, that's the truth on't—though he's my friend.

Sneer. Never.—He is as envious as an old maid verging
on the desperation of six and thirty; and then the insidious
humility with which he seduces you to give a free opinion
on any of his works, can be exceeded only by the petulant
arrogance with which he is sure to reject your observations.

Dangle. Very true, egad—though he's my friend.

Sneer. Then his affected contempt of all newspaper
strictures; though, at the same time, he is the sorest man
alive, and shrinks like scorched parchment from the fiery

ordeal of true criticism: yet he is so covetous of popularity, that he had rather be abused than not mentioned at all.

Dangle. There's no denying it—though he is my friend.

Sneer. You have read the tragedy he has just finished, haven't you?

Dangle. Oh, yes; he sent it to me yesterday.

Sneer. Well, and you think it execrable, don't you?

Dangle. Why, between ourselves, egad, I must own—though he is my friend—that it is one of the most—— He's here—[*Aside.*]—finished and most admirable perform——

Sir Fretful. [*Without.*] Mr. Sneer with him did you say?

Enter SIR FRETFUL PLAGIARY.

Dangle. Ah, my dear friend!—Egad, we were just speaking of your tragedy.—Admirable, Sir Fretful, admirable!

Sneer. You never did anything beyond it, Sir Fretful—never in your life.

Sir Fretful. You make me extremely happy; for without a compliment, my dear Sneer, there isn't a man in the world whose judgment I value as I do yours and Mr. Dangle's.

Mrs. Dangle. They are only laughing at you, Sir Fretful; for it was but just now that——

Dangle. Mrs. Dangle!—Ah, Sir Fretful, you know Mrs. Dangle.—My friend Sneer was rallying just now:—he knows how she admires you, and——

Sir Fretful. O Lord, I am sure Mr. Sneer has more taste and sincerity than to——[*Aside.*] A damned double-faced fellow!

Dangle. Yes, yes—Sneer will jest—but a better humoured——

Sir Fretful. Oh, I know——

Dangle. He has a ready turn for ridicule—his wit costs him nothing.

Sir Fretful. No, egad—or I should wonder how he came by it. [*Aside.*

Mrs. Dangle. Because his jest is always at the expense of his friend. [*Aside.*

Dangle. But, Sir Fretful, have you sent your play to the managers yet?—or can I be of any service to you?

Sir Fretful. No, no, I thank you: I believe the piece had sufficient recommendation with it.—I thank you though.—

I sent it to the manager of Covent Garden Theatre this morning.

Sneer. I should have thought now, that it might have been cast (as the actors call it) better at Drury Lane.

Sir Fretful. O Lud! no—never send a play there while I live—hark'ee!   [*Whispers* SNEER.

Sneer. Writes himself!—I know he does.

Sir Fretful. I say nothing—I take away from no man's merit—am hurt at no man's good fortune—I say nothing. —But this I will say—through all my knowledge of life, I have observed—that there is not a passion so strongly rooted in the human heart as envy.

Sneer. I believe you have reason for what you say, indeed.

Sir Fretful. Besides—I can tell you it is not always so safe to leave a play in the hands of those who write themselves.

Sneer. What, they may steal from them, hey, my dear Plagiary?

Sir Fretful. Steal!—to be sure they may; and, egad, serve your best thoughts as gypsies do stolen children, disfigure them to make 'em pass for their own.

Sneer. But your present work is a sacrifice to Melpomene, and he, you know, never——

Sir Fretful. That's no security: a dexterous plagiarist may do anything. Why, sir, for aught I know, he might take out some of the best things in my tragedy, and put them into his own comedy.

Sneer. That might be done, I dare be sworn.

Sir Fretful. And then, if such a person gives you the least hint or assistance, he is devilish apt to take the merit of the whole——

Dangle. If it succeeds.

Sir Fretful. Ay, but with regard to this piece, I think I can hit that gentleman, for I can safely swear he never read it.

Sneer. I'll tell you how you may hurt him more.

Sir Fretful. How?

Sneer. Swear he wrote it.

Sir Fretful. Plague on't now, Sneer, I shall take it ill!— I believe you want to take away my character as an author.

Sneer. Then I am sure you ought to be very much obliged to me.

Sir Fretful. Hey!—sir!——

Dangle. Oh, you know, he never means what he says.

Sir Fretful. Sincerely then—do you like the piece?

Sneer. Wonderfully!

Sir Fretful. But come, now, there must be something that you think might be mended, hey?—Mr. Dangle, has nothing struck you?

Dangle. Why, faith, it is but an ungracious thing for the most part, to——

Sir Fretful. With most authors it is just so, indeed; they are in general strangely tenacious! But, for my part, I am never so well pleased as when a judicious critic points out any defect to me; for what is the purpose of showing a work to a friend, if you don't mean to profit by his opinion?

Sneer. Very true.—Why, then, though I seriously admire the piece upon the whole, yet there is one small objection; which, if you'll give me leave, I'll mention.

Sir Fretful. Sir, you can't oblige me more.

Sneer. I think it wants incident.

Sir Fretful. Good God! you surprise me!—wants incident!

Sneer. Yes; I own I think the incidents are too few.

Sir Fretful. Good God! Believe me, Mr. Sneer, there is no person for whose judgment I have a more implicit deference. But I protest to you, Mr. Sneer, I am only apprehensive that the incidents are too crowded.—My dear Dangle, how does it strike you?

Dangle. Really I can't agree with my friend Sneer. I think the plot quite sufficient; and the four first acts by many degrees the best I ever read or saw in my life. If I might venture to suggest anything, it is that the interest rather falls off in the fifth.

Sir Fretful. Rises, I believe you mean, sir.

Dangle. No, I don't, upon my word.

Sir Fretful. Yes, yes, you do, upon my soul!—it certainly don't fall off, I assure you.—No, no; it don't fall off.

Dangle. Now, Mrs. Dangle, didn't you say it struck you in the same light?

Mrs. Dangle. No, indeed, I did not.—I did not see a fault in any part of the play, from the beginning to the end.

Sir Fretful. Upon my soul, the women are the best judges after all!

Mrs. Dangle. Or, if I made any objection, I am sure it

was to nothing in the piece; but that I was afraid it was on the whole, a little too long.

Sir Fretful. Pray, madam, do you speak as to duration of time; or do you mean that the story is tediously spun out?

Mrs. Dangle. O Lud! no.—I speak only with reference to the usual length of acting plays.

Sir Fretful. Then I am very happy—very happy indeed —because the play is a short play, a remarkably short play. I should not venture to differ with a lady on a point of taste; but on these occasions, the watch, you know, is the critic.

Mrs. Dangle. Then, I suppose, it must have been Mr. Dangle's drawling manner of reading it to me.

Sir Fretful. Oh, if Mr. Dangle read it, that's quite another affair!—But I assure you, Mrs. Dangle, the first evening you can spare me three hours and a half, I'll undertake to read you the whole, from beginning to end, with the prologue and epilogue, and allow time for the music between the acts.

Mrs. Dangle. I hope to see it on the stage next.

Dangle. Well, Sir Fretful, I wish you may be able to get rid as easily of the newspaper criticisms as you do of ours.

Sir Fretful. The newspapers! Sir, they are the most villainous—licentious—adominable—infernal.—Not that I ever read them—no—I make it a rule never to look into a newspaper.

Dangle. You are quite right; for it certainly must hurt an author of delicate feelings to see the liberties they take.

Sir Fretful. No, quite the contrary! their abuse is, in fact, the best panegyric—I like it of all things. An author's reputation is only in danger from their support.

Sneer. Why, that's true—and that attack, now, on you the other day——

Sir Fretful. What? where?

Dangle. Ay, you mean in a paper of Thursday: it was completely ill-natured, to be sure.

Sir Fretful. Oh so much the better.—Ha! Ha! Ha! I wouldn't have it otherwise.

Dangle. Certainly it is only to be laughed at; for——

Sir Fretful. You don't happen to recollect what the fellow said, do you?

Sneer. Pray, Dangle—Sir Fretful seems a little anxious——

Sir Fretful. O Lud, no!—anxious!—not I—not the least.
—I—but one may as well hear, you know.

Dangle. Sneer, do you recollect?—[*Aside to* SNEER.]
Make out something.

Sneer. [*Aside to* DANGLE.] I will.—[*Aloud.*] Yes, yes, I
remember perfectly.

Sir Fretful. Well, and pray now—not that it signifies—
what might the gentleman say?

Sneer. Why, he roundly asserts that you have not the
slightest invention or original genius whatever; though
you are the greatest traducer of all other authors living.

Sir Fretful. Ha! ha! ha!—very good!

Sneer. That as to comedy, you have not one idea of
your own, he believes, even in your commonplace-book—
where stray jokes and pilfered witticisms are kept with as
much method as the ledger of the lost and stolen office.

Sir Fretful. Ha! ha! ha!—very pleasant!

Sneer. Nay, that you are so unlucky as not to have the
skill even to steal with taste:—but that you glean from the
refuse of obscure volumes, where more judicious plagiarists
have been before you; so that the body of your work is a
composition of dregs and sentiments—like a bad tavern's
worst wine.

Sir Fretful. Ha! ha!

Sneer. In your more serious efforts, he says, your bombast would be less intolerable, if the thoughts were ever
suited to the expression; but the homeliness of the sentiment stares through the fantastic encumbrance of its fine
language, like a clown in one of the new uniforms!

Sir Fretful. Ha! ha!

Sneer. That your occasional tropes and flowers suit the
general coarseness of your style, as tambour sprigs would
a ground of linsey-woolsey; while your imitations of
Shakespeare resemble the mimicry of Falstaff's page, and
are about as near the standard as the original.

Sir Fretful. Ha!

Sneer. In short, that even the finest passages you steal
are of no service to you; for the poverty of your own
language prevents their assimilating; so that they lie on
the surface like lumps of marl on a barren moor, encum-
bering what it is not in their power to fertilize!

Sir Fretful. [*After great agitation.*] Now, another person
would be vexed at this!

Sneer. Oh! but I wouldn't have told you—only to divert you.

Sir Fretful. I know it—I am diverted.—Ha! ha! ha!—not the least invention!—Ha! ha! ha!—very good!—very good!

Sneer. Yes—no genius! ha! ha! ha!

Dangle. A severe rogue! ha! ha! ha! But you are quite right, Sir Fretful, never to read such nonsense.

Sir Fretful. To be sure—for if there is anything to one's praise, it is a foolish vanity to be gratified at it; and, if it is abuse—why one is always sure to hear of it from one damned good-natured friend or other!

Enter SERVANT.

Servant. Sir, there is an Italian gentleman, with a French interpreter, and three young ladies, and a dozen musicians, who say they are sent by Lady Rondeau and Mrs. Fugue.

Dangle. Gadso! they come by appointment!—Dear Mrs. Dangle, do let them know I'll see them directly.

Mrs. Dangle. You know, Mr. Dangle, I shan't understand a word they say.

Dangle. But you hear there's an interpreter.

Mrs. Dangle. Well, I'll try to endure their complaisance till you come.   [*Exit.*

Servant. And Mr. Puff, sir, has sent word that the last rehearsal is to be this morning, and that he'll call on you presently.

Dangle. That's true—I shall certainly be at home.—[*Exit* SERVANT.]—Now, Sir Fretful, if you have a mind to have justice done you in the way of answer, egad, Mr. Puff's your man.

Sir Fretful. Psha! sir, why should I wish to have it answered, when I tell you I am pleased at it?

Dangle. True, I had forgot that. But I hope you are not fretted at what Mr. Sneer——

Sir Fretful. Zounds! no, Mr. Dangle; don't I tell you these things never fret me in the least?

Dangle. Nay, I only thought——

Sir Fretful. And let me tell you, Mr. Dangle, 'tis damned affronting in you to suppose that I am hurt when I tell you I am not.

Sneer. But why so warm, Sir Fretful?

Sir Fretful. Gad's life! Mr. Sneer, you are as absurd as

Dangle: how often must I repeat it to you, that nothing can vex me but your supposing it possible for me to mind the damned nonsense you have been repeating to me!—and, let me tell you, if you continue to believe this, you must mean to insult me, gentlemen—and, then, your disrespect will affect me no more than the newspaper criticisms—and I shall treat it with exactly the same calm indifference and philosophic contempt—and so your servant.

[*Exit.*

Sneer. Ha! ha! ha! poor Sir Fretful! Now will he go and vent his philosophy in anonymous abuse of all modern critics and authors.—But, Dangle, you must get your friend Puff to take me to the rehearsal of his tragedy.

Dangle. I'll answer for't, he'll thank you for desiring it. But come and help me to judge of this musical family: they are recommended by people of consequence, I assure you.

Sneer. I am at your disposal the whole morning!—but I thought you had been a decided critic in music as well as in literature.

Dangle. So I am—but I have a bad ear. I'faith, Sneer, though, I am afraid we were a little too severe on Sir Fretful—though he is my friend.

Sneer. Why, 'tis certain, that unnecessarily to mortify the vanity of any writer is a cruelty which mere dulness never can deserve; but where a base and personal malignity usurps the place of literary emulation, the aggressor deserves neither quarter nor pity.

Dangle. That's true, egad!—though he's my friend!

SCENE II—*A drawing-room in* DANGLE'S *House.*

MRS. DANGLE, SIGNOR PASTICCIO RITORNELLO, SIGNORE PASTICCIO RITORNELLO, INTERPRETER, *and* MUSICIANS *discovered.*

Interpreter. Je dis, madame, j'ai l'honneur *to introduce* et de vous demander votre protection pour le Signor Pasticcio Ritornello et pour sa charmante famille.

Signor Pasticcio. Ah! vosignoria, noi vi preghiamo di favoritevi colla vostra protezione.

1 Signora Pasticcio. Vosignoria fatevi questi grazie.

2 Signora Pasticcio. Si, signora.

Interpreter. Madame—*me interpret.*—C'est à dire—*in*

English—qu'ils vous prient de leur faire l'honneur——

Mrs. Dangle. I say again, gentlemen, I don't understand a word you say.

Signor Pasticcio. Questo signore spiegheró——

Interpreter. Oui—*me interpret.*—Nous avons les lettres de recommendation pour Monsieur Dangle de——

Mrs. Dangle. Upon my word, sir, I don't understand you.

Signor Pasticcio. La Contessa Rondeau è nostra padrona.

3 *Signora Pasticcio.* Si, padre, et Miladi Fugue.

Interpreter. O!—*me interpret.*—Madame, ils disent—*in English*—Qu'ils ont l'honneur d'être protégés de ces dames.—*You understand?*

Mrs. Dangle. No, sir,—no understand!

Enter DANGLE *and* SNEER.

Interpreter. Ah, voici, Monsieur Dangle!

All Italians. Ah! Signor Dangle!

Mrs. Dangle. Mr. Dangle, here are two very civil gentlemen trying to make themselves understood, and I don't know which is the interpreter.

Dangle. Eh, bien!

> [*The* INTERPRETER *and* SIGNOR PASTICCIO *here speak at the same time.*

Interpreter. Monsieur Dangle, le grand bruit de vos talens pour la critique, et de votre intérêt avec messieurs les directeurs à tous les théâtres——

Signor Pasticcio. Vosignoria siete si famoso par la vostra conoscenza, e vostra interessa colla le direttore da——

Dangle. Egad, I think the interpreter is the hardest to be understood of the two!

Sneer. Why, I thought, Dangle, you had been an admirable linguist!

Dangle. So I am, if they would not talk so damned fast.

Sneer. Well, I'll explain that—the less time we lose in hearing them the better—for that, I suppose, is what they are brought here for.

> [*Speaks to* SIGNOR PASTICCIO—*they sing trios, &c.,* DANGLE *beating out of time.*

Enter SERVANT *and whispers* DANGLE.

Dangle. Show him up.—[*Exit* SERVANT.] Bravo! admirable! bravissimo! admirablissimo!—Ah! Sneer! where will you find voices such as these in England?

Sneer. Not easily.

Dangle. But Puff is coming.—Signor and little signoras obligatissimo!—Sposa Signora Danglena—Mrs. Dangle, shall I beg you to offer them some refreshments, and take their address in the next room.

> [*Exit* MRS. DANGLE *with* SIGNOR PASTICCIO,
> SIGNORE PASTICCIO, MUSICIANS, *and* INTER-
> PRETER, *ceremoniously*.

Re-enter SERVANT.

Servant. Mr. Puff, sir.   [*Exit*.

Enter PUFF.

Dangle. My dear Puff!

Puff. My dear Dangle, how is it with you?

Dangle. Mr. Sneer, give me leave to introduce Mr. Puff to you.

Puff. Mr. Sneer is this?—Sir, he is a gentleman whom I have long panted for the honour of knowing—a gentleman whose critical talents and transcendent judgment——

Sneer. Dear sir——

Dangle. Nay, don't be modest, Sneer; my friend Puff only talks to you in the style of his profession.

Sneer. His profession.

Puff. Yes, sir; I make no secret of the trade I follow: among friends and brother authors, Dangle knows I love to be frank on the subject, and to advertise myself *vivâ voce*.—I am, sir, a practitioner in panegyric, or, to speak more plainly, a professor of the art of puffing, at your service—or anybody else's.

Sneer. Sir, you are very obliging!—I believe, Mr. Puff, I have often admired your talents in the daily prints.

Puff. Yes, sir, I flatter myself I do as much business in that way as any six of the fraternity in town.—Devilish hard work all the summer, friend Dangle,—never worked harder! But, hark'ee,—the winter managers were a little sore, I believe.

Dangle. No; I believe they took it all in good part.

Puff. Ay! then that must have been affectation in them: for, egad, there were some of the attacks which there was no laughing at!

Sneer. Ay, the humorous ones.—But I should think, Mr. Puff, that authors would in general be able to do this sort of work for themselves.

Puff. Why, yes—but in a clumsy way. Besides, we look on that as an encroachment, and so take the opposite side. I dare say, now, you conceive half the very civil paragraphs and advertisements you see to be written by the parties concerned, or their friends? No such thing: nine out of ten manufactured by me in the way of business.

Sneer. Indeed!

Puff. Even the auctioneers now—the auctioneers, I say —though the rogues have lately got some credit for their language—not an article of the merit theirs: take them out of their pulpits, and they are as dull as catalogues!— No, sir; 'twas I first enriched their style—'twas I first taught them to crowd their advertisements with panegyrical superlatives, each epithet rising above the other, like the bidders in their own auction rooms! From me they learned to inlay their phraseology with variegated chips of exotic metaphor: by me too their inventive faculties were called forth:—yes, sir, by me they were instructed to clothe ideal walls with gratuitous fruits—to insinuate obsequious rivulets into visionary groves—to teach courteous shrubs to nod their approbation of the grateful soil, or on emergencies to raise upstart oaks, where there never had been an acorn; to create a delightful vicinage without the assistance of a neighbour; or fix the temple of Hygeia in the fens of Lincolnshire!

Dangle. I am sure you have done them infinite service; for now, when a gentleman is ruined, he parts with his house with some credit.

Sneer. Service! if they had any gratitude, they would erect a statue to him; they would figure him as a presiding Mercury, the god of traffic and fiction, with a hammer in his hand instead of a caduceus.—But pray, Mr. Puff, what first put you on exercising your talents in this way?

Puff. Egad, sir, sheer necessity!—the proper parent of an art so nearly allied to invention. You must know, Mr. Sneer, that from the first time I tried my hand at an advertisement, my success was such, that for some time after I led a most extraordinary life indeed!

Sneer. How, pray?

Puff. Sir, I supported myself two years entirely by my misfortunes.

Sneer. By your misfortunes!

Puff. Yes, sir, assisted by long sickness, and other occasional disorders: and a very comfortable living I had of it.

Sneer. From sickness and misfortunes! You practised as a doctor and an attorney at once?

Puff. No, egad; both maladies and miseries were my own.

Sneer. Hey! what the plague!

Dangle. 'Tis true, i'faith.

Puff. Hark'ee!—By advertisements—*To the charitable and humane!* and *To those whom Providence hath blessed with affluence!*

Sneer. Oh, I understand you.

Puff. And, in truth, I deserved what I got! for, I suppose never man went through such a series of calamities in the same space of time. Sir, I was five times made a bankrupt, and reduced from a state of affluence, by a train of un-avoidable misfortunes: then, sir, though a very industrious tradesman, I was twice burned out, and lost my little all both times: I lived upon those fires a month. I soon after was confined by a most excruciating disorder, and lost the use of my limbs: that told very well; for I had the case strongly attested, and went about to collect the subscrip-tions myself.

Dangle. Egad, I believe that was when you first called on me.

Puff. In November last?—O no; I was at that time a close prisoner in the Marshalsea, for a debt benevolently contracted to serve a friend. I was afterwards twice tapped for a dropsy, which declined into a very profitable con-sumption. I was then reduced to—O no—then, I became a widow with six helpless children, after having had eleven husbands pressed, and being left every time eight months gone with child, and without money to get me into an hospital!

Sneer. And you bore all with patience, I make no doubt?

Puff. Why yes; though I made some occasional attempts at *felo de se;* but as I did not find those rash actions an-swer, I left off killing myself very soon. Well, sir, at last, what with bankruptcies, fires, gout, dropsies, imprison-ments, and other valuable calamities, having got together a pretty handsome sum, I determined to quit a business which had always gone rather against my conscience, and in a more liberal way still to indulge my talents for fiction and embellishment, through my favourite channels of diurnal communication—and so, sir, you have my history.

Sneer. Most obligingly communicative indeed! and your confession, if published, might certainly serve the cause of true charity, by rescuing the most useful channels of appeal to benevolence from the cant of imposition. But surely, Mr. Puff, there is no great mystery in your present profession?

Puff. Mystery, sir! I will take upon me to say the matter was never scientifically treated nor reduced to rule before.

Sneer. Reduced to rule!

Puff. O Lud, sir, you are very ignorant, I am afraid!— Yes, sir, puffing is of various sorts; the principal are, the puff direct, the puff preliminary, the puff collateral, the puff collusive, and the puff oblique, or puff by implication. These all assume, as circumstances require, the various forms of Letter to the Editor, Occasional Anecdote, Impartial Critique, Observation from Correspondent, or Advertisement from the Party.

Sneer. The puff direct, I can conceive——

Puff. O yes, that's simple enough! For instance,—a new comedy or farce is to be produced at one of the theatres (though by-the-by they don't bring out half what they ought to do)—the author, suppose Mr. Smatter, or Mr. Dapper, or any particular friend of mine—very well; the day before it is to be performed, I write an account of the manner in which it was received; I have the plot from the author, and only add—"characters strongly drawn —highly coloured—hand of a master—fund of genuine humour—mine of invention—neat dialogue—Attic salt." Then for the performance—"Mr. Dodd was astonishingly great in the character of Sir Harry. That universal and judicious actor, Mr. Palmer, perhaps never appeared to more advantage than in the colonel;—but it is not in the power of language to do justice to Mr. King: indeed he more than merited those repeated bursts of applause which he drew from a most brilliant and judicious audience. As to the scenery—the miraculous powers of Mr. De Loutherbourg's pencil are universally acknowledged. In short, we are at a loss which to admire most, the unrivalled genius of the author, the great attention and liberality of the managers, the wonderful abilities of the painter, or the incredible exertions of all the performers."

Sneer. That's pretty well indeed, sir.

Puff. Oh, cool!—quite cool!—to what I sometimes do.

Sneer. And do you think there are any who are influenced by this?

Puff. O Lud, yes, sir! the number of those who undergo the fatigue of judging for themselves is very small indeed.

Sneer. Well, sir, the puff preliminary.

Puff. O, that, sir, does well in the form of a caution. In a matter of gallantry now—Sir Flimsy Gossamer wishes to be well with Lady Fanny Fete—he applies to me—I open trenches for him with a paragraph in the Morning Post.—"It is recommended to the beautiful and accomplished Lady F four stars F dash E to be on her guard against that dangerous character, Sir F dash G; who, however pleasing and insinuating his manners may be, is certainly not remarkable for the *constancy of his attachments!*"—in italics. Here, you see, Sir Flimsy Gossamer is introduced to the particular notice of Lady Fanny, who perhaps never thought of him before—she finds herself publicly cautioned to avoid him, which naturally makes her desirous of seeing him; the observation of their acquaintance causes a pretty kind of mutual embarrassment; this produces a sort of sympathy of interest, which if Sir Flimsy is unable to improve effectually, he at least gains the credit of having their names mentioned together, by a particular set, and in a particular way—which nine times out of ten is the full accomplishment of modern gallantry.

Dangle. Egad, Sneer, you will be quite an adept in the business.

Puff. Now, Sir, the puff collateral is much used as an appendage to advertisements, and may take the form of anecdote.—"Yesterday, as the celebrated George Bonmot was sauntering down St. James's Street, he met the lively Lady Mary Myrtle coming out of the park:—'Good God, Lady Mary, I'm surprised to meet you in a white jacket,—for I expected never to have seen you, but in a full-trimmed uniform and a light horseman's cap!'—'Heavens, George, where could you have learned that?'—'Why,' replied the wit, 'I just saw a print of you, in a new publication called the Camp Magazine; which, by-the-by, is a devilish clever thing, and is sold at No. 3, on the right hand of the way, two doors from the printing-office, the corner of Ivy Lane, Paternoster Row, price only one shilling.'"

Sneer. Very ingenious indeed!

Puff. But the puff collusive is the newest of any; for it acts in the disguise of determined hostility. It is much used by bold booksellers and enterprising poets.—"An indignant correspondent observes, that the new poem called *Beelzebub's Cotillon, or Proserpine's Fête Champêtre,* is one of the most unjustifiable performances he ever read. The severity with which certain characters are handled is quite shocking: and as there are many descriptions in it too warmly coloured for female delicacy, the shameful avidity with which this piece is bought by all people of fashion is a reproach on the taste of the times, and a disgrace to the delicacy of the age." Here you see the two strongest inducements are held forth; first, that nobody ought to read it; and secondly, that everybody buys it: on the strength of which the publisher boldly prints the tenth edition, before he had sold ten of the first; and then establishes it by threatening himself with the pillory, or absolutely indicting himself for *scan. mag.*

Dangle. Ha! ha! ha!—'gad, I know it is so.

Puff. As to the puff oblique, or puff by implication, it is too various and extensive to be illustrated by an instance: it attracts in titles and presumes in patents; it lurks in the limitation of a subscription, and invites in the assurance of crowd and incommodation at public places; it delights to draw forth concealed merit, with a most disinterested assiduity; and sometimes wears a countenance of smiling censure and tender reproach. It has a wonderful memory for parliamentary debates, and will often give the whole speech of a favoured member with the most flattering accuracy. But, above all, it is a great dealer in reports and suppositions. It has the earliest intelligence of intended preferments that will reflect honour on the patrons; and embryo promotions of modest gentlemen, who know nothing of the matter themselves. It can hint a ribbon for implied services in the air of a common report; and with the carelessness of a casual paragraph, suggest officers into commands, to which they have no pretension but their wishes. This, sir, is the last principal class of the art of puffing—an art which I hope you will now agree with me is of the highest dignity, yielding a tablature of benevolence and public spirit; befriending equally trade, gallantry, criticism, and politics: the applause of genius—the register of charity—the triumph of heroism—the self-defence of contractors—the fame of orators—and the gazette of ministers.

Sneer. Sir, I am completely a convert both to the importance and ingenuity of your profession; and now, sir, there is but one thing which can possibly increase my respect for you, and that is, your permitting me to be present this morning at the rehearsal of your new trage——

Puff. Hush, for heaven's sake!—*My* tragedy!—Egad, Dangle, I take this very ill: you know how apprehensive I am of being known to be the author.

Dangle. I'faith I would not have told—but it's in the papers, and your name at length in the Morning Chronicle.

Puff. Ah! those damned editors never can keep a secret! —Well, Mr. Sneer, no doubt you will do me great honour —I shall be infinitely happy—highly flattered——

Dangle. I believe it must be near the time—shall we go together?

Puff. No; it will not be yet this hour, for they are always late at that theatre: besides, I must meet you there, for I have some little matters here to send to the papers, and a few paragraphs to scribble before I go.—[*Looking at memorandums.*] Here is *A conscientious Baker, on the subject of the Army Bread; and a Detester of visible Brickwork, in favour of the new invented Stucco;* both in the style of Junius, and promised for to-morrow. The Thames navigation too is at a stand. Misomud or Anti-shoal must go to work again directly.—Here too are some political memorandums—I see; ay—*To take Paul Jones and get the Indiamen out of the Shannon—reinforce Byron—compel the Dutch to*—so!—I must do that in the evening papers, or reserve it for the Morning Herald; for I know that I have undertaken to-morrow, besides, to establish the unanimity of the fleet in the Public Advertiser, and to shoot Charles Fox in the Morning Post.—So, egad, I ha'n't a moment to lose.

Dangle. Well, we'll meet in the Green Room.

[*Exeunt severally.*

ACT TWO

SCENE I—*The Theatre before the Curtain*

Enter DANGLE, PUFF, *and* SNEER.

PUFF. No, no, sir; what Shakespeare says of actors may be better applied to the purpose of plays; they ought to be *the abstract and brief chronicles of the time.* Therefore when history, and particularly the history of our own country, furnishes anything like a case in point, to the time in which an author writes, if he knows his own interest, he will take advantage of it; so, sir, I call my tragedy *The Spanish Armada;* and have laid the scene before Tilbury Fort.

Sneer. A most happy thought, certainly!

Dangle. Egad it was—I told you so. But pray now, I don't understand how you have contrived to introduce any love into it.

Puff. Love! oh, nothing so easy! for it is a received point among poets, that where history gives you a good heroic outline for a play, you may fill up with a little love at your own discretion: in doing which, nine times out of ten, you only make up a deficiency in the private history of the times. Now, I rather think I have done this with some success.

Sneer. No scandal about Queen Elizabeth, I hope?

Puff. O Lud! no, no;—I only suppose the governor of Tilbury Fort's daughter to be in love with the son of the Spanish admiral.

Sneer. Oh, is that all!

Dangle. Excellent, i'faith! I see at once. But won't this appear rather improbable?

Puff. To be sure it will—but what the plague! a play is not to show occurrences that happen every day, but things just so strange, that though they never did, they might happen.

Sneer. Certainly nothing is unnatural, that is not physically impossible.

Puff. Very true—and for that matter Don Ferolo Whiskerandos, for that's the lover's name, might have been over here in the train of the Spanish ambassador, or Tilburina, for that is the lady's name, might have been in love with him, from having heard his character, or seen his picture; or from knowing that he was the last man in the world she ought to be in love with—or for any other good female reason.—However, sir, the fact is, that though she is but a knight's daughter, egad! she is in love like any princess!

Dangle. Poor young lady! I feel for her already! for I can conceive how great the conflict must be between her passion and her duty; her love for her country, and her love for Don Ferolo Whiskerandos!

Puff. Oh, amazing!—her poor susceptible heart is swayed to and fro by contending passions like——

Enter UNDER PROMPTER.

Under Prompter. Sir, the scene is set, and everything is ready to begin, if you please.

Puff. Egad, then we'll lose no time.

Under Prompter. Though, I believe, sir, you will find it very short, for all the performers have profited by the kind permission you granted them.

Puff. Hey! what?

Under Prompter. You know, sir, you gave them leave to cut out or omit whatever they found heavy or unnecessary to the plot, and I must own they have taken very liberal advantage of your indulgence.

Puff. Well, well.—They are in general very good judges, and I know I am luxuriant.—Now, Mr. Hopkins, as soon as you please.

Under Prompter. [*To the Orchestra.*] Gentlemen, will you play a few bars of something, just to——

Puff. Ay, that's right; for as we have the scenes and dresses, egad, we'll go to't, as if it was the first night's performance;—but you need not mind stopping between the acts—[*Exit* UNDER PROMPTER.—*Orchestra play—then the bell rings.*] Soh! stand clear, gentlemen. Now you know there will be a cry of down! down!—Hats off!—Silence!—Then up curtain, and let us see what our painters have done for us.　　　　　　　　[*Curtain rises.*

SCENE II—*Tilbury Fort*

"Two SENTINELS *discovered asleep."*

Dangle. Tilbury Fort!—very fine indeed!

Puff. Now, what do you think I open with?

Sneer. Faith, I can't guess——

Puff. A clock.—Hark!—[*Clock strikes.*] I open with a clock striking, to beget an awful attention in the audience: it also marks the time, which is four o'clock in the morning, and saves a description of the rising sun, and a great deal about gilding the eastern hemisphere.

Dangle. But pray, are the sentinels to be asleep?

Puff. Fast as watchmen.

Sneer. Isn't that odd though at such an alarming crisis?

Puff. To be sure it is,—but smaller things must give way to a striking scene at the opening; that's a rule. And the case is, that two great men are coming to this very spot to begin the piece; now it is not to be supposed they would open their lips, if these fellows were watching them; so, egad, I must either have sent them off their posts, or set them asleep.

Sneer. Oh, that accounts for it. But tell us, who are these coming?

Puff. These are they—Sir Walter Raleigh, and Sir Christopher Hatton. You'll know Sir Christopher by his turning out his toes—famous, you know, for his dancing. I like to preserve all the little traits of character.—Now attend.

"*Enter* Sir Walter Raleigh *and* Sir Christopher Hatton.

Sir Christopher.   True, gallant Raleigh!"

Dangle. What, they had been talking before?

Puff. O yes; all the way as they came along.—[*To the* actors.] I beg pardon, gentlemen, but these are particular friends of mine, whose remarks may be of great service to us.—[*To* Sneer *and* Dangle.] Don't mind interrupting them whenever anything strikes you.

"*Sir Christopher.*   True, gallant Raleigh!
                    But oh, thou champion of thy country's
                        fame,
                    There is a question which I yet must ask:
                    A question which I never ask'd before—
                    What mean these mighty armaments?
                    This general muster? and this throng of
                        chiefs?"

Sneer. Pray, Mr. Puff, how came Sir Christopher Hatton never to ask that question before?

Puff. What before the play began?—how the plague could he?

Dangle. That's true, i'faith!

Puff. But you will hear what he thinks of the matter.

"*Sir Christopher.*　Alas! my noble friend, when I behold
　　　　　　　　　Yon tented plains in martial symmetry
　　　　　　　　　Array'd; when I count o'er yon glittering
　　　　　　　　　　lines
　　　　　　　　　Of crested warriors, where the proud steeds'
　　　　　　　　　　neigh,
　　　　　　　　　And valour-breathing trumpet's shrill appeal,
　　　　　　　　　Responsive vibrate on my listening ear;
　　　　　　　　　When virgin majesty herself I view,
　　　　　　　　　Like her protecting Pallas, veil'd in steel,
　　　　　　　　　With graceful confidence exhort to arms!
　　　　　　　　　When, briefly, all I hear or see bears stamp
　　　　　　　　　Of martial vigilance and stern defence,
　　　　　　　　　I cannot but surmise—forgive, my friend,
　　　　　　　　　If the conjecture's rash—I cannot but
　　　　　　　　　Surmise the state some danger apprehends!"

Sneer. A very cautious conjecture that.

Puff. Yes, that's his character; not to give an opinion but on secure grounds.—Now then.

"*Sir Walter.*　　　O most accomplish'd Christopher!"——

Puff. He calls him by his christian name, to show that they are on the most familiar terms.

"*Sir Walter.*　　　O most accomplish'd Christopher! I find
　　　　　　　　　Thy staunch sagacity still tracks the future,
　　　　　　　　　In the fresh print of the o'ertaken past."

Puff. Figurative!

"*Sir Walter.*　　　Thy fears are just.
Sir Christopher.　But where? whence? when? and what
　　　　　　　　　The danger is,—methinks I fain would learn.
Sir Walter.　　　You know, my friend, scarce two revolving
　　　　　　　　　　suns,
　　　　　　　　　And three revolving moons, have closed their
　　　　　　　　　　course
　　　　　　　　　Since haughty Philip, in despite of peace,
　　　　　　　　　With hostile hand hath struck at England's
　　　　　　　　　　trade.
Sir Christopher.　I know it well.
Sir Walter.　　　Philip, you know, is proud Iberia's king!
Sir Christopher.　He is.
Sir Walter.　　　　His subjects in base bigotry
　　　　　　　　　And Catholic oppression held;—while we,
　　　　　　　　　You know, the Protestant persuasion hold.

Sir Christopher.　We do.

Sir Walter.　You know, beside, his boasted armament,
The famed Armada, by the Pope baptized,
With purpose to invade these realms——

Sir Christopher.　　　　　　　　　　　Is sailed,
Our last advices so report.

Sir Walter.　While the Iberian admiral's chief hope,
His darling son——

Sir Christopher.　　　　　Ferolo Whiskerandos hight—

Sir Walter.　The same—by chance a prisoner hath been
ta'en,
And in this fort of Tilbury——

Sir Christopher.　　　　　　　　　　Is now
Confined—'tis true, and oft from yon tall
turret's top
I've mark'd the youthful Spaniard's haughty
mien—
Unconquer'd, though in chains.

Sir Walter.　　　　　　　　　You also know"——

Dangle. Mr. Puff, as he knows all this, why does Sir
Walter go on telling him?

Puff. But the audience are not supposed to know anything of the matter, are they?

Sneer. True; but I think you manage ill: for there certainly appears no reason why Sir Walter should be so
communicative.

Puff. 'Fore Gad, now, that is one of the most ungrateful
observations I ever heard!—for the less inducement he
has to tell all this, the more, I think, you ought to be
obliged to him; for I am sure you'd know nothing of the
matter without it.

Dangle. That's very true, upon my word.

Puff. But you will find he was not going on.

"*Sir Christopher.* Enough, enough—'tis plain—and I no more
Am in amazement lost!"——

Puff. Here, now you see, Sir Christopher did not in fact
ask any one question for his own information.

Sneer. No, indeed: his has been a most disinterested
curiosity!

Dangle. Really, I find that we are very much obliged to
them both.

Puff. To be sure you are. Now then for the commander-
in-chief, the Earl of Leicester, who, you know, was no
favourite but of the queen's.—We left off—*in amazement
lost!*

"*Sir Christopher.*   Am in amazement lost.
But, see where noble Leicester comes! supreme
In honours and command.

Sir Walter.   And yet, methinks,
At such a time, so perilous, so fear'd,
That staff might well become an abler grasp.

Sir Christopher.   And so, by Heaven! think I; but soft, he's here!"

Puff. Ay, they envy him!

Sneer. But who are these with him?

Puff. Oh! very valiant knights: one is the governor of the fort, the other the master of the horse. And now, I think, you shall hear some better language: I was obliged to be plain and intelligible in the first scene, because there was so much matter of fact in it; but now, i'faith, you have trope, figure, and metaphor, as plenty as noun-substantives.

"*Enter* EARL OF LEICESTER, GOVERNOR, MASTER OF THE HORSE, KNIGHTS, &c.

Leicester.   How's this, my friends! is't thus your new-fledged zeal,
And plumed valour moulds in roosted sloth?
Why dimly glimmers that heroic flame,
Whose reddening blaze, by patriot spirit fed,
Should be the beacon of a kindling realm?
Can the quick current of a patriot heart
Thus stagnate in a cold and weedy converse,
Or freeze in tideless inactivity?
No! rather let the fountain of your valour
Spring through each stream of enterprise,
Each petty channel of conducive daring,
Till the full torrent of your foaming wrath
O'erwhelm the flats of sunk hostility!"

Puff. There it is—followed up!

"*Sir Walter.*   No more!—the freshening breath of thy rebuke
Hath fill'd the swelling canvas of our souls!
And thus, though fate should cut the cable of   [*All take hands.*
Our topmost hopes, in friendship's closing line
We'll grapple with despair, and if we fall,
We'll fall in glory's wake!

Leicester.	There spoke old England's genius! Then, are we all resolved?
All.	We are—all resolved.
Leicester.	To conquer—or be free?
All.	To conquer, or be free.
Leicester.	All?
All.	All."

Dangle. Nem. con. egad!

Puff. O yes!—where they do agree on the stage, their unanimity is wonderful!

| "*Leicester.* | Then let's embrace—and now—— [*Kneels.*" |

Sneer. What the plague, is he going to pray?

Puff. Yes; hush!—in great emergencies, there is nothing like a prayer.

| "*Leicester.* | O mighty Mars!" |

Dangle. But why should he pray to Mars?

Puff. Hush!

"*Leicester.*	If in thy homage bred, Each point of discipline I've still observed; Nor but by due promotion, and the right Of service, to the rank of major-general Have risen; assist thy votary now!
Governor.	Yet do not rise—hear me! [*Kneels.*
Master.	And me! [*Kneels.*
Knight.	And me! [*Kneels.*
Sir Walter.	And me! [*Kneels.*
Sir Christopher.	And me! [*Kneels.*"

Puff. Now pray altogether.

| "*All.* | Behold thy votaries submissive beg,
That thou wilt deign to grant them all they
ask;
Assist them to accomplish all their ends,
And sanctify whatever means they use
To gain them!" |

Sneer. A very orthodox quintetto!

Puff. Vastly well, gentlemen!—Is that well managed or not? Have you such a prayer as that on the stage?

Sneer. Not exactly.

Leicester. [*To* PUFF.] But, sir, you haven't settled how we are to get off here.

Puff. You could not go off kneeling, could you?

Sir Walter. [*To* PUFF.] O no, sir; impossible!

Puff. It would have a good effect i'faith, if you could exeunt praying!—Yes, and would vary the established mode of springing off with a glance at the pit.

Sneer. Oh, never mind, so as you get them off!—I'll answer for it, the audience won't care how.

Puff. Well, then, repeat the last line standing, and go off the old way.

> "*All.*   And sanctify whatever means we use
>   To gain them.   [*Exeunt.*"

Dangle. Bravo! a fine exit.

Sneer. Well, really, Mr. Puff——

Puff. Stay a moment!

> "*The* SENTINELS *get up.*

> 1 *Sentinel.*   All this shall to Lord Burleigh's ear.
> 2 *Sentinel.*   'Tis meet it should.   [*Exeunt.*"

Dangle. Hey!—why, I thought those fellows had been asleep?

Puff. Only a pretence; there's the art of it: they were spies of Lord Burleigh's.

Sneer. But isn't it odd they never were taken notice of, not even by the commander-in-chief?

Puff. O Lud, sir! if people who want to listen, or over-hear, were not always connived at in a tragedy, there would be no carrying on any plot in the world.

Dangle. That's certain.

Puff. But take care, my dear Dangle! the morning gun is going to fire.   [*Cannon fires.*

Dangle. Well, that will have a fine effect!

Puff. I think so, and helps to realize the scene.—[*Cannon twice.*] What the plague! three morning guns! there never is but one!—Ay, this is always the way at the theatre: give these fellows a good thing, and they never know when to have done with it.—You have no more cannon to fire?

Under Prompter. [*Within.*] No, sir.

Puff. Now, then, for soft music.

Sneer. Pray, what's that for?

Puff. It shows that Tilburina is coming!—nothing introduces you a heroine like soft music. Here she comes!

Dangle. And her confidant, I suppose?

Puff. To be sure! Here they are—inconsolable to the minuet in Ariadne! [*Soft music.*

"*Enter* Tilburina *and* Confidant.

Tilburina.   Now has the whispering breath of gentle morn
Bid Nature's voice and Nature's beauty rise;
While orient Phœbus, with unborrow'd hues,
Clothes the waked loveliness which all night slept
In heavenly drapery! Darkness is fled.
Now flowers unfold their beauties to the sun,
And, blushing, kiss the beam he sends to wake them—
The striped carnation, and the guarded rose,
The vulgar wallflower, and smart gillyflower,
The polyanthus mean—the dapper daisy,
Sweet-William, and sweet marjoram—and all
The tribe of single and of double pinks!
Now, too, the feather'd warblers tune their notes
Around, and charm the listening grove. The lark!
The linnet! chaffinch! bullfinch! goldfinch! greenfinch!
But O, to me no joy can they afford!
Nor rose, nor wallflower, nor smart gillyflower,
Nor polyanthus mean, nor dapper daisy,
Nor William sweet, nor marjoram—nor lark,
Linnet nor all the finches of the grove!"

Puff. Your white handkerchief, madam!——

Tilburina. I thought, sir, I wasn't to use that till *heart-rending woe.*

Puff. O yes, madam, at *the finches of the grove,* if you please.

"*Tilburina.*   Nor lark,
Linnet, nor all the finches of the grove!
[*Weeps.*"

Puff. Vastly well, madam!
Dangle. Vastly well, indeed!

"*Tilburina.*   For, O, too sure, heart-rending woe is now
The lot of wretched Tilburina!"

Dangle. Oh!—it's too much.
Sneer. Oh!—it is indeed.

"*Confidant.*　　　Be comforted, sweet lady; for who knows,
　　　　　　　　　But Heaven has yet some milk-white day in
　　　　　　　　　　　store?
Tilburina.　　　　Alas! my gentle Nora,
　　　　　　　　　Thy tender youth as yet hath never mourn'd
　　　　　　　　　Love's fatal dart. Else wouldst thou know,
　　　　　　　　　　　that when
　　　　　　　　　The soul is sunk in comfortless despair,
　　　　　　　　　It cannot taste of merriment."

Dangle. That's certain.

"*Confidant.*　　　But see where your stern father comes:
　　　　　　　　　It is not meet that he should find you thus."

Puff. Hey, what the plague!—what a cut is here! Why,
what is become of the description of her first meeting with
Don Whiskerandos—his gallant behavior in the sea-fight
—and the simile of the canary-bird?
　Tilburina. Indeed, sir, you'll find they will not be missed.
　Puff. Very well, very well!
　Tilburina. [*To* CONFIDANT.] The cue, ma'am, if you
please.

"*Confidant.*　　　It is not meet that he should find you thus.
Tilburina.　　　　Thou counsel'st right; but 'tis no easy task
　　　　　　　　　For barefaced grief to wear a mask of joy.

　　　　　　　　　Enter GOVERNOR.

Governor.　　　　How's this!—in tears?—O Tilburina, shame!
　　　　　　　　　Is this a time for maudling tenderness,
　　　　　　　　　And Cupid's baby woes?—Hast thou not
　　　　　　　　　　　heard
　　　　　　　　　That haughty Spain's pope-consecrated fleet
　　　　　　　　　Advances to our shores, while England's fate,
　　　　　　　　　Like a clipp'd guinea, trembles in the scale?
Tilburina.　　　　Then is the crisis of my fate at hand!
　　　　　　　　　I see the fleets approach—I see——"

Puff. Now, pray, gentlemen, mind. This is one of the
most useful figures we tragedy writers have, by which a
hero or heroine, in consideration of their being often
obliged to overlook things that are on the stage, is allowed
to hear and see a number of things that are not.
　Sneer. Yes; a kind of poetical second-sight!
　Puff. Yes.—Now then, madam.

"Tilburina.   I see their decks
                Are clear'd!—I see the signal made!
                The line is form'd!—a cable's length asunder!
                I see the frigates station'd in the rear;
                And now, I hear the thunder of the guns!
                I hear the victor's shouts—I also hear
                The vanquish'd groan!—and now 'tis smoke
                        —and now
                I see the loose sails shiver in the wind!
                I see—I see—what soon you'll see——
Governor.   Hold, daughter! peace! this love hath turn'd
                        thy brain:
                The Spanish fleet thou canst not see—be-
                        cause
                —It is not yet in sight!"

Dangle. Egad, though, the governor seems to make no
allowance for this poetical figure you talk of.

Puff. No, a plain matter-of-fact man;—that's his character.

"Tilburina.   But will you then refuse his offer?
Governor.   I must—I will—I can—I ought—I do.
Tilburina.   Think what a noble price.
Governor.   No more—you urge in vain.
Tilburina.   His liberty is all he asks."

Sneer. All who asks, Mr. Puff? Who is——

Puff. Egad, sir, I can't tell! Here has been such cutting
and slashing, I don't know where they have got to myself.

Tilburina. Indeed, sir, you will find it will connect very
well.

                    "—And your reward secure."

Puff. Oh, if they hadn't been so devilish free with their
cutting here, you would have found that Don Whiskerandos has been tampering for his liberty, and has persuaded
Tilburina to make this proposal to her father. And now,
pray observe the conciseness with which the argument is
conducted. Egad, the *pro* and *con* goes as smart as hits
in a fencing match. It is indeed a sort of small-sword-
logic, which we have borrowed from the French.

"Tilburina.   A retreat in Spain!
Governor.   Outlawry here!
Tilburina.   Your daughter's prayer!
Governor.   Your father's oath!
Tilburina.   My lover!

SCENE II] THE CRITIC 347

Governor.	My country!
Tilburina.	Tilburina!
Governor.	England!
Tilburina.	A title!
Governor.	Honour!
Tilburina.	A pension!
Governor.	Conscience!
Tilburina.	A thousand pounds!
Governor.	Ha! thou hast touch'd me nearly!"

Puff. There you see—she threw in *Tilburina.* Quick, parry Carte with *England!* Ha! thrust in tierce *a title!*—parried by *honour.* Ha! *a pension* over the arm!—put by by *conscience.* Then flankonade with *a thousand pounds*—and a palpable hit, egad!

"*Tilburina.*	Canst thou—
	Reject the suppliant, and the daughter too?
Governor.	No more; I would not hear thee plead in vain:
	The father softens—but the governor
	Is fix'd! [*Exit.*"

Dangle. Ay, that antithesis of persons is a most established figure.

"*Tilburina.*	'Tis well,—hence then, fond hopes,—fond passion hence;
	Duty, behold I am all over thine——
Whiskerandos.	[*Without.*] Where is my love—my——
Tilburina.	Ha!

Enter DON FEROLO WHISKERANDOS.

Whiskerandos.	My beauteous enemy!——"

Puff. O dear, ma'am, you must start a great deal more than that! Consider, you had just determined in favour of duty—when, in a moment, the sound of his voice revives your passion—overthrows your resolution—destroys your obedience. If you don't express all that in your start, you do nothing at all.

Tilburina. Well, we'll try again.

Dangle. Speaking from within has always a fine effect.

Sneer. Very.

"*Whiskerandos.*	My conquering Tilburina! How! is't thus
	We meet? why are thy looks averse? what means
	That falling tear—that frown of boding woe?

Ha! now indeed I am a prisoner!
Yes, now I feel the galling weight of these
Disgraceful chains—which, cruel Tilburina!
Thy doting captive gloried in before.—
But thou art false, and Whiskerandos is un-
done!

Tilburina.   O no! how little dost thou know thy Tilburina!

Whiskerandos.   Art thou then true?—Begone cares, doubts,
and fears,
I make you all a present to the winds;
And if the winds reject you—try the waves."

Puff. The wind, you know, is the established receiver of
all stolen sighs, and cast-off griefs and apprehensions.

"*Tilburina.*   Yet must we part!—stern duty seals our
doom:
Though here I call yon conscious clouds to
witness,
Could I pursue the bias of my soul,
All friends, all right of parents, I'd disclaim,
And thou, my Whiskerandos, shouldst be
father
And mother, brother, cousin, uncle, aunt,
And friend to me!

Whiskerandos.   Oh, matchless excellence! and must we
part?
Well, if—we must—we must—and in that
case
The less is said the better."

Puff. Heyday! here's a cut!—What, are all the mutual
protestations out?

Tilburina. Now, pray, sir, don't interrupt us just here:
you ruin our feelings.

Puff. Your feelings!—but, zounds, my feelings, ma'am!

Sneer. No, pray don't interrupt them.

"*Whiskerandos.*   One last embrace.
Tilburina.   Now,—farewell, for ever.
Whiskerandos.   For ever!
Tilburina.   Ay, for ever!   [*Going.*"

Puff. 'Sdeath and fury!—Gad's life!—sir! madam! if
you go out without the parting look, you might as well
dance out. Here, here!

Confidant. But pray, sir, how am I to get off here?

Puff. You! pshaw! what the devil signifies how you get

off! edge away at the top, or where you will—[*Pushes the* CONFIDANT *off.*] Now, ma'am, you see——

Tilburina. We understand you, sir.

		"Ay, for ever.
Both.	Oh!	[*Turning back, and exeunt.—*
		Scene closes."

Dangle. Oh, charming!

Puff. Hey!—'tis pretty well, I believe: you see I don't attempt to strike out anything new—but I take it I improve on the established modes.

Sneer. You do, indeed! But pray is not Queen Elizabeth to appear?

Puff. No, not once—but she is to be talked of for ever; so that, egad, you'll think a hundred times that she is on the point of coming in.

Sneer. Hang it, I think it's a pity to keep her in the green-room all the night.

Puff. O no, that always has a fine effect—it keeps up expectation.

Dangle. But are we not to have a battle?

Puff. Yes, yes, you will have a battle at last: but, egad, it's not to be by land, but by sea—and that is the only quite new thing in the piece.

Dangle. What, Drake at the Armada, hey?

Puff. Yes, i'faith—fire-ships and all; then we shall end with the procession. Hey, that will do, I think?

Sneer. No doubt on't.

Puff. Come, we must not lose time; so now for the under-plot.

Sneer. What the plague, have you another plot?

Puff. O Lord, yes; ever while you live have two plots to your tragedy. The grand point in managing them is only to let your under-plot have as little connection with your main-plot as possible.—I flatter myself nothing can be more distinct than mine; for as in my chief plot the characters are all great people, I have laid my under-plot in low life, and as the former is to end in deep distress, I make the other end as happy as a farce.—Now, Mr. Hopkins, as soon as you please.

Enter UNDER PROMPTER.

Under Prompter. Sir, the carpenter says it is impossible you can go to the park scene yet.

Puff. The park scene! no! I mean the description scene here, in the wood.

Under Prompter. Sir, the performers have cut it out.

Puff. Cut it out!

Under Prompter. Yes, sir.

Puff. What! the whole account of Queen Elizabeth?

Under Prompter. Yes, sir.

Puff. And the description of her horse and side-saddle?

Under Prompter. Yes, sir.

Puff. So, so; this is very fine indeed!—Mr. Hopkins, how the plague could you suffer this?

Mr. Hopkins. [*Within.*] Sir, indeed the pruning-knife——

Puff. The pruning-knife—zounds!—the axe! Why, here has been such lopping and topping, I shan't have the bare trunk of my play left presently!—Very well, sir—the performers must do as they please; but, upon my soul, I'll print it every word.

Sneer. That I would, indeed.

Puff. Very well, sir; then we must go on.—Zounds! I would not have parted with the description of the horse!—Well, sir, go on.—Sir, it was one of the finest and most laboured things.—Very well, sir; let them go on.—There you had him and his accoutrements, from the bit to the crupper.—Very well, sir; we must go to the park scene.

Under Prompter. Sir, there is the point: the carpenters say, that unless there is some business put in here before the drop, they sha'n't have time to clear away the fort, or sink Gravesend and the river.

Puff. So! this is a pretty dilemma, truly!—Gentlemen, you must excuse me—these fellows will never be ready, unless I go and look after them myself.

Sneer. O dear, sir, these little things will happen.

Puff. To cut out this scene!—but I'll print it—egad, I'll print it every word!   [*Exeunt.*

ACT THREE

SCENE I—*The Theatre, before the curtain*

Enter PUFF, SNEER, *and* DANGLE.

PUFF. Well, we are ready; now then for the justices.

[*Curtain rises.*

"Justices, Constables, &c., *discovered*."

Sneer. This, I suppose, is a sort of senate scene.

Puff. To be sure; there has not been one yet.

Dangle. It is the under-plot, isn't it?

Puff. Yes.—What, gentlemen, do you mean to go at once to the discovery scene?

Justice. If you please, sir.

Puff. Oh, very well!—Hark'ee, I don't choose to say anything more; but, i'faith they have mangled my play in a most shocking manner.

Dangle. It's a great pity!

Puff. Now, then, Mr. Justice, if you please.

"*Justice.*	Are all the volunteers without?
Constable.	They are.
	Some ten in fetters, and some twenty drunk.
Justice.	Attends the youth, whose most opprobrious fame
	And clear convicted crimes have stamp'd him soldier?
Constable.	He waits your pleasure; eager to repay
	The best reprieve that sends him to the fields
	Of glory, there to raise his branded hand
	In honour's cause.
Justice.	'Tis well—'tis justice arms him!
	Oh! may he now defend his country's laws
	With half the spirit he has broke them all!
	If 'tis your worship's pleasure, bid him enter.
Constable.	I fly, the herald of your will. [*Exit.*"

Puff. Quick, sir.

Sneer. But, Mr. Puff, I think not only the Justice, but the clown seems to talk in as high a style as the first hero among them.

Puff. Heaven forbid they should not in a free country! —Sir, I am not for making slavish distinctions, and giving all the fine language to the upper sort of people.

Dangle. That's very noble in you, indeed.

"*Enter* Justice's Lady."

Puff. Now, pray mark this scene.

"*Lady.*	Forgive this interruption, good my love;
	But as I just now pass'd a prisoner youth,
	Whom rude hands hither lead, strange bodings seized

	My fluttering heart, and to myself I said,
	An' if our Tom had lived, he'd surely been
	This stripling's height!
Justice.	Ha! sure some powerful sympathy directs
	Us both——

Enter CONSTABLE *with* SON.

	What is thy name?
Son.	My name is Tom Jenkins—*alias* have I
	none—
	Though orphan'd, and without a friend!
Justice.	Thy parents?
Son.	My father dwelt in Rochester—and was,
	As I have heard—a fishmonger—no more."

Puff. What, sir, do you leave out the account of your birth, parentage, and education?

Son. They have settled it so, sir, here.

Puff. Oh! oh!

"*Lady.*	How loudly nature whispers to my heart
	Had he no other name?
Son.	I've seen a bill
	Of his sign'd Tomkins, creditor.
Justice.	This does indeed confirm each circumstance
	The gipsy told!—Prepare!
Son.	I do.
Justice.	No orphan, nor without a friend art thou—
	I am thy father; here's thy mother; there
	Thy uncle—this thy first cousin, and those
	Are all your near relations!
Lady.	O ecstasy of bliss!
Son.	O most unlook'd for happiness!
Justice.	O wonderful event! [*They faint alternately*
	in each other's arms."

Puff. There, you see, relationship, like murder, will out.

"*Justice.*	Now let's revive—else were this joy ·too
	much!
	But come—and we'll unfold the rest within;
	And thou, my boy, must needs want rest and
	food.
	Hence may each orphan hope, as chance
	directs,
	To find a father—where he least expects!
	[*Exeunt."*

Puff. What do you think of that?

Dangle. One of the finest discovery-scenes I ever saw!—

Why, this under-plot would have made a tragedy itself.

Sneer. Ay, or a comedy either.

Puff. And keeps quite clear you see of the other.

"*Enter* SCENEMEN, *taking away the seats.*"

Puff. The scene remains, does it?

Sceneman. Yes, sir.

Puff. You are to leave one chair, you know.—But it is always awkward in a tragedy, to have your fellows coming in in your play-house liveries to remove things.—I wish that could be managed better.—So now for my mysterious yeoman.

"*Enter* BEEFEATER.

Beefeater.　　　　Perdition catch my soul, but I do love thee."

Sneer. Haven't I heard that line before?

Puff. No, I fancy not.—Where, pray?

Dangle. Yes, I think there is something like it in Othello.

Puff. Gad! now you put me in mind on't, I believe there is—but that's of no consequence; all that can be said is, that two people happened to hit upon the same thought—and Shakespeare made use of it first, that's all.

Sneer. Very true.

Puff. Now, sir, your soliloquy—but speak more to the pit, if you please—the soliloquy always to the pit, that's a rule.

"*Beefeater.*　　　　Though hopeless love finds comfort in despair,
　　　　　　　　　　It never can endure a rival's bliss!
　　　　　　　　　　But soft—I am observed.　　　[*Exit.*"

Dangle. That's a very short soliloquy.

Puff. Yes—but it would have been a great deal longer if he had not been observed.

Sneer. A most sentimental Beefeater that, Mr. Puff!

Puff. Hark'ee—I would not have you be too sure that he is a Beefeater.

Sneer. What, a hero in disguise?

Puff. No matter—I only give you a hint. But now for my principal character. Here he comes—Lord Burleigh in person! Pray, gentlemen, step this way—softly—I only hope the Lord High Treasurer is perfect—if he is but perfect!

"Enter Lord Burleigh, *goes slowly to a chair, and sits."*

Sneer. Mr. Puff!

Puff. Hush!—Vastly well, sir! vastly well! a most interesting gravity.

Dangle. What, isn't he to speak at all?

Puff. Egad, I thought you'd ask me that!—Yes, it is a very likely thing—that a minister in his situation, with the whole affairs of the nation on his head, should have time to talk!—But hush! or you'll put him out.

Sneer. Put him out; how the plague can that be, if he's not going to say anything?

Puff. There's the reason! why, his part is to think; and how the plague do you imagine he can think if you keep talking?

Dangle. That's very true, upon my word!

*"*Lord Burleigh *comes forward, shakes his head, and exit."*

Sneer. He is very perfect indeed! Now, pray what did he mean by that?

Puff. You don't take it?

Sneer. No, I don't, upon my soul.

Puff. Why, by that shake of the head, he gave you to understand that even though they had more justice in their cause, and wisdom in their measures—yet, if there was not a greater spirit shown on the part of the people, the country would at last fall a sacrifice to the hostile ambition of the Spanish monarchy.

Sneer. The devil! did he mean all that by shaking his head?

Puff. Every word of it—if he shook his head as I taught him.

Dangle. Ah! there certainly is a vast deal to be done on the stage by dumb show and expressions of face; and a judicious author knows how much he may trust to it.

Sneer. Oh, here are some of our old acquaintance.

"Enter Sir Christopher Hatton *and* Sir Walter Raleigh.

Sir Christopher. My niece and your niece too!
By Heaven! there's witchcraft in't.—He could not else
Have gain'd their hearts.—But see where they approach:
Some horrid purpose lowering on their brows!

Sir Walter.   Let us withdraw and mark them.

                                                [They withdraw."

  Sneer. What is all this?

  Puff. Ah! here has been more pruning!—but the fact is, these two young ladies are also in love with Don Whiskerandos.—Now, gentlemen, this scene goes entirely for what we call situation and stage effect, by which the greatest applause may be obtained, without the assistance of language, sentiment, or character: pray mark!

                    "Enter the two NIECES.

1st Niece.   Ellena here!
                    She is his scorn as much as I—that is
                    Some comfort still!"

  Puff. O dear, madam, you are not to say that to her face!—Aside, ma'am, aside.—The whole scene is to be aside.

"1st Niece.   She is his scorn as much as I—that is
                    Some comfort still.   *[Aside.*
2nd Niece.   I know he prizes not Pollina's love;
                    But Tilburina lords it o'er his heart. *[Aside.*
1st Niece.   But see the proud destroyer of my peace.
                    Revenge is all the good I've left.   *[Aside.*
2nd Niece.   He comes, the false disturber of my quiet.
                    Now vengeance do thy worst.   *[Aside.*

         Enter DON FEROLO WHISKERANDOS.

Whiskerandos.   O hateful liberty—if thus in vain
                    I seek my Tilburina!
Both Nieces.   And ever shalt!

SIR CHRISTOPHER HATTON *and* SIR WALTER RALEIGH *come forward.*

  Sir Christopher and Sir Walter. Hold! we will avenge you.
Whiskerandos.   Hold *you*—or see your nieces bleed!
                  [The two NIECES *draw their two dag-*
                    gers to strike WHISKERANDOS: *the*
                    two UNCLES *at the instant, with their*
                    two swords drawn, catch their two
                    NIECES' *arms, and turn the points of*
                    their swords to WHISKERANDOS, *who*
                    immediately draws two daggers, and
                    holds them to the two NIECES' *bos-*
                    oms."

  Puff. There's situation for you! there's an heroic group! —You see the ladies can't stab Whiskerandos—he durst not strike them, for fear of their uncles—the uncles durst not kill him, because of their nieces.—I have them all at a dead lock!—for every one of them is afraid to let go first.

Sneer. Why, then they must stand there for ever!

Puff. So they would, if I hadn't a very fine contrivance for't.—Now mind——

"*Enter* BEEFEATER, *with his halbert.*

Beefeater.	In the queen's name I charge you all to drop Your swords and daggers!
	[*They drop their swords and daggers.*"

Sneer. That is a contrivance indeed!

Puff. Ay—in the queen's name.

"*Sir Christopher.*	Come, niece!
Sir Walter.	Come, niece! [*Exeunt with the two* NIECES.
Whiskerandos	What's he, who bids us thus renounce our guard?
Beefeater.	Thou must do more—renounce thy love!
Whiskerandos	Thou liest—base Beefeater!
Beefeater.	Ha! hell! the lie! By Heaven thou'st roused the lion in my heart! Off, yeoman's habit!—base disguise! off! off! [*Discovers himself by throwing off his upper dress, and appearing in a very fine waistcoat.* Am I a Beefeater now? Or beams my crest as terrible as when In Biscay's Bay I took thy captive sloop?"

Puff. There, egad! he comes out to be the very captain of the privateer who had taken Whiskerandos prisoner—and was himself an old lover of Tilburina's.

Dangle. Admirably managed, indeed!

Puff. Now, stand out of their way.

"*Whiskerandos.*	I thank thee, Fortune, that hast thus bestowed A weapon to chastise this insolent. [*Takes up one of the swords.*
Beefeater.	I take thy challenge, Spaniard, and I thank thee, Fortune, too! [*Takes up the other sword.*"

Dangle. That's excellently contrived!—It seems as if the two uncles had left their swords on purpose for them.

Puff. No, egad, they could not help leaving them.

"Whiskerandos.	Vengeance and Tilburina!
Beefeater	Exactly so——

                  [*They fight—and after the usual number of wounds given,* WHISKERANDOS *falls.*

Whiskerandos.	O cursed parry!—that last thrust in tierce Was fatal.—Captain, thou hast fenced well! And Whiskerandos quits this bustling scene For all eter——
Beefeater.	——nity—he would have added, but stern death Cut short his being, and the noun at once!"

Puff. Oh, my dear sir, you are too slow: now mind me. —Sir, shall I trouble you to die again?

"Whiskerandos.	And Whiskerandos quits this bustling scene For all eter——
Beefeater.	——nity—he would have added,——"

Puff. No, sir—that's not it—once more, if you please.

Whiskerandos. I wish, sir, you would practise this without me—I can't stay dying here all night.

Puff. Very well; we'll go over it by-and-by.—[*Exit* WHISKERANDOS.] I must humour these gentlemen!

"Beefeater.	Farewell, brave Spaniard! and when next ——"

Puff. Dear sir, you needn't speak that speech, as the body has walked off.

Beefeater. That's true, sir—then I'll join the fleet.

Puff. If you please.—[*Exit* BEEFEATER.] Now, who comes on?

    "Enter GOVERNOR, *with his hair properly disordered.*

Governor.	A hemisphere of evil planets reign! And every planet sheds contagious frenzy! My Spanish prisoner is slain! my daughter, Meeting the dead corse borne along, has gone
	Distract! [*A loud flourish of trumpets.* But hark! I am summoned to the fort: Perhaps the fleets have met! amazing crisis! O Tilburina! from thy aged father's beard

> Thou'st pluck'd the few brown hairs which
> time had left!   [*Exit.*"

Sneer. Poor gentleman!

Puff. Yes—and no one to blame but his daughter!

Dangle. And the planets——

Puff. True.—Now enter Tilburina!

Sneer. Egad, the business comes on quick here.

Puff. Yes, sir—now she comes in stark mad in white satin.

Sneer. Why in white satin?

Puff. O Lord, sir—when a heroine goes mad, she always goes into white satin.—Don't she, Dangle?

Dangle. Always—it's a rule.

Puff. Yes—here it is—[*Looking at the book.*] "Enter Tilburina stark mad in white satin, and her confidant stark mad in white linen."

"*Enter* Tilburina *and* Confidant, *mad, according to custom.*"

Sneer. But, what the deuce! is the confidant to be mad too?

Puff. To be sure she is: the confidant is always to do whatever her mistress does; weep when she weeps, smile when she smiles, go mad when she goes mad.—Now, Madam Confidant—but keep your madness in the background, if you please.

"*Tilburina.*   The wind whistles—the moon rises—see,
                They have kill'd my squirrel in his cage:
                Is this a grasshopper?—Ha! no; it is my
                Whiskerandos—you shall not keep him—
                I know you have him in your pocket—
                An oyster may be cross'd in love!—who says
                A whale's a bird?—Ha! did you call, my
                    love?—
                He's here! he's there!—He's everywhere!
                Ah me! he's nowhere!   [*Exit.*"

Puff. There, do you ever desire to see anybody madder than that?

Sneer. Never, while I live!

Puff. You observed how she mangled the metre?

Dangle. Yes,—egad, it was the first thing made me suspect she was out of her senses!

Sneer. And pray what becomes of her?

Puff. She is gone to throw herself into the sea, to be

sure—and that brings us at once to the scene of action and so to my catastrophe—my sea-fight, I mean.

Sneer. What, you bring that in at last?

Puff. Yes, yes—you know my play is called *The Spanish Armada;* otherwise, egad, I have no occasion for the battle at all.—Now then for my magnificence!—my battle!—my noise!—and my procession!—You are all ready?

Under Prompter. [*Within.*] Yes, sir.

Puff. Is the Thames dressed?

"Enter THAMES *with two* ATTENDANTS.*"*

Thames. Here I am, sir.

Puff. Very well, indeed!—See, gentlemen, there's a river for you!—This is blending a little of the masque with my tragedy—a new fancy, you know—and very useful in my case; for as there must be a procession, I suppose Thames, and all his tributary rivers, to compliment Britannia with a fête in honour of the victory.

Sneer. But pray, who are these gentlemen in green with him?

Puff. Those?—those are his banks.

Sneer. His banks?

Puff. Yes, one crowned with alders, and the other with a villa!—you take the allusions?—But hey! what the plague!—you have got both your banks on one side.— Here, sir, come round.—Ever while you live, Thames, go between your banks.—[*Bell rings.*] There, so! now for't! —Stand aside, my dear friends!—Away, Thames!

[*Exit* THAMES *between his banks.*

[*Flourish of drums, trumpets, cannon, &c., &c. Scene changes to the sea—the fleets engage—the music plays—"Britons strike home."—Spanish fleet destroyed by fire-ships, &c.—English fleet advances —music plays, "Rule Britannia."—The procession of all the English rivers, and their tributaries, with their emblems, &c., begins with Handel's water music, ends with a chorus to the march in Judas Maccabæus.—During this scene,* PUFF *directs and applauds everything—then*

Puff. Well, pretty well—but not quite perfect. So, ladies and gentlemen, if you please, we'll rehearse this piece again to-morrow.   [*Curtain drops.*

THE MERMAID SERIES

THE MERMAID SERIES of English dramatists was the brain-child of a twenty-six year old medical student, later a famous sexologist. "At that time," Havelock Ellis writes in his autobiography,* speaking of the year 1886, "it happened that a London publisher, Henry Vizetelly, was conspicuous by the way in which he had published fairly literal translations of the chief contemporary French novelists. My friend Eleanor Marx Aveling [daughter of Karl Marx] had translated *Madame Bovary* for him, and he had issued translations—it is true by no means always literal—of a large number of Zola's novels. He had himself been a distinguished journalist in earlier days, he was familiar with France, and he was really engaged in a quite honorable and useful work. It occurred to me that a series of volumes of the best plays, unexpurgated, of the Elizabethan dramatists—for which I devised at the suggestion of Beaumont's poem the name Mermaid Series—would be an excellent scheme for Vizetelly to undertake. I had no idea of proposing myself for editor, and indeed could hardly feel competent for the post. I wrote to Vizetelly putting the scheme before him, and almost by return of post he replied accepting it, asking me to undertake the work of general editor, and inquiring what remuneration I would wish to receive. Such a proposal seemed too tempting for a young unknown man to put aside, whatever his disabilities, and even though he was in the midst of training for an arduous profession. I accepted with alacrity, and speedily repaired, so far as I could, my incompetence. I knew nothing as to what fees a general editor was entitled, and the sum I asked (three guineas per volume) was, no doubt, too small . . . I selected the dramatists, the space to be devoted to each, and I chose the editors [though Vizetelly told Ellis that he needed 'one or two names of mark' to launch the project] cooperating in their work, besides myself editing Marlowe, Middleton, Ford and Porter. . . ."†

Ellis then relates how Vizetelly was sent to jail as the publisher of that famous pornographer, Emile Zola; and how, soon afterwards, he died. At this point, Ellis continues, "the Mermaid Series was taken over [by T. Fisher Unwin, a publisher], without any word of explanation or apology to me, or any word of protest from me, though I do not flatter myself he [Unwin] knew that my silence was contempt. I was well aware that for a publisher the editor of a series is an insignificant figure even though he may be altogether responsible for its conception, mainly responsible for its production, and largely responsible for its success. I had, of course, arranged for volumes ahead, many of them nearly ready for publication; the editors of these were equally disregarded by the new publisher. . . . The Mermaid Series swiftly passed away so far as I was concerned, and languished to death after it was taken out of my hands. But it was not superseded. I am pleased to be assured—as I revise these lines some forty years later, a paper on 'Havelock Ellis and the English Drama' comes to hand, written by a devoted student of the drama, Montague Summers —that 'the Mermaid Series remains a magnificent service rendered to the English drama, a pioneer work, a work that demanded courage, scholarship, and enthusiasm.' "

* *My Life*, by Havelock Ellis. Quoted by permission of the publisher, Houghton Mifflin Co.

† Instigated, as Houston Peterson tells in his life of Ellis, by the protest of "a well-meaning woman" but put through with rather hysterical despatch by Vizetelly.

In 1917, the firm of T. Fisher Unwin arranged for publication of the Mermaid Series in the United States by Charles Scribner's Sons. In 1926 Unwin was absorbed by Ernest Benn Limited who continued supplying Scribner's with the Mermaid volumes until 1945. After the Second World War some 12 of the Mermaid volumes were re-issued in London by Ernest Benn Limited and A. A. Wyn Incorporated in New York. On this occasion, the Curator of the Brander Matthews Dramatic Museum at Columbia University (Henry W. Wells) wrote: "If a class of students in our century was to know the Elizabethan drama through any more attractive medium than an anthology, this series provided the almost certain means. Earlier editions . . . were directed to . . . British gentlemen. The new library . . . was addressed to a very much larger and democratic public. It always sold well in America. Yet one by one these books went out of print. . . . The gradual strangulation of the Mermaid Series seemed a mark of doom upon the popular success of Elizabethan studies themselves. . . . But lovers of the most humane movement in all English literature have at present cause for congratulation . . . the Mermaid Series is being re-issued." But the price of this 1948-49 hard-back edition was beyond the means of the academic and democratic public Mr. Wells speaks about. The necessary next step was to issue the books—completely reset—in paper-back form at little more than one dollar each.

It also seemed high time to continue the work itself where Ellis, so long ago, had left off. In 1887 were issued the Marlowe, the Dekker, the Congreve, Middleton Volume I, and Massinger Volume I. In 1888 followed Heywood, Ford, Shirley, Wycherley, Otway, Webster and Tourneur, and an anthology entitled *Nero and Other Plays;* in 1889-90, the second volumes of Middleton and Massinger, respectively. In the nineties came Steele, Chapman, Vanbrugh, and three volumes of Jonson. In the nineteen-hundreds, Shadwell, Farquhar, Greene, and two volumes each of Dryden and Beaumont & Fletcher. The rest was silence.*

Hill and Wang Incorporated, in addition to bringing out the original Mermaids, plans to issue several new Mermaids a year, beginning with Sheridan, edited by Louis Kronenberger, and *Camille and Other Plays,* edited by Stephen S. Stanton. The new titles indicate two ramifications: one down, as it were, towards the present, the other across towards the drama of other lands. No longer confined to the Elizabethan and Restoration periods, the Mermaid Series will include more recent English plays and also non-English plays. And it will be part of a larger series—Dramabooks—which will also include studies of theatre and dramatic literature by leading writers.

Eric Bentley is Advisory Editor to Dramabooks.

The Publishers
New York, 1957

---

* Ellis's editors—aside from those whose work never appeared—were Alexander C. Ewald, H. P. Horne, Edmund Gosse, Roden Noel, Ernest Rhys, A. C. Swinburne, John Addington Symonds, Arthur Symons, A. W. Verity, and W. C. Ward. The choice of editors after 1890 was presumably made by T. Fisher Unwin. Those chosen were: G. A. Aitken, William Archer, T. H. Dickinson, C. H. Herford, Brinsley Nicholson, William Lyon Phelps, George Saintsbury, J. St. Loe Strachey, A. E. H. Swain.

DRAMABOOKS

HILL AND WANG aims to establish DRAMABOOKS as a permanent library of the great classics of the theatre of all countries, in an attractive, low-priced format.

Eric Bentley, Advisory Editor to Dramabooks, is Brander Matthews Professor of Dramatic Literature at Columbia University.

Published

Christopher Marlowe edited by Havelock Ellis. Introduction by John Addington Symonds   MD 1
(Tamburlaine the Great, Parts I & II, Doctor Faustus, The Jew of Malta, Edward the Second)

William Congreve edited by Alexander Charles Ewald. Introduction by Macaulay. (Complete Plays)   MD 2

Webster and Tourneur Introduction by John Addington Symonds   MD 3
(The White Devil, The Duchess of Malfi, The Atheist's Tragedy, The Revenger's Tragedy)

John Ford edited by Havelock Ellis   MD 4
(The Lover's Melancholy, 'Tis Pity She's a Whore, The Broken Heart, Love's Sacrifice, Perkin Warbeck)

Richard Brinsley Sheridan edited with an Introduction by Louis Kronenberger   MD 5
(The Rivals, St. Patrick's Day, The Duenna, A Trip to Scarborough, The School for Scandal, The Critic)

Camille and Other Plays edited, with an Introduction to the well-made play by Stephen S. Stanton   MD 6
(Scribe: A Peculiar Position, and The Glass of Water; Sardou: A Scrap of Paper; Dumas, fils: Camille; Augier: Olympe's Marriage)

Shakespeare and the Elizabethans by Henri Fluchère, Foreword by T. S. Eliot   D 1

On Dramatic Method by Harley Granville-Barker   D 2

George Bernard Shaw by G. K. Chesterton   D 3

The Paradox of Acting by Denis Diderot and *Masks or Faces?* by William Archer, Introduction by Lee Strasberg   D 4

The Scenic Art by Henry James. Edited, with an Introduction and Notes by Allan Wade   D 5

Preface to Hamlet by Harley Granville-Barker   D 6

In Preparation

Hazlitt on Theatre edited by Archer and Lowe   D 7

The Fervent Years by Harold Clurman   D 8

The Quintessence of Ibsenism by Bernard Shaw   D 9

John Dryden edited, and with an Introduction by George Saintsbury   MD 7
(The Conquest of Granada, Parts I and II, Marriage à la Mode, Aureng-Zebe)

Ben Jonson edited, with an Introduction and Notes by Brinsley Nicholson and C. H. Herford   MD 8
(Volpone, Epicoene, The Alchemist)

Oliver Goldsmith edited by George P. Baker. Introduction by Austin Dobson   MD 9
(The Good Natur'd Man, She Stoops to Conquer, An Essay on the Theatre, A Register of Scotch Marriages)